pwc

Manual of Accounting – Narrative reporting 2013

UK Accounting Consulting Services
PricewaterhouseCoopers LLP, Chartered Accountants

Published by

Bloomsbury Professional

Bloomsbury Professional, an imprint of Bloomsbury Publishing Plc, Maxwelton House, 41–43 Boltro Road, Haywards Heath, West Sussex, RH16 1BJ

ISBN - 978 1 78043 105 5

British Library Cataloguing-in-Publication Data.
A catalogue record for this book is available from the British Library.

Printed in Great Britain.
Typeset by YHT Ltd, 4 Hercies Road, Hillingdon, Middlesex UB10 9NA

Authors

PricewaterhouseCoopers' Manual of Accounting – Management Reports and Governance is written by the PricewaterhouseCoopers LLP's UK Accounting Consulting Services team.

Writing team led by
Barry Johnson
Peter Holgate

Authors, contributors and reviewers

Michelle Amjad	Michael Gaull	Avni Mashru	Iain Selfridge
Claire Burke	Imre Guba	Helen McCann	Mike Simpson
Joanne Clarke	Margaret Heneghan	Michelle Millar	Alfredo Ramirez
Lucy Crofts	Peter Hogarth	Janet Milligan	Thomas Roberts
Howard Crossland	Claire Howells	Steve Mosley	Richard Tattershall
Roz Crawford	Jayne Kerr	Armon Nakhai	Laura Taylor
Luis de Leon Ortiz	Hannah King	Hari Patel	Sandra Thompson
Sallie Deysel	Sabine Koch	John Patterson	Sarah Troughton
Peter Dymoke	Sheetal Kumar	Peter Piga	Simon Whitehead
Elaine Forrest	Marian Lovelace	Olaf Pusch	Barbara Willis
Phil Garcia	Joanna Malvern	Tom Quinn	Michelle Winarto
			Katie Woods

Preface

PricewaterhouseCoopers' Manual of Accounting – Narrative reporting is a practical guide to the legal and other regulatory requirements that impact elements of financial statements that are common to users of both IFRS and UK GAAP, often referred to as the 'front half' of the financial statements. The Manual includes practical advice based on our work in the PricewaterhouseCoopers LLP's UK Accounting Consulting Services team in advising the firm's clients, partners and staff.

The Manual deals with the requirements of the Combined Code on corporate governance and looks at the rules for the business review and expanded guidance on the operating and financial review. Also explained are the directors' report and their remuneration report. This book has been produced in an A4 format to allow us to include more examples from financial statements and to reproduce them in their original layout to illustrate the diversity of presentation techniques used especially in the operating and financial review. This book supplements our two books which deal with the latter half of the financial statements: 'PricewaterhouseCoopers' Manual of Accounting – IFRS for the UK' and 'PricewaterhouseCoopers' Manual of Accounting – UK GAAP'.

Even in a work of this size it is not possible to cover every aspect of company reporting.

We hope that finance directors, accountants, legal practitioners, company administrators, financial advisers and auditors will find this manual useful.

Barry Johnson, Peter Holgate
PricewaterhouseCoopers LLP
London
October 2012

Contents

Abbreviations and terms used

AAPA	Association of Authorised Public Accountants
ABI	Association of British Insurers
AC	Appeal Cases, law reports
ACG	Audit Committees guidance
Accounts	financial statements
ADR	american depositary receipts
AESOP	all employee share ownership plan
the 1985 Act	the Companies Act 1985 (as amended by the Companies Act 1989)
the 1989 Act	the Companies Act 1989
the 2006 Act	the Companies Act 2006
ACCA	Association of Chartered Certified Accountants
ACT	advance corporation tax
AFS	available-for-sale
AG	Application Guidance
AGM	Annual General Meeting
AIC	Association of Investment Companies
AIM	Alternative Investment Market
AIMR	Alternative Investment Market Rules
AITC	Association of Investment Trust Companies
All ER	All England Law Reports
AMPS	auction market preferred shares
APB	Auditing Practices Board
APC	Auditing Practices Committee
App	Application note of a Financial Reporting Standard
App	Appendix
ARC	Accounting Regulatory Committee
ARSs	auction rate securities
ASB	Accounting Standards Board
ASC	Accounting Standards Committee
AVC	additional voluntary contribution
BBA	British Bankers' Association
BC	Basis for Conclusions (to an accounting standard)
BCLC	Butterworths Company Law Cases
BERR	Department for Business, Enterprise and Regulatory Reform (formerly the DTI and now BIS)
BEV	business enterprise value
BIS	Department for Business, Innovation and Skills (formerly BERR before that DTI)
BNA 1985	Business Names Act 1985
BOFI	banks and other financial industry entities
BVCA	British Venture Capital Association
C	currency unit
CA85	the Companies Act 1985
CA06	the Companies Act 2006
CCA	current cost accounting
CCAB	Consultative Committee of Accountancy Bodies Limited
CC	The Combined Code – Principles of good governance and code of best practice
CC(CP)	Companies Consolidation (Consequential Provisions) Act 1985
CEO	chief executive officer
CESR	Committee of European Securities Regulators
CGAA	Co-ordinating Group on Audit and Accounting Issues
CGU	cash-generating unit
Ch	Chancery Division, law reports
Chp	Chapter
chapter (1)	'PricewaterhouseCoopers' Manual of accounting' – chapter (1)
CIF	cost, insurance, freight
CIMA	Chartered Institute of Management Accountants
CIPFA	Chartered Institute of Public Finance and Accountancy

CISCO	The City Group for Smaller Companies
Cmnd	Command Paper
CBO	collateralised bond obligation
CDO	collateralised debt obligation
CLO	collateralised loan obligation
CMO	collateralised mortgage obligation
CODM	chief operating decision maker
COSO	Committee of Sponsoring Organisations of the Treadway Commission
CPP	current purchasing power
CR	Report of the committee on The Financial Aspects of Corporate Governance (the 'Cadbury Report')
CSR	corporate social responsibility
CTD	cumulative translation difference
CUV	continuing use value
DCF	discounted cash flow
DG XV	Directorate General XV
the 7th Directive	EC 7th Directive on Company Law
DP	discussion paper
DRC	depreciated replacement cost
DTI	Department of Trade and Industry
DTR	Disclosure rules and transparency rules
EASDAQ	European Association of Securities Dealers Automated Quotation
EBIT	earnings before interest and tax
EBITDA	earnings before interest, tax, depreciation and amortisation
EC	European Community
ECU	european currency unit
ED	exposure draft
EEA	European Economic Area
EEE	electrical and electronic equipment
EFRAG	European Financial Reporting Advisory Group
EGM	extraordinary general meeting
EITF	Emerging Issues Task Force (US)
EPS	earnings per share
ESOP	employee share ownership plan
ESOT	employee share ownership trust
EU	European Union
EU 2005 Regulation	Regulation (EC) No 1606/2002 on the application of International Accounting Standards
EUV	existing use value
FASB	Financial Accounting Standards Board (US)
FEE	The European Federation of Accountants
FIFO	first-in, first-out
financial statements	Accounts
FLA	Finance and Leasing Association
FM	facilities management
FOB	free on board
FPI	foreign private investors (US-listed)
FRAG	Financial Reporting and Auditing Group of the ICAEW
Framework	Framework for the preparation and presentation of financial statements
FRED	Financial Reporting Exposure Draft
FRA	forward rate agreement
FRC	Financial Reporting Council
FRN	floating rate note
FRRP	Financial Reporting Review Panel
FRS	Financial Reporting Standard
FRSSE	Financial Reporting Standard for Smaller Entities
FSA	Financial Services Authority
FTSE	The Financial Times Stock Exchange
FVLCS	fair value less costs to sell
FVTPL	at fair value through profit or loss
GAAP	generally accepted accounting principles (and practices)
GAAS	generally accepted auditing standards
GB	Great Britain

GCFR	Going Concern and Financial Reporting - published by the joint working group of the Hundred Group of finance directors, ICAEW and ICAS
GRI guidelines	Global Reporting Initiative guidelines
HEFCE	Higher Education Funding Council for England
HMSO	Her Majesty's Stationery Office
HP	hire purchase
HMRC	HM Revenue & Customs
HR	human resources
IAASB	International Auditing and Assurance Standards Board
IAS	International Accounting Standard (see also IFRS)
IASB	International Accounting Standards Board
IASC	International Accounting Standards Committee
IBF	Irish Bankers' Federation
IBNR	incurred but not reported
ICAEW	Institute of Chartered Accountants in England and Wales
ICAI	Institute of Chartered Accountants in Ireland
ICAS	Institute of Chartered Accountants of Scotland
ICFR	Internal Control and Financial Reporting - published by the joint working group of the Hundred Group of finance directors, ICAEW and ICAS
ICR	Industrial Cases Reports
ICSA	Institute of Chartered Secretaries and Administrators
ICTA	Income and Corporation Taxes Act 1988
IFAC	International Federation of Accountants
IFRIC	International Financial Reporting Interpretations Committee
IFRS	International Financial Reporting Standard (see also IAS)
IG	Implementation Guidance (to an accounting standard)
IGU	income-generating unit
IIMR	Institute of Investment Management and Research (see SIP)
IIR	internal rate of return
IIRC	International Integrated Reporting Committee
IoD	Institute of Directors
IOSCO	International Organisation of Securities Commissions
IPO	initial public offering
IPR&D	in-process research and development
IR	Statement on interim reporting issued by ASB
ISA	International Standard on Auditing
ISA (UK & Ire)	International Standard on Auditing (UK and Ireland)
ISDA	International Swap Dealers Association
ISP	internet service provider
IVSC	International Valuation Standards Committee
JWG	Joint Working Group
LIBID	London inter-bank bid rate
LIBOR	London inter-bank offered rate
LIFFE	the London International Financial Futures and Options Exchange
LIFO	last-in, first-out
LR	UK Listing Authority's Listing Rules
LTIP	long-term incentive plan
MBO	management buy-out
MD&A	management's discussion and analysis
MEEM	multi-period excess earnings method
MR	Master of the Rolls
NASDAQ	National Association of Securities Dealers Automated Quotations
NAPF	National Association of Pension Funds
NCI	non-controlling interest
NCU	national currency unit
NIC	national insurance contributions
OECD	Organisation for Economic Co-operation and Development
OEICs	open-ended investment companies
OFT	Office of Fair Trading

OFR	operating and financial review
OIAC	Oil Industry Accounting Committee
OTC	over-the-counter market
PA	preliminary announcement
para(s)	paragraph(s) of Schedules to the Companies Acts, or IFRSs or IASs or FRSs, or SSAPs, or FREDs, or EDs, or DPs, or text
PCAOB	Public Company Accounting Oversight Board (US)
PE	price-earnings
PHEI	previously held equity interest
PFI	Private Finance Initiative
PLUSR	Plus Rules for Issuers (for PLUS-quoted entities)
PPE	property, plant and equipment
PPERA	Political Parties, Elections and Referendums Act 2000
PPF	Pension Protection Fund
PRAG	Pensions Research Accountants Group
PS	Practice Statements
QC	Queen's Counsel
QCA	Quoted Companies Alliance
QUEST	qualifying employee share ownership trust
R&D	research and development
RCN	replacement cost new
RCNLD	replacement cost new less depreciation
RDG	regional development grant
Reg	regulation of a statutory instrument (for example, SI 1995/2092 Reg 5 = regulation 5 of The Companies (Summary Financial Statements) Regulations 1995)
RFR	relief-from-royalty
RICS	Royal Institution of Chartered Surveyors
ROI	return on investment
RS	Reporting Standard
SAC	the Standards Advisory Council
SAS	Statement of Auditing Standards
SC	Session Cases
Sch	Schedule to the Companies Act 1985 (eg CA85 4A Sch 85 = Schedule 4A, paragraph 85)
SDC	Standards Development Committee
SEC	Securities and Exchange Commission (US)
Sec(s)	Section(s) of the 1985 Act/Sections(s) of the 2006 Act
SEE	social, environmental and ethical
SERPS	State earnings related pension scheme
SFAC	Statement of Financial Accounting Concepts issued in the US
SFAS	Statement of Financial Accounting Standards issued in the US
SI	Statutory Instrument
SIC	Standing Interpretation Committee of the IASC (see IFRIC)
SIP	Society of Investment Professionals (formerly IIMR)
SIPs	share incentive plans
SMEs	small and medium-sized entities
SOI	Statement of Intent
SoP	Statement of principles
SORIE	statement of recognised income and expense
SORP	Statement of Recommended Practice
SPE	special purpose entity
SPV	special purpose vehicle
SSAP	Statement of Standard Accounting Practice
Stock Exchange (or LSE)	the London Stock Exchange
STRGL	statement of total recognised gains and losses
TR	Technical Release of the ICAEW
TSR	total shareholder return
TUPE	Transfer of Undertakings (Protection of Employment) Regulations
UITF	Urgent Issues Task Force
UK	United Kingdom
UKCGC	UK Corporate Governance Code

US	United States of America
VAT	value added tax
VIU	value in use
VIE	variable interest entity
WACC	weighted average cost of capital
WARA	weighted average return analysis
WEEE	Waste electrical and electronic equipment
WLR	Weekly Law Reports

Chapter 1

Introduction

Introduction

Corporate reporting today

1.1 Recent years have seen major changes in financial reporting worldwide. It would be difficult to argue with the assertion that the biggest single change has been the process of global harmonisation around international financial reporting standards (IFRS), including their adoption for the consolidated financial statements of listed companies in the UK and the rest of the EU. But an important further trend has been the increasing importance and role of the various constituents of what is often called the 'front half' of the annual report, that is: management's commentary on how the business has fared since the last report and on its future prospects; governance reports; reports on directors' remuneration; and indeed the statutory directors' report. This second trend is the subject of this book.

1.2 It is widely recognised that pure accounting numbers, however good the accounting policies and however extensive the notes disclosure, are only part of the story. To be really useful to investors and other users, they need to be supplemented by additional information – often in narrative form – that seeks to give a sense of context, an explanation of what is going on and a sense of what might happen in the future. This, taken in aggregate, can be described as 'narrative/corporate reporting', as opposed to financial reporting.

1.3 The Companies Act 2006 requires management to provide a fair review of the company's business along with a description of its principal risks and uncertainties, in other words a business review. The requirement to present a business review is noteworthy in two respects. First, it applies to all companies, except those that are 'small' according to the definitions in the Companies Act. So many medium-sized private companies, including wholly-owned subsidiaries of groups, have to produce business reviews. Second, the requirements are flexible and tailored to the circumstances. For example, the review should be *"a balanced and comprehensive analysis of the development and performance of the business of the company during the financial year, and the position of the company at the end of that year, consistent with the size and complexity of the business"*. Also, key performance indicators need to be disclosed *"to the extent necessary for an understanding of the development, performance or position of the business of the company"*. This is sensible, in that it expects more when there is more to tell and where, in practice, there is a significant public interest to satisfy.

1.4 For a large diverse company, the business review can be detailed and complex. The ASB has issued non-mandatory guidance to assist companies preparing operating and financial reviews (OFRs), which although not written with the business review specifically in mind, does deal with a number of its required disclosures. The guidance is principles based; that is, information should be presented through the eyes of management focussing on matters relevant to members in a way that is comprehensive, understandable and forward-looking as well as being balanced, neutral and comparable over time.

1.5 A well-managed company has a clear vision of its ambitions, of how it will achieve its goals, measure its progress along the way and remunerate its people. By reflecting effective internal management in transparent external reporting, a company can give confidence to stakeholders that the company's management have the company on the right track. That is why it is important that the various components of the annual report are linked; for example, that the company's stated objectives are not just a 'wish list' but are linked to specific actions to be taken to drive the achievement of strategy.

1.6 Under current government proposals, the narrative reporting regime will be changed. It is proposed that a 'strategic report' and an on-line annual directors' statement will replace the business review and directors' report. The strategic report would incorporate the current business review content into a concise report of the company's strategy, risks and business model. This information would be linked to high level financial information and, for quoted companies, to key information of corporate governance and remuneration. These proposals are not dealt with further in this book.

The politics of corporate reporting

1.7 The emphasis on a broader notion of corporate reporting is to some extent a social and political trend. There has been much debate in the last years about whether companies should have as their objectives a narrow focus on the shareholders or a wider focus on a range of stakeholders.

1.8 Some aspects of the front half owe more to politics than to financial reporting. Politics, in a broad sense, is already taking narrative reporting into more fields. Corporate reporting is increasingly covering environmental reporting and social reporting of various kinds, some of which are requirements of the Companies Act 2006.

1.9 Politics, rather than accounting, lies behind the UK's extensive disclosure requirements for directors' remuneration. Executive pay levels, particularly in the financial sector, have been the subject of much comment in recent times. The government has expressed concern that there is a disconnect between executive pay and performance, with pay levels in recent years increasing at rates that are out of line with the rates of improvement in company performance. To improve shareholder engagement with companies, the government intends to introduce legislation that will give shareholders a binding vote on pay policy. The detailed disclosure requirements for executive remuneration will be amended to give greater transparency; the intention is to give shareholders more transparent, good quality information to enable them to hold companies to account so that executive pay is better linked to company performance.

International practice

1.10 Although it is seen in the UK as part of the directors' report, the requirement for a business review has an EU origin, namely a 2003 amendment to the earlier 4th and 7th accounting directives. The recitals to the 2003 directive say: *"The annual report and consolidated annual report are important elements of financial reporting. Enhancement, in line with current best practice, of the existing requirement for these to present a fair review of the development of the business and of its position, in a manner consistent with the size and complexity of the business, is necessary to promote greater consistency and give additional guidance concerning the information a "fair review" is expected to contain. The information should not be restricted to the financial aspects of the company's business...".*

1.11 There are also further international comparisons that can be made. For example, both Australia and Canada have similar guidance and principles to those used by the ASB in its OFR guidance. The US SEC requires a Management Discussion and Analysis (MD&A), which while differing in detail, is largely based on the same objectives and principles as used by the ASB.

1.12 The IASB's practice statement, 'Management commentary', provides non-mandatory guidance for entities that present management commentary relating to financial statements that have been prepared in accordance with IFRS. This guidance is very similar to the ASB's OFR guidance.

1.13 For UK listed companies applying IFRS, IFRS 8, 'Operating segments', requires that the segmental information disclosed in the financial statements is based on the information that is reported to the chief operating decisions maker (CODM). IFRS 8 uses a 'through management's eyes' approach requiring information to be reported on which the management governs the business. Hence, it is also important that the information given in the 'front half' is consistent with this segmental information. IFRS 8 also requires a reconciliation between the management information and the results prepared in accordance with IFRS.

1.14 Narrative reporting is developing worldwide. As in the UK, 'integrated reporting' is seen as important internationally. The International Integrated Reporting Committee (IIRC) comprises a global cross-section of people from the corporate, investment, accounting, securities, regulatory, academic and standard-setting sectors as well as civil society. It promotes corporate reporting that demonstrates the linkages between a company's strategy, governance and financial performance and the social, environmental and economic context within which it operates.

Corporate governance

1.15 The UK has a well established corporate governance regime that stems from the early 1990s when the Cadbury Committee reported in response to a series of scandals, fuelled by the then recession. Some governance issues have attracted significant political and public interest because they strike at the root of companies' objectives – none more so than the accountability of boards to shareholders in relation to executive pay.

1.16   The regime in the UK is set out in a corporate governance code – the UK Corporate Governance Code – which uses a 'comply or explain' principle, whereby if a company has not complied with the Code's provisions during the year it provides an explanation for those provisions with which it did not comply. The Code applies to all Premium listed companies, including overseas companies. It includes amongst other matters annual re-election of all directors and external facilitation of board performance reviews at least every three years (both these provision apply for FTSE 350 companies only).

The approach in this Manual

1.17   Considerations relating to the front half apply to all UK companies at least to some extent. Even the smallest company has to prepare a directors' report. Other requirements come into play once a company achieves a certain size, becomes listed or pays its directors above a certain amount. For these various reports, we give our views on what the requirements or recommendations mean and on what is good disclosure in the areas in which there are no rules or guidance. As part of that approach, this Manual contains many examples and extracts from financial reports.

1.18   This Manual can be viewed as a supplement to two other works. One is the 'PricewaterhouseCoopers' Manual of Accounting – UK GAAP', which gives guidance to the many UK companies that still follow UK GAAP. The second is the 'PricewaterhouseCoopers' Manual of Accounting – IFRS for the UK', which applies to those UK listed groups that have to follow IFRS and other entities that have opted to apply IFRS. The issues described in this Manual relating to the 'front half' apply to some extent to both categories of company, though the requirements and expectations for listed companies are greater than for others.

Chapter 2

Directors' report

Directors' report

Introduction

2.1 The directors' report is one of the mandatory components of a company's annual financial statements and reports for members. It must also be delivered to the Registrar of Companies by all companies except those entitled to the small companies exemption (see from para 2.143). [CA06 Secs 444(1), 444A(1), 445(1), 446(1), 447(1)].

2.2 The duty to prepare a directors' report is contained in section 415 of the Companies Act 2006. However, the Companies Act 2006 does not contain all the disclosure requirements: many of the detailed requirements are contained in Schedule 5 to SI 2008/409, 'The Small Companies and Groups (Accounts and Directors' Report) Regulations 2008', for companies or groups falling within the definition of 'small' (see chapter 31 of the Manual of Accounting – UK GAAP) and Schedule 7 to SI 2008/410, 'The Large and Medium-sized Companies and Groups (Accounts and Reports) Regulations 2008' for all other companies.

2.3 Directors have a responsibility to prepare the report even if none of the directors at the time the report is produced were directors during the period covered by the report. They cannot avoid this responsibility simply because they were not responsible for all or some of the activities that are being reported on.

2.4 The principal objectives of the directors' report are to supplement the information in the financial statements with discussions and explanations about the company's activities and its future and also to provide details of other non-financial matters. The purpose of the narrative information is to give the user of the financial statements a more complete picture of the company.

2.5 Listed companies regard the annual report and financial statements as an important mode of communication with shareholders. They, therefore, use the annual report to provide shareholders with information about all aspects of the company's activities and the environment in which it operates, the company's objectives and its values. Such information may be presented outside the statutory directors' report, for example, in the chairman's statement or in a separate operating and financial review (see further chapter 3).

2.6 Companies structure the 'front half' of their annual reports (that is, the elements of the annual report that come before the financial statements) in a variety of ways. The Companies Act 2006 gives directors safe harbour from civil liability for statements or omissions in the directors' report (and also the directors' remuneration report prepared by quoted companies) and as a result many identify the entire front half as the directors' report. (See para 2.150.1.) Others name the majority of the front half 'business review', or alternatively have separate sections for an operating, financial and/or business review, directors' report, corporate governance statement and directors' remuneration report.

2.7 In this chapter, we deal with the mandatory disclosure requirements that apply to the directors' report, including the business review. In addition to those requirements, the ASB has published non-mandatory good practice guidance on the operating and financial review (OFR). In deciding how to comply with the some of the disclosure requirements, companies may wish to consider that guidance. In discussing the various disclosure requirements in this chapter, we refer to chapter 3 on the OFR, when the ASB's statement provides guidance on the particular point under discussion.

[The next paragraph is 2.11.]

Companies reporting under IFRS

2.11 The requirements relating to the directors' report are contained within the body of the Companies Act and, thus, apply to all companies, regardless of whether the financial statements are prepared under IFRS or UK GAAP.

Consolidated financial statements

2.12 The Companies Act 2006 requires that, where an entity is a parent company and the directors prepare consolidated financial statements, the directors' report must be a consolidated report covering the company and its subsidiary undertakings included in the consolidation. [CA06 Sec 415(2)].

2.13 Where appropriate, the consolidated report should give greater emphasis to matters that are significant to the company and its subsidiary undertakings included in the consolidation, taken as a whole. [CA06 Sec 415(3)].

[The next paragraph is 2.16.]

Matters to be dealt with in the directors' report

Principal activities

2.16 The principal activities of both the company and of its subsidiaries during the year should be stated. [CA06 Sec 416(1)]. It is appropriate to include details of any significant change in the group's activities. Listed companies are required to go further and describe their business model (see para 2.21.40).

2.16.1 It is worth noting that a 'listed company' is not the same as a 'quoted company'. Rules applying to listed companies are set out in the FSA Handbook, which includes the Listing Rules, Disclosure Rules and Transparency Rules. Rules applying to quoted companies are set out in the Companies Act 2006. A company may be both 'listed' and 'quoted'; as such, it has to comply with both sets of rules. A 'listed company' is defined in the FSA Handbook as one that has any class of it securities listed. A 'quoted company' is defined as a company whose equity share capital:

- has been included in the official list in accordance with the provisions of Part VI of the Financial Services and Markets Act 2000;

- is officially listed in an EEA State; or

- is admitted to dealing on either the New York Stock Exchange or the exchange known as NASDAQ.

[CA06 Sec 385].

2.16.2 The application of the definitions to different categories of company is set out in the table below.

Status of company's securities	FSA Handbook: 'listed company'	Companies Act 2006: 'quoted company'
Equity shares listed in the UK official list	✓	✓
Debt securities (but not equity shares) listed in the UK official list	✓	✗
Equity shares listed in another EEA state or admitted to dealing on New York Stock Exchange or NASDAQ, but not on UK official list	✗	✓
Equity shares traded on AIM	✗	✗

2.17 The term 'principal activities' is not defined in the Companies Act 2006. A useful description of a company's principal activities would describe what the company does to make money (or to achieve whatever other objective it has). Often, a company's activities are in diverse industries or classes of business, which represent segments for the purposes of its financial statements. Guidance is provided in SSAP 25, which defines a separate class of business as the distinguishable component of the entity that provides a separate product or service or a separate group of related products or services. [SSAP 25 para 11]. Distinguishable components of an entity may include, for example, mining, textiles, electrical etc. Broad categories such as manufacturing, wholesaling and retailing are not indicative of the industries in which the entity operates. Those terms should not generally be used to describe an entity's industry segments without identification of the products or services. IFRS 8 considers segments entirely differently and uses a 'through the eyes of management' approach. Under this approach, the operating segments reported externally are those that management uses as a basis for its decision-making.

[The next paragraph is 2.19.]

2.19 The categories of principal activities described in the directors' report should, as far as possible, be consistent with the information that is provided for segmental reporting purposes. So that investors can build a picture of the company from its component parts, it is desirable to have consistency between the description of the company's activities and the measurement of its performance. There are various factors that should be taken into account when deciding whether or not an entity operates in different industry segments and these are discussed further in chapter 10 on segmental reporting in both the Manual of Accounting – UK GAAP and the Manual of Accounting – IFRS for the UK.

2.20 A change in activity should be reported whenever there has been a commencement of a new activity or a complete withdrawal from a previous activity rather than a change in the degree of the activity undertaken. Such a change may be brought about by the acquisition or disposal of a subsidiary undertaking. In order to provide meaningful disclosure of the changes in activities, the extent to which the acquisition or disposal has impacted on any resultant change in the group's activities should be considered. Indeed, FRS 3 requires that if an acquisition, a sale or a termination has a material impact on a major business segment, this impact should be disclosed and explained. [FRS 3 para 53]. IFRS 8's predecessor, IAS 14 encouraged entities to disclose the nature and amount of any items of segment revenue and segment expense that were of such size, nature or incidence that their disclosure was relevant to explain the performance of each reportable segment for the period. [IAS 14 para 59]. Although there are no equivalent requirements in IFRS 8 or in UK GAAP, we consider such disclosure to be strongly recommended.

2.21 The degree of detail that should be given under principal activities will obviously depend upon the nature of the company's business. For companies operating in one or two business segments, the relevant information is normally given in the directors' report. Multinational corporations engaged in a wide range of business activities tend to include the relevant details elsewhere in the annual report and accounts, for example, in a separate statement that sets out a detailed review of their operations. Where this is done, a reference should be given in the directors' report to where the necessary information can be found. Table 2.1 provides an illustration of the disclosure of principal activities.

Table 2.1 — Principal activities

Smiths Group plc — Annual report and accounts — 31 July 2011

Group directors' report (extract)

Principal activities

The principal activities of the Company and its subsidiaries (the Group) are and, during the year ended 31 July 2011, were the development, manufacture, sale and support of:

- advanced security equipment, including trace detection, millimetre-wave, infrared, biological detection and diagnostics, that detect and identify explosives, narcotics, weapons, chemical agents, biohazards and contraband;

- mechanical seals, seal support systems, engineered bearings, power transmission couplings, specialist filtration systems and other hardware for the oil and gas, chemical, pharmaceutical, pulp and paper and mining sectors;

- medical devices aligned to specific therapies, principally airway, pain and temperature management, infusion, needle protection, critical care monitoring and vascular access;

- specialised electronic and radio frequency products that connect, protect and control critical systems for the global wireless telecommunications, aerospace, defence, space, medical, rail, test and industrial markets; and

- engineered components including ducting, hose assemblies and heating elements that move and heat fluids and gases for the aerospace, medical, industrial, construction and domestic markets.

The main manufacturing operations are in the UK, the Americas, Continental Europe and China.

Business review

2.21.1 The directors should include in their report a review of the business of the company and its subsidiaries. [CA06 Sec 417(1)]. Where it is not included within the directors' report, the business review should be incorporated into the directors' report by specific cross-reference. Where a company is entitled to either the small companies or medium sized companies exemption (see further the Manual of Accounting – Interim financial reporting, there are reduced disclosure requirements (see para 2.21.4 below).

2.21.2 The purpose of the business review is to inform the company's members and help them assess how the directors have performed their duty to promote the company's success. [CA06 Sec 417(2)].

2.21.3   In promoting the company's success, directors must, in particular, have regard to the following:

- The likely consequences of any decision in the long-term.

- The interests of the company's employees.

- The need to foster the company's business relationships with suppliers, customers and others.

- The impact of the company's operations on the community and the environment.

- The desirability for the company maintaining a reputation for high standards of business conduct.

- The need to act fairly as between the company's members.

[CA06 Sec 172].

2.21.3.1   The business review must be 'balanced and comprehensive'. [Sec 417(4)]. A balanced review is one that reports both good and bad news. In a press notice, the FRRP reported that it had held discussions with Rio Tinto plc on whether additional information about some of the company's operations referred to in the 2008 business review ought to have been included in the review to comply with the legal requirement for a balanced analysis. Following those discussions, in their report and accounts for the year ended 31 December 2010, the directors of Rio Tinto plc included more information about environmental matters, social and community issues and related reputational risk.

2.21.3.2   Little authoritative guidance is available on the practical aspects of preparing a business review, which, for a large diverse company, could be detailed and complex. Although not written with the business review specifically in mind, the ASB's reporting statement on the OFR ('RS (OFR)') does deal with a number of its required disclosures, as shown in the table above. So, it is common for those preparing an OFR — which incorporates a statutory business review — or those simply preparing a business review as part of the directors' report to comply with the RS (OFR), to ensure that investors receive the most appropriate information. Hence, the example disclosures within the chapter on the OFR may also be considered when preparing a business review. See chapter 3 for guidance on the RS (OFR). Chapter 3 also provides information about publications that will be of assistance to companies preparing a business review, whether complying with the RS (OFR) or not. These publications and other good practice examples can be found at www.corporatereporting.com.

2.21.4   The legal requirements vary according to the type of company: a small company does not have to prepare a business review; all other companies must do so; but the reporting requirements vary depending on the company's size and status. A company will comply with the legal requirements for a business review if it elects to comply with the ASB's RS (OFR) (see chapter 3). This overlap between the law and the RS (OFR) is expressed diagrammatically below and described more fully in the subsequent paragraphs.

Interaction of legal requirements and non-mandatory guidance on the business review

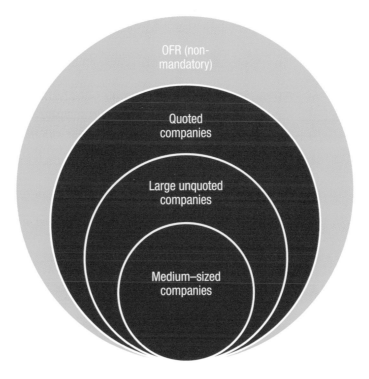

 Sec 417 requirements

 Non-mandatory guidance in the ASB's RS (OFR)

2.21.4.1 The legal requirements applying to different types of company are set out in the table below. The table includes references to the relevant paragraphs of the non-mandatory RS (OFR) for each of the legal disclosure requirements.

Type of company	Disclosure requirement	Non-mandatory guidance in the RS (OFR) paragraphs
Small company (see from para 2.143)	Business review not required. [Sec 417(1)].	
Medium-sized company	■ The business review must contain, at a minimum:	
	■ A fair review of the company's business.	22, 30-32, 36-37
	■ A description of the principal risks and uncertainties facing the company.	27(c), 52-56
	■ The review should be consistent with the business' size and complexity and provide a balanced and comprehensive analysis of:	
	■ The development and performance of the company's business during the financial year.	27(b), 30-32, 43-46
	■ The company's position at the end of the year.	27(d), 30-32, 50-51, 60-74
	■ The review should also include, to the extent necessary for an understanding of the company's business, analysis using *financial* key performance indicators (KPIs).	38-42, 75-77
	■ The review must contain, where appropriate, references to and additional explanation of amounts included in the financial statements. [Sec 417 (3), (4), (6)(a), (7), (8)].	13-15
Large unquoted company	All of the above plus, where appropriate, analysis using other KPIs, including information on environmental and employee matters. [Sec 417(6)(b)].	38-42,75-77
Quoted company (see para 2.16.1)	■ The main trends and factors likely to affect the future development, performance and position of the company's business (see from para 2.37.6 below).	8-12, 27(b), 33-35, 47-49
	■ *Information about persons with whom the company has contractual or other arrangements that are essential to the company's business (see from para 2.21.35).	28(d),57-59
	■ *Information about ■ environmental matters (including the impact of the company's business on the environment) (see from para 2.28); ■ the company's employees (see from para 2.28); ■ social and community issues (see from para 2.28); and ■ including information about any of the company's policies in relation to those matters and the effectiveness of those policies. [CA06 Sec 417(5)]. The disclosures above are required *"to the extent necessary for an understanding of the development, performance or position of the company's business".* *If the review does not contain information on any of the items asterisked above, it must state that fact. [CA06 Sec 417(5)].	28(a), (b), (c) 29,35

2.21.4.2   The meaning of 'quoted company' is discussed in paragraph 2.16.1.

2.21.4.3   Balanced reporting is discussed further in chapter 3.

2.21.5   Where an entity is a parent company and prepares consolidated financial statements, the business review should be a consolidated review covering the company and its subsidiary undertakings included in the consolidation. [CA06 Sec 417(9)]. There is no requirement for the parent company to prepare a separate review for the company alone.

[The next paragraph is 2.21.9.]

Applying the requirements to different types of company

2.21.9   As mentioned above, all companies must prepare a business review, other than those entitled to the small companies exemption (see para 2.21.1). The ASB's RS (OFR) offers some guidance on practically implementing the various business review requirements; this guidance is most often used by listed companies (see chapter 3). Guidance to assist directors in preparing a business review is limited for private entities, although it is open to them to use the RS (OFR) if they wish to do so.

2.21.10   Many of the requirements of the business review are preceded with the words *"to the extent necessary for an understanding of the development, performance or position of the company's business"*; this gives directors some discretion over the level of detail that should be presented in the business review.

2.21.11   Bearing in mind that the overriding purpose of the business review is as a tool for communicating with members (see para 2.21.2), we believe that the type and extent of disclosure required depends on the extent to which an entity's share ownership is dispersed and how close/involved the owners are to the business' management. This distinction can be illustrated as follows:

- *Owner-managed companies*: Members already have a good understanding of the company's development, performance and position. The minimum information to comply with the legislation is all that is needed to present a clear picture to members.

- *Wholly owned subsidiaries:* The position for wholly-owned subsidiaries of a parent company that actively monitors the business performance on an ongoing basis is similar to that for owner-managed companies. Often both the management and reporting of risk and key performance indicators for wholly-owned subsidiaries are undertaken at the group level. In such circumstances, it is appropriate to clarify this position and also to state that the company's directors believe that analysis using key performance indicators is not necessary or appropriate to understand the business' development, performance or position. The statement should usefully refer to further information available in the group annual report, making clear that it does not form part of the company's annual report. The cross-reference should be to a specific paragraph, heading, or page in the group annual report. See further paragraph 2.21.13 below.

- *Public interest, AIM-listed or separately managed private companies:* For public interest companies, AIM-listed (or PLUS-quoted) companies and private companies (including non-wholly owned subsidiaries) where ownership is distinct from those who manage the entity on members' behalf, the amount of information disclosed should reflect the explicit requirements implied by BIS in its pronouncements and guidance (for example, *"the business review would include information on objectives, strategies and resources where necessary to provide a fair review of the company"*). The minimum disclosures described for owner-managed entities should be supplemented by additional contextual information around risk and key performance indicators, as well as a description of the entity's strategy and business environment.

- *Quoted companies:* Fuller disclosure is necessary for quoted companies, to assist members in understanding the entity's development, performance and position. The most appropriate guidance is in the recommendations of the ASB's RS (OFR). (See chapter 3).

2.21.12   Given the broad nature of the categories set out above, and particularly public interest entities with dispersed ownership, there needs to be a degree of flexibility in the approach chosen by companies depending on their circumstances.

2.21.13 As mentioned above, a pragmatic approach to disclosing principal risks and KPIs for a wholly-owned subsidiary of a UK parent company may be taken where the subsidiary is managed as part of a wider unit, on a group basis rather than a statutory basis. Wording such as that provided below is typical:

"*Principal risks and uncertainties*

From the perspective of the company, the principal risks and uncertainties are integrated with the principal risks of the group and are not managed separately. Accordingly, the principal risks and uncertainties of R Group Ltd, which include those of the company, are discussed on page x of the group's annual report which does not form part of this report.

Key performance indicators (KPIs)

The directors of R Group Ltd manage the group's operations on a divisional basis. For this reason, the company's directors believe that analysis using key performance indicators for the company is not necessary or appropriate for an understanding of the development, performance or position of the business of R Ltd. The development, performance and position of the retail division of R Group Ltd, which includes the company, is discussed on page y of the group's annual report, which does not form part of this report."

[The next paragraph is 2.21.15.]

2.21.15 The table below provides a guide to the type of information that we believe should be included in a business review for private companies with dispersed ownership and public interest companies (other than those for whom compliance with the ASB's RS (OFR) is more relevant).

Heading	Suggested type of content
Principal activities	Nature of the business, extent of operations. Results in terms of revenues and profits. Net debt position and net cash inflow.
Business environment	Description of the market and competitive environment – market factors and dynamics that can affect the business environment, for example, competitors and market outlook. Regulatory environment – legal, agency or other regulatory factors that impose requirements on the conduct of business activities; for example, deregulation and privatisation. Macro environment – factors that could have a material impact on corporate performance; for example, interest rates, demographics and economic outlook.
Strategy	Overriding objectives of the company and, where relevant, the group. The company's and, where relevant, the group's strategy for achieving these objectives, including the priorities for action, and an explanation of each strategy, as well as how successful implementation of the strategy is measured.
Research and development (R&D)	Actions taken in the area of R&D and how these link into the group's strategy.
Future outlook	Expected development of the business environment, including factors that may affect the quality and sustainability of performance, and any planned actions to address these developments.

Principal risks and uncertainties	The principal risks and uncertainties that have the focus of the directors' attention – not simply a list of all risk factors that the group faces – as well as the approach taken by management to these risks.
Key performance indicators	The measures used to assess progress against objectives and strategies – including quantifying of these measures, trend data, definition, method of calculation and any relevant narrative.

Principal risks and uncertainties

2.21.16   As noted in paragraph 2.21.4.1 above, the business review should include disclosure of the principal risks and uncertainties facing the company. [Sec 417]. The FRRP has expressed concern at the quality of reporting of principal risks and uncertainties in the business review. In Practice Note 130, the FRRP states that in reviewing the business review of certain companies, it has commented on a number of occasions on the issues it has encountered in assessing whether directors' reports comply with this requirement of the Companies Act 2006. In particular, the Panel has challenged a number of companies where:

■ the directors' report does not clearly identify which risks and uncertainties the directors believe to be the principal ones facing the business;

■ a long list of principal risks and uncertainties is given and the list raises a question as to whether all the risks and uncertainties on the list are actually principal ones;

■ the description given of a risk or uncertainty is in generic terms and it is not clear how that risk or uncertainty applies to the company's circumstances;

■ the disclosure is of a risk framework rather than of the risks or uncertainties themselves;

■ the principal risks and uncertainties disclosed are not consistent with other information given in the report and accounts; and

■ the directors' report does not state how the company manages its principal risks and uncertainties. As the purpose of the business review is to inform members of the company and to help them assess how the directors have performed their duty to promote the success of the company, the FRRP believes that a Board should state how the company manages its principal risks and uncertainties.

2.21.17   The FRRP encourages boards of directors to consider their disclosure of the principal risks and uncertainties facing their businesses by considering the following questions:

■ Do the disclosures state clearly which are the principal risks and uncertainties facing the business?

■ Are those risks and uncertainties described as principal; that is the main risks and uncertainties that currently face the business? For example, have the risks and uncertainties listed as principal been the subject of recent discussions at board or audit committee meetings? Are there risks which have been the subject of such discussions that should be considered as principal?

■ Is the description of each principal risk and uncertainty sufficient for shareholders to understand the nature of that risk or uncertainty and how it might affect the company?

■ Are the principal risks and uncertainties described in a manner consistent with the way in which they are discussed within the company?

■ Are the principal risks and uncertainties shown consistent with the rest of the report and accounts? Are there risks and uncertainties on the list which are not referred to elsewhere or are there significant risks and uncertainties discussed elsewhere which do not appear on the list?

■ Is there a description, in the directors' report, or elsewhere in the report and accounts and explicitly cross-referenced from the directors' report, of how the company manages each of the principal risks and uncertainties?

2.21.18   In addition, the FRC report, 'An update for directors of listed companies: Responding to increased country and currency risk in financial reports', draws attention to issues that directors should consider when providing a balanced and understandable assessment of a company's position and prospects in the context of increased country and currency risk. The issues directors could consider include, where relevant:

- The company's exposure to country risk, direct or to the extent practical indirect, through financial instruments, through foreign operations and through exposure to trading counterparties (customers and suppliers).
- The impact of austerity measures being adopted in a number of countries on the company's forecasts, impairment testing, going concern considerations, etc.
- Possible consequences of currency events that are not factored into forecasts but may impact reported exposures and the sensitivity testing of impairment or going concern considerations.
- A post balance sheet date event requiring enhanced disclosures to adequately inform investors and other users.

2.21.19   Disclosure of principal risks and uncertainties is discussed further in chapter 3.

Key performance indicators

2.21.20   Key performance indicators (KPIs) are defined as "*factors by reference to which the development, performance or position of the business of the company can be measured effectively*". [CA06 Sec 417(6)]. The ASB's RS (OFR) provides a more detailed definition, describing KPIs as "*...quantified measurements that reflect the critical success factors of an entity and disclose progress towards achieving a particular objective or objectives*". [RS (OFR) para 3].

2.21.21   The Companies Act 2006 does not prescribe specific KPIs that entities should disclose. Entities use a variety of different KPIs and the relevance of a particular KPI varies from industry to industry and even from one entity to another within an industry. In addition, methods of calculating particular KPIs may vary from one entity to another. Directors will, therefore, need to determine which KPIs are necessary for an understanding of the business.

2.21.22   Directors may look to RS (OFR) for further guidance on disclosure of KPIs. The RS (OFR) sets out the recommendations for disclosure for each KPI. In addition, RS (OFR)'s implementation guidance contains examples of disclosure of KPIs. Further guidance on KPIs, including example disclosures, is provided in chapter 3.

Cross-referencing between the directors' report, business review and OFR

2.21.23   If companies that prepare an OFR in accordance with the RS (OFR) were also required to give information to meet the business review requirements in their directors' report, there would be considerable duplication.

2.21.24   The BIS publication 'Guidance on changes to the directors' report requirements in the Companies Act 1985 – April and December 2005' clarified that where the directors' report and a voluntary OFR are published together, it is acceptable to cross-refer from the directors' report to the OFR. This guidance is considered to be relevant to similar provisions of the Companies Act 2006. The cross-reference must clearly refer (by page numbers, paragraph numbers or headings) to the specific section in the OFR. The guidance provides example wording for such a cross-reference as follows:

> "*The information that fulfils the requirements of the business review can be found in the OFR on pages x to y, which are incorporated in this report by reference.*"

Likely future developments

2.21.25   Paragraph 7(b) of Schedule 7 to SI 2008/410 requires the directors' report to contain an indication of the likely future developments in the company's business. Companies subject to the small companies' regime are not required to make this disclosure.

2.21.25.1   In addition, for quoted companies, as noted in paragraph 2.21.4, section 417(5)(a) of the Companies Act 2006 requires the directors' report to contain an indication of the main trends and factors likely to affect the future development, performance and position of the company's business.

2.21.26   As with the provisions relating to a review of the company's business during the year, the Companies Act 2006 contains no amplification as to the extent and the scope of this commentary. In practice, directors tend to interpret this requirement by providing information that will have a significant impact on future earnings and profitability of the company or the group. For example, information on development of new products or services, business expansion or rationalisation plans, capital expenditure plans and proposed disposals and acquisitions is fairly common.

2.21.27 Companies can refer to RS (OFR) for further guidance in this area (see chapter 3).

[The next paragraph is 2.21.35.]

Contractual arrangements

2.21.35 Quoted companies should disclose information about persons with whom the company has contractual or other arrangements that are essential to the company's business (but see para 2.21.39). Some contractual arrangements should be disclosed as part of the disclosure on the principal risk disclosures (see para 2.21.16 above).

2.21.36 An example disclosure of contractual arrangements is given in Table 2.1.1.

Table 2.1.1 – Contractual and other arrangements essential to the business

Lonmin plc – Report and accounts – 30 September 2011

Directors' Report – Governance (extract)

4.12 Essential contractual arrangements

Group companies are party to contracts and other arrangements which the Board judges are essential to the business of the Company:

- **Mineral rights** – for any mining company, its mineral titles are of crucial importance and therefore the New Order Prospecting Rights and New Order Mining Licences granted by the South African Department of Mineral Resources in respect of our operations in that country fall into this category, as do the various Old Order prospecting and mining rights currently held pending conversion into New Order rights.

- **Contracts for the purchase of materials and services** – while most of the inputs needed by the Group's mines and refining facilities are secured through competitive tendering in the open market, the Group is heavily dependent on two State-owned near-monopolies, Eskom for the supply of electricity, and Rand Water in respect of the supply of water. Long term contracts are in place with both vendors and there is extensive engagement, both at industry and Lonmin levels, with these critical suppliers.

- **Financing arrangements** – the Company and Group have a number of loan and other funding facilities with South African and international banks. These facilities were restructured during the year and are described in more detail in Note 18.

- **Contracts relating to labour** – we have formal recognition and collective agreements with trade unions representing the vast majority of the Group's employees in South Africa, most notably in the NUM, but also CEPPWAWU, Solidarity and UASA. These govern the relationships between the parties and the basis on which wages and other allowances paid to our employees will be determined.

- **Contracts for the sale of goods** – the majority of the Group's production of PGMs in the year was sold to either BASF or Mitsubishi. The Group has highly valued long term relationships and contracts with both companies.

2.21.37 The ASB's RS (OFR) provides further guidance on disclosure around relationships. See chapter 3.

Seriously prejudicial

2.21.38 A limited exemption has been provided under the Companies Act 2006 such that disclosure of information is not required regarding *"information about impending developments or matters in the course of negotiation if the disclosure would, in the opinion of the directors, be seriously prejudicial to the interests of the company"*. [CA06 Sec 417(10)].

2.21.39 In addition, quoted companies need not disclose information about essential contractual or other arrangements if such disclosure would, in the directors' opinion, be seriously prejudicial to the counterparty of those arrangements or contrary to the public interest. [CA06 Sec 417(11)].

Disclosure of business model for listed entities — UK Corporate Governance Code

2.21.40 The UK Corporate Governance Code (2010) recommends that a listed company's annual report should include an explanation of the basis on which the company generates or preserves value over the longer term (the business model) and the strategy for delivering the company's objectives. [UK CGC C.1.2].

2.21.41 The recommendation goes further than the statutory requirement for a business review for quoted companies. However, the footnote accompanying the recommendation to disclose the business model states that it would be desirable if the explanation were located in the same part of the annual report as the business review. It goes on to say that guidance on what should be considered in an explanation of the business model is provided in paragraphs 30 to 32 of the ASB's RS (OFR) – see chapter 3. The FRC considers that companies that are properly applying the ASB's RS (OFR) will already be meeting the new recommendation.

[The next paragraph is 2.28.]

Environmental and social matters

2.28   The Companies Act 2006 requires the directors of quoted companies to disclose information about the following in their directors' report:

- environmental matters (including the impact of the company's business on the environment),

- the company's employees; and

- social and community issues,

including information about any policies of the company in relation to those matters and the effectiveness of those policies. [CA06 Sec 417(5)].

2.29   The disclosures are required *"to the extent necessary for an understanding of the development, performance or position of the company's business".* If the review does not contain information about environmental and employee matters and social and community issues, it must state that fact. In our view, the business review should include only information that is relevant to an understanding of the company's business model, development, performance and position. Environmental and social matters that fall outside that category are, in our view, more suitably reported through channels other than the annual report; these might include, for example, disclosure on the company's web site.

2.30   The government expressed the view that the additional disclosures would add value to the quality of reporting without imposing unnecessary costs. Further guidance on making disclosures in these areas is included in chapter 3.

2.31   In recent years there has been a growing tendency on the part of listed companies to comment on environmental issues in their annual report and accounts. Public pressures matched by legislation, in particular the Environmental Protection Act 1990 and various EC Regulations, have been instrumental in many companies submitting their environmental practice to external scrutiny.

2.32   As mentioned above, section 417(5)(b)(i) of the Companies Act 2006 requires quoted companies to disclose information about environmental matters (including the impact of the company's business on the environment) in their directors' report. Companies producing an OFR are not required to repeat the information that is given in the OFR, for example on environmental matters, in their directors' report provided that a reference is given in the directors' report to the specific paragraph or section in the OFR.

2.33   Many leading companies go further than the requirements for reporting within the directors' report and publish separate environmental or corporate social responsibility (CSR) reports. Guidance on what is regarded as good practice can be found on the PwC web site (www.corporatereporting.com). The Department of the Environment, Food and Rural Affairs (Defra) issues 'Environmental reporting guidelines – key performance indicators' (available via www.defra.gov.uk). The guidelines aim to help companies measure, manage and report on their environmental impacts.

2.34   An example of disclosure of essential (and other) contractual relationships is set out in Table 2.2.

Table 2.2 – Essential relationships

Stagecoach Group plc – Annual report – 30 April 2012

2. Operating and Financial Review (extract)

2.3.5 What we need to do what we do (resources and relationships)

Stagecoach Group has a range of resources and relationships, including contractual relationships, that underpin its business and support its strategy. These assist in giving the Group a competitive advantage in the markets in which it operates.

Customers
Millions of people use our services and our relationship with our customers is important to us. To deliver organic growth in revenue, a key element of our strategy, we need to provide services that people want to use.

We conduct extensive customer research to monitor our performance and to determine how we can improve the delivery and accessibility of our services. We are passionate about providing good customer service and indeed, the theme of our 2012 Group-wide management conference was customer service.

Our businesses have a regular and ongoing dialogue with bus and rail user groups. This includes presentations from managers on detailed aspects of our service as well as consultation and information sharing on particular issues.

Employees
Human resources are key to the Group's business and the Group's relationship with its employees is therefore fundamental to achieving its objectives. We seek to recruit and retain the best employees in our sector, offering an excellent package of benefits, which allows us to deliver good customer service to our passengers. The Group's individual divisions invest significantly in the training and development of our people and we operate a successful graduate training scheme which provides one source of training for the managers of the future. We have established strong working relationships with trade unions and work in partnership with them on a range of issues, including training and development, occupational health matters, pensions and other employee benefits. We also communicate with our people face to face and through a number of internal publications.

The financial community
Our shareholders and lenders are critical to our business success. We have a regular programme of meetings with investors and provide frequent updates to the markets and financial community on our performance.

We have contractual arrangements with banks and other finance providers for the provision of funds and financial products to the Group.

Government and regulatory bodies
Our managers have ongoing relationships with national and local government in all our countries of operation to ensure the effective delivery of government transport policy and to assist in meeting wider objectives. We work with local authorities, including passenger transport executives, regional transport committees and transit authorities, in the delivery and planning of bus and rail services. Many of our businesses have partnership agreements in place to improve the delivery of public transport in their areas. In the UK, we work closely with the DfT, the Scottish Executive, Transport Scotland, the Welsh Assembly, and Transport for London.

We contract with local authorities, government bodies and other parties for the supply of bus services on a contracted or tendered basis. We have franchise agreements with the DfT governing the supply of franchised rail services in the UK.

We have constructive dialogue with organisations such as the Commission for Integrated Transport, which provides advice to the UK Government, and lobbying groups such as the Campaign for Better Transport.

Suppliers
We rely on a range of suppliers to provide goods and services linked to our bus and rail operations. All of our businesses have various contractual relationships with suppliers including purchase contracts with fuel suppliers, vehicle suppliers, IT companies and spare part suppliers.

The operation of our rail franchises depends upon a number of contractual relationships with suppliers, including contracts with Network Rail governing station and track access arrangements, leases with rolling stock companies for the lease of trains and maintenance contracts for the maintenance of trains.

Corporate reputation, brand strength, and market position
Stagecoach is one of the best-known public transport operators in the UK and is consistently rated highly for the quality of its services in research by Government and other independent organisations. We value our reputation, both as a public transport provider and as a key part of the communities in which we operate. Stagecoach has a strong set of brands that support our strategy of organic growth in our business and that help maintain our leading market position.

Natural resources and manufacturing technology
Operating our bus and rail services requires considerable use of natural resources, including diesel and electricity. We have arrangements in place to ensure that these resources are sourced as efficiently as possible and that our supplies are maintained to ensure the smooth functioning of our business. A number of experienced manufacturers supply our buses, coaches, trains and trams, which are produced to detailed specifications relevant to the individual markets in which they are required.

Licences
Various licences are held by Stagecoach giving authority to operate our public transport services and these are maintained up to date as required.

Transport and Industry Representation Groups
We are active members of industry groups, such as the Confederation of Passenger Transport UK (which covers buses and light rail), the Association of Train Operating Companies and the American Bus Association.

[The next paragraph is 2.43.]

Dividends

2.43   The amount (if any) that the directors recommend should be paid as dividend must be stated except in the case of a company that is entitled to the small companies exemption under the Companies Act 2006 (see from para 2.143). [CA06 Sec 416(3)]. Where the directors do not propose a dividend, then it is customary to state this fact. An example of the relevant disclosure is given in Table 2.3 below.

Table 2.3 – Dividend payment

Imperial Tobacco Group PLC – Annual Report – 30 September 2011

Directors' Report (extract)
Corporate Governance Report (extract)
Financial Results and Dividends

We include a review of our operational and financial performance, current position and future developments in our Directors' Report: Strategy, Risks, Performance and Governance sections on pages 8 to 74.

The profit attributable to equity holders of the Company for the financial year was £1,796 million, as shown in our consolidated income statement on page 77. Note 1 to the Financial Statements gives an analysis of revenue and profit from operations (page 88).

An analysis of net assets is provided in the Consolidated Balance Sheet on page 79 and the related Notes to the Financial Statements.

The Directors have declared and proposed dividends as follows:

£ million	2011	2010
Ordinary Shares		
Interim paid, 28.1p per share (2010: 24.3p)	284	246
Proposed final, 67.0p per share (2010: 60.0p)	674	609
Total ordinary dividends, 95.1p (2010: 84.3p)	958	855

The final dividend, if approved, will be paid on 17 February 2012 to our shareholders on the Register of Members at the close of business on 20 January 2012. The associated ex dividend date will be 18 January 2012. We paid an interim dividend on 19 August 2011 to shareholders on the register at the close of business on 22 July 2011.

2.43.1   In addition to giving information about the recommended dividend, as required by the Companies Act 2006, SSE plc, shown in Table 2.3.1 below, provides information about the growth in dividends and future targets.

Table 2.3.1 –Dividend growth and targets

SSE plc – Annual Report – 31 March 2012

Financial overview (extract)

Dividend

Increasing the dividend for 2011/12

SSE's first financial responsibility to its shareholders is to remunerate their investment through the delivery of sustained, above-inflation increases in the dividend. The Board is recommending a final dividend of 56.1p, compared with 52.6p in the previous year, an increase of 6.7%. This will make a full-year dividend of 80.1p, which is:

■ an increase of 6.8% compared with 2010/11;

■ a real-terms increase of 2.0%, based on the average annual rate of RPI inflation in the UK between April 2011 and March 2012, which meets the target set for the year;

■ the thirteenth successive above-inflation dividend increase since the first full-year dividend paid by SSE, for 1998/99;

■ more than three times the first full-year dividend paid by SSE, for 1998/99; and

■ covered 1.41 times by SSE's adjusted earnings per share*.

SSE is now one of just five companies to have delivered better-than-inflation dividend growth every year since 1999, while remaining part of the FTSE 100 for at least 50% of that time, and ranks third amongst that group in terms of compound annual growth rate over that period.

Targeting further dividend increases in 2012/13 and beyond
SSE's key financial objective will remain the delivery of increases in the dividend paid to shareholders, and its targets are to deliver:

■ a full-year dividend increase of at least 2% more than RPI inflation for 2012/13; and

■ annual dividend increases from 2013/14 onwards which are greater than RPI inflation.

Inside this report… (extract)
The Directors' Report is set out on pages 1 to 88.

* Unless otherwise stated, this Annual Report describes adjusted operating profit before exceptional items, remeasurements arising from IAS 39 and after the removal of taxation and interest on profits from jointly-controlled entities and associates. In addition, it describes adjusted profit before tax before exceptional items, remeasurements arising from IAS 39 and after the removal of taxation on profits from jointly-controlled entities and associates. It also describes adjusted earnings and earnings per share before exceptional items, remeasurements arising from IAS 39 and deferred tax.

2.43.2 Listed entities are required by the Listing Rules to give details of arrangements under which any shareholder has waived or agreed to waive any dividends. See paragraph 2.138 for further details.

Post balance sheet events

2.44 Particulars of any important events affecting the reporting entity that have occurred since the end of the financial year must be disclosed by all companies other than those subject to the small companies regime under the Companies Act 2006. [SI 2008/410 7 Sch 7(1)(a)]. This requirement gives rise to two potential inconsistencies between the law and FRS 21 and IAS 10.

■ FRS 21 and IAS 10 distinguish between events that require adjustments to the amounts reported in the financial statements but do not require separate disclosure ('adjusting events') and events that are only required to be noted ('non-adjusting events'). However, the law does not make such a distinction and requires disclosure of important post balance sheet events whether adjusting or non-adjusting.

■ The law requires material events after the balance sheet date to be disclosed in the directors' report, whereas FRS 21 and IAS 10 require disclosure of non-adjusting events in the notes to the financial statements. Where a post balance sheet event requires disclosure under both the Companies Act 2006 and the standard, then theoretically disclosure ought to be made both in the directors' report as well as in the notes to the financial statements. In practice, however, companies normally disclose the information only in one place – usually the notes – so as to avoid duplication. A cross-reference should be given in the directors' report to the precise location of the information.

These standards are considered further in the Manual of Accounting – UK GAAP and the Manual of Accounting – IFRS for the UK.

Research and development activities

2.45 An indication of the activities (if any) of the reporting entity in the field of research and development should be provided in the directors' report by all companies except those subject to the small companies regime. [SI 2008/410 7 Sch 7(1)(c)].

2.46 As the law does not indicate how much detail needs to be given, the extent of disclosure varies considerably in practice. Some companies, particularly those in the pharmaceutical sector, give significant details about their research and development activities. In other cases, a broadly-based note that considers the commercial aspects of the research and development activities and their impact on the activities of the company or group may be sufficient. An illustration of this disclosure is shown in Table 2.5.

Table 2.4 – Research and development

British American Tobacco plc – Annual report – 31 December 2011

DIRECTORS' REPORT (extract)

Research and development

Our Group Research & Development (R&D) activities are concentrated on our harm reduction efforts but also encompass the exploration of new products and innovative technologies. Group R&D also provides guidance on the use of ingredients to ensure our products comply with national legislative requirements and our own Group standards.

Our principal R&D facilities are located in Southampton and Cambridge in the UK and at Cachoeirinha in Brazil. In 2011, investment in Group R&D, including Marketing Futures and Nicoventures, was £166 million, compared to £164 million in 2010.

2.47 The requirement to give an indication of the research and development activities of the company and its subsidiaries does not mean that the accounting policy for research and development should be disclosed in the directors' report. It should, instead, supplement the accounting policy and the other disclosure requirements of SSAP 13 (see also the Manual of Accounting – UK GAAP), and IAS 38 (see also the Manual of Accounting – IFRS for the UK).

Differences between market and balance sheet value of land

2.48 Substantial differences between the market value and the balance sheet value of any interest in land held by the reporting entity should be disclosed in the report of any company other than one subject to the small companies regime if, in the opinion of the directors, the difference is of such significance that it should be brought to the shareholders' or debenture holders' attention. 'Land' includes the buildings and other structures. [Sch 1 Interpretation Act 1978]. The difference has to be shown with such degree of precision as is practicable. [SI 2008/410 7 Sch 2]. Although there is no requirement to make a negative statement that the difference is not significant, many companies do make this statement where there might otherwise be doubt. An example of disclosure is provided in Table 2.5.

Table 2.5 – Differences between market and book value of land

Marks and Spencer Group plc – Report and accounts – 3 April 2010

Directors' report (extract)

Other disclosures (extract)

Market value of properties

The last formal valuation of the Group's properties was carried out in September 2006. Taking into account movements in the Group's property portfolio since that date, the directors are of the opinion that the market value of the Group's properties, at 3 April 2010 exceeded their net book value (including prepayments in respect of leasehold land) of the fixed asset and leasehold properties by approximately £0.8bn.

2.49 It is recommended that, where there are several interests in land, the aggregate market value and the aggregate book value should be compared to see if the difference is substantial. When it is considered that a substantial difference exists, it is preferable to state both the aggregate market value and the basis on which the market value has been arrived at. In this regard, for financial statements prepared in accordance with UK GAAP, FRS 19 also requires disclosure of the tax effects, if any, that would arise if the asset were realised at a price equal to the estimated market value. [FRS 19 para 64(b)]. There is no equivalent requirement in IAS 12 for financial statements prepared in accordance with IFRS. An independent professional valuation is not required if the directors are competent to arrive at the market value themselves, but the wording should make the position clear in this respect. Where property is situated overseas, especially in territories subject to political unrest or where the remittance of currencies is restricted, it may not always be practicable, and may be misleading, to give the information required. In such circumstances, the wording should make this clear.

Details of directors

2.50 Disclosure is required of the names of the persons who were directors of the company at any time during the financial year. [CA06 Sec 416(1)(a)]. This can be achieved either by listing the names of the directors in the report or by referring to the page where this information may be found (for example, see Table 2.6 below). When cross-referring to a list elsewhere in the annual report, the list of directors is often at the balance sheet date or at the date the report and accounts were approved. Where there have been changes in directors during the year (or since the year end if the list is at the date the report and accounts were approved), it is necessary to provide details. In group financial statements, disclosure is required of the names of the parent company's directors only. Identification of directors and their roles is also required by the DTR – see paragraph 2.127.7.

2.51 Although not required by law, it has become customary to include the following information:

■ The dates of appointments or resignations of directors occurring during the financial year.

■ Changes in the directors since the end of the financial year.

■ Retirement of directors at the AGM and whether they offer themselves for election.

[The next paragraph is 2.57.]

Directors' service contracts for listed companies

2.57 Information on service contracts is usually given in the directors' remuneration report with a cross-reference from the directors' report as in the example in Table 2.6. The directors' remuneration report for listed companies must state the unexpired term of the directors' service contracts of any director who is proposed for election or re-election at the forthcoming AGM (see Table 2.6 below). If the directors proposed for election or re-election do not have service contracts, the directors' remuneration report must state that fact. [LR 9.8.8R (9)]. Directors' service contracts for this purpose are defined by reference to section 227 of the Companies Act 2006. For further guidance on the directors' remuneration report, see chapter 5.

Table 2.6 – Directors' service contracts

Cookson Group plc – Annual Report – 31 December 2011

DIRECTORS' REPORT (extract)

DIRECTORS
Dr FitzGerald and Messrs Butterworth, Harris, Hewitt, Hill, Oosterveld, Perry, Salmon, Sussens and Wanecq all served as Directors of the Company during the year. Mr Perry retired from the Board at the close of the AGM on 12 May 2011 and Dr FitzGerald was appointed as a Director on 1 August 2011. Biographical information for all the current Directors of the Company is given on page 21. All the Directors will retire at the AGM and offer themselves for election. Further information on the contractual arrangements of the executive Directors is given on page 46. The Non-executive Directors do not have service agreements.

DIRECTORS' REMUNERATION REPORT (extract)

DIRECTORS' CONTRACTS

The following paragraphs summarise the main terms and conditions of the contracts of the Directors:

Executive Directors

In line with the policy of the Committee, Messrs Butterworth and Salmon have UK service contracts which have 12 month unexpired terms and provide for 12 months' notice being given by the Company and six months by them. Mr Salmon's contract was dated 14 June 2004 and Mr Butterworth's 25 May 2005. Each contract provides for compensation to be paid on early termination by the Company based on one times salary, pension allowance and benefits payable half in a lump sum and the balance in six separate monthly instalments commencing six months after leaving, mitigated by any salary earned from any new paid occupation. Mr Wanecq is contracted to Vesuvius Group NV/SA, under a Belgian services agreement dated 1 March 2006 for which his remuneration is in the form of fees. His appointment to the Cookson Group plc Board is subject to a separate appointment agreement for which no fee is payable. His termination arrangements are structured to effectively mirror Messrs Butterworth's and Salmon's arrangements including the notice period and mitigation obligations.

None of the executive Directors' contracts contain any change of control provisions and they all contain a duty to mitigate should the Director find an alternative paid occupation in any period during which the Company must otherwise pay compensation on early termination. Other than as described for Mr Wanecq, no Directors had any material interest in a contract of significance (other than service agreements) with the Company or any subsidiary company during the year.

Non-executive Directors

Each Non-executive Director is appointed for an initial fixed term of three years subject to their election at the Company's first Annual General Meeting following their appointment and re-election at intervening Annual General Meetings. Thereafter, subject to approval of the Board and their continued re-election by shareholders, they are appointed for a further three-year term.

	Date of appointment	Annual General Meeting at which current term is expected to expire/ expired	Unexpired notice period
Current Non-executive Directors			
Emma FitzGerald	1 August 2011	2015	Not required
Jeff Hewitt	1 June 2005	2015	Not required
Peter Hill	1 February 2010	2013	Not required
Jan Oosterveld	15 June 2004	2013	Not required
John Sussens	1 May 2004	2013	Not required
Former Non-executive Director			
Barry Perry	1 January 2002	2011	Not required

The Chairman, Mr Harris, was appointed as a Non-executive Director on 1 April 2010 and succeeded Mr Beeston as Chairman at the conclusion of the 2010 Annual General Meeting. Mr Harris was appointed for a fixed period which is due to expire at the conclusion of the Annual General Meeting in 2016. He is entitled to six months' notice from the Company. Any compensation for loss of office would be based upon his fee. None of the other Non-executive Directors are entitled to receive compensation for loss of office at any time.

All Directors are subject to retirement, and election or re-election, in accordance with the Company's Articles of Association.

The Board sets the remuneration of the Non-executive Directors after considering the role and responsibilities of each Director and the practice of other companies. The Non-executive Directors do not participate in Board discussions on their own remuneration.

2.58 The UK Corporate Governance Code states that notice or contract periods should be set at one year or less. If it is necessary to offer longer notice or contract periods to new directors recruited from outside, such periods should reduce to one year or less after the initial period. [UK CGC D.1.5].

2.59 If a service contract does not specify a term, the term can be ascertained in one of the following ways:

■ If the contract is terminable on giving of notice, the expiration of the notice period will indicate the earliest date at which the contract could end.

■ If no notice period is stated in the contract, there may be a custom or practice as to the length of the notice.

■ In the absence of an express provision as to duration or expiry of a customary arrangement, there is a presumption in common law that (subject to the statutory minimum entitlements to notice) every contract of employment is terminable on reasonable notice by either party.

Where the length of the unexpired period of a director's service contract has been determined in one of the ways above, the details should be fully disclosed in the directors' report.

Directors' interests in contracts

2.60 Under the Companies Act 2006, disclosure of directors' interests in contracts is not required in the directors' report. Disclosure is required in the financial statements of transactions and arrangements in which the director of a company has, directly or indirectly, a material interest (for example, contracts between a director and a company for the sale of non-cash assets). [SI 2008/410 1 Sch 72].

2.61 In addition, the Listing Rules require listed entities to disclose in the annual report and accounts particulars of any contract of significance subsisting during the period under review. The disclosure does not have to be provided in the directors' report, but in practice is often given there. See paragraph 2.137.11 for further details.

Corporate governance for listed companies

2.62 The Listing Rules require companies to give a two part narrative statement, to explain how they have applied the UK Corporate Governance Code's main principles and confirm that they have complied throughout the year with its provisions – or provide an explanation where they have not complied.

2.63 The Disclosure and Transparency Rules require the corporate governance statement to be included in the directors' report. [DTR 7.2.1R]. In practice, many companies prepare a separate corporate governance statement. Where this is the case, a cross-reference should be provided in the directors' report to the specific location of the corporate governance statement elsewhere in the annual report. [DTR 7.2.9R].

2.64 DTR 7.2.10R states that the directors' report must include a description of the main features of the group's internal control and risk management systems in relation to the process for preparing consolidated accounts.

2.65 See chapter 4 for further discussion of corporate governance matters, including the principles and provisions of the UK Corporate Governance Code and the disclosures required by the DTR in the corporate governance statement.

[The next paragraph is 2.75.]

Purchase of own shares and sales of treasury shares

2.75 Where the company has an interest in its own shares, the directors' report is required to include certain information. The directors' report must contain the details set out in paragraph 2.76 below where any of the following circumstances occur:

Acquisition of shares by the company

■ A company purchases its own shares (including treasury shares) or otherwise acquires them by forfeiture, or by surrender in lieu of forfeiture, or by way of a gift, or in a reduction of capital duly made, or by order of the Court. [SI 2008/409 5 Sch 6(1)(a); SI 2008/410 7 Sch 8(a); CA06 659(1)(2)].

Acquisition of shares in a public company by another person

■ A nominee of a public company acquires shares in the company from a third party without the company providing any financial assistance directly or indirectly and the company has a beneficial interest in those shares. [SI 2008/409 5 Sch 6(1)(b); SI 2008/410 7 Sch 8(b); CA06 Sec 662(1)(d)].

■ Any person acquires shares in a public company with the financial assistance of the company and the company has a beneficial interest in those shares. [SI 2008/409 5 Sch 6(1)(b); SI 2008/410 7 Sch 8(b); CA06 Sec 662(1)(e), 671].

Lien or charges on own shares held by the company

■ A company takes a lien or a charge (either express or implied) on its own shares for any amount that is payable in respect of those shares. [SI 2008/409 5 Sch 6(1)(c), SI 2008/410 7 Sch 8(c); CA06 Sec 670(2)].

■ A company that has re-registered under section 1040 of the Companies Act 2006, holds a lien or a charge (either express or implied) on its own shares, and that lien or charge existed immediately before the company applied to be re-registered as a public company. [SI 2008/409 5 Sch 6(1)(c); SI 2008/410 7 Sch 8(c); CA06 Sec 670(4)].

2.76 Where any of the above circumstances has occurred, the directors' report must state the following details:

In respect of shares purchased

■ The number and the nominal value of the shares that have been purchased in the financial year and the percentage of the called-up share capital which shares of that description represent.

■ The aggregate amount of consideration paid and the reasons for their purchase.

An example is given in Table 2.7 below.

Directors' report

In respect of shares acquired other than by purchase or charged

- The number and the nominal value of any shares that have been otherwise acquired (whether by the company or by its nominee or any other person) or charged at any time during the financial year.

- The maximum number and the nominal value of shares which, having been so acquired or charged (whether or not during the year) are held at any time during the financial year.

- The number and the nominal value of such shares that were disposed of by the company (or any other person holding them on behalf of the company) during the year, or that were cancelled by the company during the year.

- For each of the above, the percentage of the called-up share capital which shares of that description represent.

- The amount of any charge.

In addition to the above, there should be disclosed the amount or the value of any consideration for any shares that either the company or the other person disposed of during the financial year that the company or the other person acquired for money or money's worth.

[SI 2008/409 5 Sch 6(2); SI 2008/410 7 Sch 9].

Table 2.7 – Repurchase of own shares

AstraZeneca PLC – Annual Report and Accounts – 31 December 2011

Directors' report (extract)

Corporate Governance Report (extract)

Other matters (extract)

Distributions to shareholders and dividends for 2011

Our distribution policy comprises both a regular cash dividend and a share repurchase component, further details of which are set out in the Financial Review on page 90 and Notes 20 and 21 to the Financial Statements on page 170.

The Company's dividends for 2011 of $2.80 (175.5 pence, SEK 18.54) per Ordinary Share amount to, in aggregate, a total dividend payment to shareholders of $3,678 million. Two of our employee share trusts, AstraZeneca Share Trust Limited and AstraZeneca Quest Limited, waive their right to a dividend on the Ordinary Shares that they hold and instead receive a nominal dividend.

A shareholders' resolution was passed at the 2011 AGM authorising the Company to purchase its own shares. Pursuant to this resolution, the Company repurchased (and subsequently cancelled) 127.4 million Ordinary Shares with a nominal value of $0.25 each, at an aggregate cost of $6,015 million, representing 9.9% of the total issued share capital of the Company. The Company will seek a renewal of permission from shareholders to purchase its own shares at the AGM on 26 April 2012.

During our share repurchase programmes that operated between 1999 and 2011, a total of 557.4 million Ordinary Shares were repurchased, and subsequently cancelled, at an average price of 2767 pence per share for a consideration, including expenses, of $26,717 million.

Financial Review (extract from page 90)

Dividend and share repurchases
In recognition of the Group's strong balance sheet, sustainable significant cash flow and the Board's confidence in the strategic direction and long-term prospects for the business, the Board has adopted a progressive dividend policy, intending to maintain or grow the dividend each year.

The Board has recommended a 5% increase in the second interim dividend to $1.95 (123.6 pence, 13.21 SEK) to be paid on 19 March 2012. This brings the full year dividend to $2.80 (175.5 pence per share, 18.54 SEK), an increase of 10%.

In 2010, the Group recommenced its share repurchase programme. The Group completed net share repurchases of $5,606 million in 2011 (2010: $2,110 million). The Board has announced that the Group intends to complete net share repurchases in the amount of $4.5 billion during 2012, subject to market conditions and business needs. In setting the distribution policy and the overall financial strategy, the Board's aim is to continue to strike a balance between the interests of the business, our financial creditors and our shareholders. After providing for business investment, funding the progressive dividend policy and meeting our debt service obligations, the Board will keep under review the opportunity to return cash in excess of these requirements to shareholders through periodic share repurchases.

Additional disclosure under the Listing Rules for companies purchasing own shares or selling treasury shares

2.77 A listed company must give the following additional information concerning purchases or proposed purchases of the company's own shares and sales of treasury shares:

- Particulars of any authority given by the shareholders in general meeting for the company to purchase its own shares that is still effective at the year end (that is, authority that has not yet been exercised and has not expired).

- In relation to purchases other than through the market or by tender to all shareholders, the names of the sellers of the shares that have been purchased, or are to be purchased, by the company.

- If the company has purchased any of its own shares since the year end, or has either been granted an option or entered into a contract to purchase its own shares since the year end, then the directors' report should disclose the equivalent information to that required under the Act as detailed in paragraph 2.76 above.

- In relation to sales of treasury shares made other than through the market, or in connection with an employees' share scheme, or other than pursuant to an opportunity available to all shareholders on the same terms, the names of the purchasers of such shares sold, or proposed to be sold, during the year.

[LR 9.8.6R (4)].

2.78 Examples of the relevant disclosures are given in chapters 23 of the PwC Manual of Accounting – UK GAAP and the Manual of Accounting – IFRS for the UK dealing with treasury shares.

Employee information

2.79 All companies are required to include in the directors' report information regarding the company's policy in respect of the employment of disabled persons. In addition, companies other than those subject to the small companies' regime must include information regarding employee involvement.

Employment of disabled persons

2.80 If the company employed, on average, more than 250 employees in the UK in each week of the financial year, the directors' report must contain a statement that describes the company's policy during the year in respect of the following:

- Giving full and fair consideration (having regard to the persons' particular aptitudes and abilities) to applications for employment that disabled persons (as defined in the Disability Discrimination Act 1995) make to the company. The definition of 'disabled person' in the 1995 Act is a person who has a physical or mental impairment that has a substantial and long term adverse effect on their ability to carry out normal day-to-day activities. [Disability Discrimination Act 1995 Sec 1.]

- Continuing the employment of, and arranging appropriate training for, any of the company's employees who have become disabled during the period in which the company employed them.

- Otherwise providing for the training, the career development and the promotion of those disabled persons the company employs.

[SI 2008/409 5 Sch 5; SI 2008/410 7 Sch 10].

An illustration of this disclosure is given in Table 2.8 below.

Table 2.8 – Employment of disabled persons

Yell Group plc – Annual report – 31 March 2012

Directors' Report (extract)

People with disabilities

Yell is an Equal Opportunities Employer and is committed to the employment of people with disabilities and guarantees an interview for those who meet minimum selection criteria. Yell provides training and development for people with disabilities, tailored where appropriate, to ensure they have the opportunity to achieve their potential. If a Yell person becomes disabled while in our employment, Yell will do its best to retain them, including consulting them about their requirements, making reasonable and appropriate adjustments, and providing alternative suitable provisions.

Employee involvement

2.81 The directors' report of any company other than one subject to the small companies regime should describe the action the company has taken during the financial year to introduce, maintain, or develop arrangements aimed at:

■ Providing employees systematically with information on matters of concern to them as employees.

■ Consulting employees or their representatives on a regular basis, so that the company can take the views of employees into account in making decisions that are likely to affect their interests.

■ Encouraging the involvement of employees in the company's performance through (for example) an employees' share scheme.

■ Achieving a common awareness on the part of all employees of the financial and the economic factors that affect the company's performance.

[SI 2008/410 7 Sch 11].

2.82 The above requirements apply only to the directors' report of a reporting entity that employs, on average, more than 250 employees in the UK each week during the financial year. [SI 2008/410 7 Sch 11(1)].

Creditor payment policy

2.83 Company law requires a reporting entity to disclose its payment policy for its suppliers. The provision applies to public companies and large private companies (that is, neither small nor medium-sized companies) that are members of a group whose parent is a public company. [SI 2008/410 7 Sch 12(1)(a)(b)]. The provisions apply at a company level and not to the group as a whole. The requirement is for the directors to state with respect to the financial year *following* that covered by the annual report whether it is the company's policy to follow any code or standard on payment practice. Only where a company follows a particular code does it have to give the name of the code or standard together with an indication of where information about, and copies of, the code or standard can be obtained. [SI 2008/410 7 Sch 12(2)(a)]]. The directors also have to state whether it is the company's policy in respect of some or all of its suppliers:

■ To settle the terms of payment with those suppliers when agreeing the terms of each transaction.

■ To ensure that those suppliers are made aware of the terms of payment.

■ To abide by the terms of payment.

[SI 2008/410 7 Sch 12(2)(b)].

2.84 Where the company's policy is different in respect of some or all of its suppliers from that outlined above, the directors must also state the company's policy in respect of those suppliers. In addition, where the company's policy is different for different suppliers or classes of suppliers, the directors must identify in their report the suppliers or classes of suppliers to which the different policy applies. [SI 2008/410 7 Sch 12(2)]. An example of a payment policy is given in Table 2.9.

Table 2.9 – Creditor payment policy

Marks and Spencer Group plc – Annual report and financial statements – 31 March 2012

Directors' report (extract)

Creditor payment policy

For all trade creditors, it is the Group's policy to:

● agree the terms of payment at the start of business with that supplier;

● ensure that suppliers are aware of the terms of payment; and

● pay in accordance with its contractual and other legal obligations.

The main trading company, Marks and Spencer plc, has a policy concerning the payment of trade creditors as follows:

● general merchandise payments are received between 25 and 60 days after the stock was invoiced;

● food payments are received between 19 and 25 days after the stock was invoiced; and

● distribution suppliers are paid monthly, for costs incurred in that month, based on estimates, and payments are adjusted quarterly to reflect any variations to estimate.

> Trade creditor days for Marks and Spencer plc for the year ended 31 March 2012 were 26 days, or 17 working days (last year 26 days, or 17 working days), based on the ratio of Company trade creditors at the end of the year to the amounts invoiced during the year by trade creditors.

2.85 The directors' report is also required to state the number of days represented by trade creditors falling due for payment within one year at the year end (for example, UK GAAP balance sheet Format 1 item E4) compared to the total amounts invoiced to suppliers during the year. The requirement is to disclose the number of days that bears to the number of days in the financial year in the same proportion as X bears to Y where:

- X = the aggregate of the amounts that were owed to trade creditors at the end of the year.

- Y = the aggregate of the amounts invoiced by suppliers during the year.

[SI 2008/410 7 Sch 12(3)].

2.86 The calculation of the number of creditor days is illustrated in the example below.

> **Example**
>
> Trade creditors (all due within one year) at the end of the year are £30 million. Amounts invoiced during the year by suppliers are £300 million. Number of days in the financial year is 365.
>
> $$\frac{30 \times 365}{300} = 36.5 \text{ days}$$

2.87 For the purposes of the above provisions, a person will be a supplier of the company at any time if:

- At the time, the person is owed an amount in respect of the goods and services supplied.

- The amount owed would be included within trade creditors (item E4 in Format 1) if the financial statements were prepared at that time, were prepared in accordance with Schedule 1 to SI 2008/410 and that format was adopted.

[SI 2008/410 7 Sch 12(4)].

2.88 If a company does not draw up its accounts under balance sheet Format 1 in Schedule 1 to SI 2008/410, it still has to comply with the disclosures outlined above. If, for example, the company prepares its financial statements in accordance with IFRS or is a banking or insurance company, the disclosure has to be given in respect of creditors for goods and services that would have been included under trade creditors, had the company drawn up its financial statements in accordance with Schedule 1. Therefore, for an insurance company, although insurance and reinsurance creditors would not be classified as trade creditors, creditors for stationery and rent would be and the required disclosure has to be given in respect of these creditors.

2.89 There is no requirement to disclose comparative information in the directors' report but it is common and best practice to do so.

[The next paragraph is 2.100.]

Political and charitable donations

Summary of the provisions for disclosure and control

2.100 Company law requires a company to make disclosure in the directors' report of political donations and expenditure in the UK/EU and outside the EU. [SI 2008/409 5 Sch 2, 3; SI 2008/410 7 Sch 3, 4]. It also requires a company to control its political donations and expenditure in the UK and in other EU Member States by requiring directors to seek prior shareholder authorisation.

Definitions

2.101 Sections 362 to 379 of the Companies Act 2006 concern political donations and expenditure in the UK.

2.101.1 The legislation relates to political expenditure and to political donations made by companies to:

- Political parties (both those registered in the UK and those acting in connection with any election to public office in any other EU member State).

- Political organisations other than political parties, which are any organisation:

    - Carrying on, or proposing to carry on, activities capable of being reasonably regarded as intended to affect public support for any political party (as defined in the first bullet point in this paragraph) or for independent candidates at elections to public office held in an EU Member State other than the UK.

    - Carrying on, or proposing to carry on, activities capable of being reasonably regarded as intended to influence voters in national or regional referendums held under the law of any EU Member State.

- Independent election candidates at any election to public office in the UK or another EU Member State.

[CA06 Sec 363].

2.101.2 The definition of a political donation is wide. It includes:

- Any gift of money or other property.

- Any sponsorship provided to cover expenses relating to any party conference, meeting or event, the preparation, publication or dissemination of any party publication or any party political study or research (or to ensure that such expenses are not incurred).

- Any fee or subscription paid for membership of or affiliation to a political party or organisation.

- Any money spent in paying expenses incurred directly or indirectly by a political party, organisation or election candidate.

- Any money lent to a political party, organisation or election candidate otherwise than on a commercial basis.

- The provision (other than on a commercial basis) of property, services or facilities (including the services of any person).

The definition includes donations to any officer, member, trustee or agent of a political party, in his/her capacity as such. Further, it includes any donation made through a third party. [CA06 Sec 364].

2.101.3 Section 364 of the Companies Act 2006 defines a 'political donation' by reference to sections 50 to 52 of the Political Parties, Elections and Referendums Act 2000 (disregarding amendments made by the Electoral Administration Act 2006, which remove from the definition of 'donation' loans made otherwise than on commercial terms).

2.101.4 Political expenditure means any expenditure incurred by a company in respect of:

- the preparation, publication or dissemination of advertising, promotional or publicity material of any kind that is capable of being reasonably regarded as intended to affect public support for a political party or other political organisation, or an independent election candidate; or

- any of the company's activities of the kind referred to in the definition of 'political organisation' (second bullet point of para 2.101.1).

[CA06 Sec 365].

Prohibition on political donations and expenditure

2.102 A company is prohibited from making any political donation to a political party, political organisation or independent election candidate, or incurring any political expenditure unless the donation or EU political expenditure has been authorised by the company using an 'approval resolution' (see para 2.105). [CA06 Sec 366(1)].

2.103 This resolution must be passed before the donation or political expenditure is made or incurred or, if earlier, any relevant contract entered into. See also the special rules for subsidiaries in paragraph 2.107.

Shareholder approval is not required of donations or expenditure for purposes that are not connected with party politics in any EU Member State, but these still require disclosure.

[The next paragraph is 2.105.]

2.105 An approval resolution is a resolution passed by the company that:

■ Authorises the company to make donations not exceeding a specified total or incur political expenditure (including EU political expenditure) not exceeding a specified total for a period of not more than four years beginning with the date on which the resolution is passed.

■ Is expressed in general terms (accordingly, it must not purport to authorise particular donations or expenditure).

[CA06 Sec 367, 368].

Exemptions for donations

2.106 Sections 374 to 378 of the Companies Act 2006 set out five exemptions from the requirement for prior shareholder authorisation:

■ Donations to trade unions (including those in countries other than the UK). The exemption covers donations such as the provision of company rooms for trade union meetings, the use of company vehicles by trade union officials and paid time off for trade union officials to act in that capacity. However, a donation to a trade union's political fund is not covered by the exemption. [CA06 Sec 374].

■ Subscriptions paid to EU trade associations for membership (including trade associations that carry out their activities outside the EU). [CA06 Sec 375].

■ Donations to all-party parliamentary groups. [CA06 Sec 376].

■ Political expenditure that is exempt by virtue of an order by the Secretary of State. [CA06 Sec 377].

■ Small political donations: authorisation is not required unless the political donation and the aggregate amount of the political donations by the company in the 12 months ending on the date of the donation exceeds £5,000. Donations by other group companies (including subsidiaries) must be taken into account in calculating whether the £5,000 threshold has been exceeded. [CA06 Sec 378].

Subsidiaries incorporated in the UK

2.107 If the company is a subsidiary of another company (its holding company), an approval resolution may need to be passed by the holding company's shareholders as well as or instead of those of the company. This is relevant where the company is not a wholly-owned subsidiary of a UK-registered company. In addition to the resolution of the company, a resolution must be passed by its 'relevant holding company'. The relevant holding company is the ultimate holding company or, where such a company is not a UK-registered company, the holding company highest up the chain that is a UK-registered company. [CA06 Sec 366].

2.108 A wholly-owned subsidiary of a UK-registered company is not required to pass a resolution approving political donations or expenditure, although its relevant holding company is required to do so. [CA06 Sec 366(3)].

Example 1

X limited wishes to make a political donation. It is an 80% subsidiary of Y limited, which is a subsidiary of Z plc. Approval resolutions must be passed by X limited (the company) and Z plc (the ultimate holding company).

Example 2

The facts are the same as in example 1 except that entity Z is incorporated outside the UK. Approval resolutions must be passed by X limited and Y limited (the highest UK-registered holding company of X limited).

Example 3

The facts are the same as in example 2 except that X limited is a 100% subsidiary of Y limited. An approval resolution must be passed by Y limited, but need not be passed by X limited.

Directors' liability

2.109 There are no criminal sanctions in relation to making unauthorised political donations or incurring unauthorised political expenditure. Civil remedies are available to a company in the event of a breach of the prohibitions and may be pursued in the normal manner by the company.

2.110 If the company makes an unauthorised payment, the directors and (unless they took all available steps to prevent the political donation being made or the political expenditure being incurred), the directors of the relevant holding company are liable to reimburse the company for the amount of the political donation or political expenditure and damages for any loss it suffers together with interest until the amount is repaid to the company. [CA06 Sec 369].

2.111 Action may be taken against the directors for reimbursement by not less than 50 members or members holding not less than 5% of the issued share capital. In addition, in any such action, the members are entitled to require the company to provide all relevant information. If the company refuses to do so, the court may make an order directing the company or its officers or employees to provide the information. [CA06 Secs 370(3), 373(1)].

Disclosure of political donations and expenditure

2.112 There are separate disclosure regimes for:

■ Political donations and expenditure within the UK/EU area.

■ Contributions to political parties in the rest of the world.

Company with no subsidiaries — not wholly-owned by a UK parent

2.113 If a company has made any donation to a political party, other political organisation or independent election candidate or has incurred any political expenditure, and the aggregate of those exceeds £2,000 in a financial year, it must disclose the following particulars in the directors' report for the year:

■ For political donations, the name of each political party, political organisation or independent election candidate and the amount given to each in the financial year.

■ The total amount of political expenditure incurred in the financial year.

[SI 2008/409 5 Sch 2(2); SI 2008/410 7 Sch 3(2)].

2.114 All contributions made by the company to non-EU political parties also require disclosure (although there is no requirement to name the parties). There is no threshold for these disclosures. Therefore, if the company has in the financial year made any contribution to a non-EU political party the directors' report for the year must contain:

■ A statement of the amount contributed.

■ If it has made more than one contribution in the year, a statement of the total contributions.

[SI 2008/409 5 Sch 3(1); SI 2008/410 7 Sch 4(1)].

Company with subsidiary — not wholly-owned by a UK parent

2.115 The following applies where the company has subsidiaries. If the amount of the combined political donations and the political expenditure of the company and its subsidiaries exceeds £2,000, the directors' report for the year must disclose the particulars mentioned in paragraph 2.114 above in relation to the company and each subsidiary by whom any such political donation or political expenditure has been made or incurred. [SI 2008/409 5 Sch 2(3); SI 2008/410 7 Sch 3(3)].

2.116 Where the company has subsidiaries that have made any contributions to a non-EU political party in the financial year the following applies. The directors' report of the company is not required to disclose the amount of the company's own contributions, but should instead contain a statement of the total amount of the contributions made by the company and its subsidiaries in the year. There is no threshold for these disclosures. [SI 2008/409 5 Sch 3(2); SI 2008/410 7 Sch 4(2)].

Company that is a wholly-owned subsidiary of a UK parent

2.117 A wholly-owned subsidiary of a company incorporated in the UK does not have to disclose its donations, expenditure or contributions in its own directors' report, but these must be disclosed by its holding company as mentioned above.

2.117.1 An example of disclosure is given in Table 2.10.

Table 2.10 – Political and charitable donations

Rolls-Royce Holdings plc – Report and Accounts – 31 December 2011

Community investment

Rolls-Royce has a firm, long-standing commitment to the communities in which we operate around the world. During 2011, the Group's total contributions (including money, employee time and gifts in kind) were £7.1 million.

Our community investment activities support the Group's strategy and future success, particularly in the areas of: recruitment and employee retention, employee engagement, professional development and the Group's reputation in the community.

During the year, the Group approved a new global charitable contributions and social sponsorships policy and procedure, confirming our major areas of support as:

- education and skills, particularly in the areas of STEM which are key to our future success;

- environment, adding value to the Group's environment strategy;

- social investment, making a positive difference to the communities in which we operate;

- arts and culture, contributing to the cultural vibrancy in geographic areas in which we operate; and

- requests relating to the Group's business such as armed services related, engineering and aviation.

The new policy and procedure also sets out a clear structure for global governance, ensuring consistency of approach and global visibility of contributions.

2011 charitable contributions and sponsorships, and payroll giving	£m
Charitable contributions and social sponsorships	
– UK	2.1
– Asia and Middle East £0.3m, Americas £0.7m, Europe £0.6m	1.6
Commercial sponsorship	0.7
Employee time	2.6
Gifts in kind	0.1
Total	7.1
Payroll giving UK £0.5m and North America £0.3m	0.8

Political donations

In line with its established policy, the Group made no political donations pursuant to the authority granted at the 2011 AGM. Although the Company does not make, and does not intend to make, donations to political parties, within the normal meaning of that expression, the definition of political donations under the Companies Act 2006 is very broad and includes expenses legitimately incurred as part of the process of talking to members of parliament and opinion formers to ensure that the issues and concerns of the Group are considered and addressed. These activities are not intended to support any political party and the Group's policy is not to make any donations for political purposes in the normally accepted sense.

A resolution will therefore be proposed at the 2012 AGM seeking shareholder approval for the directors to be given authority to make donations and incur expenditure which might otherwise be caught by the terms of the Companies Act 2006. The authority sought will be limited to a maximum amount of £25,000 per Group company but so as not to exceed £50,000 for the entire Group in aggregate.

During the year, the business expenses incurred by Rolls-Royce North America Inc. towards the operation of the Rolls-Royce North America Political Action Committee (RRNAPAC) in the USA was US$44,436 (2010: nil). PACs are a common feature of the US political system and are governed by the Federal Election Campaign Act.

The PAC is independent of the Company and independent of any political party. The PAC funds are contributed voluntarily by employees and the Company cannot affect how they are applied, although under US Law, the business expenses are paid by the Company.

Such contributions do not require authorisation by shareholders under the Companies Act 2006 and therefore do not count towards the £25,000 and £50,000 limits for political donations and expenditure for which shareholder approval will be sought at the AGM.

Disclosure of charitable gifts

2.118 The disclosures required in relation to charitable gifts are as follows:

- *By a company that is not a wholly-owned subsidiary of a company incorporated in the UK.*

  If such a company has given money exceeding £2,000 for charitable purposes in a financial year, its directors' report for the year must contain, for each of the purposes for which money has been given, a statement of the amount of money given for that purpose. [SI 2008/409 5 Sch 4(1); SI 2008/410 7 Sch 5(1)].

- *By a company, that is not a wholly-owned subsidiary of a company incorporated in the UK, with subsidiaries that have given money for charitable purposes.*

  In this case, the requirements in the bullet point above do not apply to the company. But if the amount given in the year for charitable purposes by the company and its subsidiaries exceeds £2,000, the directors' report for the year must contain, for each of the purposes for which money has been given by the company and its subsidiaries between them, a statement of the amount given for that purpose. [SI 2008/409 5 Sch 4(2); SI 2008/410 7 Sch 5(2)].

2.119 For these disclosures 'charitable purposes' means purposes that are exclusively charitable and in Scotland, 'charitable' is defined in section 7(2) of the Charities and Trustee Investment (Scotland) Act 2005. Money given for charitable purposes to a person, who at the time of the gift, was ordinarily resident outside the UK is to be left out of account for these purposes. [SI 2008/409 5 Sch 4(3)(4); SI 2008/410 7 Sch 5(3)(4)].

2.120 Money given for purposes that include either a political or a commercial element would not come within the disclosure of charitable donations. However, a donation with a political element may be disclosable as a political donation and require shareholder approval. Some companies may consider it good practice to seek shareholders' approval for charitable gifts, although, unlike political donations, this is not a statutory requirement.

2.121 An example of disclosure is provided in Table 2.10 above (see para 2.117.1).

Financial instruments

2.122 Companies (other than those subject to the small companies regime) are required to provide the following disclosures in the directors' report in relation to the entity as a whole:

- The entity's financial risk management objectives and policies, including the policy for hedging each major type of forecasted transaction for which hedge accounting is used.
- The entity's exposure to price risk, credit risk, liquidity risk and cash flow risk.

The disclosure is not required where such information is not material for the assessment of the entity's assets, liabilities, financial position and profit or loss. [SI 2008/410 7 Sch 6(1)].

2.123 These requirements are consistent with IFRS 7 and FRS 29. Although not all companies preparing Companies Act financial statements are required to comply with FRS 29, the standard provides additional guidance as to appropriate disclosure.

2.124 FRS 29 and IFRS 7 require an entity to provide disclosures *"that enable users to evaluate: (a) the significance of financial instruments for the entity's financial position and performance; and (b) the nature and extent of risks arising from financial instruments to which the entity is exposed during the period and at the reporting date, and how the entity manages those risks"*. [FRS 29 para 1; IFRS 7 para 1]. Extensive quantitative and qualitative disclosures of each type of risk arising from financial instruments (credit risk, market risk and liquidity risk) are required. [FRS 29 paras 31-42; IFRS 7 paras 31-42]. (See the Manual of Accounting – Financial instruments.)

2.125 Both IFRS 7 and FRS 29 require the disclosures to be given in the notes to the financial statements. For companies that comply with either IFRS 7 or FRS 29, to avoid the need for duplication, a specific cross-reference may be included in the directors' report to the relevant note.

Disclosure of overseas branches

2.126 Companies (other than unlimited companies and those subject to the small companies regime) must give an indication of the existence of branches that they operate outside the UK. [SI 2008/410 7 Sch 7(1)(d)]. For this purpose, a branch is defined in section 1046(3) of the Companies Act 2006 to mean only branches within the EU (see further the Manual of Accounting – UK GAAP). Therefore, branches operated in the US, for example, would not require disclosure. It should be noted that disclosure is required only of the company's branches, not those of its subsidiaries. This means that the directors' report of a parent company need only refer to the existence of branches that it operates outside the UK and not to those that are operated outside the UK by its subsidiaries. Branches operated by its subsidiaries would fall to be disclosed in the subsidiaries' directors' reports.

Directors' responsibility statements

2.127 There is no Companies Act requirement for a company's directors to include a statement of their responsibilities anywhere in the annual report. For listed companies, however, there is a recommendation, in the UK Corporate Governance Code, for directors to make a statement of their responsibilities. [UK CGC C.1.1]. In addition, the Disclosure and Transparency Rules of the FSA require listed companies to make certain disclosures about directors' responsibilities (see further from para 2.127.5).

2.127.1 ISA (UK&I) 700 (revised), 'The auditor's report on the financial statements (2009)', refers to the responsibilities of those charged with governance (which, in a UK context, is the company's directors) and states that:

> *"The auditor's report should include a statement that those charged with governance are responsible for the preparation of the financial statements and a statement that the responsibility of the auditor is to audit and express an opinion on the financial statements in accordance with applicable legal requirements and International Standards on Auditing (UK and Ireland)."*
> [ISA (UK&I) 700 (revised) para 15].

2.127.2 To complement ISA (UK&I) 700 (revised), the APB has included specimen wording describing the directors' responsibilities for inclusion in the annual report of a non-publicly traded company applying UK GAAP. This wording is found in Appendix 11 of Bulletin 2009/02, 'Auditor's reports on financial statements in the United Kingdom'. In addition, the example financial statements for GAAP UK Plc, IFRS GAAP Plc and UK GAAP Ltd (see 'Illustrative financial statements: IFRS and UK GAAP 2010') each contain example wording for directors' responsibility statements.

2.127.3 In more complicated situations, for example, where the company is listed in a market outside the UK where different requirements may apply, the directors may need to take legal advice on what to include in the statement of directors' responsibilities.

2.127.4 It is now usual for a company to post its financial reports on its web site — indeed, it is a requirement for quoted companies. [CA06 Sec 430]. The example in the APB's previous Bulletin (2006/06) on the same subject included a statement that the directors take responsibility for the maintenance and integrity of financial information contained on the company's web site, which should be included where that web site includes financial reports and it continues to be appropriate to include such a statement. Table 2.10A shows an example from published financial statements that reflects such responsibility. The inclusion of this responsibility in the directors' responsibilities statement negates the requirement to include it in the audit report.

Table 2.10A – Directors' responsibilities

Dixons Retail plc – Annual Report and Accounts – 28 April 2012

Directors' Responsibilities

The directors are responsible for preparing the Annual Report and the financial statements in accordance with applicable law and regulations. English company law requires the directors to prepare financial statements for each financial year and under that law, the directors have prepared the Group and the Company financial statements in accordance with International Financial Reporting Standards (IFRS) as adopted by the European Union.

The financial statements are required by law to give a true and fair view of the state of affairs of the Group and the Company and of the profit or loss of the Group for the period. In preparing the financial statements, the directors are also required to:

● Properly select and apply accounting policies;

● Present information, including accounting policies, in a manner that provides relevant, reliable, comparable and understandable information; and

● Provide additional disclosures when compliance with the specific requirements of IFRS is insufficient to enable users to understand the impact of particular transactions, other events and conditions on the financial position and financial performance.

In preparing both the Group and the Company financial statements, suitable accounting policies have been used and applied consistently, and reasonable and prudent judgements and estimates have been made. Applicable accounting standards have been followed. The financial statements have been prepared on the going concern basis as disclosed in the Statutory Information section of the Directors' Report and Business Review.

The directors are responsible for maintaining adequate accounting records and sufficient internal controls to safeguard the assets of the Company and to take reasonable steps for the prevention and detection of fraud or any other irregularities and for the preparation of a directors' report and directors' remuneration report which comply with the requirements of the Companies Act 2006 and, as regards the Group financial statements, Article 4 of the IAS Regulation. The directors are responsible for the maintenance and integrity of the corporate and financial information included on the Company's website. Legislation in the UK governing the preparation and dissemination of financial statements may differ from legislation in other jurisdictions.

Each of the directors confirm that to the best of their knowledge:

● The Group and Company financial statements give a true and fair view of the assets, liabilities, financial position and profit / (loss) of the Group and Company, respectively; and

● The business and financial review contained in this Annual Report and Accounts includes a fair review of the development and performance of the business and the position of the Group and Company together with a description of the principal risks and uncertainties they face.

By Order of the Board
Sebastian James   Humphrey Singer
Group Chief Executive   Group Finance Director
21 June 2012   21 June 2012

2.127.5 For entities that are included in the official list maintained by the FSA, the Disclosure and Transparency Rules of the FSA require the annual financial report to include a responsibility statement. [DTR 4.1.5R]. The DTR require that the persons responsible within the listed company (that is, the directors) state that, to the best of their knowledge:

■ The financial statements, prepared in accordance with the applicable set of accounting standards, give a true and fair view of the assets, liabilities, financial position and profit or loss of the listed company and the undertakings included in the consolidation taken as a whole.

■ The management report includes a fair review of the development and performance of the business and the position of the company and the undertakings included in the consolidation taken as a whole, together with a description of the principal risks and uncertainties that they face (the same wording as is used in the directors' report business review requirements in Section 417 of the Companies Act 2006 – see further chapter 2).

[DTR 4.1.12R].

This requirement does not extend to companies traded on AIM or the Plus Market's PLUS-quoted market.

2.127.6 The directors already have a responsibility under section 393 of the Companies Act 2006 to provide financial statements, prepared in accordance with applicable accounting standards that give a true and fair view. They are also responsible for preparing a business review (see further from para 2.21.1). The DTR simply require the directors to make positive statements regarding their responsibilities.

2.127.7   The name and function of each person making a responsibility statement under the DTR must be clearly indicated in the responsibility statement. [DTR 4.1.12R]. If the responsibility statement is provided collectively by the board (and, for example, signed by the company secretary or a director on its behalf), all directors are, in substance, making the responsibility statement. It is usual for the directors' names and job titles to be listed elsewhere in the annual report and hence, to avoid duplication, a specific cross-reference from the directors' report would fulfil the DTR requirements.

Statement on disclosure of information to the auditors

2.127.8   Unless the entity is exempt from the requirement to audit the accounts and has taken advantage of that exemption, the directors' report must contain a statement to confirm, for all directors in office at the time the report is approved, the following:

■   So far as each director is aware, there is no relevant audit information of which the company's auditors are unaware. Relevant information is defined as *"information needed by the company's auditor in connection with preparing his report"*.

■   Each director has taken all the steps that he ought to have taken in his duty as a director in order to make himself aware of any relevant audit information and to establish that the company's auditor is aware of that information.

Steps that a director ought to have taken would include making enquiries of other directors and the auditor and any other steps required by the director's duty to exercise due care, skill and diligence.

[CA06 Secs 418(1) to (4)].

2.127.9   Table 2.10B gives an example of disclosure.

Table 2.10B – Statement on disclosure to auditors

Diageo plc – Report and accounts – 30 June 2011

DIRECTORS' REPORT (extract)

Disclosure of information to the auditor

The directors who held office at the date of approval of this directors' report confirm that, so far as they are each aware, there is no relevant audit information of which the company's auditor is unaware; and each director has taken all the steps that they ought to have taken as a director to make themselves aware of any relevant audit information and to establish that the company's auditor is aware of that information.

2.127.10   In determining the extent of each director's duty, the Companies Act 2006 states that the following considerations are relevant:

■   The knowledge, skill and experience that may reasonably be expected of a person carrying out the functions of the company director.

■   The knowledge, skill and experience that the director actually has.

[CA06 Sec 174].

2.127.11   The penalty for *'knowingly or recklessly'* making a false statement in this regard, and failing to take reasonable steps to prevent the directors' report being approved, may be imprisonment or a fine, or both, for each director indicted. [CA06 Sec 418(5)(6)].

Re-appointment of auditors

2.128   It is customary, but not a statutory requirement, to state at the end of the directors' report that a resolution will be put to the general meeting, regarding the appointment or re-appointment of the auditors. Where a private company is deemed to have reappointed its auditors in accordance with section 487(2) of the Companies Act 2006, such a statement will of course not be relevant. In that situation, companies may wish to include a statement indicating that in the absence of a notice proposing that the appointment be terminated, the auditors will be deemed to be re-appointed for the next financial year.

Disclosure of qualifying third party and pension scheme indemnity provisions

2.128.1   Where a qualifying third party indemnity provision and/or a qualifying pension scheme indemnity provision (made by the company or otherwise) was in force for the benefit of one or more directors at any time during the financial year, or at the time when the report is approved, a statement should be made in the directors' report to confirm this fact. [CA06 Sec 236(2)(3)]. An example of disclosure is provided in Table 2.10C.

Table 2.10C – Disclosure of directors' indemnities

Mitchells & Butlers plc – Report and accounts – 24 September 2011

Directors' report (extract)

Directors' indemnity

As permitted by the Articles of Association, the Directors have the benefit of an indemnity which is a qualifying third party indemnity provision as defined by Section 234 of the Companies Act 2006. The indemnity was in force throughout the last financial year, and is currently in force. The Company also purchased and maintained throughout the financial year Directors' and Officers' liability insurance in respect of itself and its Directors. No indemnity is provided for the Company's auditor.

2.128.2   A statement is also required in the directors' report where a qualifying indemnity provision has been made during the year, or at the time when the report is approved, by the company for the benefit of one or more directors of an associated company. [CA06 Sec 236(4)(5)]. An associated company is defined in section 256 of the Companies Act 2006. A holding company is associated with all its subsidiaries and a subsidiary is associated with its holding company and all the other subsidiaries of its holding company.

2.128.3   Section 234 of the Companies Act 2006 defines a qualifying third party indemnity provision as one where the provision does not provide indemnity for any liability incurred by the director in respect of each of the following:

- An amount due to the company or any associated company.

- A fine imposed by criminal proceedings.

- A penalty payable to a regulatory authority in respect of non-compliance with any requirement of a regulatory nature.

- An amount payable.

  - in defending criminal proceedings in which the director is convicted;

  - in defending civil proceedings brought by the company (or an associated company) in which judgement is given against the director; or

  - in connection with any application in which the court refused to grant the director relief.

[CA06 Sec 234(2)(3)].

2.128.4   The Companies Act 2006 defines a qualifying pension scheme indemnity provision as a provision indemnifying a director of a company that is a trustee of an occupational pension scheme against liability incurred in connection with the company's activities as a trustee of the scheme, provided the provision does not provide indemnity against any liability of the director:

- To pay a fine imposed by criminal proceedings.

- To pay a sum to a regulatory authority due to a penalty in respect of non-compliance with any regulatory requirement.

- Incurred by the director in defending criminal proceedings in which he is convicted.

[CA06 Sec 235(2)(3)].

Change of name

2.128.5   A company may change its name either during the financial year or after the year end. Although there are no specific disclosure requirements set out in law, it is convention and best practice that an explanation of the change of name is given in the directors' report, whether the change of name occurred before or after the year end. The financial statements and reports should be in the new name followed by the words 'formerly (old name)' .The name should also be stated this way on the front of the financial statements (and at the top of each page if the company's name is stated there).

Additional matters for publicly traded companies

2.129 The directors' report of companies with publicly traded securities should give information on further matters in addition to those already discussed above. These additional matters are considered in the paragraphs that follow.

Control and share structures

2.129.1 These are general requirements designed to bring greater transparency to the market and apply to companies whether or not they are involved in a takeover. The disclosure requirements apply to companies with voting shares that were admitted to trading on a regulated market at the end of the year. [SI 2008/410 7 Sch 13(1)].

2.129.2 The specific disclosure requirements must be provided either in the directors' report or, by virtue of DTR 7.2.9R, in a document accompanying the annual report provided that there is a specific cross-reference to the disclosures from the directors' report. The disclosure requirements are set out in Part 6 of Schedule 7 to SI 2008/410 and include the following, which are to be given by reference to the end of the financial year:

- The structure of the company's capital, including the rights and obligations attached to the shares.

- Any restrictions on the transfer of securities.

- Any restriction on voting rights.

- Where a person has a significant direct or indirect holding, the identity of the person, the size of the holding and the nature of the holding (see further from para 2.130).

- Where any person holds shares with specific rights regarding control of the company:

    - the identity of the person; and

    - the nature of those rights.

- Where the company has an employee share scheme but shares relating to that scheme have rights regarding the control of the company that are not directly exercisable by the employees, how those rights are exercisable.

- Agreements between holders of securities known to the company that may result in restrictions on the transfer of securities or voting rights.

- Any rules that the company has about the appointment of directors, powers of directors or amendments to the company's articles of association.

- Significant agreements that the company is a party to that will be affected by a change in control of the company, together with the effects of such agreements (see further from para 2.129.4).

- Any agreements with employees (including directors) of the company providing for compensation for loss of office or employment on the takeover of the company.

2.129.3 Failure to include either the information concerning control and share structures or explanatory material in the annual report will attract criminal sanctions under sections 415(4), (5), and 419(3), (4) of the Companies Act 2006 (directors responsible for the failure to comply with provisions related to the directors' report are liable to a fine).

Agreements affected by a change of control

2.129.4 The extent to which agreements that a company has entered into will be affected by a change of control will vary, as will the nature of those contracts. Examples of agreements that may be affected (other than those specifically mentioned by the Act) are:

- Bank loan/facility agreements.

Directors' report

- Convertible and listed debt.
- Sale/supply agreements.
- Leases.
- Joint venture agreements.

An example showing both disclosure of agreements that would be affected by a change of control and a restriction of voting rights (that is also affected by a change of control) is given in Table 2.11.

Table 2.11 – Disclosure of agreements affected by change of control

Xstrata plc plc – Annual Report – 31 December 2011

Directors' report – (extract)

Significant contractual arrangements (extract)

The Companies Act 2006 requires the Company to disclose the following significant agreements that contain provisions entitling the counterparties to exercise termination or other rights in the event of a change of control of the Company:

Relationship Agreement

The Company is party to the Relationship Agreement with Glencore International AG (Glencore) dated 20 March 2002. The Agreement regulates the continuing relationship between the parties. In particular it ensures that (a) the Company is capable of carrying on its business independently of Glencore as a controlling shareholder (as such term is defined in the Agreement); (b) transactions and relationships between Glencore (or any of its subsidiaries or affiliates) and the Company are at an arm's length and on normal commercial terms; (c) Glencore shall be entitled to nominate up to three directors or (if lower or higher) such number of directors equal to one less than the number of directors who are independent directors; and, (d) directors of the Company nominated by Glencore shall not be permitted to vote on any Board resolution, unless otherwise agreed by the independent directors, to approve any aspect of the Company's involvement in or enforcement of any arrangements, agreements or transactions with Glencore or any of its subsidiaries or affiliates. The Agreement provides that, save to the extent required by law, the parties agree that they shall exercise their powers so that the Company is managed in accordance with the principles of good governance set out in the Combined Code and that the provisions of the Code of Best Practice set out in the Combined Code are complied with by the Company. It is expressed that the Agreement terminates in the event that Glencore ceases to be a controlling shareholder of the Company following a sale or disposal of shares in the Company or if the Company ceases to be listed on the Official List and traded on the London Stock Exchange.

US$500 million notes due 2037

On 30 November 2007, Xstrata Finance (Canada) Limited issued $500 million 6.90% notes due 2037, guaranteed by the Company, Xstrata (Schweiz) AG and Xstrata Finance (Dubai) Limited. The terms of these notes require Xstrata Finance (Canada) Limited to make an offer to each noteholder to repurchase all or any part of such holder's notes at a repurchase price in cash equal to 101% of the aggregate principal amount of the notes so repurchased plus any accrued and unpaid interest on the principal amount of the notes repurchased to the date of repurchase, if both of the following occur:

(i)   a change of control (as defined in the terms and conditions of the notes) of Xstrata; and

(ii) the notes are rated below investment grade by each of Moody's and Standard & Poor's on any date from 30 days prior to the date of the public notice of an arrangement that could result in a change of control (as defined in the terms and conditions of the notes) until the end of the 60-day period following public notice of the occurrence of a change of control.

€600 million notes due 2015

On 23 May 2008, Xstrata Canada Financial Corporation issued €600,000,000 6.25% guaranteed notes due 2015 and £500,000,000 7.375% guaranteed notes due 2020 (the 2008 MTN Notes). The 2008 MTN Notes are guaranteed by each of Xstrata plc, Xstrata (Schweiz) AG, Xstrata Finance (Dubai) Limited and Xstrata Finance (Canada) Limited and were issued pursuant to the $6,000,000,000 Euro Medium Term Note Programme.

Pursuant to the terms and conditions of the 2008 MTN Notes, if:

(i)   a change of control occurs (as defined in the terms and conditions of the 2008 MTN Notes); and

(ii) the 2008 MTN Notes carry, on the relevant announcement date of the change of control:

    (a)   an investment grade credit rating is either downgraded to a non-investment grade credit rating or is withdrawn; or

    (b)   a non-investment grade credit rating is downgraded by one or more notches or is withdrawn; or

    (c)   no credit rating and a negative rating event (as defined in the terms and conditions of the 2008 MTN Notes) occurs, each holder has the option to require Xstrata Canada Financial Corp. to redeem such 2008 MTN Notes in cash at the principal amount plus interest accrued to (but excluding) the date of redemption.

US$6.0 billion syndicated facility

On 24 October 2011, Xstrata (Schweiz) AG and the Company entered into a $6.0 billion multicurrency revolving syndicated loan facility agreement with the banks and financial institutions named therein as lenders (the Syndicated Facilities Agreement) and Barclays Capital acting as facility agent.

Upon a change of control, no borrower may make a further utilisation unless otherwise agreed. The majority lenders, as defined in the agreement, can also require that the Syndicated Facilities Agreement is immediately terminated and declared that all

---

outstanding loans become immediately payable. Alternatively, if the majority lenders do not require cancellation, but a specific lender does on the basis of internal policy, that particular lender can require that its commitments are cancelled and all amounts outstanding in respect of that lender's commitments shall become immediately payable.

US$3.0 billion multi-tranche notes

On 3 November 2011, Xstrata Finance (Canada) Limited issued $800 million 2.85% notes due 2014, $700 million 3.6% notes due 2017, $1.0 billion 4.95% notes due 2021 and $500 million 6.0% notes due 2041. The notes are guaranteed by the Company. The terms of the notes contain change of control provisions, in substance, identical to those set out in the referenced US$500 million notes due 2037 above.

Xstrata plc Long Term Incentive Plan

The rules of our employee share plans set out the consequences of any change of control of the Company on employees' rights under the plans. Generally such rights will vest on a change of control and participants will become entitled to acquire shares in the Company or, in some cases, to the payment of a cash sum of equivalent value.

Matters for listed companies

2.129.5 The following requirements apply to those companies that are subject to the UKLA's Listing Rules (for example, companies traded on the main market of the LSE or the Plus Market's PLUS-listed market).

Major interest in company's shares

2.130 A statement should be given of particulars of the nature and extent of the interests of any person, in any holding of 3% or more of the nominal value of any class of capital carrying rights to vote in all circumstances at general meetings of the company. The statement must be made at a date not more than one month prior to the date of notice of the annual general meeting. [LR 9.8.6R (2)]. The 3% threshold is higher for certain entities, for example market makers only disclose interests of 10% or more. [DTR 5.1.3R].

2.131 The particulars to be disclosed include the names of the persons and the amount of their interests. This information should be that which has been disclosed to the company in accordance with DTR 5. If there is no such interest, that fact should also be stated. [LR 9.8.6R (2)]. It is customary to give this information in the directors' report. An example is given in Table 2.12 below. It should be noted that the Companies Act requirement to disclose significant shareholdings (described in para 2.129.2 above) requires such holdings to be disclosed as at the end of the financial year, whereas the Listing Rules require disclosures as at not more than one month prior to the date of the notice of AGM. The Companies Act requirement also requires the nature of the interest (direct or indirect) to be disclosed.

Table 2.12 — Major interest in company's shares

3i Group plc – Report and accounts – 31 March 2012

Directors' report – statutory and corporate governance information (extract)

Major interests in ordinary shares

Notifications of the following voting interests in the Company's ordinary share capital (which are notifiable in accordance with Chapter 5 of the FSA's Disclosure and Transparency Rules and section 793 Companies Act 2006) had been received by the Company as at 31 March 2012 and 10 May 2012

	As at 31 March 2012	% of issued share capital	10 May 2012	% of issued share capital	Nature of holding
BlackRock, Inc	106,259,273	10.943	106,259,273	10.943	Indirect
Ameriprise Financial, Inc. and its group	66,041,715	6.805	66,041,715	6.805	Direct and Indirect
Standard Life Investments plc	48,482,387	4.996	48,482,387	4.996	Direct and Indirect
Schroders Plc	47,870,160	4.933	47,870,160	4.933	Indirect
Legal & General Group Plc and/or its subsidiaries	38,620,595	3.979	38,620,595	3.979	Direct

---

2.132 In order to ensure that the share register is up to date, the Companies Act 2006 gives listed companies the right to write to any person who it believes is (or has been during the previous three years) interested in the company's shares and ask them to confirm that fact, or to state the person to whom the interest was transferred. [CA06 Sec 793]. Further, the DTR require holders of more than 3% (or a higher threshold in certain circumstances – see para 2.130) of a company's qualifying financial instruments to notify the company if that holding increases above or falls below any integer percentage holding equal to or higher than 3%.

[The next paragraph is 2.135.]

Transactions with a controlling shareholder

2.135   The annual report should include particulars of any contract of significance between the company (or one of its subsidiary undertakings) and a controlling shareholder subsisting during the year. [LR 9.8.4R (10)(b)]. For this purpose, a 'contract of significance' is one which is determined in accordance with the rules set out in paragraph 2.137.11 below. An example is given in Table 2.13 below. In the example, the company cross-references from the directors' report to the notes to the financial statements, where extensive disclosure of contracts with the controlling shareholder is provided.

2.135.1   A 'controlling shareholder' is defined within the definition of an associate in the Listing Rules and is taken to mean any person who is:

■   entitled to exercise, or control the exercise of, at least 30% of the voting power at the company's general meetings; or

■   is in a position to control the composition of a majority of the company's board of directors.

[LR App 1.1].

2.135.2   In addition, the directors' report should disclose details of any contract with a controlling shareholder (as defined above) to provide services to the company or to one of its subsidiaries (see Table 2.13 below). This information is not required if the shareholder is providing services that it normally provides as part of its principal business and it is not a contract of significance that is required to be disclosed. [LR 9.8.4R (11)].

Table 2.13 — Contract with a controlling shareholder

Xstrata plc — Annual Report — 31 December 2011

Directors' Report (extract)

Significant contractual arrangements (extract)

Glencore International AG is Xstrata's major shareholder and at the date of this document holds 33.64% of Xstrata's issued share capital. A Relationship Agreement regulates the relationship between Xstrata and Glencore to ensure all commercial arrangements are transacted on an arm's-length basis. Glencore is the sole distributor of Xstrata's nickel, cobalt and ferronickel production, has sales agreements with Xstrata Copper for some of its copper concentrate and copper cathode and is the marketing agent for much of Xstrata Alloys' ferrochrome and vanadium. Glencore has a market advisory role with Xstrata Coal. Full details of related party contractual arrangements are provided in Note 35 of the financial statements.

[The next paragraph is 2.137.]

Disclosure of directors' interests

2.137   The UKLA's Listing Rules require a listed company's annual financial report to include a statement setting out all the interests, as at the year end, of each person who is a director of the company as at the end of the period under review including:

■   all changes in the interests of each director that have occurred between the end of the period under review and a date not more than one month prior to the date of the notice of the annual general meeting; or

■   if there have been no changes in the interests of each director in the period described above, a statement that there have been no changes.

[LR 9.8.6R (1)].

2.137.1   An example of disclosure is set out in Table 2.14.

Table 2.14 – Directors' share interests

3i Group plc – Report and accounts – 31 March 2012

Directors' report – statutory and corporate governance information (extract)

Directors' interests

In accordance with FSA Listing Rule 9.8.6(R)(1), Directors' interests in the shares of the Company (in respect of which transactions are notifiable to the Company under FSA Disclosure and Transparency Rule 3.1.2(R)) as at 31 March 2011 are shown below:

	Ordinary shares	B shares
Sir Adrian Montague	57,758	0
J P Asquith	2,500	0
S A Burrows	1,567,158	0
A R Cox	4,900	0
R H Meddings	18,460	0
W Mesdag	224,174	0
M J Queen	1,703,162	6,227
M G Verluyten	0	0
J S Wilson	59,686	1,038

The share interests shown for Mr M J Queen and Mrs J S Wilson include shares held in the 3i Group Share Incentive Plan and share bonus awards under the 3i Group Deferred Bonus Plan. The share interests shown exclude share option and performance share awards detailed in the Directors' remuneration report. From 1 April 2012 to 10 May 2012, Mr M J Queen and Mrs J S Wilson became interested in an additional 201 and 198 ordinary shares respectively, and there were no other changes to Directors' share interests.

2.137.2 The interests required to be disclosed are those in respect of transactions that are notifiable to the company under DTR 3.1.2R. Under that rule, persons discharging managerial responsibilities (which includes, but is not restricted to, directors) and their connected persons, must notify the issuer in writing of the occurrence of all transactions conducted on their own account in the shares of the issuer, or derivatives or any other financial instruments relating to those shares within four business days of the day on which the transaction occurred. Connected persons are considered further from paragraph 2.137.7.

2.137.3 Persons who are directors during, but not at the end of, the period under review need not be included. [LR 9.8.6AG (1)].

2.137.4 The UKLA's Listing Rules note that a listed company unable to compile the statement in LR 9.8.6R (1) from information already available to it may need to seek the relevant information, or confirmation, from the director, including that in relation to connected persons, but would not be expected to obtain information directly from connected persons. [LR 9.8.6AG (2)].

[The next paragraph is 2.137.6.]

2.137.6 Listed companies are required by Schedule 8 to SI 2008/410, 'The Large and Medium-sized Companies and Groups (Accounts and Reports) Regulations 2008', to make detailed disclosure in the directors' remuneration report about directors' share options. These are considered in detail in chapter 5. In practice, the disclosure of directors' interests in shares and options are sometimes combined and presented in a tabular manner, usually in the directors' remuneration report. A cross-reference may be given in the directors' report to the precise location of the information. Examples of how a company discloses its directors' interests in accordance with the Listing Rules are included in chapter 5.

Connected persons

2.137.7 The definition of 'connected persons' contained in the Listing Rules is wider than that contained in section 252 of the Companies Act 2006 (see para 2.137.10).

2.137.8 The definition of 'connected persons' in the Companies Act 2006 includes:

- Members of the director's family, including:
  - The director's spouse, civil partner or any other person with whom the director lives as a partner in an enduring family relationship.
  - The director's children or step-children.

- - Any children or step-children (under the age of 18) of the director's enduring life partner who live with the director.

  - The director's parents.

- A body corporate with which the director is connected (see para 2.137.9).

- A trustee of a trust of which the beneficiary is (or can be, at the discretion of the trustee) the director (or a family member or connected body corporate as defined above) other than a trust for the purposes of an employee share scheme or pension scheme.

- A person acting in capacity as partner of the director (or any person connected with him).

- A partnership that is a legal person in which the director (or any person connected with him) is a partner.

- A partnership that is a legal person with a partner that is, itself, a partnership, where the director (or a connected person of his) is a partner.

[CA06 Secs 252, 253].

2.137.9 A body corporate is a connected person of a director if the director and his connected persons are interested in at least 20% of the nominal value of the body corporate's equity share capital (excluding treasury shares), or are entitled to control at least 20 percent of the voting power at any general meeting (excluding votes attached to treasury shares). [CA06 Sec 254]. For this purpose, an 'interest' in shares is defined in Schedule 1 to the Companies Act 2006 and is taken to mean any interest whatsoever and includes any right to acquire shares or control of the voting rights attached to the shares. The definition of 'equity share capital' is contained in section 548 of the Companies Act 2006 and is considered further in chapter 23 of the Manual of Accounting – IFRS for the UK and chapter 23 of the Manual of Accounting – UK GAAP.

2.137.10 In addition to those that fall within the Companies Act 2006's definition of connected persons, the Listing Rules definition includes:

- Any relative of the director who, on the date of the transaction in question has shared the same household as the director for at least 12 months.

- A body corporate in which the director (or a person connected to him under the Companies Act 2006 or the bullet point above) is a director or a senior executive who has the power to make management decisions affecting the future development and business prospects of that body corporate.

[LR Glossary].

Directors' interests in contracts of significance

2.137.11 The Listing Rules require disclosure of particulars of any contract of significance (including substantial property transactions) subsisting during the period under review, to which the company, or one of its subsidiary undertakings, is a party and in which a director of the company is, or was, materially interested. [LR 9.8.4R (10)]. In this context, 'a contract of significance' is one which represents in value a sum equal to 1% or more, calculated on a group basis where relevant, of:

- The aggregate of the group's share capital and reserves for a capital transaction or for a transaction of which the principal purpose is the granting of credit.

- The group's total purchases, sales, payments or receipts, as appropriate for other transactions.

[LR App 1.1].

Waiver of dividends

2.138 Particulars of any arrangements under which any shareholder has waived or agreed to waive any dividends should be disclosed. This requirement applies to waivers of future dividends as well as to waivers of dividends payable during the past financial year. Waivers of dividend of less than 1% of the total value of any dividend may be disregarded provided that some payment has been made on each share of the relevant class during the year. [LR 9.8.5G].

[The next paragraph is 2.140.]

Special business

2.140 Holders of listed securities who are sent a notice of a meeting that is to occur on the same day as an AGM, which includes business that is considered not to be routine business of an AGM must be provided with an explanation in the directors' report of such business, unless an explanatory circular accompanies the notice. [LR 13.8.8R (1)]. An example of matters that are regarded as special business in an AGM is given in Table 2.15 below.

Table 2.15 — Special business in an AGM

WH Smith PLC — Annual report and accounts — 31 August 2011

Corporate governance, AGM and other matters (extract)

Annual General Meeting
The AGM of the Company will be held at JPMorgan Cazenove, 20 Moorgate, London EC2R 6DA on 25 January 2012 at 11.30am. The Notice of Annual General Meeting is given, together with explanatory notes, in the booklet which accompanies this report.

Notice of Annual General Meeting (extract)

Special business

The following 3 resolutions will be proposed as ordinary resolutions.

Authority to make political donations
Resolution 13: to resolve that, in accordance with Section 366 of the Companies Act 2006, the Company and all companies that are subsidiaries of the Company at any time during the period for which this resolution has effect be and are hereby authorised to:

(a) make political donations to political parties or independent election candidates not exceeding £50,000 in total;

(b) make political donations to political organisations other than political parties not exceeding £50,000 in total; and

(c) incur political expenditure not exceeding £50,000 in total, during the period from the date of passing this resolution up to and including the conclusion of the next Annual General Meeting or up to and including 28 February 2013, whichever is the earlier.

For the purpose of this resolution the terms 'political donations', 'political parties', 'independent election candidates', 'political organisations' and 'political expenditure' have the meanings set out in Sections 363 to 365 of the Companies Act 2006.

WH Smith 2012 Co-Investment Plan
Resolution 14: to resolve that:

(a) the rules of the WH Smith 2012 Co-Investment Plan ('CIP'), the main features of which are summarised in the explanatory notes and a copy of which is produced to the meeting and for the purpose of identification marked 'A' and signed by the Chairman be and are hereby approved and adopted and the directors, or a duly authorised committee of them, be and are hereby authorised to do all things as they may consider necessary or expedient to carry the CIP into effect; and

(b) the directors, or a duly authorised committee of them, be authorised to establish any schedule to the CIP they consider necessary in relation to any employees in jurisdictions outside the United Kingdom, with any modifications necessary or desirable to take account of local securities laws, exchange control and tax legislation, provided that any ordinary shares made available under any schedule are treated as counting against the relevant limits on individual and overall participation in the CIP.

Authority to allot shares
Resolution 15: to resolve that:

(a) the directors be authorised to allot shares in the Company or grant rights to subscribe for, or convert any security into, shares in the Company:

    (i) in accordance with Article 7 of the Company's Articles of Association, up to a maximum nominal amount of £10,225,196 (such amount to be reduced by the nominal amount of any equity securities (as defined in Article 8 of the Company's Articles of Association) allotted under paragraph (ii) below in excess of £10,225,196); and

    (ii) comprising equity securities (as defined in Article 8 of the Company's Articles of Association), up to a maximum nominal amount of £20,453,460 (such amount to be reduced by any shares allotted or rights granted under paragraph (i) above) in connection with an offer by way of a rights issue (as defined in Article 8 of the Company's Articles of Association);

(b) this authority shall expire at the conclusion of the next Annual General Meeting of the Company after the passing of this resolution or, if earlier, at the close of business on 28 February 2013;

(c) all previous unutilised authorities under Section 551 of the Companies Act 2006 shall cease to have effect (save to the extent that the same are exercisable pursuant to Section 551(7) of the Companies Act 2006 by reason of any offer or agreement made prior to the date of this resolution which would or might require shares to be allotted or rights to be granted on or after that date).

The following 3 resolutions will be proposed as special resolutions.

Disapplication of pre-emption rights

Resolution 16: to resolve that:

(a) in accordance with Article 8 of the Company's Articles of Association, the directors be given power to allot equity securities for cash;

(b) the directors be given power to allot equity securities for cash within Section 560(3) of the Companies Act 2006 (sale of treasury shares) as if Section 561 of that Act did not apply;

(c) the powers under paragraphs (a) and (b) above (other than in connection with a rights issue, as defined in Article 8(b)(ii) of the Company's Articles of Association) shall be limited to the allotment of equity securities having a nominal amount not exceeding in aggregate £1,533,933;

(d) these authorities shall expire at the conclusion of the next Annual General Meeting of the Company after the passing of this resolution or, if earlier, at the close of business on 28 February 2013; and

(e) all previous unutilised authorities under Sections 570 and 573 of the Companies Act 2006 shall cease to have effect.

Market purchases of ordinary shares

Resolution 17: to resolve that, pursuant to Section 701 of the Companies Act 2006, the Company be and is hereby generally and unconditionally authorised to make market purchases (as defined in Section 693(4) of the Companies Act 2006) of any of its own ordinary shares in such manner and on such terms as the directors may from time to time determine provided that:

(a) the maximum aggregate number of ordinary shares that may be purchased under this authority is 20,763,024;

(b) the minimum price which may be paid for each ordinary share is $22^6/_{67}$p (exclusive of all expenses);

(c) the maximum price which may be paid for each ordinary share is an amount (exclusive of all expenses) equal to the higher of:

    (i) 105 per cent of the average of the middle market quotations for an ordinary share as derived from the London Stock Exchange Daily Official List for the five business days immediately preceding the day on which the ordinary share is purchased; and

    (ii) the price stipulated by Article 5(1) of the Buy-back and Stabilisation Regulation 2003;

(d) the authority shall, unless previously varied, revoked or renewed, expire at the conclusion of the next Annual General Meeting of the Company or at close of business on 28 February 2013, whichever is the earlier, save that the Company shall be entitled under such authority to make at any time before such expiry any contract or contracts to purchase its own shares which will or might be executed wholly or partly after such expiry and make a purchase of shares in pursuance of any such contract or contracts; and

(e) all existing authorities for the Company to make market purchases of ordinary shares are revoked, except in relation to the purchase of shares under a contract or contracts concluded before the date of this resolution and which has or have not been executed.

Notice of general meetings

Resolution 18: to resolve that a general meeting (other than an annual general meeting) may be called on not less than 14 clear days' notice.

Explanatory notes

[Not reproduced in this example]

[The next paragraph is 2.143.]

Small companies

2.143 The disclosures required for directors' reports for small companies depend on the type of small company involved. The requirements distinguish between two types of small company, described here as Type A and Type B companies:

■ Type A: A company that is entitled to prepare financial statements in accordance with the small companies regime (see further chapter 31 of the Manual of Accounting – UK GAAP).

■ Type B: A company that is not entitled to prepare financial statements in accordance with the small companies' regime, but would be so entitled if it was not a member of an ineligible group.

2.144 An ineligible group is a group in which any of its members is (or was, at any time within the financial year) any one of the following:

■ A public company.

■ An authorised insurance company, a banking company, an e-money issuer, a MiFiD investment firm or a UCITS management company.

■ Carrying on insurance market activity.

■ A body corporate (other than a company, but including a foreign company) whose shares are admitted to trading on a regulated market in an EEA member State.

[CA06 Sec 384(2)].

2.144.1 Both of the types of small company set out in paragraph 2.143 are permitted, but not required, to exclude the directors' report from the financial statements filed with the Registrar of Companies. [CA06 Secs 444(1), 444A(1)].

2.145 This does not affect the requirement for companies to prepare a directors' report: all companies are required to do so, but small companies do not have to give all the disclosures that would be required of larger companies. Large and medium-sized companies must prepare their directors' reports in accordance with Schedule 7 of SI 2008/410. This statutory instrument does not apply to small companies that avail themselves of the small companies' regime (Type A companies); instead, these companies apply Schedule 5 of SI 2008/ 409. The small companies' regime is not available to a company that is a member of an ineligible group (Type B companies).

2.145.1 The table below sets out the disclosures that are *not* required for each type of company.

Disclosures	Type A companies (see para 2.143)	Type B companies (see para 2.143)
(✓ indicates disclosure is *not* required)		
A business review. [CA06 Sec 417(1)].	✓	✓
The dividends recommended by the directors. [CA06 Sec 416(3)].	✓	✓
Disclosures relating to financial instruments (para 2.122).	✓	✗
Particulars of important events that have occurred between the end of the financial year and the date of approval of the financial statements (para 2.44).	✓	✗
An indication of likely future developments in the business (para 2.21.25).	✓	✗
An indication of the activities, if any, in the field of research and development (para 2.45).	✓	✗
An indication of the existence of branches, as defined in section 698(2), of the company outside the UK (para 2.126).	✓	✗
Any information in respect of employee involvement in the company where the average weekly number of employees during the year exceeded 250 (para 2.79).	✓	✗

2.145.2 If, in preparing the directors' report, advantage has been taken of the small companies' exemption, a statement to that effect must be included in the directors' report in a prominent position above the signature. [CA06 Sec 419(2)].

Approval and signing of directors' report

2.146 The board of directors must formally approve the directors' report and it must be signed on behalf of the board by a director or the secretary of the company. [CA06 Sec 419(1)].

2.147 Every copy of the directors' report that is laid before the company in general meeting, or that is otherwise circulated, published or issued, must state the name of the person who signed it on behalf of the board. [CA06 Sec 433(1) to (3)]. A copy of the directors' report that is to be delivered to the Registrar of Companies must also be signed on behalf of the board by a director or secretary of the company. [CA06 Sec 444 to 447].

2.147.1 As noted in paragraph 2.145.1 above, a directors' report prepared in accordance with the small companies regime must contain a statement to that effect in a prominent position above the signature. [CA06 Sec 419(2)].

Liability for contravention

2.148   Every person who was a director of the company at the end of the period within which the company's financial statements must be laid before the company in general meeting and be delivered to the Registrar of Companies may be guilty of an offence if the directors' report fails to comply with the Act's requirements. This offence is punishable by a fine. [CA06 Secs 415(4)(5), 419(3)(4)].

2.149   It is a defence in such a situation for a director to prove that he took all reasonable steps to ensure that the directors' report complied with all the Act's requirements. [CA06 Secs 415(4), 419(3)].

2.150   Furthermore, where the company does not comply with the requirements for the approval and signing of the directors' report as set out in paragraphs 2.146 and 2.147 above, the company and every officer of it who is in default will be guilty of an offence and liable to a fine. [CA06 Secs 419(4), 433(5)].

Directors' liability: safe harbour

2.150.1   The Companies Act 2006 contains a statutory liability regime for directors in respect of narrative reporting. [CA06 Sec 463]. This effectively incorporates a 'safe harbour' for information in the directors' reports (including the business review) under section 417 of the Companies Act 2006, the directors' remuneration reports under section 420 of the Companies Act 2006 and any summary financial statement, so far as it is derived from either of these reports. A director is not subject to any liability to a person other than the company resulting from reliance, by that person or another, on information in such a report. A director is liable to compensate the company for any loss suffered by it as a result of any untrue or misleading statement in such a report, or the omission from such a report of anything required to be included in it. However, the director is liable only if he knew the statement to be untrue or misleading, or was reckless as to whether it was untrue or misleading, or he knew the omission to be dishonest concealment of a material fact. An explicit statement is not required in the annual report for the 'safe harbour' protection to be invoked.

2.150.2   The 'safe harbour' applies to the reports described above and BIS has indicated that it extends to information cross-referenced from those reports to other parts of the annual report. Safe harbour will, therefore, cover, for example, separate voluntary OFR or narrative reporting outside the directors' report, provided that cross-referencing from the directors' report to the OFR is provided explicitly.

Position of the auditor

2.151   The auditors are required to state in their report whether, in their opinion, *"the information given in the directors' report for the financial year for which the accounts are prepared is consistent with those accounts"*. [CA06 Sec 496]. There is no exemption from this requirement for auditors of small and medium-sized companies (other than those exempt from the audit requirement.

2.152   Auditors have a statutory responsibility to review the directors' report for consistency with the financial statements. This approach is supported by the Auditing Practices Board's ISA (UK&I) 720B (revised), 'The auditor's statutory reporting responsibility in relation to directors' reports (2009)', and by APB Bulletin 2009/02, 'Auditor's reports on financial statements in the United Kingdom'.

2.153   ISA (UK&I) 720B (revised) deals specifically with the auditor's statutory reporting responsibility in relation to directors' reports and requires the auditor to read the information in the directors' report and assess whether it is consistent with the financial statements.

2.154   The auditor should seek to resolve any inconsistencies identified between the information in the directors' report and the financial statements. If a material inconsistency between the directors' report and the financial statements is not resolved, details should be provided in the audit report. In addition, a qualified or adverse opinion would be necessary where an amendment that is necessary to the financial statements has not been made.

2.155   ISA (UK&I) 720B (revised) confirms that the information given in the directors' report includes information that is included by way of a cross reference to other information presented separately from the directors' report. For example the auditor has a statutory responsibility to review a business review presented within a separate voluntary OFR for consistency with the financial statements. [ISA (UK & I) 720B (revised) para 3].

Enforcement

2.156 The Financial Reporting Review Panel (FRRP), part of the Financial Reporting Council, is responsible for ensuring that both public and large private companies comply with relevant reporting requirements including the directors' report (and, thus, the business review). The Secretary of State (through Companies House) is responsible for enforcement in respect of other companies. [Companies (Audit, Investigation and Community Enterprise) Act 2004 Sec 14].

2.157 Under the existing enforcement regime in respect of defective accounts, a company may be required to revise its directors' report where it is not compliant with the Act's requirements. In cases of non-compliance the FRRP will have the power, if necessary, to go to the court to compel a company to revise its report. Press notices and Practice Notes issued by the FRRP include those discussed from paragraph 2.21.3.1 and from paragraph 2.21.16.

Chapter 3

Operating and financial review

Operating and financial review

Introduction

3.1 This chapter deals with the voluntary and good practice corporate reporting often set out in the front section ('front half') of a company's annual report as an operating and financial review (OFR) or similar.

3.2 To assist directors in preparing OFRs, the ASB issued a non-mandatory reporting statement, 'Operating and financial review' (referred to in this chapter as RS (OFR) or the reporting statement). Although non-mandatory, it is recommended for quoted companies and any other companies that purport to prepare an OFR and it is generally accepted that directors of a company preparing an OFR will give due regard to it.

3.3 The statutory business review is a disclosure required within the directors' report by the Companies Act 2006. (See further chapter 2 for guidance relating to other parts of the directors' report).A company that includes an OFR in its directors' report, either directly or by cross reference, also complies with the statutory requirement to include a business review in its directors' report. As such, the example disclosures within the OFR section of this chapter may also be considered when preparing a business review. Some of the examples in this chapter relate to non-UK companies that do not prepare an OFR (or statutory business review), as defined in the UK; nevertheless, the reports they prepare contain information that addresses some or all of the matters recommended for inclusion in an OFR.

3.4 While there is no UK statutory requirement for an entity to prepare an operating and financial review, many UK listed and public interest entities produce one voluntarily and consider it a key mechanism for communicating with investors. Often, companies present information equivalent to that which would be included in an OFR but either include it in the annual report under a different title or include the information under a number of headings within the 'front half'.

3.5 Further PwC publications that may provide additional guidance to companies in preparing an OFR include:

Title of publication	Description
Guide to forward-looking information – Don't fear the future: communicating with confidence	This guide provides practical guidance on how the reporting of forward-looking information can be achieved, together with examples from progressive companies, both in the UK and elsewhere, who are already adopting a forward-looking orientation in their narrative reporting.
Guide to key performance indicators – Communicating the measures that matter	A practical publication that has been developed to highlight the increasing demand for reporting of key performance indicators (KPIs). It addresses many of the questions posed by these demands and demonstrates what good reporting of KPIs looks like with a collection of examples drawn from the UK and elsewhere.
Report Leadership: Tomorrow's reporting today	Provides a framework, strategic thinking and practical ideas for improving the content of annual reports, including the narrative section.
Integrated reporting: What does your reporting say about you?	Sets out a picture of the information that can help present a cohesive and persuasive picture of a business, including the way it is managed and governed.
11 Reporting Tips	Simple actions and examples of best practice to make company reporting more accessible and to ensure effective communication.

These publications are equally relevant to companies preparing a business review to form part of a directors' report (see chapter 2). All of these publications can be found at www.corporatereporting.com, which also provides further examples of good narrative reporting. The publications are located under the 'Toolkit' and the 'Research and insights' tabs. Many illustrative examples of OFR reporting can be found on www.pwcinform.com.

Location of the OFR within the annual report

3.6   Historically, many listed companies have presented an OFR as a separate statement within the annual report. As explained in chapter 2, the business review is required to be included within the directors' report, although BIS has indicated that cross-referencing to information contained elsewhere in the annual report (for example, in the OFR) is acceptable.

3.7   However, the Companies Act 2006 contains provisions that give directors a 'safe harbour' in respect of civil liability arising out of the content of the directors' report (see further chapter 2). Thus, companies may wish to include the OFR within the directors' report in order to benefit from the 'safe harbour' provisions.

Good practice reporting

3.8   Users of financial statements can benefit enormously from accompanying narrative reporting that explains the company's performance, cash flows and financial position in the context of its objectives, strategies and future prospects. Financial statements are mainly backward-looking, reflecting what has already happened. Although the financial statements give important information, particularly in judging the quality of management's stewardship, they do not fully explain why the entity's performance was what it was or what is likely to happen next.

3.9   The global financial crisis has raised questions about the adequacy of corporate reporting in its broadest sense. Investors want to know, not just what the company does and how it performed, but also whether that performance is sustainable, given the risks and market conditions that face it. Our ongoing research programme with investors has shown that they often have insufficient contextual and non-financial information to enable them to model future cash flows. An OFR is intended to meet the shortfall between the information provided by financial statements and the information sought by investors.

3.10   In recent years, narrative reporting has come to be viewed as increasingly important, providing an opportunity to present integrated and comprehensive information about a company to the capital markets and other user groups. The OFR gives management an opportunity to present a complete picture of the company to the outside world. Management need to consider whether their external communications describe fairly and comprehensively the company's value (however measured) and their ability to increase that value. Investors need to know the ways in which the entity and its management is organised, and the actions they will take, to ensure that value-creation actually happens.

3.11   The corporate reporting agenda is broadening. In 'Tomorrow's corporate reporting', the May 2011 report of a collaborative research study undertaken by the Chartered Institute of Management Accountants, the UK firm of PwC and the London-based think-tank Tomorrow's Company, Prof Mervyn E. King states:

> *"The world has accepted that people, planet and profit are inextricably intertwined, and nowhere was this better illustrated that in July last year in London, when the International Integrated Reporting Committee was formed. The disparate bodies sitting round the table, such as A4S, GRI, the FASB of America, IASB, IFAC, IOSCO, WWF, Big Four etc., established within one hour an identity of purpose, namely that financial reporting was not sufficient to make an informed assessment about the sustainability of a business in the new economy, It was accepted that the annual report had to be an integrated one, that is one where there is a holistic representation of the financial and non-financial performance of the company. In short how the financial impacted on the non-financial and vice-versa."*

Integrated reporting – an overview

3.12   Effective reporting presents information about a company in a logical and connected way. When this information is presented externally, it answers the questions investors want answered and excludes information that is irrelevant. The type of information and the method of presentation will vary between companies, depending on the nature and organisation of the business. For example, businesses comprising various segments should explain the objectives, strategy, performance and risks for each segment.

3.13 Effective reporting integrates the information presented by linking the various pieces of information together so that the user gains an understanding of the entity as a whole. There are various ways in which this integration can be achieved. An integrated approach connects not just the various elements of the narrative reporting, but also connects the information in the financial statements with the 'front half'. For example, the explanation of performance in the OFR or business review should be linked to the performance statements in the financial statements.

3.14 Integrated reporting should seek to answer the following questions (by segment, where appropriate):

- What is the nature of the entity's business? In which industries does the entity operate? (See further from para 3.91.)

- What are the entity's objectives? What is the entity's business model? How does the entity create value? (See further from para 3.91.)

- What are the entity's strategies for achieving its objectives? (See further from para 3.103.)

- What are the resources and relationships that are essential to the achievement of those objectives? (See further from para 3.143.)

- How does the entity measure the extent to which it has achieved its objectives? (See further from para 3.209.)

- How has the entity performed in the current year compared with the objectives it set in previous periods? (See further from para 3.39 and from para 3.118.)

- Is that performance sustainable? What are the risks that will affect the sustainability of the performance? To what extent is the performance based on recurring transactions or 'one-off' events? (See from para 3.146.)

- What are the entity's future prospects? What will the entity do to ensure it meets its objectives? What constraints exist that may hamper the entity's plans? (See further from para 3.135.)

3.15 The model in the diagram set out below highlights the scope of the information set that we believe companies need to have at their disposal if they are to be on top of the dynamics of a modern business. Communication of clear and focused management thought processes to the outside world is essential for companies to build trust with their stakeholders. It is these communications that are at the heart of OFR reporting.

Integrated reporting model

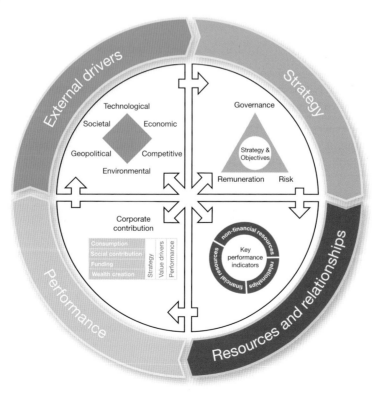

External drivers

- Management's capability to understand and explain external market drivers is fundamental to effective decision-making and reporting.

- The credit crunch and subsequent economic downturn have highlighted the need for companies to understand, monitor, manage and explain emerging risks and opportunities.

- Processes must capture macro, competitive, regulatory and political factors shaping the market place, as well as changing societal expectations.

- Understanding sustainability 'mega trends' and their impact on the business model will shed light on risks and opportunities.

Strategy

- A clear strategy is fundamental to business success and consequently should underpin reporting.

- Effective strategies are developed in the context of market drivers and are aligned with the core competencies of the resources and relationships of the business.

- Strategic priorities should be clearly aligned with remuneration policies and the risks assumed.

- An understanding of the culture/values and governance practices in place is increasingly important to determine how a strategy is embedded into the company and its risk appetite to pursue strategic success.

Resources and relationships

- Greater collaboration between businesses within the value chain means an understanding of the scope of the business model is key.

- Access to natural capital in a resource-constrained world will have profound implications for how business is carried out. The relative importance of resources (financial, human and natural capital) and relationships (customers, employees, suppliers, etc) will flex, depending on changing market dynamics and strategies.

- Information on the relative strength of resources and relationships and how they are being managed, developed and protected, is critical.

- This information should go beyond qualitative statements to a clear set of KPIs.

Performance

- The outputs of corporate activity need to be added to the other three categories in the integrated information set to complete the picture.

- Financial performance is currently the dominant output and it will remain critical, but we expect other outputs to play an increasingly significant role.

- Society's changing expectations will demand a more balanced assessment of corporate contribution. Resource consumption, wealth creation and wealth distribution, for example, can provide real insight into long-term sustainability of a business.

3.16 The suggested model provides a logical structure for thinking about the information needs of a business and the critical links and interdependencies that exist between the various information sets – external, strategic, business and performance. The suggested model is grounded in years of PwC research and work with investors and companies.

3.17 The model's insight and value become apparent when each category is considered in the context of another, rather than in isolation. It succeeds when governance interfaces with remuneration and risk; when strategy is designed to exploit a changing market environment; and when strategic priorities align with key performance indicators (KPIs). It is this joined-up thinking that is so critical and that lies at the heart of the model.

3.18 Today, few companies excel in integrated reporting. But we believe that it is a key determinant of corporate success.

3.19 Increasingly, a number of key dynamics influence strategy and the way businesses operate. These factors also change the information that management needs to make effective decisions and the external reporting needed to meet both society's and shareholders' expectations. These dynamics include:

- *Macro trends*: – Emerging issues such as climate change, resource scarcity and demographics all mean that the business environment is becoming more challenging and more intrusive. This results in a changed 'licence to operate' for business — one driven more by the balance between consumption and contribution, fairness, trust and integrity.

- *Technological advancements:* – The reporting environment is becoming more 'demand-pull' than 'supply-push'. This has clear benefits for companies that can collate a clear, consistent and integrated information set and use this consistently when tailoring their communications for different audiences. In response to these and other dynamics, we expect businesses to be more collaborative in the development of business solutions. In this more integrated world, the ability to build and maintain key business relationships will be critical to long-term success and insightful intelligence will become a 'must-have' capability.

3.20 The four core categories in our model are common to all industries and companies, but their relative importance and the information that sits beneath each category will need to flex depending on how these dynamics impact industries and influence corporate strategies and business/operating models.

3.21 The model is consistent with the OFR's disclosure framework (see paragraph 3.87).

ASB's reporting statement: operating and financial review

Scope and definitions

3.22 The ASB's reporting statement has been written with quoted companies in mind, but applies to any entity that purports to prepare an OFR. [RS (OFR) para 2].

3.23 The term 'quoted company' is defined in the Companies Act as a company whose equity share capital:

- has been included in the official list in accordance with the provisions of Part VI of the Financial Services and Markets Act 2000;

- is officially listed in an EEA State; or

- is admitted to dealing on either the New York Stock Exchange or the exchange known as NASDAQ.

[CA06 Sec 385].

3.24 This means, for instance, that companies traded on AIM and other public companies, that are not 'quoted' as defined in the Act, are not specifically covered by the reporting statement's scope. Nor are large private companies. However, many such companies may voluntarily prepare an OFR. The reporting statement applies to them if they 'purport' to prepare an OFR. [RS (OFR) para 2]. 'Purporting' to prepare an OFR would normally mean that the entity uses the words 'operating and financial review'.

3.25 An OFR is defined as *"a narrative explanation, provided in or accompanying the annual report, of the main trends and factors underlying the development, performance and position of an entity during the financial year covered by the financial statements, and those which are likely to affect the entity's future development, performance and position"*. [RS (OFR) para 3].

Approach adopted by the ASB

3.26 The ASB sets out in its OFR reporting statement a number of principles that directors should follow in developing an OFR and the key elements of a disclosure framework that directors should address.

Objective

3.27 The objective of an OFR is to provide a balanced and comprehensive analysis, consistent with the business' size and complexity, of:

- The development and performance of the entity's business during the year.

- The position of the entity at the end of the year.

- The main trends and factors underlying the development, performance and position of the entity's business during the year.

- The main trends and factors that are likely to affect the entity's future development, performance and position.

The analysis should be prepared so as to assist members to assess the strategies adopted by the entity and the potential for those strategies to succeed. [RS (OFR) para 1].

3.28   To get an appreciation of the overall position of the business, it is important that users are able to navigate the OFR. Key information can get lost in a sea of narrative, especially if it contains lots of jargon. In Table 3.1, ICAP plc uses a ten point overview of its business at the front of its annual report; its business is specialised and these explanations and clear diagrams assist the reader's understanding. Some of the ten points are shown here for illustration purposes.

Table 3.1 Navigation of the annual report

ICAP plc – Annual report – 31 March 2010

ICAP in ten (extract)

Welcome to ICAP in 10

ICAP is the world's premier voice and electronic interdealer broker and provider of post trade risk and information services.

In this section we provide a ten-point overview of ICAP, what we do and how we have performed.

05

ICAP plc Annual Report 2010

ICAP in ten
01 – 15 | Business review
17 – 41 | Governance
43 – 63 | Financial statements
65 – 140 | Information for shareholders
141 – 143

3

What we do

ICAP is the world's premier voice and electronic interdealer broker and provider of post trade risk and information services. The Group is active in the wholesale markets in interest rates, credit, commodities, FX, emerging markets and equity derivatives.

Read more
on page 24

Electronic and voice broking

An interdealer broker draws together willingness to buy and sell in wholesale markets. ICAP uses voice broking or electronic networks to bring these buyers and sellers together, facilitating price discovery and receiving a commission when a transaction is entered into. In many of the markets where ICAP operates, voice brokers help to create liquidity and facilitate the price discovery process. This is particularly important in non-standardised, bespoke markets where the number of parties willing to enter certain transactions may be limited. In more standardised markets with higher and more frequent participation, such as spot FX and government bonds, ICAP operates electronic broking platforms. ICAP's combined solution offers access to markets across all asset classes and levels of liquidity.

Customer A
Customer A is interested in selling certain securities and contracts to dealer 1

Dealer 1
Dealer 1 places a sell order with ICAP

ICAP
- Voice broking
- Electronic broking
- Post trade risk

Dealer 2
The dealer who buys the securities will in turn sell them on to a customer

Customer B
Customer B buys the securities from dealer 2

Post trade risk

ICAP also provides a range of post trade risk services to help its customers reduce operational and systemic risk in their markets. This increases their capacity, reduces their costs and creates new trading opportunities, which in turn benefits ICAP. As regulatory and market demand for such products and services increases, ICAP expects this business to grow.

ICAP in ten

5

Our strategic goals

Read more on page 19

ICAP's strategic goals are clear. We want to be:

→ the leading global intermediary;

→ the leading post trade risk provider; and

→ the main infrastructure provider to the world's wholesale financial markets.

We aim to have at least 35% of overall interdealer market revenues and to generate operating profit evenly distributed between voice broking, electronic broking and post trade risk and information.

There are three components to our strategy:

→ the expansion of our leading voice broking business;

→ the growth of our global electronic broking business both through increasing volumes of existing products and by developing new markets; and

→ the development of our post trade risk and information businesses to provide innovative services that enable our customers to reduce their costs and risks and to increase their efficiency, return on capital and capacity to process trades.

6
How we measure our progress

7
How we have performed

9
How we are rewarded

8
Managing risk

Principles

3.29 The ASB's reporting statement 'Operating and financial review' adopts a principles-based approach.

3.30 Seven principles are set out in bold in the reporting statement. These are:

■ The OFR should set out an analysis of the business through the eyes of the board of directors (see further from para 3.31).

■ The OFR should focus on matters that are relevant to the interests of members (see further from para 3.34).

■ The OFR should have a forward-looking orientation, identifying those trends and factors relevant to the members' assessment of the current and future performance of the business and the progress towards the achievement of long-term business objectives (see further from para 3.39).

■ The OFR should complement as well as supplement the financial statements, in order to enhance the overall corporate disclosure (see further from para 3.52).

■ The OFR should be comprehensive and understandable (see further from para 3.66).

■ The OFR should be balanced and neutral, dealing even-handedly with both good and bad aspects (see further from para 3.80).

■ The OFR should be comparable over time (see further from para 3.82).

Principle 1 — Business analysis through the board's eyes

3.31 This principle states that *"The OFR should set out an analysis of the business through the eyes of the board of directors"*. [RS (OFR) para 4]. It ensures that the matters that are reported to the company's members are those of most interest to the board; for example, the strategies the board will implement to achieve the company's objectives, specific performance measures they regularly review and significant risks.
3.32 The reporting statement notes that the directors should disclose appropriate elements of information used in managing the entity and its subsidiaries. More emphasis is given in a group situation to matters that are significant to the group as a whole. [RS (OFR) para 5]. Significant matters may include matters relating to a specific business segment where this is relevant to understanding the business as a whole; for example, particular emphasis on a geographical segment where developments in a new market are significant to the entity as a whole, because expansion in that area is a major part of the strategy.

3.33 Where a company is organised into different segments, the OFR should reflect that segmentation. Each segment will be operating in a different market and will be subject to, for example, distinct market conditions and risk factors. Table 3.2 is an example where the company has disclosed its objectives and then disclosed how each segment has performed in meeting those objectives. Each segment section includes information on market environment, segment strategy, performance against objectives and financial performance. Table 3.2 shows only performance against one of the company's objectives for one of the segments, for illustration purposes, but the report goes on to discuss performance against each of the company's objectives for each of the segments.

Table 3.2 Business analysis by segment

National Grid plc – Annual Report and Accounts – 31 March 2010

Operating and Financial Review (extract)

Company objectives

The objectives are the building blocks of the strategy and are fundamental to our business – what we are doing now.

- Driving improvements in our safety, customer and operational performance
- Delivering strong, sustainable regulatory and long-term contracts with good returns
- Modernising and extending our transmission and distribution networks
- Expanding our capabilities and identifying new financeable opportunities to grow

- Becoming more efficient through transforming our operating model and increasingly aligning our processes
- Building trust, transparency and an inclusive and engaged workforce
- Developing our talent, leadership skills and capabilities
- Positively shaping the energy and climate change agenda with our external stakeholders in both regions

Transmission

Performance against our objectives

National Grid's progress against the Company objectives is set out on pages 30 to 45. We include below further information specific to Transmission with respect to the objectives that are closely aligned to the lines of business.

Driving improvements in our safety, customer and operational performance

Our objectives are to reduce employee lost time injuries to zero and to support generators and distribution network customers, including our own networks operated by Gas Distribution in the UK and Electricity Distribution & Generation in the US, in delivering energy efficiently and effectively to consumers, in particular in connecting new sources of supply to our transmission networks.

Safety

In the UK, during 2009/10 there were 10 lost time injuries compared with 8 in 2008/09 and 15 in 2007/08. The lost time injury frequency rate was 0.17 in 2009/10 compared with 0.14 in 2008/09 and 0.28 in 2007/08.

Our US electricity transmission lost time injury frequency rate decreased to zero in 2009/10 from 0.20 in 2008/09. There were no lost time injuries in 2009/10 compared with 2 in 2008/09.

Customer service

Our transmission customer service activities principally relate to facilitating new connections and maintaining existing relationships with the customers who are already connected. In the US, much of the interconnection work with our transmission customers is performed in conjunction with the system operators in the areas within which we operate.

Principle 2 — Focus on matters relevant to members

3.34 Principle 2 states that *"The OFR should focus on matters that are relevant to the interests of members"*. [RS (OFR) para 6]. This is consistent with directors' and auditors' reporting on the financial statements.

3.35 The priority of the OFR is to report to members, however, it will also be of interest to other users, such as other investors, potential investors, creditors, customers, suppliers and society more widely. The directors should consider the extent to which they should report on issues relevant to these other users where they are also of importance to members, because those issues influence the business' performance and its value. The OFR should not, however, be used as a replacement for other forms of reporting addressed to a wider stakeholder group. [RS (OFR) paras 7, 27, 28].

3.36 The interests of other OFR users may significantly affect the directors' perspective, because they also affect the members' assessment. Factors that may contribute to the relative importance include relationships with key resources (for example, reliance on skilled employees, dependence on a few large customers or suppliers) and the power of other users to affect the entity's business (for example, actions of regulators and unions).

3.37 These issues should be covered by the OFR where they are significant, because the actions of the other users may affect the business and thus the interests of members.

3.38 Although the OFR audience is the company's shareholders, companies frequently include cross references to other reports (within the annual report or elsewhere) or to information on their web sites where information relevant to a broader group of stakeholders can be found.

Principle 3 – Forward-looking

3.39 Principle 3 states that *"The OFR should have a forward-looking orientation, identifying those trends and factors relevant to the members' assessment of the current and future performance of the business and the progress towards the achievement of long-term business objectives"*. [RS (OFR) para 8].

3.40 Issues that should be addressed are those that have affected development, performance and position during the year and those that are likely to affect the entity's future development, performance and position. [RS (OFR) para 9].

3.41 There are no rules dictating what forward-looking information a company must provide in its OFR. Directors must decide which information to include on the basis of their own business dynamics and those of the industry sectors in which they operate.

3.42 Topics might include:

- An explanation of the resources, principal risks and uncertainties and relationships that may affect the entities long-term value, for example development of new products or services.

- An analysis of the trends and factors the directors believe are likely to impact future prospects, for example introduction of new technology.

- Information on future targets, for example, for key performance indicators.

3.43 The reporting statement acknowledges directors' concerns regarding the disclosure of forward-looking information. It notes that some forward-looking information cannot be objectively verified, even though it has been given in good faith. It states that directors may want to include a statement in the OFR that such information should be treated with caution and explain the uncertainties inherent in such information. [RS (OFR) para 10].

3.44 For any company, there will be certain information that, were it to be disclosed, would undermine its market position. But this should not be used to avoid full and frank disclosure. For example, pharmaceutical companies disclose details of their products in the pipeline without disclosing the underlying patent formulations. With this approach, they provide investors with information they need to understand the sustainability of the company's performance, without compromising the company's interests..

3.45 As noted in paragraph 3.7, directors may wish to include forward-looking information in the directors' report, rather than a separate OFR in order to benefit from the 'safe harbour' provisions contained within the Companies Act 2006, protecting them from civil liability for forward-looking statements made in the directors' report.

3.46 An example of a cautionary statement used by a UK company that conveys a warning similar to that suggested by the reporting statement is given in Table 3.3.

Table 3.3 – Cautionary statement

Smiths Group plc – Annual Report and Accounts – 31 July 2011

Operating and financial review – extract

The purpose of this document is to provide information to the members of the Company. This document contains certain statements that are forward-looking statements. They appear in a number of places throughout this document and include statements regarding our intentions, beliefs or current expectations and those of our officers, directors and employees concerning, amongst other things, our results of operations, financial condition, liquidity, prospects, growth, strategies and the business we operate. By their nature, these statements involve uncertainty since future events and circumstances can cause results and developments to differ materially from those anticipated. The forward-looking statements reflect knowledge and information available at the date of preparation of this document and unless otherwise required by applicable law the Company undertakes no obligation to update or revise these forward-looking statements. Nothing in this document should be construed as a profit forecast. The Company and its directors accept no liability to third parties in respect of this document save as would arise under English law.

3.47 The reporting statement also recommends commentary on the impact on future performance of significant events after the balance sheet date. [RS (OFR) para 11]. An example is provided in Table 3.3A.

Table 3.3A – Significant events after the balance sheet date

Logica plc – Annual Report 31 December 2010

Delivering our strategy (extract)

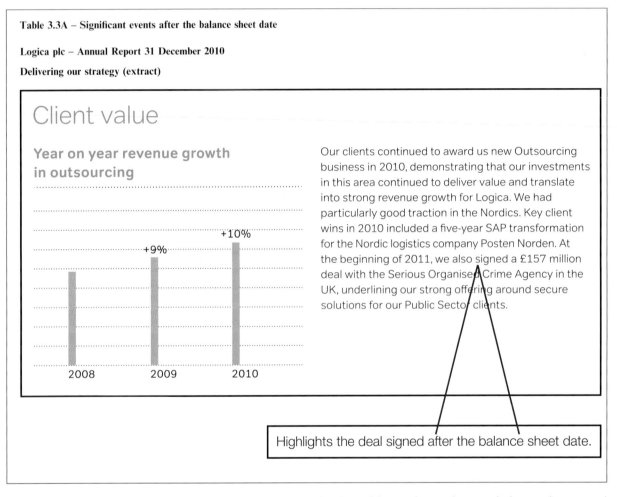

Highlights the deal signed after the balance sheet date.

3.48 OFRs should discuss forward-looking comments, both positive and negative, made in previous years' reviews, whether or not these have been borne out by events. [RS (OFR) para 12]. The discussion would usefully include the reasons why any previous predictions have not been fulfilled.

3.49 Such comments might include previous discussions around likely trends and factors impacting the business – for example whether 'gross domestic product' (GDP) growth rates have matched forecasts. They may also include goals or targets set by the company and an explanation comparing actual performance with those goals.

3.50 As shown in Table 3.4, Telus Corporation sets out in tabular form the current year performance compared with the target performance. Target performance for the next year is also included. There is accompanying narrative (not included in table below) to explain why certain targets were not met.

Table 3.4 — Performance against targets

Telus Corporation – Annual Report — 31 December 2010

Management's Discussion and Analysis (extract)

	2010 performance			2011 targets (IFRS-IASB)	
Scorecards	Actual results and growth	Original targets and estimated growth	Result	2010 unaudited *pro forma* IFRS-based comparative results	2011 targets and estimated growth over 2010 IFRS
Consolidated					
Revenues	**$9.779 billion** 2%	$9.8 to $10.1 billion 2 to 5%	✗	$9.792 billion	**$9.925 to $10.225 billion 1 to 4%**
EBITDA[1]	**$3.643 billion** 4%	$3.5 to $3.7 billion flat to 6%	✓	$3.650 billion	**$3.675 to $3.875 billion 1 to 6%**
EPS – basic[2]	**$3.23** 3%	$2.90 to $3.30 (8) to 5%	✓	$3.27	**$3.50 to $3.90 7 to 19%**
Capital expenditures	**$1.721 billion** (18)%	Approx. $1.7 billion (19)%	✓	$1.721 billion	**Approx. $1.7 billion**
Wireless segment					
Revenue (external)	**$5.014 billion** 6.5%	$4.95 to $5.1 billion 5 to 8%	✓	$5.014 billion	**$5.2 to $5.35 billion 4 to 7%**
EBITDA	**$2.031 billion** 5%	$1.925 to $2.025 billion flat to 5%	✓✓	$2.022 billion	**$2.15 to $2.25 billion 6 to 11%**
Wireline segment					
Revenue (external)	**$4.765 billion** (3)%	$4.85 to $5.0 billion (1) to 2%	✗	$4.778 billion	**$4.725 to $4.875 billion (1) to 2%**
EBITDA	**$1.612 billion** 3.5%	$1.575 to $1.675 billion 1 to 8%	✓	$1.628 billion	**$1.525 to $1.625 billion (6) to 0%**

(1) A non-GAAP measure. *See Section 11.1 Earnings before interest, taxes, depreciation and amortization (EBITDA)* for the definition.
(2) Actual EPS for 2010 includes approximately nine cents for favourable income tax-related adjustments and a 12-cent charge for early partial redemption of long-term debt that were not contemplated in the original target for EPS.

✓✓ Exceeded target
✓ Met target
✗ Missed target

3.51 As set out in Table 3.4A, Telus Corporation's MD&A also describes the assumptions made in creating the 2010 targets and compares each of these assumptions with what actually happened. The table below is provided for illustration purposes only and shows only the first few assumptions.

Operating and financial review

Table 3.4A — Assumptions compared with actual experience

Telus Corporation – Annual Report — 31 December 2010

Management's Discussion and Analysis (extract)

The following key assumptions were made at the time the 2010 targets were announced in December 2009.

Assumptions for 2010 original targets	Result or expectation for 2010
Ongoing wireline and wireless competition in both business and consumer markets	Confirmed by frequent promotional offers by the primary cable-TV competitor in Western Canada (Shaw Communications), a new brand launch (Chatr) by an incumbent wireless competitor (Rogers Communications), and a brand re-launch (Solo) by an incumbent wireless competitor (Bell Canada).
Canadian wireless industry market penetration gain of approximately four percentage points for the year (approximately 3.6 percentage points in 2009)	The Company's estimate is a gain of approximately 4.4 percentage points in industry market penetration for 2010, with an increasing proportion from postpaid subscribers associated with growing data usage and smartphone adoption.
Increased wireless subscriber loading in smartphones	Smartphones represented 46% of postpaid gross additions in the fourth quarter of 2010, compared to 25% in the fourth quarter of 2009. Smartphones represent 33% of the postpaid subscriber base at the end of 2010 compared to 20% at the end of 2009.
Reduced downward pressure on wireless ARPU	Confirmed by the 1.9% year-over-year increase in wireless ARPU in the fourth quarter of 2010 and 1.4% decrease for the full year of 2010, as compared to decreases of 7.7% and 6.8%, respectively, in the fourth quarter and full year of 2009.
New competitive wireless entry in early 2010 following one competitive launch in December 2009	After its initial launch in Calgary and Toronto in December 2009, Globalive (Wind brand) launched in Edmonton and Ottawa in the first quarter of 2010, and Vancouver in the second quarter, and announced that it expects to launch in Victoria in 2011.

Other new entrants began launching services in the second quarter of 2010. Mobilicity launched services in the Toronto area in the second quarter, in Edmonton, Vancouver and Ottawa in the fourth quarter, and in Calgary in early 2011. Public Mobile turned up services in the Toronto and Montreal areas. Quebecor (Videotron brand) launched its services in September 2010, initially in Montreal and Quebec City. Videotron previously offered wireless services in Quebec as a mobile virtual network operator. Shaw Communications stated it expects to begin launching wireless services in early 2012.

In addition, during the third quarter of 2010, one incumbent national competitor launched a new brand and the other incumbent national competitor re-launched one of its brands. |
| In wireline, stable residential network access line losses and continued competitive pressure in small and medium business market from cable-TV and voice over IP (VoIP) companies | Residential access line losses moderated in the second half of 2010 when compared to the same period in 2009, due to improved bundle and retention offers. Residential access lines decreased by 8.0% in 2010, resulting from promotional activity by the primary Western cable-TV competitor Shaw for voice and Internet services, particularly in the first half of 2010. Business line losses were 2.9% in 2010 due to increased competition in the small and medium business market and conversion of voice lines to more efficient IP services. See *Section 5.4*. |
| Continued wireline broadband expansion | See *Section 2: Core business and strategy*. |
| Significant increase in cost of acquisition and retention expenses for smartphones and TELUS TV loading | Wireless cost of acquisition (COA) per gross subscriber addition was $350 in 2010, an increase of 3.9% from 2009. Retention spending as a percentage of growing network revenue was 11.6% in 2010, up from 10.9% in 2009.

TELUS TV loading was 144,000 in 2010, an increase of 57% from 2009. TELUS TV programming and other costs have increased, as well, due to the 85% increase in total TV subscribers compared to 2009. |
EBITDA savings of approximately $135 million from efficiency initiatives	Savings of approximately $134 million were realized in 2010.
Approximately $75 million of restructuring expenses ($190 million in 2009)	Restructuring charges were $74 million.
A blended statutory tax rate of approximately 28.5 to 29.5% (30.3% in 2009). The expected decrease is based on enacted changes in federal and provincial income tax rates	The blended statutory income tax rate was 29% and the effective income tax rate was 24%.

Cash income taxes peaking at approximately $385 to $425 million (net $266 million in 2009) due to the timing of instalment payments	Cash income tax payments net of refunds received were $311 million in 2010, comprised of instalments for 2010 and final payments for the 2009 tax year made in the first quarter, net of $41 million of refunds for the settlement of prior years' matters. The expectation for the full year was revised to a range of $300 to $350 million on November 5, 2010, and was previously revised to a range of $330 to $370 million on August 6, 2010.
A pension accounting discount rate was estimated at 5.75% and subsequently set at 5.85% (140 basis points lower than 2009). The expected long-term return of 7.25% is unchanged from 2009 and consistent with the Company's long-run returns and its future expectations. ■ Defined benefit pension plans net expenses were estimated to be $28 million in 2010 (compared to $18 million in 2009), based on projected pension fund returns ■ Defined benefit pension plans contributions were estimated to be approximately $143 million in 2010, down from $179 million in 2009, largely due to the stock market recovery in 2009 and proposed federal pension reforms.	Defined benefit pension plan expenses were $28 million in 2010 and are set at the beginning of the year. The Company's contributions to defined benefit pension plans in 2010 were $137 million. A $200 million voluntary contribution was announced in mid-December 2010 and made in January 2011. See *Assumptions for 2011 targets in Section 1.5*.

Principle 4 — Complement and supplement the financial statements

3.52   Principle 4 states that *"The OFR should complement as well as supplement the financial statements, in order to enhance the overall corporate disclosure"*. [RS (OFR) para 13].

Supplementing the financial statements

3.53   Supplementing the financial statements means:

■   providing additional explanations of amounts recorded in the financial statements; and

■   explaining the conditions and events that shaped the information contained in the financial statements.

[RS (OFR) para 15].

3.54   The information recorded in the financial statements is increasingly complex. For example, pension liabilities are significant for many companies – an understanding of these is essential for investors. The OFR (and the financial statements themselves) can be used to provide additional information to aid that understanding. Events and conditions also shape amounts recorded in the financial statements.

3.55   Taking the example of pensions, it is difficult to truly understand the risks inherent in a scheme and the chances of increased cash contributions or other action being needed in the future.

3.56   Table 3.5 shows an example of additional disclosure given in respect of defined benefit pension schemes. In addition to the narrative commentary, Bombardier Inc also provides a diagrammatic representation of the movement in the actuarial deficit over a number of years. The company discloses the causes of the movement in the deficit in the year, separately identifying, for example, the impact of the changes in assumptions. Changes in assumptions are of particular interest to users because they are an area of judgement.

Table 3.5 Diagrammatic presentation of pension deficit

Bombardier Inc – Annual Report – 31 January 2010

Management's Discussion and Analysis (extract)

PENSION

Pension deficit remains at a manageable level

We sponsor several domestic and foreign funded and unfunded defined benefit pension plans. Funded plans are plans for which segregated plan assets are invested in trusts. Unfunded plans are plans for which there are no segregated plan assets, as the establishment of segregated plan assets is generally not permitted or not in line with local practice because of adverse tax consequences. There will therefore always be a deficit for unfunded plans. We also manage several defined contribution plans which specify how contributions are determined rather than the amount of benefits an employee is to receive at retirement. There is no deficit or surplus for defined contribution plans.

While we work closely with the trustees of our various pension plans to implement risk-management measures, including aligning plan assets with the terms of the plan obligations, our future cash contributions to the funded pension plans will nonetheless be dependent on changes in discount rates, actual returns on plan assets and other factors such as plan amendments.

The defined benefit pension contributions of $318 million for calendar year 2009 are lower than the $400-million anticipated last year. The decrease is mainly due to positive variations in foreign exchange rates and lower funding requirements in some countries, arising from the finalization of our funding calculations or from funding reliefs provided by some governments to alleviate the impact of the financial crisis.

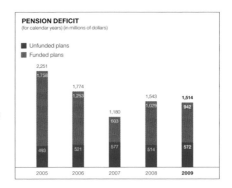

PENSION DEFICIT
(for calendar years) (in millions of dollars)

■ Unfunded plans
■ Funded plans

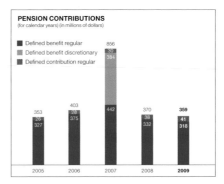

PENSION CONTRIBUTIONS
(for calendar years) (in millions of dollars)

■ Defined benefit regular
■ Defined benefit discretionary
■ Defined contribution regular

PENSION CONTRIBUTIONS	Calendar year 2009 Actual	Calendar year 2010 Estimate
Defined benefit pension plans	$318	$336
Defined contribution pension plans	41	45
	$359	$381

Our pension deficit totalled $1.5 billion as at December 31, 2009, essentially unchanged compared to December 31, 2008.

VARIATION IN PENSION DEFICIT	
Balance as at December 31, 2008[1]	$ 1,543
Actual return on plan assets[2]	(753)
Interest cost[3]	363
Employer contributions	(318)
Changes in discount rate assumptions[4]	238
Effect of changes in foreign exchange rates	177
Current service cost[5]	172
Change in inflation assumptions	67
Change in compensation increase assumptions	(33)
Plan amendments and other	58
Balance as at December 31, 2009[1]	**$1,514**

1 Of which $572 million is related to unfunded plans as at December 31, 2009 ($514 million as at December 31, 2008).
2 The performance of stock markets is a key driver in determining the pension fund's asset performance, since our targeted allocation for pension plan assets invested in publicly traded equity securities is 57%. Most of the remaining plan assets are invested in publicly traded long-term fixed-income securities.
3 Represents the expected increase in pension obligation due to the passage of time.
4 The discount rate is used to determine the present value of the estimated future benefit payments at the measurement date. A higher discount rate decreases the benefit obligation and pension deficit. The discount rate must represent the market rate for high-quality corporate fixed-income investments available for the period to maturity of the benefits, and thus management has little discretion in its selection.
5 Current service cost represents the present value of retirement benefits earned by participants during the current year.

The pension cost of defined benefit pension plans is estimated at $302 million for fiscal year 2011, compared to an actual pension cost of $234 million for fiscal year 2010. The expected increase is mainly due to:

- the negative impact in fiscal year 2011 of the three-year smoothing of net losses realized on equity investments over the proceeding three-year period; and
- the negative variation in discount rates, reflecting the recent decrease in high-quality corporate fixed-income rates in Canada.

SENSITIVITY ANALYSIS		Impact of a 0.25% increase on:
Increase (decrease)	Pension cost for fiscal year 2011	Pension deficit as at December 31, 2009
Discount rate	$(32)	$ (283)
Expected return on plan assets	$(13)	n/a
Rate of compensation increase	$17	$ 85

[The next paragraph is 3.57].

Complementing the financial statements

3.57 Complementing the financial statements means providing useful financial and non-financial information about the business and its performance that is not reported in the financial statements, but which is judged by the directors to be relevant to the members in evaluating past results and assessing future prospects. [RS (OFR) para 14].

3.58 Our ongoing research programme with investors over the past decade has clearly shown that, as investors model the future, they typically have insufficient contextual and non-financial information to underpin their cash flow projections. Traditional reporting focuses on past financial performance, which is not the only guide to future returns. The OFR's requirement to complement the financial statements addresses that need.

3.59 Contextual information can be defined broadly and will be unique to each company and its industry sector. It may include information about the markets in which the company operates and expectation for growth. How the company plans to achieve its objectives and the resource and relationships it will need to manage to do so, are key pieces of information to allow investors to evaluate the company. The disclosure framework included in the reporting statement (discussed from para 3.85) provides guidance on the type of information to be reported, much of it contextual in nature. In Table 3.5.1 below, Severn Trent plc describes diagrammatically the policy and regulatory framework within which the company operates.

Table 3.5.1 — Policy and regulatory context

Severn Trent Plc – Annual Report and Accounts 31 March 2010

Overview (extract)

Severn Trent Water – Our Industry

The achievements of the water industry in the 20 years since privatisation are well documented – service to customers has improved, new drinking water standards have been met, tighter environmental standards have been achieved and new investment attracted.

These successes have been driven by an effective regulatory framework which has incentivised companies to become more efficient, so keeping bills lower than they would

otherwise have been. The framework has also provided investor confidence, allowing companies to attract financing for an investment programme of around £85 billion over the last 20 years to deliver the improvements.

However, the successes of the last 20 years have not been without consequences. Water company debt has increased significantly, customers face higher bills and carbon emissions have increased.

Organisations that have an influence on how Severn Trent Water is run

The policy and regulatory context for the water sector is complex, with a number of different stakeholders having different remits in relation to regulating the industry and developing the policy framework. This is shown below.

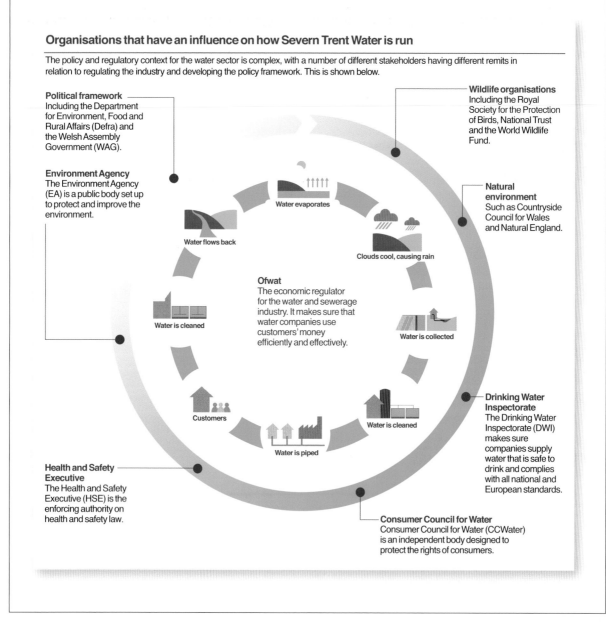

Political framework
Including the Department for Environment, Food and Rural Affairs (Defra) and the Welsh Assembly Government (WAG).

Environment Agency
The Environment Agency (EA) is a public body set up to protect and improve the environment.

Health and Safety Executive
The Health and Safety Executive (HSE) is the enforcing authority on health and safety law.

Wildlife organisations
Including the Royal Society for the Protection of Birds, National Trust and the World Wildlife Fund.

Natural environment
Such as Countryside Council for Wales and Natural England.

Drinking Water Inspectorate
The Drinking Water Inspectorate (DWI) makes sure companies supply water that is safe to drink and complies with all national and European standards.

Consumer Council for Water
Consumer Council for Water (CCWater) is an independent body designed to protect the rights of consumers.

Ofwat
The economic regulator for the water and sewerage industry. It makes sure that water companies use customers' money efficiently and effectively.

Water evaporates

Clouds cool, causing rain

Water is collected

Water is cleaned

Water is piped

Customers

Water is cleaned

Water flows back

3.60 Similarly, an entity might use the OFR to disclose non-financial information that is relevant to business performance. Examples might include health and safety statistics, such as accident rates, environmental information such as total carbon dioxide emissions and community and social issues. Such factors may have major impacts on the business and, where they are significant, disclosure may be necessary for an assessment of the business' development, performance and position. The impacts are potentially limitless and can include regulatory penalties for underperformance, litigation, employee loyalty, reputation and customer confidence.

Providing non-GAAP financial information

3.61 Frequently, companies report non-GAAP information, particularly non-GAAP measures of performance. Many argue that the presentation of such measures permits companies to present their 'underlying performance', stripping out 'one off' events. Companies often present 'EBITDA' (earnings before interest, taxes, depreciation and amortisation'). The counter argument to the presentation of such items is that they tend to undermine the GAAP numbers and that entities may be biased in the adjustments they make to GAAP numbers (for example, only adjusting to exclude bad news). However, we believe there is a difference between proper analysis and distortion of financial information; non-GAAP measures can be useful, subject to compliance with some basic principles (see below). Investment analysts use non-GAAP measures widely; it makes sense to provide them with the information they want, provided the measures are properly explained.

3.62 Where amounts from the financial statements have been adjusted for inclusion in the OFR, that fact should be highlighted and a reconciliation provided. [RS (OFR) para 15].

3.63 This is an important recommendation and mirrors guidance issued by the European Securities and Markets Authority (ESMA) (formerly Committee of European Securities Regulators (CESR)) in November 2005, 'Recommendations on alternative performance measures'. This contained a number of recommendations relating to alternative measures produced by companies that have adopted IFRS. These recommendations extend to the 'highlights' sections, press releases and commentary sections related to both preliminary and interim announcements, interim management statements and reports and elsewhere in annual reports. See chapter 4 of the Manual of Accounting – IFRS for the UK and chapter 31 of the Manual of Accounting – UK GAAP for further information.

3.64 An example of a company providing alternative performance measures in accordance with the ESMA guidelines is shown in Table 3.6. As well as discussing such measures in its 'Business review', this company includes non-GAAP information on the face of its primary financial statements, a practice that is acceptable under IFRS and UK company law, where the ESMA guidance has been followed.

Table 3.6 Alternative performance measures

Diploma plc – Annual report and accounts – 30 September 2010

Consolidated Income Statement
For the year ended 30 September 2010

Continuing businesses	Note	2010 £m	2009 £m
Revenue	3,4	183.5	160.0
Cost of sales		(115.5)	(101.7)
Gross profit		68.0	58.3
Distribution costs		(4.4)	(4.1)
Administration costs		(35.0)	(31.7)
Operating profit	3	28.6	22.5
Financial expense, net	6	(1.9)	(2.0)
Profit before tax		26.7	20.6
Tax expense	7	(8.8)	(7.1)
Profit for the year from continuing businesses		17.9	13.4
Profit from discontinued businesses	22	5.1	0.9
Profit for the year		23.0	14.3
Attributable to			
Shareholders of the Company		21.5	13.0
Minority interests	20	1.5	1.3
		23.0	14.3
Earnings per share	9		
Basic and diluted earnings - continuing		14.8p	10.9p
Basic and diluted earnings - discontinued		4.5p	0.8p
Basic and diluted earnings - continuing and discontinued		19.1p	11.6p

Alternative Performance Measures (note 2)

	Note	2010 £m	2009 £m
Operating profit		28.6	22.5
Add: Acquisition related charges	11	3.5	3.1
Adjusted operating profit	3,4	32.1	25.6
Add/(deduct): Net interest income/(expense)	6	0.1	(0.1)
Adjusted profit before tax		32.2	25.5
Adjusted earnings per share	9	18.9p	14.8p

Cross referenced to definitions in the notes to the consolidated financial statements (see below).

Consolidated Cash Flow Statement
For the year ended 30 September 2010

Continuing businesses	Note	2010 £m	2009 £m
Cash flow from operating activities			
Cash flow from operations	23	34.3	34.2
Interest income received, net		0.1	–
Tax paid		(9.3)	(9.0)
Net cash from operating activities		25.1	25.2
Cash flow from investing activities			
Acquisition of subsidiaries (net of cash acquired)	21	(8.1)	(11.1)
Acquisition of minority interests	21	(2.5)	–
Disposal of subsidiaries (net of cash disposed)	22	6.4	–
Deferred consideration paid	19	(0.4)	(1.1)
Proceeds from the sale of property, plant and equipment		–	0.1
Purchase of property, plant and equipment	12	(1.2)	(1.5)
Purchase of other intangible assets	11	(0.1)	(0.3)
Net cash used in investing activities		(5.9)	(13.9)
Cash flow from financing activities			
Dividends paid to shareholders	8	(9.1)	(8.4)
Dividends paid to minority interests	20	(1.1)	(0.7)
Purchase of own shares		(0.4)	–
Net cash used in financing activities		(10.6)	(9.1)
Net cash (used in)/from discontinued businesses	22	(0.5)	1.7
Net increase in cash and cash equivalents		8.1	3.9
Cash and cash equivalents at beginning of year		21.3	15.7
Effect of exchange rates on cash and cash equivalents		0.7	1.7
Cash and cash equivalents at end of year	17	30.1	21.3

Alternative Performance Measures (note 2)

	2010 £m	2009 £m
Net increase in cash and cash equivalents	8.1	3.9
Add: Dividends paid to shareholders	9.1	8.4
Dividends paid to minority interests	1.1	0.7
Acquisition of subsidiaries/minority interests	10.6	11.1
Deferred consideration paid	0.4	1.1
Free cash flow – continuing and discontinued businesses	29.3	25.2
Add/(deduct): Free cash flow – discontinued businesses	0.5	(1.7)
Free cash flow – continuing businesses	29.8	23.5

Free cash flow is identified as a key performance indicator (see below).

Key Performance Indicators (extract)

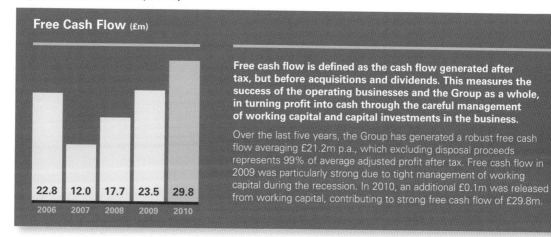

Free Cash Flow (£m)

| 22.8 | 12.0 | 17.7 | 23.5 | 29.8 |
| 2006 | 2007 | 2008 | 2009 | 2010 |

Free cash flow is defined as the cash flow generated after tax, but before acquisitions and dividends. This measures the success of the operating businesses and the Group as a whole, in turning profit into cash through the careful management of working capital and capital investments in the business.

Over the last five years, the Group has generated a robust free cash flow averaging £21.2m p.a., which excluding disposal proceeds represents 99% of average adjusted profit after tax. Free cash flow in 2009 was particularly strong due to tight management of working capital during the recession. In 2010, an additional £0.1m was released from working capital, contributing to strong free cash flow of £29.8m.

Notes to the consolidated financial statements (extract)

2. Alternative Performance Measures

The Group uses a number of alternative (non-Generally Accepted Accounting Practice ("non-GAAP")) financial measures which are not defined within IFRS. The Directors use these measures in order to assess the underlying operational performance of the Group and as such, these measures are important and should be considered alongside the IFRS measures. The following non-GAAP measures are referred to in this Annual Report.

2.1 Adjusted operating profit

At the foot of the consolidated income statement, "adjusted operating profit" is defined as operating profit before amortisation and impairment of acquisition intangible assets, acquisition costs and adjustments to deferred consideration (collectively, "acquisition related charges"). The Directors believe that adjusted operating profit is an important measure of the underlying operational performance of the Group.

2.2 Adjusted profit before tax

At the foot of the consolidated income statement, "adjusted profit before tax" is separately disclosed, being defined as profit before tax and before the costs of restructuring or rationalisation of operations, the profit or loss relating to the sale of property, fair value remeasurements under IAS 32 and IAS 39 in respect of future purchases of minority interests, and acquisition related charges. The Directors believe that adjusted profit before tax is an important measure of the underlying performance of the Group.

2.3 Adjusted earnings per share

"Adjusted earnings per share" is calculated as the total of adjusted profit, less income tax costs, but excluding the tax impact on the items included in the calculation of adjusted profit and the tax effects of goodwill in overseas jurisdictions, less profit attributable to minority interests, divided by the weighted average number of ordinary shares in issue during the year. The Directors believe that adjusted earnings per share provides an important measure of the underlying earning capacity of the Group.

2.4 Free cash flow

At the foot of the consolidated cash flow statement, "free cash flow" is reported, being defined as net cash flow from operating activities, after net capital expenditure on fixed assets and including proceeds received from business disposals, but before expenditure on business combinations and dividends paid to both minority shareholders and the Company's shareholders. The Directors believe that free cash flow gives an important measure of the cash flow of the Group, available for future investment.

3.65 Some companies present an analysis that uses widely accepted measures, such as profitability measured in terms of constant exchange rates, or accepted industry-specific measures, such as replacement cost profit (as used in the oil and gas industry) or the achieved profits method (used in the insurance industry). Despite being widely understood, any such measures should be defined in the annual report. The use of consistent measures across an industry will aid comparison by users. In the example below, the company shows its constant currency performance alongside its reported performance.

Table 3.7 – Constant currency

Glanbia plc– Annual Report – 1 January 2011

Directors' Report: Divisional Performance (extract)

US Cheese & Global Nutritionals

	Constant Currency			Reported	
	2010	**2009**	**Change**	**2010**	**Change**
Revenue	€971.5m	€792.4m	+ 22.6%	€1,021.9m	+ 29.0%
Operating profit	€93.9m	€90.0m	+ 4.3%	€93.8m	+ 4.2%
Operating margin	9.7%	11.4%	- 170bps	9.2%	- 220bps
EBITA	€104.6m	€100.3m	+ 4.3%	€104.5m	+ 4.2%
EBITA margin	10.8%	12.7%	- 190bps	10.2%	- 250bps
EBITDA	€116.8m	€110.0m	+ 6.2%	€116.7m	+ 6.1%

Results are stated pre exceptional items

Principle 5 — Comprehensive and understandable

3.66 This principle states that *"The OFR should be comprehensive and understandable"*. [RS (OFR) para 16]. The reporting statement adds to this principle by stating that directors should consider whether the omission of information might reasonably be expected to influence significantly the assessment by members. [RS (OFR) para 17]. This is similar wording to that used in defining materiality in IAS 1, 'Presentation of financial statements', and the Statement of Principles in the UK (see further chapter 4 of the Manual of Accounting – IFRS for the UK and chapter 2 of the Manual of Accounting – UK GAAP) and is, perhaps another way of saying that all material information should be included.

3.67 The reporting statement notes that the recommendation for the OFR to be comprehensive does not mean that it should cover all possible matters. The objective is quality not quantity. It is not possible for a reporting statement to list all of the elements that might need to be included, as these will vary depending on the nature and circumstances of the particular business and how it is run. [RS (OFR) para 18].

3.68 A simple example of what types of information might be relevant to one entity's OFR, but not to another's might be:

	Company A (Operates internationally)	Company B (Operates solely in the UK, sourcing its product and making sales in the UK)
Exchange rates	Relevant	Less relevant
Political disturbances	Relevant	Less relevant
Cross border tax rules	Relevant	Less relevant
Hyperinflation	Possibly relevant	Less relevant
Global market trends	Relevant	Less relevant

3.69 The question of whether information is comprehensive may be particularly difficult to assess when dealing with the future and forward-looking statements. This is a natural consequence of the increased uncertainty inherent in predicting the future.

3.70 The reporting statement notes that, where relevant, directors should explain the source of information and the degree to which the information is objectively supportable, so that members can assess the reliability of the information for themselves. [RS (OFR) para 19]. Table 3.8 shows an example of disclosure of sources and provides both trend data and a forward-looking orientation to the information.

3.71 It is likely that directors, as well as making the 'cautionary statement' referred to above in paragraph 3.45, may, in particular, wish to explain fully the basis for predictive (forward-looking) statements and the degree of objective evidence supporting the statements. This is not to say that objective evidence does not exist for predictive statements or that uncertainty should, in itself, restrict directors' predictive statements, but rather that appropriate caveats may need to be given.

3.72 One type of forward-looking statement for which objective evidence should exist, is the expected growth rate for a particular country in which the entity may wish to expand its business. Such growth rates or rates of consumer spending may be based on estimates made by governments or by international organisations such as the World Bank. Another example is forecast growth rates for an industry sector where a recognised and reputable organisation provides industry specific data. An example of the latter is provided in Table 3.8, explaining the source and its objectivity.

Table 3.8 — Objective evidence for forecasts

Amec plc – Annual report — 31 December 2010

Business and financial review (extract)

Oil and gas

Markets

The International Energy Agency (IEA) latest World Energy Outlook forecasts primary oil demand in their 'New Policies Scenario' to increase from 84.0mb/d in 2009 to 89.2mb/d in 2015 and 99.0mb/d by 2035. A decline in OECD countries is expected, offset by growth elsewhere, particularly in China and India. Satisfying this demand will require an average annual development of nine billion barrels of new discoveries from 2015 onwards. The IEA forecasts an upstream oil and gas capital spending requirement between 2010 and 2035 of about $440 billion per annum.

In the near term, the Deutsche Bank/Wood Mackenzie annual survey of global capex forecasts growth of six per cent across 2010 to 2012 and expects US$440 billion of Engineering and Construction capex in 2011 (of which NOCs represent 40 per cent). By 2013, they expect that levels of spend should surpass the 2008 peak.

There is a continued trend of resources being more difficult to extract, and AMEC's experience of Arctic, deepwater and complex projects gives the group a good position. At the same time, environmental pressures have increased and this is another area where AMEC can demonstrate a strong track record in helping its customers.

The mature oil and gas sector has ageing infrastructure and increasingly depleting reserves which AMEC is well positioned to service, both in terms of asset support services, performance and efficiency improvements, and decommissioning and cessation of production.

Opex activity is set to grow in part because globally the number of complex facilities continues to increase. These facilities are at different, and ever increasing, stages of maturity and therefore require a growing amount of maintenance input. More importantly, AMEC is increasingly providing more sophisticated solutions which adapt existing facilities to handle new reservoirs, for example by using tie-backs.

With leading market positions in mature markets and frontier regions, early life cycle visibility, a balanced portfolio of services and a carefully selected yet diversified customer base, AMEC is well positioned to grow.

AMEC estimates that its accessible markets will grow by between 8 and 10 per cent per annum in the period to 2015.

3.73 The directors should consider the key issues to be included in the OFR. The inclusion of too much information may obscure judgements and will not promote understanding. Where additional information is included elsewhere in the annual report or other reports or on the company's web site, cross-referencing to those sources will assist members. [RS (OFR) para 20].

3.74 However, where information, such as environmental or employee information, is included in a separate corporate social responsibility (CSR) report, the relevant information should still be included in the OFR to the extent necessary to enable members to assess the entity's development, performance and position. Any cross-referencing should be to additional information in the CSR or other report that is not essential for the purpose of the OFR.

3.75 The reporting statement recommends that the OFR should be written in a clear and readily understandable style. [RS (OFR) para 21].

3.76 Management should consider what it needs to communicate, and what investors want to know, to prevent key messages from getting lost. For example, some form of narrative sequence and clear linkage from the company's markets to their strategy to their key performance indicators and future goals. An integrated structure, where important issues are linked throughout the report, can aid the reader's retention of the information provided.

Table 3.9 Clear linkage

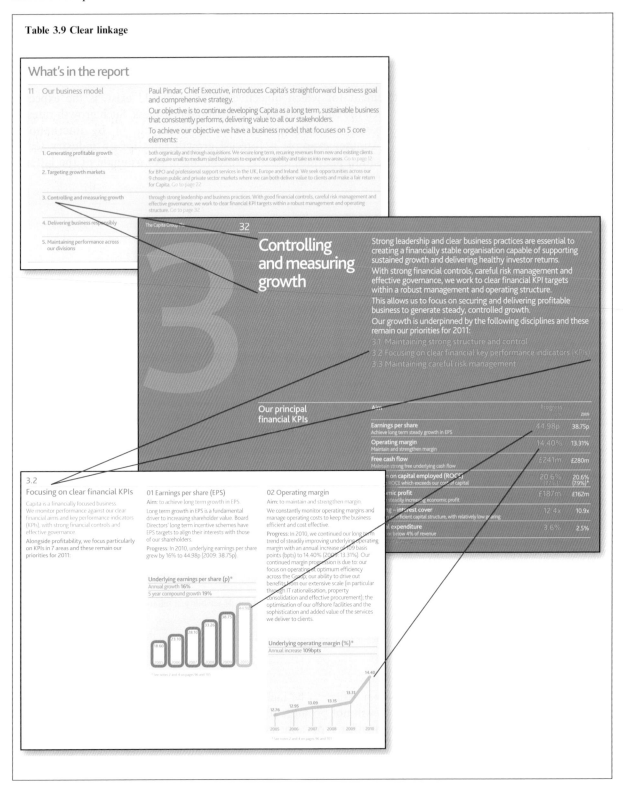

3.77 Making the messages within the OFR understandable is imperative. Directors can help readers to navigate their reporting by explaining the critical issues for the company, highlighting them in quotes, titles, bullet points, etc. Graphical summaries can be used to present complex information visually. Use of plain English with clear explanations of technical terms and avoidance of jargon will help companies meet the aim of the principle of clarity and understandability.

3.78 It will not be possible (or even desirable, given the volume of explanation that would be required) to explain every technical aspect of an entity's business. Besides, the reader of the OFR is most likely to be a person with either some knowledge of the industry or of the entity itself. So, the reader is likely to have more knowledge than the layman and entities should take that into account when preparing the OFR. The OFR should not try to be 'all things to all men'. Despite this, simplification of the description of the entity's business may be necessary in some cases. For example, while the use of technical terms and scientific names may be unavoidable in an explanation of a drug development pipeline, application of this principle might mean additional information being given to describe as simply as possible what the drug does in relation to diseases or other conditions and how development will benefit both the company and the sufferers. Many pharmaceutical companies also include a brief description of the various stages (phases) of the approval process for new drugs. Table 3.9.1 shows an extract of the 'Pipeline overview' for diabetes drugs being developed by Novo Nordisk A/S.

Table 3.9.1 — Pharmaceutical pipeline

NovoNordisk A/S – Annual Report and Accounts – 31 December 2010

Pipeline overview (extract)

Pipeline overview

In 2010, significant progress was made throughout Novo Nordisk's clinical development pipeline. This overview illustrates key development activities, including entries into the pipeline and progression of development compounds.

See more at novonordisk.com/investors/rd_pipeline/rd_pipeline.asp and clinicaltrials.gov.

Phase 1
Studies in a small group of healthy volunteers, and sometimes patients, usually between 10 and 100, to investigate how the body handles new medication and establish maximum tolerated dose.

Phase 2
Testing a drug at various dose levels in a larger group of patients to learn about its effect on the condition and its side effects.

Therapy area	Indication	Compound	Description
Diabetes care			
	Type 1 and 2 diabetes	Degludec	Ultra-long-acting basal insulin. Enrolment in the phase 3a programme completed in June 2010. First phase 3a study results announced in October 2010.
	Type 1 and 2 diabetes	DegludecPlus	Ultra-long-acting basal insulin with a bolus boost. Enrolment in the phase 3a programme completed in June 2010. First phase 3a study results announced in August 2010.
	Type 2 diabetes	Semaglutide	Once-weekly GLP-1 analogue. Phase 3 initiation was postponed in June 2010 pending a long-acting portfolio development strategy decision.
Diabetes	Type 2 diabetes	NN9068	GLP-1 and basal insulin combination. Phase 1 studies are ongoing.
	Type 1 and 2 diabetes	NN1218	Ultra-fast-acting insulin analogue. First phase 1 studies initiated during the second quarter of 2010.
	Type 1 and 2 diabetes	NN1952	Fast-acting oral insulin analogue. First phase 1 study completed during the fourth quarter of 2010.
	Type 2 diabetes	NN9924	Long-acting oral GLP-1 analogue. First phase 1 study initiated in the first quarter of 2010.
Obesity	Obesity	Liraglutide	Once-daily GLP-1 analogue. First phase 3a study completed during the third quarter of 2010. The remaining phase 3a studies are expected to be initiated mid-2011.

Phase 2a
Pilot clinical trials to evaluate efficacy (and safety) in selected populations of patients.

Phase 2b
Well controlled trials to evaluate efficacy (and safety) in patients with the disease. Sometimes referred to as pivotal trials.

Phase 3
Studies in large groups of patients worldwide comparing the new medication with a commonly used drug or placebo for both safety and efficacy in order to establish its risk–benefit relationship.

Phase 3a
Trials conducted after efficacy of the medicine is demonstrated, but prior to regulatory submission.

Phase 3b
Clinical trials conducted after regulatory submission, but prior to the medicine's approval and launch.

Filed/regulatory approval
A New Drug Application is submitted for review by various government regulatory agencies.

Intended clinical benefit	Phase 1	Phase 2	Phase 3	Filed/regulatory approval
Long-acting basal insulin with duration of action of 24 hours and an improved safety profile.				
A soluble fixed combination of fast-acting and long-acting insulin combining 24-hour basal insulin coverage with a distinct meal peak.				
Provide the pharmacological actions of a GLP-1 analogue with fewer injections.				
Combination of a basal insulin and a GLP-1 analogue intended to combine the benefits of the two hormones in a single preparation.				
Fast-acting insulin for improvement of glycaemic control during a meal.				
Insulin delivered as a tablet.				
A GLP-1 analogue delivered as a tablet.				
Sustainable weight loss for people with obesity, including those at risk of developing diabetes.				

3.79 Helpful navigation ensures that readers can find the information they need. A clear table of contents and an index, use of colour-coded sections or tabs and clarity in headings and sub-headings will all help achieve this. Companies can also repeat information or provide cross-referencing to other areas of the report to provide context and use box-outs to highlight key issues or figures.

Principle 6 — Balanced and neutral

3.80 Principle 6 states that *"The OFR should be balanced and neutral, dealing even-handedly with both good and bad aspects"*. [RS (OFR) para 22]. It means that directors should maintain a balance between good and bad news, give details of unfavourable events and include information about setbacks or misjudgements. [RS (OFR) para 23]. The FRRP has drawn attention to the legal requirement that the business review is 'balanced and comprehensive.' See chapter 2 for more details.

3.81 Highlighting only the positives when, for example, the company's profitability has declined, is unrealistic and, worse still, may give the impression that management has not focused on a strategic plan for improving performance. Investors want to know which parts of the business have experienced difficulties and what management's plans are for improving the position. The OFR should discuss current year performance against target, highlighting good and bad performance. The principle of providing balanced and neutral analysis should also be observed when providing forward-looking information. Investors need to know the challenges that management see as likely to affect future performance. An example of a chairman's statement that balances positive and negative aspects of the business is shown in Table 3.10.

Table 3.10 – Positive and negative aspects of the business

Xchanging plc – Annual report and accounts — 31 December 2010

We expect 2011 to be a year of transition for the company.

2010 was a difficult year, characterised by performance issues with parts of the Cambridge business and a weak economic background in our principal markets.

In 2010, revenue increased by 4%. Underlying operating profit was £67.3 million (FY 2009: £63.9 million), helped by contract settlements and consultancy income totalling £11.8 million (FY 2009 £8.0 million). In addition, exceptional items totalling £112.5 million have been recorded, including an impairment provision against goodwill arising from the Cambridge acquisition. The operating cash flow of the year was similar to 2009 and the net cash balance of £24.8 million at the year end was slightly higher than at the end of 2009 (£22.1 million).

Cambridge
Cambridge was purchased at the beginning of 2009 and the results to date, particularly in the American workers' compensation and ITO businesses, have been very disappointing. The business in India is performing well. The results from the Australian and the other Asian businesses have been mixed but do provide a platform for the future. The acquisition has been costly in terms of profitability, cash flow and management distraction. A plan is underway to resolve the major issues as quickly as possible.

Board changes
In October, Richard Houghton stood down from the Board and his role as Chief Financial Officer (CFO), and Ken Lever was appointed his successor.

On 9 February, we announced that David Andrews had decided to step down from the Board and his role as Chief Executive Officer (CEO) with immediate effect. As David was the founder and successful creator of Xchanging as a business, I am delighted he has agreed to take on a new role as Senior Adviser to me, to support Xchanging's business development initiatives.

We have begun the search for David's successor as CEO. Whilst this is ongoing, Ken Lever will be acting CEO in addition to his responsibilities as CFO, and I will support him as Executive Chairman.

Our people
It is in difficult circumstances that we recognise the strength and resolve of our people, our most valuable resource. The last few weeks have been challenging but I am confident that our employees have the determination to meet these challenges and to put Xchanging back on the path to becoming the global business processor of choice.

Our customers
Xchanging's strength is based on unrelenting attention to customer service. We have been reassured by the continued support of all of our customers and partners during 2010 and look forward to building on these relationships in 2011.

Liquidity
The Group's liquidity and cash position remain sound and cash generation will be a primary focus in the coming year.

Dividend
Shareholders will be disappointed by our decision not to declare a dividend in respect of 2010. However, we want to conserve our cash resources in the business for the changes we are effecting in 2011 and to fund the growth opportunities we see. We will review this again at the end of the year.

Action plan

We have developed a four-part action plan to overhaul our entire business, seeking value creation through regenerated profitable revenue growth and cash flow improvement. Where value is best created through disposal, we will pursue this option. The first part of our plan, a fundamental value assessment of our entire business, is complete, and we have already started taking specific action. We will report on progress at the half year. There will be costs associated with any such restructuring but we believe this will put the company in a better position to resume growth in 2012.

Outlook

We expect 2011 to be a year of transition for the company. We will continue to drive the successful and profitable parts of our business, focusing our sales efforts on our existing customer base and some potential new ones. I believe that the initiatives now underway will enable us to start rebuilding shareholder confidence and value.

Nigel Rich CBE
Executive Chairman

1 March 2011

Principle 7 — Comparable

3.82 Principle 7 states that *"The OFR should be comparable over time"*. [RS (OFR) para 24]. This ensures that directors do not change from one performance measure to another from year to year depending on which gives the more favourable impression of the business. Similarly, if information is given in one year about a particular aspect of the business, similar information should be given in subsequent years if that aspect of the business remains significant. The aim is for information to be sufficient for members to compare it with similar information about the entity for previous financial years. Information on particular aspects of the business given over several years enables members to identify and analyse trends and other factors over successive years. [RS (OFR) para 25]. Of course, although consistency is desirable, relevance is key and, therefore, management are not precluded from introducing new performance measures when there is a change in the business or when the old measures are, for whatever reason, deemed no longer appropriate and are no longer used in the management of the business.

3.83 An analysis of revenues over several years is shown in Table 3.11.

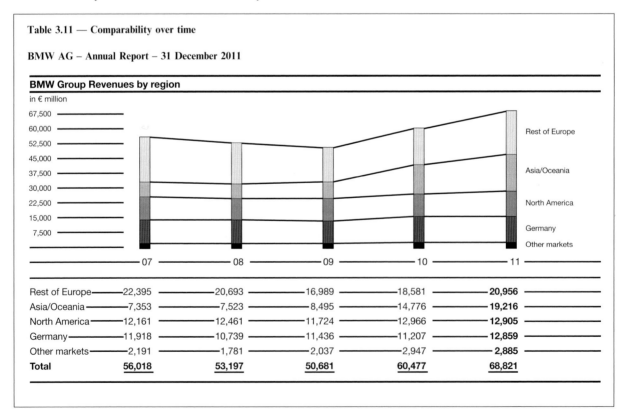

Table 3.11 — Comparability over time

BMW AG – Annual Report – 31 December 2011

BMW Group Revenues by region
in € million

	07	08	09	10	11
Rest of Europe	22,395	20,693	16,989	18,581	**20,956**
Asia/Oceania	7,353	7,523	8,495	14,776	**19,216**
North America	12,161	12,461	11,724	12,966	**12,905**
Germany	11,918	10,739	11,436	11,207	**12,859**
Other markets	2,191	1,781	2,037	2,947	**2,885**
Total	**56,018**	**53,197**	**50,681**	**60,477**	**68,821**

3.84 The reporting statement notes that directors may wish to consider the extent to which the OFR is consistent with reviews prepared by other entities in the same industry or geographical sector. [RS (OFR) para 25].

Table 3.12 – Comparability across industry sector

Prudential plc – Annual Report and Accounts – 31 December 2010

Business review (extract)

Other corporate information (extract)

In May 2004 the CFO Forum, representing the Chief Financial Officers of 19 European insurers, published the European Embedded Value Principles (expanded by the Additional Guidance of EEV Disclosures published in October 2005), thatprovide consistent definitions, a framework for setting actuarial assumptions, and a more explicit approach to the underlying methodology and disclosures. So for example:

- The allowance for risk is explicit for EEV through: (i) an allowance for the cost of capital (at the higher of economic capital and the local statutory minimum) (ii) stochastic or other appropriate modelling of financial options and guarantees toensure that an allowance for their cost is irrespective of theirvalue at the balance sheet date, and (iii) an explicit allowance in the risk discount rate for financial and non-financial risks;

- EEV specifically allows for the look-through into profits arising in shareholder service companies, most notably the profit arising in investment management companies from managing the insurance companies funds for covered business; and

- There are extensive disclosures required for EEV on all aspects of the calculations, including the methodology adopted and the analysis of return.

It is thought that the EEV basis not only provides a good indication of the value being added by management in a given accounting period, but also helps demonstrate whether shareholder capital is being deployed to best effect. Indeed insurance companies in many countries use comparable bases of accounting for management purposes.

Disclosure framework

3.85   The reporting statement provides a framework for the disclosures to be provided by the directors in an OFR. The purpose of the framework is to prescribe the key content elements that should be addressed in the OFR. It is for directors to consider how best to use the framework to structure the OFR, given the entity's circumstances. These circumstances may include:

- The industry or industries in which the entity operates.

- The range of products, services or processes that the entity offers.

- The number of markets served by the entity.

[RS (OFR) para 26].

3.86   The OFR should provide information to assist members to assess the strategies adopted by the entity and the potential for those strategies to succeed. The key elements of the disclosure framework necessary to achieve this are:

- The nature of the business, including a description of the market, competitive and regulatory environment in which the entity operates and the entity's objectives and strategies.

- The business' development and performance, both in the financial year under review and in the future.

- The resources, principal risks and uncertainties and relationships that may affect the entity's long-term value.

- Position of the business including a description of the entity's capital structure, treasury policies and objectives, and liquidity, both in the financial year under review and the future.

[RS (OFR) para 27].

3.87   To assist companies in structuring their OFR information more effectively, the reporting statement sets out the above disclosure framework, which can be represented in a logical flow as shown in Table 3.13. The first column of Table 3.13 connects the main headings of the OFR's disclosure framework to our integrated reporting model shown in paragraph 3.20.

Table 3.13 – Disclosure framework

Integrated reporting model (see para 3.20)	OFR disclosure framework (see para 3.87)	
External drivers	The nature, objectives and strategies of the business (see from para 3.91)	– Description of business and external environment.
Strategy*		– Objectives to generate or preserve value over the longer term. – Strategies for achieving the objectives.
Resources and relationships	Resources, risks* and uncertainties, and relationships (see from para 3.143)	– Description of resources, tangible and intangible, available and how they are managed. – Description of principal risks and uncertainties and the directors' approach to them. – Information about significant relationships and stakeholders other than investors who may directly impact performance.
Performance	Current and future development of performance (see from para 3.118)	– Significant features of the development and performance of the business. – Main trends and factors likely to impact future performance.
	Financial position (see from paragraph 3.169)	– Analysis of the financial position and critical accounting policies. – Discussion of the capital structure. – Discussion of the cash inflows and outflows, ability to generate cash to meet commitments and fund growth. – Discussion of current and prospective liquidity.
Underpinned by the financial and non-financial KPIs used to assess progress against stated objectives, as well as other measures and evidence.		

*Strategy is affected by the risks facing the business and by management's appetite for risk.

3.88 The OFR should also include the following information to the extent necessary to meet the recommendations set out in paragraph 27 of the reporting statement:

- Environmental matters (including the impact of the entity's business on the environment).

- The entity's employees.

- Social and community issues.

- Persons with whom the entity has contractual or other arrangements that are essential to the entity's business.

- Receipts from, and returns to, the entity's members in respect of members' shareholdings.

- All other matters the directors consider to be relevant.

[RS (OFR) para 28].

3.89 The OFR should also include the following items relating to environmental matters, the entity's employees and social and community issues:

- The entity's policies in each area mentioned.

- The extent to which those policies have been successfully implemented.

[RS (OFR) para 29].

3.90 The disclosures set out in paragraphs 3.88 and 3.89 above are only included to the extent they are necessary to meet the objectives set out in paragraph 27 of the reporting statement. In other words, they are only disclosed where they are relevant to the company's business. Increasingly, these matters will be relevant to businesses because, for example, they affect their reputation or ability to obtain scarce resources. But the purpose of the OFR is not to demonstrate a company's 'green' or 'good employer' credentials but to explain the company's business development and performance and so on. It is, of course, open to companies to prepare other reports to address the needs of stakeholders other than investors. In Table 3.13.1 the company links its good environmental practice to its business development.

Table 3.13.1 Sustainable development

Rio Tinto plc – Annual Report — 31 December 2010

Group strategy (extract)

The way we work: Governance, Sustainable Development and Values (extract)

The way we work is equally important to achieving our vision, as we integrate sustainable development practices into everything we do, wherever we operate: building on improvements to health and safety performance and extending leadership in areas such as community and government engagement, biodiversity and management of land, carbon, energy and water.

Success in these areas helps strengthen our licence to operate. We are recognised as a socially responsible developer, and one that builds strong relationships that bring lasting benefits to our neighbours and to the places where we work. Our approach gives us improved access to land, people and capital – all of which are essential to our future success.

> Makes the link between good environmental practice and business development.

Collectively, our strengths provide us with our strategic advantage. And this advantage is allowing us to meet responsibly the needs of a wide variety of customers while generating superior returns for our shareholders.

Sustainable Development Review (extract)

Our approach

Group strategy on p.18

Sustainable development has been identified as an area crucial to the delivery of the Group's long term strategy.

> Sustainable development is key part of strategy.

The minerals and metals produced at our operations contribute to society's needs, delivering financial dividends for our shareholders, paying wages and salaries for our employees, and creating wealth to support community infrastructure, health care and education. Our activities also provide the means and opportunity to develop new approaches to the environmental and human development challenges confronting society, such as climate change and poverty.

We recognise that some aspects of our activities can lead to unavoidable impacts, such as limiting options for the future use of land and water, impacts on local communities, and greenhouse gas emissions from our operations and the use of our products. We strive to minimise these impacts through good management of our operations.

The extended timeframes associated with our operations from exploration, through development and operation to closure provide us with opportunities to plan, implement and deliver sustainable contributions to social wellbeing, environmental stewardship and economic prosperity, within our strong governance systems.

Our continued licence to operate is subject to the ever increasing expectations of society. Consequently, we have developed and implemented a structured framework to ensure that we meet our goal of contributing to the global transition to sustainable development. This framework contains the "must have" building blocks, which must all work together to achieve leading performance and manage risk effectively.

We are communicating and raising our awareness of our approach to our internal and external stakeholders.

In 2010 we commenced a review of our approach to sustainable development to ensure it remains focused on the risks most relevant to delivering our business strategy.

Sustainable development framework

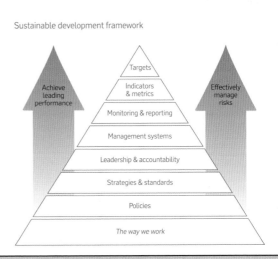

Detailed guidance within the disclosure framework

The business' nature, objectives and strategies

Nature of the business

3.91 The OFR should include a description of the business and the external environment in which it operates. This is to provide a context for the discussion and analysis of the entity's development, performance and financial position. [RS (OFR) para 30].

3.92 Depending on the nature of the business, the OFR should include discussion of matters such as:

- The industries in which the business operates.

- The entity's major markets and competitive position within those markets.

- Significant features of the legal, regulatory, macro-economic and social environment that influence the business.

- The main products and services, business processes and distribution methods.

- The business' structure and its economic model, including an overview of the main operating facilities and their location.

[RS (OFR) paras 31, 32].

3.93 From the business description, a user of the financial statements can expect to get an overall picture of the business model. Listed companies are required by the UK Corporate Governance Code to disclose the business model (see chapter 2), but it is a key disclosure for any company that wishes to communicate effectively with investors and other interested parties. How does the business work? What does the business do to add value and how does it do it? In Table 3.13.2, ARM Holdings plc gives an overview of its business model.

Table 3.13.2 – Business model

ARM Holdings plc – Annual Report – 31 December 2010

Overview (extract)

How ARM makes money

ARM is the world's leading semiconductor intellectual property (IP) supplier. The technology we design was at the heart of many of the digital electronic products sold in 2010.

ARM has an innovative business model. We licence our technology to a network of Partners, mainly leading semiconductor manufacturers. These Partners incorporate our designs alongside their own technology to create smart, low-energy chips suitable for modern electronic devices.

Why semiconductor companies use ARM technology

ARM designs technology that once was developed by our Partners' R&D teams, but it is cheaper for them to licence the technology from ARM. The design of a processor requires a large amount of R&D investment and expertise. We estimate that every semiconductor company would need to spend about $100 million every year to reproduce what ARM does. This represents an additional $20 billion of annual costs for the industry. By designing once and licensing many

times, ARM spreads the R&D costs over the whole industry, making digital electronics cheaper.

Technologies that are suitable for the ARM business model

ARM's licensing business started in the early 1990s with the development of our first processor. The processor is like the brain of the chip; it is where the software runs and controls the functionality of the product that the chip is in. ARM designs each processor to be applicable to a broad range of end-markets to maximise the number of companies that can licence each processor. In most years ARM introduces 2-3 new processor designs.

Recently, ARM has developed other technologies suitable for a licensing and royalty business model, such as graphics processors and physical IP components.

How ARM creates value

ARM endeavours to recover its costs from the licence revenues of each technology, leaving the majority of royalties as profits. Over the medium term, we expect royalties to grow faster than licence revenues, and we expect that revenues will grow faster than costs, making ARM increasingly profitable.

As our customers are the world's largest semiconductor manufacturers, their regular royalty payments have become a highly reliable cash flow. ARM's business model is strongly cash generative. In 2010 we generated £180 million of cash. Since 2004, ARM has returned over £400 million of cash to shareholders through a combination of share buybacks and dividends.

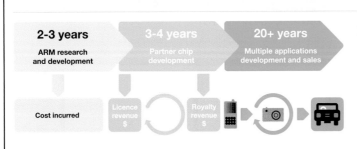

ARM business model

The companies who choose ARM technology pay an up-front licence fee to gain access to a design. They incorporate the ARM technology into their chip – a process that often takes 3-4 years. When the chip starts to ship, ARM receives a royalty on every chip that uses the design. Typically our royalty is based on the price of the chip. Each ARM processor design is suitable for a wide range of end applications and so can be reused in different chip families addressing multiple markets. Each new chip family generates a new stream of royalties. An ARM processor design may be used in many different chips and may ship for over 20 years.

3.94 To understand and evaluate a company's strategy and performance, investors need a clear grasp of its business environment and the impact this has on the company. Frequently, when management discusses market conditions and other factors, they do so only to explain past behaviour and performance. Management should also discuss its expectations for the future and how this will impact on the delivery of business strategy. Often, performance has been reported in isolation with only high level commentary on the business environment such as *"...against intensifying competition..."* or *"...prospects are good...".*

3.95 Investors who are familiar with the company are interested in management's interpretation of market developments and trends; some may be less familiar and need the information to judge performance and the logic of the company's strategies.

3.96 In its 2010 annual report, as illustrated in Table 3.14 below, Logica plc discusses current and potential future trends within the group's market. It uses graphics to support the narrative discussion, in respect of market concentration and market position. The table below sets out extracts for illustrative purposes only. Considerable further detail is included in the report. In addition, within the annual report, there are references to an online annual report, which includes videos of members of the management team speaking on the main subjects of interest.

Table 3.14 — Business trends

Logica plc – Annual report 31 December 2010

Our markets in 2010 (extracts)

> Throughout 2010 we have seen signs of the market returning to growth. The IT Services market has continued to evolve with growth in global IT spend expected to be solid in 2011 and the European IT services sector is now expected to total £134 billion. Outsourcing continues to be the driver of growth across Europe.

Our market share

We grew revenue ahead of the market and our major European peers in 2010.

Within the European markets where we operate, we maintain a strong position as one of the top five suppliers with particularly good market share in the Nordics, France and Portugal. In the UK, our market position remains solid based on our position with the UK government. In 2010, we were one of the 19 key suppliers invited to sign the government's Memorandum of Understanding.

In Europe, buying patterns varied by country and this has played to our strength of local presence, allowing us to tailor solutions locally for our clients with a blended delivery of services. Such a specialist offering will be paramount to remaining competitive and maintaining market share as all geographies return to growth.

Our approach to clients

As outlined on pages 10 to 15, we approach our clients by industry but organise ourselves by geography.

Growth patterns in different geographies are closely related to GDP growth, so 2010 was a mixed year. Despite recovery in the Northern and Central European and French economies, the UK, Benelux and Portuguese economies remained weaker. Across all geographies the blended delivery model has proved successful this year in creating efficienc for both us and our clients while still maintaining service close to them.

We have seen significant growth in Morocco, for example, from where we support the relationships with our French clients.

Similarly, as the industry remains fragmented, clients increasingly want IT suppliers with good vertical industry knowledge. This is one of our strengths. Our contracts in energy and utilities, transport and logistics and the public sector give us good visibility for 2011.

The Public Sector represented 31% of Group revenue in 2010. This sector declined as a result of the elections held in a number of countries. Following the change in UK government in May, we saw a reduction in short-term demand. But the signing of our £157 million, 10-year contract with the UK Serious Organised Crime Agency at the beginning of 2011 was a welcome sign that high quality IT solutions remain important in the government's agenda. We expect demand to improve as government departments absorb spending reductions and allocate their spending priorities. Clients such as the UK Crown Prosecution Service remain focused on reducing costs, using shared services for front and back office to deliver savings, and want suppliers with a reputation for security. Throughout this, Logica has been well-placed as a valued and trusted supplier and we remain confident that there are significant medium-term opportunities.

In the Energy & Utilities sector, we have continued to develop long-term partnerships. Our contract with EDP in Portugal is a good example of how we can successfully evolve and how our client intimacy approach produces best in class, innovative solutions.

Financial services has seen a return to growth as a result of improving conditions in the sector and client need for systems improvements and upgrades. Revenue drivers include consulting work around payments, risk and regulation, and integration support resulting from disposals and acquisitions. Within this, Logica remains a top three supplier for key clients in managing their risk.

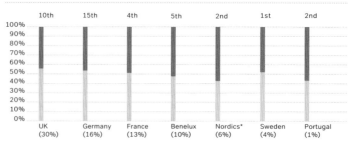

Market concentration and Logica market position at end of 2009

Share of market: ⬤ Top 10 players ⬤ Others
Source: Logica, based on 2009 data.
Number in brackets indicates size of country market.
* Nordics includes Finland, Norway and Denmark. Sweden is excluded.

3.97 From the business description, a user of the financial statements can expect to get an overall picture of the business. For example:

- Whether it operates internationally.

- Whether it operates in unstable economic and political regions.

- The entity's relative strength in the markets/industry compared to its competitors, including its strongest and weakest business and geographic areas.

- Whether the entity is highly regulated, or subject to significant legal actions against it.

- The performance and outlook for the economies, markets and sectors in which the business operates.

- The environmental and social factors that influence the business.

- The products or services the entity provides, whether they involve significant R&D or advertising support and the product risk involved; whether there is significant dependency on a small number of customers or suppliers or scarcity of sources of supply for raw materials that affect the business.

- Whether there are significant factors involved in manufacturing or distributing the entity's products.

- How the business is organised and monitored by the board, for example by business or geographic sectors or a combination of both. Whether the business is run centrally or if the individual units have a high degree of autonomy.

- Where the main operating facilities are located, giving an idea of the business's size.

Business objectives

3.98 The OFR should discuss the objectives of the business to generate or preserve value over the longer-term. [RS (OFR) para 33]. The reporting statement notes that objectives will often be defined in terms of financial performance, but that objectives in non-financial areas should also be discussed, where appropriate. [RS (OFR) para 34].

3.99 For many businesses, financial objectives and general interests are best served by having increased regard to social, environmental and other non-financial factors. As a result, an entity's objectives, whilst generally continuing to focus on achieving returns for members, include or refer to non-financial objectives or factors, particularly in those industries that have the potential to significantly affect the environment in which they operate. The theme of increasing responsibility is now a trend or factor that influences the development of businesses. It emerges even more clearly in the development of strategies as can be seen in the example in Table 3.13.1. Where creating value for the company is partly dependent on the company's response to social and environmental issues, this is built into management's strategies and these strategies should be presented in the OFR. In such cases, management's action in social and environmental fields is not an optional 'add on' designed only to improve the image of the business, but is part of core strategy to promote the quality and sustainability of business performance. Where social and environmental issues are not particularly important in delivering the company's business objectives, they should not be included in the OFR as this will tend to obscure the important disclosures.

3.100 Many companies now produce separate corporate social responsibility reports. Thus, whilst in some cases the OFR may contain details of a company's policy and performance in this area, in other cases a separate report is often prepared. Sometimes such a report is separate from the annual report and accounts, with only a summary appearing in the latter document. On other occasions a full corporate social responsibility report is included with the annual report, either separate from the OFR or incorporated within it.

3.101 Whilst discussion of corporate social responsibility is outside the scope of this chapter, it is worth noting that there are a number of organisations dedicated to improving corporate reporting in this area. Among them is Business in the Community and The Business Impact Review Group, who work together to develop a common approach to social and environmental reporting. As part of this work they developed guidance for disclosures under five major headings: marketplace, environment, workplace, community and human rights.

3.102 Examples of where financial objectives are qualified by non-financial considerations in the extractive industry, one of the industries where such factors are most significant, are given in Tables 3.13.1 and 3.14.1.

Table 3.14.1 – Social, environmental and other non-financial factors

BHP Billiton plc Annual Report – 31 December 2010

3.2 Our strategy (extract)

Our objective and commitments are pursued through our six strategic drivers:

- *People* – the foundation of our business is our people. We require people to find resources, develop those resources, operate the businesses that produce our products, and then deliver those products to our customers. Talented and motivated people are our most precious resource.
- *Licence to operate* – we aim to ensure that the communities in which we operate value our citizenship. Licence to operate means win-win relationships and partnerships. This includes a central focus on health, safety, environment and the community, and making a positive difference to our host communities.
- *World-class assets* – our world-class assets provide the cash flows that are required to build new projects, to contribute to the economies of the countries in which we operate, to meet our obligations to our employees, suppliers and partners, and ultimately to pay dividends to our shareholders. We maintain high-quality assets by managing them in the most effective and efficient way.
- *Financial strength and discipline* – we have a solid 'A' credit rating, which balances financial flexibility with the cost of finance. Our capital management program has three priorities:
  - To return excess capital to shareholders.
  - To reinvest in our extensive pipeline of world-class projects that carry attractive rates of return regardless of the economic climate.
  - To ensure a solid balance sheet.
- *Project pipeline* – we are focused on delivering an enhanced resource endowment to underpin future generations of growth. We have an abundance of tier one resources in stable countries that provide us with a unique set of options to deliver brownfield growth.
- *Growth options* – we use exploration, technology and our global footprint to look beyond our current pipeline to secure a foundation of growth for future generations. We pursue growth options in several ways – covering the range from extending existing operations to new projects in emerging regions, through exploration, technology and, on occasion, merger and acquisition activity.

Links strategy on people and licence to operate to key measures

3.3 Key measures (extract)

People and licence to operate
These foundational strategic drivers bring together health, safety, environment and community (HSEC) related measures. These measures are a subset of the HSEC Targets Scorecard, which can be found in each corresponding section of our Sustainability Report at *www.bhpbilliton.com*.

We monitor a comprehensive set of health, safety, environment and community contribution indicators. Two key measures are the Total Recordable Injury Frequency (TRIF) and community investment.

	2010	2009	2008
People and licence to operate – health, safety, environment and community			
Total Recordable Injury Frequency (TRIF) [1]	**5.3**	5.6	5.9
Community investment (US$M) [1]	**200.5**	197.8	141.0

[1] See section 10 for glossary definitions.

Safety – Despite strong performance improvement across the organisation, sadly we experienced the loss of five colleagues at our operations during the year.

We made an incremental improvement in Total Recordable Injury Frequency (which comprises fatalities, lost-time cases, restricted work cases and medical treatment cases per million hours worked) from 5.6 to 5.3 per million hours worked. This is over halfway towards our target of a 50 per cent reduction on 2007 TRIF performance of 7.4 by 2012.

Health – We are progressing well with our health performance objectives. We had 164 new cases of occupational disease reported in FY2010, 52 fewer new cases compared with the FY2007 base year. The overall reduction in occupational disease since FY2007 is 27 per cent, which is on track to meet our target of a 30 per cent reduction in incidences in occupational disease among our employees by June 2012.

It is mandatory for our employees who may be potentially exposed to airborne substances or noise in excess of our occupational exposure limits (OELs) to wear personal protective equipment. Compared with the FY2007 base year there was a 3.9 per cent reduction in the proportion of employees potentially exposed in excess of OELs in FY2010, which is behind schedule to meet our target of a 15 per cent reduction in potential employee exposures over our occupational exposure limits.

Environment – In FY2010, we reduced absolute greenhouse gas emissions by more than three million tonnes compared with FY2009.

We have five-year targets of a six per cent reduction in our greenhouse gas emissions intensity index and a 13 per cent reduction in our carbon-based energy intensity index, both by 30 June 2012. Our greenhouse intensity index is currently tracking at seven per cent below our FY2006 base year. Our carbon-based energy intensity index is currently tracking at six per cent below our FY2006 base year.

We have a five-year target of a 10 per cent improvement in our land rehabilitation index by 2012. This index is based on a ratio of land rehabilitated compared with our land footprint. In FY2010, the index improved by one per cent due to the development of new green and brownfield projects and the divestment of a number of operations, including Optimum Colliery in 2008, which had large areas of land under rehabilitation.

We have a five-year target of a 10 per cent improvement in the ratio of water recycled to high-quality water consumed by 30 June 2012. This water use index has improved seven per cent on our FY2007 base year.

We define a significant environmental incident as one with a severity rating of four or above based on our internal severity rating scale (tiered from one to five by increasing severity). One significant incident occurred during FY2010 at our Pinto Valley Operations (US) involving a tailings release. The majority of the eroded tailings and cover material were recovered. Metal concentrations in surface water and sediments appear to be well below levels that could present a hazard.

Community – We continue to invest one per cent of our pre-tax profits in community programs, based on the average of the previous three years' pre-tax profit publicly reported in each of those years. During FY2010, our voluntary investment totalled US$200.5 million comprising cash, in-kind support and administrative costs and includes a US$80 million contribution to BHP Billiton Sustainable Communities.

Despite the global financial crisis, our direct expenditure on community programs during the year was similar to our expenditure in FY2009.

Business strategy

3.103 The OFR should set out the directors' strategies for achieving the business' objectives. To assess the quality and sustainability of a company's performance, investors need to be clear about its objectives and the strategies for achieving those objectives. They need to know how management intends to address market trends and the threats and opportunities that they represent. They also need to understand the relationship between strategic objectives, management actions and executive remuneration. (Directors' remuneration is dealt with in chapter 5.) This enables them to judge the appropriateness and success of management actions in delivering the strategy and what to expect in the future.

3.104 Statements of objectives and strategies should provide the detail that enables investors to understand the priorities for action or the resources that must be managed to deliver results, as well as explaining how success will be measured and over what period of time it should be assessed.

3.105 The reporting statement notes that objectives will often be defined in terms of financial performance, but that objectives in non-financial areas should also be discussed, where appropriate. [RS (OFR) para 34].

3.106 Many strategic objectives focus on achieving value for shareholders and financial success. However, a company's strategy should also be based on an understanding of the key areas in which a company has competitive advantage, for example, a market-leading customer base or a highly skilled workforce. The company's success in creating value will depend on management's ability to invest resources in these areas and manage them so that they deliver the financial performance investors expect.

3.107 In its 2011 annual report, Premier Farnell plc describes its strategy and breaks it down in into areas of strategic focus. The company describes what has happened in relation to each of these focus areas in the current year and sets out priorities for action in 2012. Table 3.14.2 shows an extract of the strategy and an extract of the related area of strategic focus.

Table 3.14.2 — Strategy – Priorities for action

Premier Farnell plc – Annual Report – 30 January 2011

Strategy (extract)

> **Focus on EDE**
> Central to the strategy is Electronic Design Engineering – an attractive market which offers above average gross margins and growth rates. Through providing an industry leading high service proposition together with an increasingly rich offering of design solutions, EDEs truly appreciate the value of our model and reward us with loyalty and high purchase frequency.
>
> The global EDE market consists of customers involved in the design of electronic products and components. EDE customers have similar service requirements wherever they are located around the world – a broad product offering, latest technology, technical support, accurate design and legislative information and reliable and prompt delivery – which means we can leverage our global organisation to meet those needs. Increasingly EDEs also want to collaborate and discuss their work through social media, a trend which led us to launch the pioneering element14 community in 2009. This convergence of community with commerce is a trend we expect to increase and is central to our brand and eCommerce strategies.
>
> We set a goal for this part of our strategy that 50% of MDD revenue would come from EDE customers by the end of 2010 and in many regions we exceeded that goal. That journey continues and we are now aiming for 50%–70% of our business to come from EDE by the end of our 2013 financial year. In the final quarter of 2011 EDE sales accounted for 53.7% of sales from our electronics distribution businesses.

Strategic Focus 1 (extract)

Strategic Focus 1
Profitable growth through
focusing on
EDEs globally

The world of the EDE is changing rapidly. Electronics is becoming increasingly ubiquitous across all aspects of life.

The demand for electronics in more end products is rising, while the importance of aesthetics and environmental compliance is driving an increase in the redesign of electronics. The speed-to-market requirements in the modern design world are also placing greater pressures on our core EDE customer group as they strive to take their designs from concept through to creation as quickly as possible. Such change is presenting us with much opportunity to develop solutions and enhance our proposition to meet the evolving needs of EDEs and win market share.

Designs have to work first time and comply with the latest legislation, as well as reflecting market focus on miniaturisation, green technology and the demands of aesthetics. In this climate the needs of the EDE go beyond the component – they require a wealth of data and information, design tools, software and, increasingly, the views of their global peers to inform their decisions. Once the pressure on time-to-market is factored in, the opportunity for meeting all those needs in a single converged web environment is clear. The element14 brand and our enhanced proposition are delivering just that – high service access to all the latest products, design and legislative information and the leading global EDE community.

The investments we continue to make in building such a holistic, industry leading proposition means we are able to meet more of an EDE's needs. This is reflected in our EDE active customer base growing 7.5% year-on-year as we concentrated on leveraging our powerful proposition to deliver accelerated market share gains and help to ensure customer loyalty.

During the year we enhanced the design support we provide EDEs through our own technical services department. We are continuing to invest to provide our engineering customers no matter where they are in the world, with 24 hour, five day a week access to our own dedicated technical support team. We have also introduced live chat as another method for customers to communicate with our own engineers, as we look to build a technical offering which fully complements our growing suite of services within our EDE ecosystem. Our acquisition of CadSoft, developer of the EAGLE CAD software, has enabled another step towards offering engineers a holistic solution to meet all their needs no matter what stage of the design cycle they are at. EAGLE and its ongoing development is just one aspect of our next 1,000 day services beyond product programme which is focused on introducing new technology or service based propositional enhancements that meet the needs of EDEs as they move through the design cycle. Indeed, towards the end of the year we launched a new service that combines the power of element14, the Eagle software and our franchise relationship with Pentalogix to allow customers to order a prototype directly from their virtual design environment.

EDE customers depend on our high service model to get their products to them exactly when they need them. Our delivery service is best-in-class, with 99.6% of our orders delivered either the same day or the next day, supported by our distribution facilities located in seven different locations around the world. However, to ensure we remain at the forefront of our industry, we hold numerous customer focus groups to ensure we stay in touch with and listen closely to the needs of our customers. This helps us to understand the challenges they are facing today and into the future. It also helps us to understand how we can meet those needs and where best to invest when developing our proposition to drive market share growth.

Achievements in 2011

- Our full year sales growth in the EDE sector outperformed our sales growth in the MRO sector by 20.8 percentage points, while EDE sales accounted for 52.5% of our distribution business' sales. This is within our target range of 50%–70%.

- Market launch in Asia Pacific of our enhanced value proposition and the first convergence of community and transactional web offerings under the element14 brand.

- Ongoing development of the element14 EDE community, with close to 50,000 registrants and over 1.5 million customers visiting the site in 2011. This has helped drive a 7.5% year-on-year increase in our EDE active customer base.

- Successful integration of CadSoft and the market launch of further enhancements to the EAGLE software, in conjunction with the launch of a rapid prototyping service accessible from within an EDE's CAD environment or directly on element14.

- Added 72,500 new EDE products to our stocked range, 43 new suppliers, and nearly doubled the locally stocked range in Asia Pacific to 122,000.

- Successfully enhanced our technical support services and global technology centres, located in Bangalore and Chengdu, with over 200 technical experts now employed within the organisation globally.

Priorities in 2012

- Leveraging the convergence of community, information and transaction under the element14 brand to drive customer acquisition and loyalty.

- Accelerate our services beyond product initiative to create and launch a holistic ecosystem for design engineers that offers EDEs the solutions and services they require at each stage of the design cycle.

- Build on our work in 2011 to draw together design tools, software and partners into a truly collaborative workspace for EDEs.

- Focus on customer acquisition in the world's developing markets and key high growth vertical markets globally, such as lighting, solar and wind while also targeting universities to attract tomorrow's engineers to the element14 brand.

- Provide our supplier partners with rich insights into customer behaviour from our global online environment as we seed the market with their latest technology and supporting information.

- Ensure efficient and cost effective stocking processes are in place, purchasing products around the world, making the most of Premier Farnell's global footprint.

- Continue to invest in technical skills, software and services to build a global brand with EDEs.

- Engage with customers and suppliers to find new ways to reduce our environmental footprint.

3.108 Strategies and objectives may also embed environmental, social and ethical values of particular importance to the company, as shown in Table 3.16. In this example, Marks and Spencer Group PLC set out how Plan A is important to its brand value as well as helping to reduce costs.

Table 3.15 Embedding non-financial values in strategy

Marks and Spencer Group PLC – Annual Report and Financial Statements – 2 April 2011

About M&S (extract)

Our performance (extract)

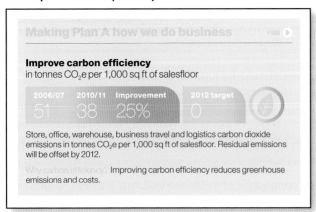

Governance: Accountability (extract)

Risk description	Mitigating activities
Brand and reputation Our founding principles of Quality, Value, Service, Innovation and Trust continue to influence how we do business and our reputation for being one of the UK's most trusted brands.	
Corporate reputation External expectations relating to our Plan A, ethical or corporate governance commitments are not adequately managed Our brand continues to be trusted in the marketplace with Plan A being an integral component of the M&S brand. With such a strong brand comes high expectations and the need to consistently deliver quality and value to our wide stakeholder base.	– Our commitment to Plan A and becoming the world's most sustainable major retailer by 2015 continues to be a priority for the Group with one of our key objectives being for all M&S products to have at least one Plan A attribute by 2020. – We have recently launched 'Only at Your M&S' emphasising to customers that they will find exclusive and innovative products that are unique to M&S. – We are ensuring that adequate policies and procedures are in place to meet the requirements of the Bribery Act 2010 which comes into force in July this year.

Financial Review (extract)

Looking ahead

Plan A is an integral part of the M&S brand, which sets us apart from the competition. In the year ahead we aim to retain our leadership position and make Plan A even more relevant to our customers.

3.109 The OFR should discuss the business' objectives to generate or preserve value over the longer-term. [RS (OFR) para 33].

3.110 The nature of the industry will affect the directors' determination of an appropriate time frame for the OFR. [RS (OFR) para 35]. The reporting statement gives, as an example, a business that focuses on long-term projects and that has to plan over the full project life cycle, which may be 20 years or more. It also states that if a project has a long-term impact on the environment, this is likely to affect long-term value and, therefore, determines the time perspective for reporting in the OFR. Industries with such long-term perspectives include, for example, the extractive industry, where the development and exploitation of a mine may extend for 20 years or more.

3.111 This contrasts with a service industry having few physical assets and depending on the supply of particular employee skills for its competitive advantage. Such an industry, it says, will plan over a period consistent with its ability to recruit, train and develop its staff, which may be a much shorter period than the industries cited above.

3.112 As noted above, the OFR should set out the directors' strategies for achieving the business' objectives. [RS (OFR) para 36].The reporting statement says that disclosure of the directors' strategies is recommended in order for members to assess the current and past actions undertaken by directors in respect of the stated objectives. [RS (OFR) para 37].

3.113 When describing an entity's strategies, directors should include information about any changes in strategies. This is particularly important where past strategies have not been successful, resulting in poor performance. In such circumstances, it is important for directors, in seeking to restore lost confidence in the entity, to spell out in detail the revised strategies for the future. In doing so, they may have particular regard, when discussing past strategy, to the principle that the OFR should be balanced and neutral, dealing even-handedly with both good and bad aspects.

3.114 In Transnet Limited's 2010 annual report, the company's new 'Quantum Leap Strategy' is described; the new strategy sets targets for a five year period. Table 3.18 gives an overview of the change in strategy while Table 3.18.1 shows the projections for capital investment, one of the key areas of focus under the new strategy.

Table 3.16 — Changes in strategy

Transnet Limited – Annual Report – 31 March 2010

Review of strategy execution

Review of strategy execution

The successful turnaround of the Company laid the foundation for the Growth Strategy adopted in 2008. Achieving the targeted growth in volumes has been impacted by the global economic crisis – given the high correlation between commodity volumes and containers handled by Transnet and global economic growth. Despite the impact of the global economic crisis the outcome of the Growth Strategy is evident in the performance of the Company during the year. While operational performance has improved in many areas of the Company, the **rate of improvement has not met our expectations**. Progress has been slow and at best incremental.

During the year the Board approved a strategic shift from the Growth Strategy. This shift constitutes a number of focus areas and initiatives to be implemented in the medium-term, and will enhance Transnet's ability to deliver on its mandate and position the Company to support the long-term competitiveness of the South African economy.

The strategy going forward will be on realising a **Quantum Leap** improvement in **customer service** by improving **operational efficiency** in all areas of the business together with **volume growth** while maintaining the **financial stability** of the Company.

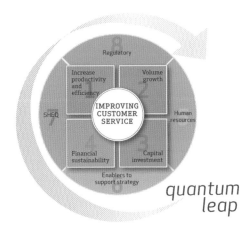

Achieving objectives within a framework of
corporate governance, internal controls, dynamic
management reporting, leading environmental practices and
legal compliance.

This is embodied in the Quantum Leap Strategy as set out below:

- Harnessing **volume growth** opportunities;
- Achieving substantial improvement in **customer service**;
- Increasing **productivity** and operating **efficiencies**;
- Implementing effective **cost-control** and reducing the cost base;
- Continuous **improvement** in **safety** and environmental compliance; and
- Improving asset utilisation to achieve **appropriate returns**.

The overarching theme for 2011 is a Quantum Leap improvement in customer service, volume growth and operational efficiency. The Quantum Leap initiatives aims to change the trajectory of performance improvement to a significantly higher level.

This will be achieved by enhancing operational efficiencies across the Company which will result in an improvement in the reliability and predictability of services while maintaining the financial sustainability for the Company.

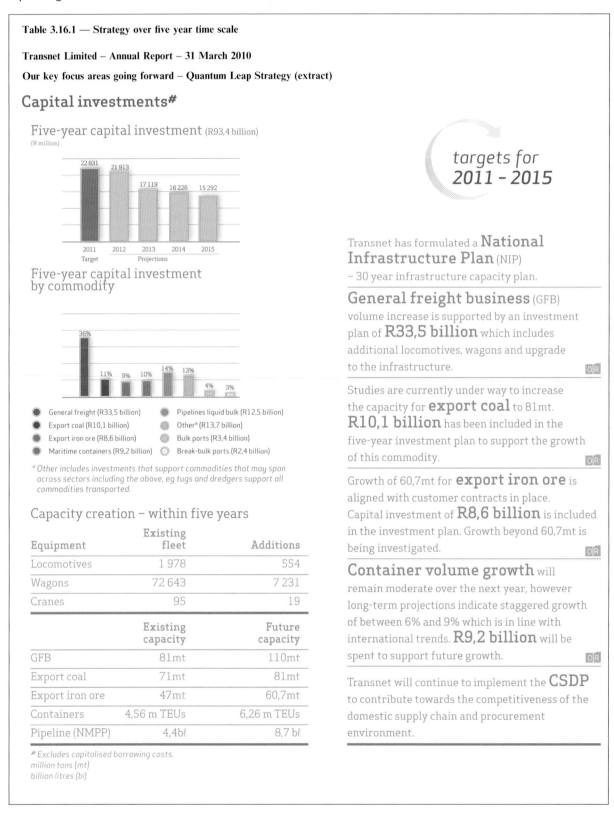

Table 3.16.1 — Strategy over five year time scale

Transnet Limited – Annual Report – 31 March 2010

Our key focus areas going forward – Quantum Leap Strategy (extract)

Capital investments#

Five-year capital investment (R93,4 billion)
(R million)

	2011 Target	2012	2013	2014	2015
	22 831	21 913	17 119	16 226	15 292
			Projections		

Five-year capital investment by commodity

- General freight (R33,5 billion) — 36%
- Export coal (R10,1 billion) — 11%
- Export iron ore (R8,6 billion) — 9%
- Maritime containers (R9,2 billion) — 10%
- Pipelines liquid bulk (R12,5 billion) — 14%
- Other* (R13,7 billion) — 13%
- Bulk ports (R3,4 billion) — 4%
- Break-bulk ports (R2,4 billion) — 3%

Other includes investments that support commodities that may span across sectors including the above, eg tugs and dredgers support all commodities transported.

Capacity creation – within five years

Equipment	Existing fleet	Additions
Locomotives	1 978	554
Wagons	72 643	7 231
Cranes	95	19

	Existing capacity	Future capacity
GFB	81mt	110mt
Export coal	71mt	81mt
Export iron ore	47mt	60,7mt
Containers	4,56 m TEUs	6,26 m TEUs
Pipeline (NMPP)	4,4bℓ	8,7 bℓ

 # Excludes capitalised borrowing costs.
million tons (mt)
billion litres (bℓ)

targets for 2011 - 2015

Transnet has formulated a **National Infrastructure Plan** (NIP) – 30 year infrastructure capacity plan.

General freight business (GFB) volume increase is supported by an investment plan of **R33,5 billion** which includes additional locomotives, wagons and upgrade to the infrastructure.

Studies are currently under way to increase the capacity for **export coal** to 81mt. **R10,1 billion** has been included in the five-year investment plan to support the growth of this commodity.

Growth of 60,7mt for **export iron ore** is aligned with customer contracts in place. Capital investment of **R8,6 billion** is included in the investment plan. Growth beyond 60,7mt is being investigated.

Container volume growth will remain moderate over the next year, however long-term projections indicate staggered growth of between 6% and 9% which is in line with international trends. **R9,2 billion** will be spent to support future growth.

Transnet will continue to implement the **CSDP** to contribute towards the competitiveness of the domestic supply chain and procurement environment.

3.115 To the extent necessary, the OFR should include the key performance indicators, both financial and non-financial, used by the directors to assess progress against their stated objectives. [RS (OFR) para 38]. The KPIs disclosed should be those that the directors judge are effective in measuring the delivery of their strategies and managing their business. Regular measurement using KPIs will enable an entity to set and communicate its performance targets and to measure whether it is achieving them. [RS (OFR) para 39]. Comparability will be enhanced if KPIs are widely used, either within the industry sector or more generally. [RS (OFR) para 40]. However, it is important that the KPIs used are appropriate for measuring the entity's performance from year to year.

3.116 KPIs are discussed from paragraph 3.209 and examples are given in Tables 3.44 and 3.45.

3.117   Directors should also consider the extent to which other performance indicators and evidence should be included. [RS (OFR) para 41]. Other performance indicators may be narrative evidence describing how the directors manage the business or indicators that are used to monitor the entity's external environment and/or its progress towards achieving its objectives. [RS (OFR) para 42]. Other performance indicators are discussed from paragraph 3.222 below.

Current and future development and performance

Development and performance in the year

3.118   The OFR should describe the significant features of the business' development and performance in the financial year, focusing on business (including geographical) segments that are relevant to an understanding of the development and performance as a whole. [RS (OFR) para 43]. The example in Table 3.16.2 shows performance by region and by product type, together with a high-level explanation of that performance. (Only one region and one product type are shown here, for illustration purposes.)

Table 3.16.2 — Financial performance

Unilever PLC — Annual Report and Accounts — 31 December 2011

Financial review (extract)

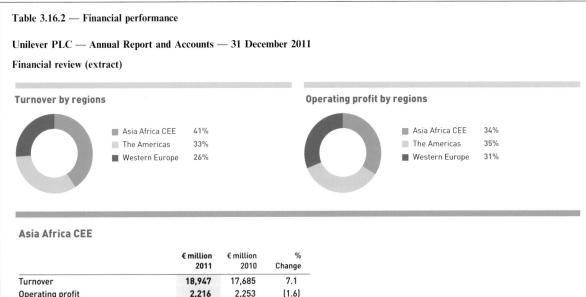

Turnover by regions

■ Asia Africa CEE	41%
■ The Americas	33%
■ Western Europe	26%

Operating profit by regions

■ Asia Africa CEE	34%
■ The Americas	35%
■ Western Europe	31%

Asia Africa CEE

	€ million 2011	€ million 2010	% Change
Turnover	18,947	17,685	7.1
Operating profit	2,216	2,253	(1.6)
Underlying operating margin (%)	12.7	13.4	(0.7)
Underlying sales growth (%)	10.5	7.7	
Underlying volume growth (%)	4.5	10.2	
Effect of price changes (%)	5.8	(2.2)	

Key developments
- Market growth remained strong throughout the region, with high single digit increases particularly in buoyant markets across East and South Asia. Conditions in Russia and CEE, however, were more subdued.
- Underlying sales growth of 10.5% was ahead of our markets and well balanced between volume and price. China and India both contributed double digit volume growth; South Africa, Turkey and Indonesia also performed strongly.
- Value market shares were up for the region as a whole, driven by strong growth in Home Care, while Foods value shares were slightly down. Share gains were seen across many key markets, including China, Indonesia, the Philippines and South Africa. Volume shares were flat.
- Underlying operating margin was down 0.7%, primarily reflecting the impact of higher commodity costs.
- Other key developments included further progress on the roll-out of the regional IT system and the acquisition of the Concern Kalina business in Russia.

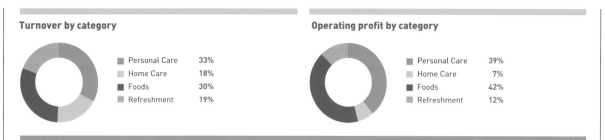

Personal Care

	€ million 2011	€ million 2010	% Change
Turnover	**15,471**	13,767	12.4
Operating profit	**2,536**	2,296	10.5
Underlying operating margin (%)	**18.0**	18.0	–
Underlying sales growth (%)	**8.2**	6.4	
Underlying volume growth (%)	**4.2**	7.9	
Effect of price changes (%)	**3.8**	(1.4)	

Key developments
- Personal Care grew strongly in 2011 to become Unilever's largest category, with underlying sales growth of 8.2%. The acquisitions of Alberto Culver and the Sara Lee brands started to contribute positively.
- Growth was well balanced between volume and price, and reflected strong performance across the portfolio, particularly in deodorants, hair care and skin cleansing.
- Value market shares were up overall, with strong gains in North America where hair care and deodorants performed well, and in China where skin cleansing and hair care saw strong gains.
- Underlying operating margin was stable at 18.0%.

3.119 Trends and factors in development and performance suggested by an analysis of current and previous financial years should be highlighted. Development and performance should be described in the context of the business' strategic objectives. [RS (OFR) para 44]. It should also be set in the context of the entity's key performance indicators (see further from para 3.209).

3.120 Comparison over a number of years may be appropriate where, for example, the entity has a particular strategic objective with a duration of several years.

3.121 The OFR should cover significant aspects of the statements of financial performance and, where appropriate, should be linked to other aspects of performance. [RS (OFR) para 45]. The example in Table 3.20 shows a graphical explanation of the revenue and profit from operations included in the financial statements. There is a clear indication of reasons for changes in these figures from one period to the next. Further information on each element of the movement is given in detailed narrative explanations of financial performance.

Table 3.17 – Explaining financial performance

Tomkins plc – Annual Report – 2 January 2010

OPERATING AND FINANCIAL REVIEW (extract)

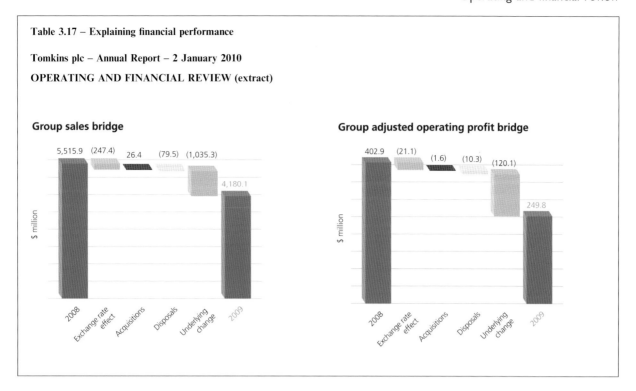

3.122 Unusual, non-recurring or exceptional items should be discussed and fully explained. Such items may include gains and losses on sales of businesses, reorganisation costs, fines and penalties, impairments, litigation costs and other material items that have been separately disclosed in the financial statements.

3.123 The OFR should include the directors' analysis of the effect on current development and performance of changes in the industry or external environment in which the business operates and developments within the business. Such changes include market conditions impacting the business and new products or services introduced by the company. [RS (OFR) para 46].

3.124 Competition, regulation and macro-economics can all affect a company's current development and performance. The introduction of a new competitor may result in changes to pricing decisions, as may regulatory pressure. Macro-economics and other broad market factors such as geopolitical events can also impact how the company has performed.

3.125 Table 3.18 provides an illustration of how market conditions have impacted a company's performance. This disclosure is part of a 'Management Speak' section which presents highlights of conversations held by management with stakeholders during the period. In Table 3.19, another company describes the impact of economic conditions on the current period and considers the likely impact of planned government spending cuts.

Table 3.18 Market conditions

Tata Steel Limited – 103rd Annual Report – 31 March 2010

Management Speak (extract)

 How has the global economic crisis affected the Steel Industry in the last 12 months?

This has been the worst global crisis in living memory. The global financial landscape has changed significantly since September 2008 and this has had a severe impact on the global economy in the last 18 months. The lack of capital had resulted in a significant decline in demand across most sectors globally and in steel too we saw demand contracting in many end-user segments in the first half of 2009-10. The Eurozone economy contracted by 2.7%, with the UK falling by 3.7% in the 12 months ended December 2009.

The collapse in private business investment and decline in consumption levels due to high unemployment rates led to low capacity utilisation in the steel industry in the first half of the year. Europe and the US were the most affected regions, being in the eye of the storm, but there were cascading effects across other geographies as well, including emerging economies like India.

The immediate impact on the steel industry was the sharp decline in volume due to the lack of credit among customers. As a consequence steel prices across the world declined significantly. In order to match the reduced demand, steel companies, especially in the US and Europe, reduced their capacity utilisation by temporarily taking capacity off stream. However in emerging economies like India, the credit shortage was not as acute as in the western world and so demand conditions continued to be relatively stable, even though prices dropped significantly in line with the global pricing scenario. The South East Asian economies too witnessed a demand contraction in 2009, partly due to domestic issues, as in Thailand, or due to lower economic activity, especially in the construction sector, resulting from risk aversion and credit concerns.

 Tata Steel Europe recorded a turnaround in the second half of the year. How was this achieved?

2009-10 was really a year of two halves for Tata Steel Europe (TSE). During the first half of the year the European operations were significantly affected by market conditions, which led us to temporarily shut down one Blast Furnace in each of our sites at IJmuiden, Port Talbot and Scunthorpe. This led to capacity utilisation rates falling to as low as 53% in the first quarter of the financial year. In addition the Company faced serious challenges at its Teesside facility due to the sudden and unilateral termination of a 10-year Offtake Agreement by 4 international customers of the slab produced in Teesside. The Company was consequently left exposed to the highly volatile international slab market, as Teesside slab cannot be used internally beyond the volumes agreed under the Offtake agreement. These unforeseeable developments affected the Company severely and resulted in significant losses in the first half of the year. A detailed financial analysis shows the majority of the full year EBITDA losses at TSE resulted from the action of the Offtakers.

Despite these adversities, the Company's employees exhibited remarkable tenacity in weathering the downturn during this challenging period. The Company continued on its path towards delivering the savings identified under the 'Weathering the Storm' programme, which totalled almost £ 866 million during the year, as well as implementing the 'Fit for the Future' restructuring programme. While top-line revenues at the European operations declined by almost 35% due to lower volumes and prices, very significant measures to bring about operating cost savings were undertaken to offset some of the resulting losses. Cost reduction is a continuing activity across our businesses in Europe, as is productivity improvement and working capital management. These enormous achievements have been realised despite very serious challenges in the market.

In the second half of the financial year market conditions started to improve gradually and the Company began to bring back on stream some of capacity it had idled, although pricing pressures continued throughout virtually the whole year. The Company launched several initiatives aimed at serving the market and customers better through the 'Customer First' programme and also started investments to improve the supply chain process across the Company. Increased capacity utilisation rates, a better cost base and an improved pricing scenario helped the Company post a turnaround in the European operations from the December 2009 quarter onwards. However, having run the Teesside operations for almost 10 months after the Offtakers walked out of the Agreement and having incurred severe losses, the Company had regrettably to take the decision to partially mothball the iron and steel making facilities in Teesside, while continuing to seek long-term solutions for the site.

On a year-end analysis, Tata Steel Europe registered a significant turnaround in the second half of the year with an EBITDA of around £ 297 million compared to an EBITDA loss of £ 476 million in the first half of the year. The recently launched initiatives on 'Customer First' and supply chain management are expected to help the Company's performance further in the future.

Table 3.19 – Market Conditions

Go-Ahead Group Plc – 30 June 2010

Directors' Report – Business Review – Market Overview (extract)

The economic downturn has presented some challenging market conditions for the industry and the impact of public spending cuts remains unclear. However, the fundamentals of public transport remain strong. Growth in the sector is essential to the economic and sustainable future of the UK.

Impact of economic downturn

Two important drivers of transport businesses are economic growth (GDP) and employment. In the 12 months ended June 2010, UK GDP declined by 1.7% and employment rose marginally by 0.36%[1]. Whilst the economic climate made UK market conditions difficult, in particular causing a reduction in discretionary travel, urban bus operations proved to be relatively resilient and the impact on commuter rail franchises was less than some had predicted. This may be in part due to further improvements in service quality and value for money compared with other modes of transport. In addition, there has been a focus on cost reduction across the industry to limit the adverse impact of the economic downturn on margins.

Rail franchise reform

The recession has highlighted issues with the existing rail franchise model. In November 2009, the East Coast inter-city franchise was handed back to the Government. At present almost all franchises which are eligible for revenue support are receiving it. This situation is not beneficial to the Government or the industry and as a result in July 2010 the new Government published a consultation document entitled "Shaping the future of rail franchising." Whilst this is still at the consultation stage we see the potential changes outlined in the document as a positive step for the rail industry and look forward to working with the new Government.

Department for Transport public spending cuts

In June 2010 the Government announced its initial cuts to transport spending. It stated that £683m will be cut from the Department for Transport's £22bn budget for the 2010/11 financial year as part of the programme of cuts to tackle the national budget deficit.

To date, little additional detail around the proposed cuts has been published. More information and further spending reductions are expected in the Comprehensive Spending Review in October 2010. It is believed that many of the savings will come from large scale infrastructure projects which would not directly affect day-to-day public transport services. However, there are some risks to public transport operators, with the bus industry potentially exposed to cuts. The table opposite shows the main risks, consequences and certain mitigating factors.

Broadly speaking, rail operators are protected from cuts in transport spending because franchise contracts, which typically last for around eight years, are legally binding.

Sector activity

In April 2010 Deutsche Bahn announced that a recommended cash offer had been agreed to purchase Arriva. The transaction completed in August 2010 and this means there are now four listed UK public transport groups in the UK: Go-Ahead, FirstGroup, National Express and Stagecoach. The UK public transport market is the most liberalised in Europe but the Continental European market is in the process of becoming more deregulated. A number of European players operate in the UK public transport market, including SNCF, Ned Railways, Transdev and Deutsche Bahn.

Long term growth

We remain cautious on the near term outlook for the UK economy as the new Government begins to tackle the UK's budget deficit. However, despite the near term uncertainty, we believe in the fundamental strengths of public transport and long term growth in the sector. An efficient public transport system strengthens the economy, creates jobs, reduces traffic congestion and air pollution, and helps tackle social exclusion. This is recognised by the Government and other major political parties, with a clear acceptance that the private sector is best placed to deliver and grow these services.

"THE GOVERNMENT BELIEVES THAT A MODERN TRANSPORT INFRASTRUCTURE IS ESSENTIAL FOR A DYNAMIC AND ENTREPRENEURIAL ECONOMY."

New Government, May 2010

Potential impacts of Government transport spending cuts

Description	Approximate total Government funding per annum[2]	Relevance to Go-Ahead	Potential consequences/ mitigation
Bus service operators grant (BSOG) Typically bus operators receive a fuel duty rebate of 43 pence per litre. See page 34 for more information on the composition of Go-Ahead's fuel costs.	£500 million	Go-Ahead receives approximately £48m through BSOG, with just over half in London. Equivalent to around 8% of bus revenue.	In London any changes to BSOG are likely to be passed on to TfL on contract renewal. Outside London, operators would need to look at ways to recover the extra costs, potentially through network reduction and fare increases.
Bus concessionary fares Currently anyone aged 60 or over is eligible to travel for free on any off peak local bus service in England. Local authorities receive a fund from the Government which they use to reimburse bus operators a percentage of the full fare.	£1.2 billion	Concessionary passengers represent around 30% of Go-Ahead's deregulated bus passengers and around 20% of deregulated bus revenue, equivalent to approximately £60 million. Overall, our average reimbursement rates are around 50-60%. In London we are not exposed to the scheme as we do not collect passenger revenue.	The concessionary fares scheme has proved very popular and it is believed it would be difficult for the Government to withdraw it completely. However, if the fund reduced and eligibility changed, operators would need to look at ways to recover the extra costs, potentially through network reduction and fare increases.
Tendered bus services Transport for London (TfL) tenders bus routes in the capital. Outside London, bus routes which are not commercially viable, such as non-frequent rural services, are tendered by local authorities.	£1.2 billion Includes subsidy to TfL of c.£600m	Go-Ahead operates around 21% of the London bus market. Less than 10% of Go-Ahead's deregulated operations are tendered. We focus on high density commuter areas where we operate commercially run services.	Bus is the most frequently used mode of transport in London and is vital to the capital. TfL's business plan 2009/10-2017/18 outlines ways to reduce the bus subsidy whilst maintaining the network. Outside London, some rural routes could be withdrawn but it is unlikely to have a material effect on Go-Ahead.

3.126 The introduction of new products or services is often a factor that affects a company's performance. The example in Table 3.20 gives a company's explanation of the impact of new products.

Table 3.20 –Effect of new products on performance

Johnson & Johnson – Annual Report – 2 January 2011

Management's Discussion and Analysis of Results of Operations and Financial Condition (extract)

> **MANAGEMENT'S OBJECTIVES**
> The Company manages within a strategic framework aimed at achieving sustainable growth. To accomplish this, the Company's management operates the business consistent with certain strategic principles that have proven successful over time. To this end, the Company participates in growth areas in human health care and is committed to attaining leadership positions in these growth areas through the development of high quality, innovative products and services. New products introduced within the past five years accounted for approximately 25% of 2010 sales. In 2010, $6.8 billion, or 11.1% of sales, was invested in research and development. This investment reflects management's commitment to the importance of ongoing development of new and differentiated products and services to sustain long-term growth.

3.127 Where a company operates in a number of different territories and has a number of different product lines that are affected by different trends and factors (either economic or non-economic), analysis of performance showing this level of detail should be given. In Table 3.21, Group Five Limited explains the geographic drivers of its business and presents information about each of those geographic areas (only west Africa is shown here for illustration purposes).

Table 3.21 Geographic drivers

Group Five Limited Annual Report – 30 June 2010

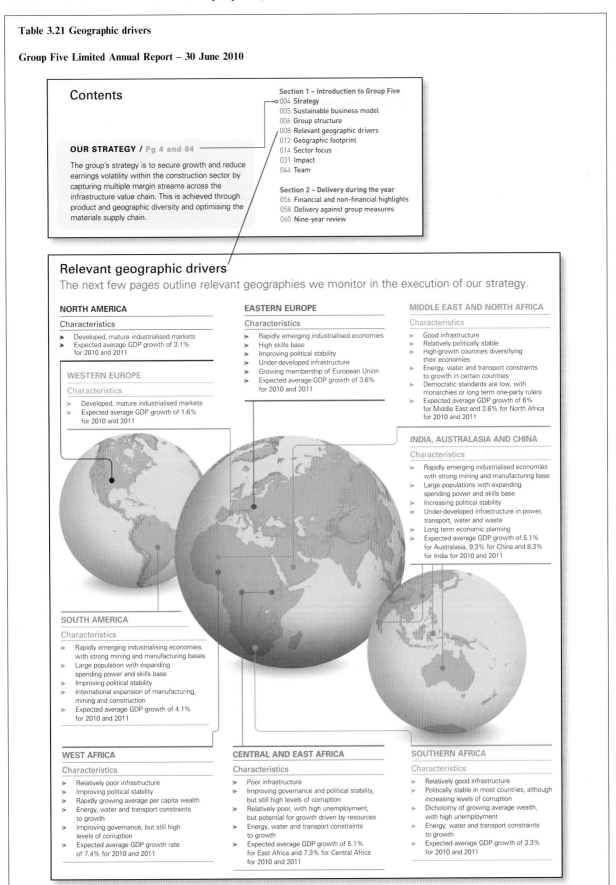

Contents

OUR STRATEGY / Pg 4 and 84

The group's strategy is to secure growth and reduce earnings volatility within the construction sector by capturing multiple margin streams across the infrastructure value chain. This is achieved through product and geographic diversity and optimising the materials supply chain.

Relevant geographic drivers

The next few pages outline relevant geographies we monitor in the execution of our strategy.

NORTH AMERICA

Characteristics

- Developed, mature industrialised markets
- Expected average GDP growth of 3.1% for 2010 and 2011

WESTERN EUROPE

Characteristics

- Developed, mature industrialised markets
- Expected average GDP growth of 1.6% for 2010 and 2011

EASTERN EUROPE

Characteristics

- Rapidly emerging industrialised economies
- High skills base
- Improving political stability
- Under-developed infrastructure
- Growing membership of European Union
- Expected average GDP growth of 3.6% for 2010 and 2011

MIDDLE EAST AND NORTH AFRICA

Characteristics

- Good infrastructure
- Relatively politically stable
- High-growth countries diversifying their economies
- Energy, water and transport constraints to growth in certain countries
- Democratic standards are low, with monarchies or long term one-party rulers
- Expected average GDP growth of 6% for Middle East and 3.6% for North Africa for 2010 and 2011

INDIA, AUSTRALASIA AND CHINA

Characteristics

- Rapidly emerging industrialised economies with strong mining and manufacturing base
- Large populations with expanding spending power and skills base
- Increasing political stability
- Under-developed infrastructure in power, transport, water and waste
- Long term economic planning
- Expected average GDP growth of 5.1% for Australasia, 9.3% for China and 8.3% for India for 2010 and 2011

SOUTH AMERICA

Characteristics

- Rapidly emerging industrialising economies, with strong mining and manufacturing bases
- Large population with expanding spending power and skills base
- Improving political stability
- International expansion of manufacturing, mining and construction
- Expected average GDP growth of 4.1% for 2010 and 2011

WEST AFRICA

Characteristics

- Relatively poor infrastructure
- Improving political stability
- Rapidly growing average per capita wealth
- Energy, water and transport constraints to growth
- Improving governance, but still high levels of corruption
- Expected average GDP growth rate of 7.4% for 2010 and 2011

CENTRAL AND EAST AFRICA

Characteristics

- Poor infrastructure
- Improving governance and political stability, but still high levels of corruption
- Relatively poor, with high unemployment, but potential for growth driven by resources
- Energy, water and transport constraints to growth
- Expected average GDP growth of 5.1% for East Africa and 7.3% for Central Africa for 2010 and 2011

SOUTHERN AFRICA

Characteristics

- Relatively good infrastructure
- Politically stable in most countries, although increasing levels of corruption
- Dichotomy of growing average wealth, with high unemployment
- Energy, water and transport constraints to growth
- Expected average GDP growth of 3.3% for 2010 and 2011

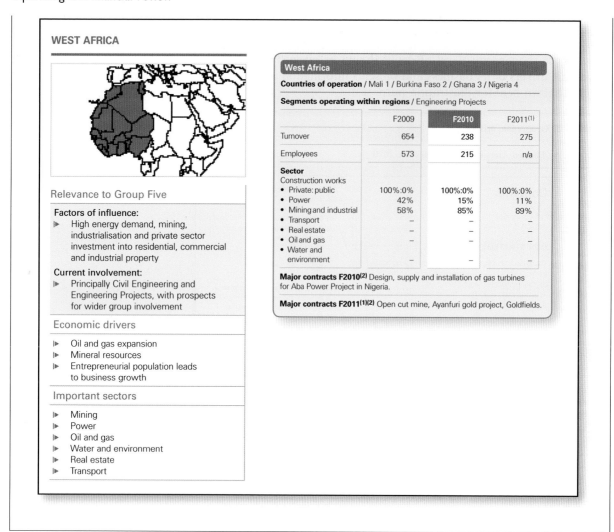

WEST AFRICA

Relevance to Group Five

Factors of influence:

▸ High energy demand, mining, industrialisation and private sector investment into residential, commercial and industrial property

Current involvement:

▸ Principally Civil Engineering and Engineering Projects, with prospects for wider group involvement

Economic drivers

▸ Oil and gas expansion
▸ Mineral resources
▸ Entrepreneurial population leads to business growth

Important sectors

▸ Mining
▸ Power
▸ Oil and gas
▸ Water and environment
▸ Real estate
▸ Transport

West Africa

Countries of operation / Mali 1 / Burkina Faso 2 / Ghana 3 / Nigeria 4

Segments operating within regions / Engineering Projects

	F2009	F2010	F2011[1]
Turnover	654	238	275
Employees	573	215	n/a
Sector			
Construction works			
• Private:public	100%:0%	100%:0%	100%:0%
• Power	42%	15%	11%
• Mining and industrial	58%	85%	89%
• Transport	–	–	–
• Real estate	–	–	–
• Oil and gas	–	–	–
• Water and environment	–	–	–

Major contracts F2010[2] Design, supply and installation of gas turbines for Aba Power Project in Nigeria.

Major contracts F2011[1][2] Open cut mine, Ayanfuri gold project, Goldfields.

Acquisitions and disposals

3.128 Another factor that can have significant impact on a company's current development and performance is changes in the business from acquisitions or disposals. Investors want to know the rationale for any acquisitions and whether the acquisitions have delivered value to the entity. In Table 3.22, United Business Media plc describes the basis for selecting targets for acquisition and describes what the company expects from its investments.

Table 3.22 – Acquisition strategy and returns on investment

United Business Media Limited Annual Report and Accounts–31 December 2010

UBM Strategy (extract)

2.
Growth through acquisition
We invest in strategic acquisitions in order
to strengthen our existing portfolio or provide
exposure to markets we feel are attractive.

Target selection

We select targets which are complementary to our existing business in terms of geography, segment or community. Below is a table showing the acquisitions made in 2010.

Integration process

In order to facilitate a smooth process, executives are given responsibility for integration. The integration of the Canon acquisition, completed in October, is progressing well.

Strict financial discipline

A target acquisition also has to satisfy financial criteria with projected post tax ROI* exceeding 8% within the first full year of ownership.

	Consideration £m	Pre tax return on investment % 2008	2009	2010
2008 acquisitions	49.9	12.4	6.5	7.8
2009 acquisitions	26.5	–	14.8	4.5[1]
2010 acquisitions[2]	258.0	–	–	10.6
Total	334.4			10.0

2010 acquisitions	Geography	Segment	Community	Initial consideration net of cash acquired* £m	Expected contingent and deferred consideration £m	Estimated total consideration £m
E Commerce Expo	UK	Events	Technology	0.4	1.2	1.6
Sign China	China	Events	Other	6.3	4.3	10.6
DesignCon	USA	Events	Technology	0.9	–	0.9
Sienna – Concrete show	Brazil	Events	Built Environment	6.5	6.8	13.3
NavalShore	Brazil	Events	Trade & Transport	1.2	0.1	1.3
Children – Baby – Maternity – Expo	China	Events	Lifestyle	6.3	4.2	10.5
The Routes Development Group	UK	Events	Trade & Transport	6.8	1.3	8.1
Canon Communications	USA	Events	Technology/Health	182.9	–	182.9
Publishing Expo	UK	Events	Other	0.2	–	0.2
DNA-13	Canada	TD&M	News Distribution	4.0	0.6	4.6
PR Newswire do Brasil	Brazil	TD&M	News Distribution	0.7	0.1	0.8
PR Newswire Argentina	Argentina	TD&M	News Distribution	0.0	–	0.0
Corporate360	Hong Kong	TD&M	News Distribution	0.2	0.7	0.9
Hors Antenne	Europe	TD&M	News Distribution	5.3	2.7	8.0
SharedVue	USA	DS	Technology	0.2	4.9	5.1
CenTradeX	USA	DS	Trade & Transport	0.3	0.1	0.4
UM Paper	China	DS	Paper	0.1	0.2	0.3
JOC Exchange (Triton)	USA	DS	Trade & Transport	0.3	1.7	2.0
Lead-In Research	UK	DS	Built Environment	0.9	0.3	1.2
Game Advertising Online	New Zealand	Online	Technology	0.6	3.0	3.6
Astound	USA	Online	Technology	0.1	1.0	1.1
OBGYN.net	USA	Online	Health	0.5	0.1	0.6
Total				224.7	33.3	258.0

1 Performance reflects reported results for The Fuel Team which was integrated into PR Newswire in 2010. Excluding it, the pre tax return on acquisition would have been 8.6% for 2009 acquisitions.
2 2010 return on investment calculated on a full year pro-forma basis.
* See explanation of UBM's business measures on page 51.

3.129   The example in Table 3.23 illustrates the impact on performance of acquisitions for a drinks company in total and by division. The performance of the acquired businesses is set out separately and the divisional analysis of results distinguishes between the organic and acquired businesses (only the distribution segment is shown here).

Table 3.23 – Acquired businesses

c&c group plc – Annual Report – 28 February 2010

Operations review (extract)

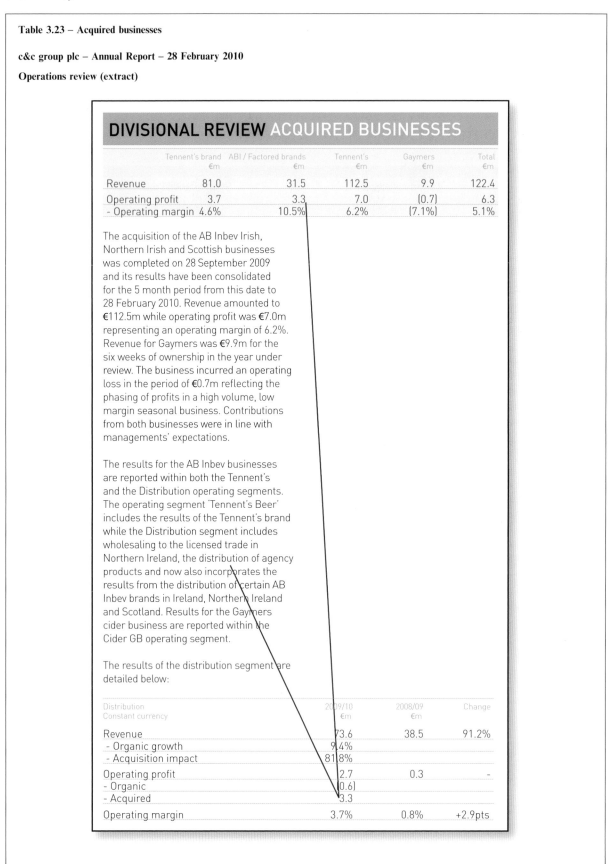

DIVISIONAL REVIEW ACQUIRED BUSINESSES

	Tennent's brand €m	ABI / Factored brands €m	Tennent's €m	Gaymers €m	Total €m
Revenue	81.0	31.5	112.5	9.9	122.4
Operating profit	3.7	3.3	7.0	(0.7)	6.3
- Operating margin	4.6%	10.5%	6.2%	(7.1%)	5.1%

The acquisition of the AB Inbev Irish, Northern Irish and Scottish businesses was completed on 28 September 2009 and its results have been consolidated for the 5 month period from this date to 28 February 2010. Revenue amounted to €112.5m while operating profit was €7.0m representing an operating margin of 6.2%. Revenue for Gaymers was €9.9m for the six weeks of ownership in the year under review. The business incurred an operating loss in the period of €0.7m reflecting the phasing of profits in a high volume, low margin seasonal business. Contributions from both businesses were in line with managements' expectations.

The results for the AB Inbev businesses are reported within both the Tennent's and the Distribution operating segments. The operating segment 'Tennent's Beer' includes the results of the Tennent's brand while the Distribution segment includes wholesaling to the licensed trade in Northern Ireland, the distribution of agency products and now also incorporates the results from the distribution of certain AB Inbev brands in Ireland, Northern Ireland and Scotland. Results for the Gaymers cider business are reported within the Cider GB operating segment.

The results of the distribution segment are detailed below:

Distribution Constant currency	2009/10 €m	2008/09 €m	Change
Revenue	73.6	38.5	91.2%
- Organic growth	9.4%		
- Acquisition impact	81.8%		
Operating profit	2.7	0.3	-
- Organic	(0.6)		
- Acquired	3.3		
Operating margin	3.7%	0.8%	+2.9pts

3.130 Similarly, the disposal of operations will affect a company's development and performance. Table 3.23.1 shows an example of a company that made disposals of businesses during the year and shows the impact of one of the disposals on the relevant division.

Table 3.23.1 — Disposal of operation

Greencore group plc – Annual Report and Accounts – 24 September 2010

Chairman's statement (extract)

A key highlight of the year was the successful disposal programme with the Group's Malt, Water and Continental convenience food businesses disposed of for an aggregate total consideration of €142.3m[4], including cash received on completion of €129.4m[5], with an aggregate surplus on disposal of €2.3m. Convenience Foods trading was very strong in the year with operating profit[2] from continuing operations[1] 21.1% ahead of FY09. The Group exited FY10 as a focused, strong performing convenience foods business with 31.8% less net debt than at the end of September 2009. Net debt was €193.4m on 24 September 2010 compared to €283.5m at the end of the previous financial year.

Divisional review ingredients and property (extract)

Ingredients & Property
Less than 10% of Group Activity
Ingredients & Property represents less than 10% of overall Group activity following the disposal of Malt. The performance of Malt, previously reported within this division, has been separately disclosed as a discontinued activity. The Group's remaining Ingredients & Property activity recorded a solid year in difficult market conditions. An operating profit of €5.6m was recorded compared to a profit of €6.1m in FY09 reflecting reduced molasses and edible oils volumes in the year.

Malt
Disposed of in March 2010
Malt was disposed of on 26 March 2010 and as a consequence the FY10 performance reflects its contribution for half the financial year compared to a full year in FY09. The overall malt margin was maintained due to carry-over volumes on long-term agreement contracts entered into in previous years.

Foreign exchange

3.131 Where an entity undertakes a significant volume of transactions in foreign currencies, the impact of currency exchange rates may be a useful disclosure in the OFR.

3.132 Table 3.23.2 illustrates the effect of changes in exchange rates on net income.

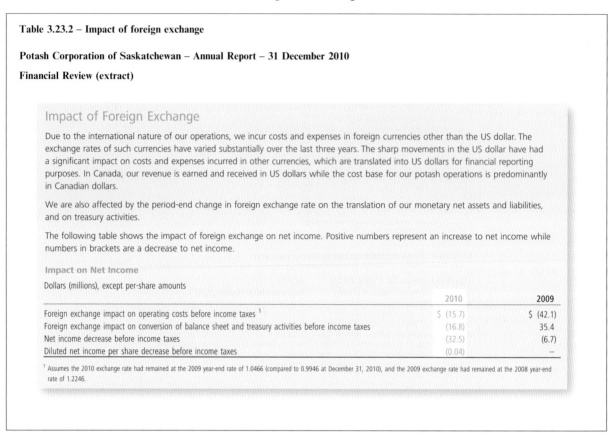

Table 3.23.2 – Impact of foreign exchange

Potash Corporation of Saskatchewan – Annual Report – 31 December 2010

Financial Review (extract)

Impact of Foreign Exchange

Due to the international nature of our operations, we incur costs and expenses in foreign currencies other than the US dollar. The exchange rates of such currencies have varied substantially over the last three years. The sharp movements in the US dollar have had a significant impact on costs and expenses incurred in other currencies, which are translated into US dollars for financial reporting purposes. In Canada, our revenue is earned and received in US dollars while the cost base for our potash operations is predominantly in Canadian dollars.

We are also affected by the period-end change in foreign exchange rate on the translation of our monetary net assets and liabilities, and on treasury activities.

The following table shows the impact of foreign exchange on net income. Positive numbers represent an increase to net income while numbers in brackets are a decrease to net income.

Impact on Net Income

Dollars (millions), except per-share amounts

	2010	2009
Foreign exchange impact on operating costs before income taxes [1]	$ (15.7)	$ (42.1)
Foreign exchange impact on conversion of balance sheet and treasury activities before income taxes	(16.8)	35.4
Net income decrease before income taxes	(32.5)	(6.7)
Diluted net income per share decrease before income taxes	(0.04)	–

[1] Assumes the 2010 exchange rate had remained at the 2009 year-end rate of 1.0466 (compared to 0.9946 at December 31, 2010), and the 2009 exchange rate had remained at the 2008 year-end rate of 1.2246.

3.133 Many companies express figures in the OFR in terms of constant currency, so as to show the trends in performance, excluding the effect of exchange rates. (See para 3.65)

Other factors affecting performance

3.134 The discussion and analysis should also include any other factors that have affected performance in the period under review. This includes those for which the effect cannot be specifically quantified, as well as any specific exceptional items that are quantified and disclosed in the financial statements. Events range from natural disasters that may affect entities operating in the geographical regions affected, to wars and terrorist attacks, fraud and other irregularities, major strategy changes involving acquisitions and disposals or major reorganisations, regulatory fines and sanctions and so on.

3.135 The OFR should analyse the main trends and factors that the directors consider are likely to affect future prospects. [RS (OFR) para 47]. The directors will, therefore, need to consider the potential future significance of issues in deciding whether or not to include an analysis of them in the OFR. [RS (OFR) para 49].

3.136 An example of disclosure relating to trends and factors likely to affect future prospects is given in Table 3.8. Market conditions are described for each segment, with an indication of the key parameters that the directors consider of potential significance for the company's future development and performance. Only one segment is included in the example for illustration purposes.

3.137 Paragraph 48 of the reporting statement states:

"The main trends and factors likely to affect the future development and performance will vary according to the nature of the business, but could include the development of known new products and services or the benefits expected from capital investment. The OFR should discuss the current level of

investment expenditure together with planned future expenditure and shall explain how that investment is directed to assist the achievement of business objectives. Any assumptions underlying the main trends and factors should be disclosed." [RS (OFR) para 48].

3.138 Investment expenditure is not defined in the reporting statement. The definition used by a company should be disclosed in the OFR to avoid ambiguity and should be wide enough that it enables users of financial statements to obtain an understanding of its impact on the company's future. The definition used may be wider than the definition of 'investing cash flows' used in the preparation of the cash flow statement (see further chapter 30 of the Manual of Accounting — IFRS for the UK and the Manual of Accounting — UK GAAP) and may include:

■ Development of new products and services.

■ Expansion into new markets.

■ Pure and applied research that may lead to potential new products, services or processes.

■ Investment in brand equity, for example through advertising and marketing activities.

■ Technical support to customers.

■ Personnel policies and practices, including employee training.

■ Refurbishment and maintenance programmes.

3.139 In Table 3.24, Royal Mail Holdings plc describes its modernisation programme.

Table 3.24 Modernisation programme

Royal Mail Holdings plc – Annual Reports and Financial Statements – 27 March 2011

Modernising Royal Mail (extract)

Modernising Royal Mail

Our modernisation programme is one of the biggest transformations in UK industry.

A major programme
A major programme to modernise Royal Mail is under way – it is one of the biggest transformations in UK industry. Significant progress has been made over the last year, but much remains to be done.

Before the current modernisation programme started in 2007, Royal Mail did not have the latest technology to sequence mail to the order of a postman and woman's walk. Most of the mail was still hand sorted before being delivered. Postmen and women carried the full mail weight on their shoulders. All this is changing – fast.

The programme is led by Mark Higson, Executive Director and Managing Director, Operations and Modernisation. A dedicated team is working to update every aspect of our operations – collections, processing, sorting and delivery.

Around £400 million was invested by Royal Mail Group in modernisation this year.

Why is modernisation important for customers and external stakeholders?
Revenues are falling as the mail market continues to decline. Fewer mail items are being handled every year and we have too much capacity given this smaller mail market.

Modernisation is about generating cost savings faster than the decline in revenues. It is at the heart of ensuring a sound, secure and sustainable Universal Service for everybody in the UK. It is as fundamental as that.

Modernisation is about a more innovative Royal Mail and a more customer-responsive business. While traditional 'white letters' have seen a dramatic decline, packet volumes are increasing following the boom in online retailing. Modernisation enables us to provide new customer solutions such as tracking to the doorstep that better reflect the reality of a changed – and changing – mail market, and crucial to the competitiveness and commercial success of Royal Mail.

The pace will intensify
We are committed to fully engaging and involving our people as we implement these changes, which are affecting the working lives of more than 100,000 colleagues. We are working closely with the Communication Workers Union (CWU) under the Business Transformation agreement reached in early 2010. As our Chief Executive said: "The peak period of change is under way – now".

Our postmen and women are our main asset and modernisation is challenging for many of them. They may need to work differently, there are changes to their start and finish times, more efficient working methods and different delivery rounds. We are also significantly reducing the size of our workforce. Since 2002, around 45,000 people have left Royal Mail Group as part of our ongoing change programme.

As part of the Group's modernisation programme, 378 walk sequencing machines have been installed at mail centres across the UK to improve efficiencies in the sorting process. The equipment automatically sorts the mail into the exact sequence of a postman or woman's walk.

We are committed to working with our people and the CWU to manage operational job reductions on a voluntary basis.

Many of the changes are improving the working lives of our colleagues. They include the installation of modern technology and better equipment for our postmen and women, including more trolleys, shared vans to handle packets and parcels, and handheld devices to record signatures when mail is delivered.

Most importantly of all, modernisation is about ensuring that our core letters business is placed on a sound, secure and sustainable footing. That is the key to ensuring a viable business and protecting as many jobs as possible.

Our recent progress
In the 12 months since we signed the Business Transformation agreement with the CWU, we have made significant progress. A significant number of delivery office revisions have been completed and major changes have been made to our mail centre and transport networks. We have also reduced accidents in the workplace by 25% in 2010-11 – a key and vital improvement – and met our licence targets for First Class and Second Class mail quality of service after force majeure adjustments for volcanic ash and extreme weather in December and January.

Nevertheless, the programme has taken longer to start fully delivering results than we planned. So, much more needs to be done.

Modernising Royal Mail continued

Key examples of significant progress

- Installed 378 sequencing machines

- Introduced 38 'intelligent' Letter Sorting Machines which can sort 38,500 letters an hour, nearly twice the speed of older machines

- Upgraded and extended 138 Integrated Mail Processing machines

- Sequencing 34% of the mail

- Closed 12 mail centres, and, following extensive consultations, announced the closure of a further 16

Modernisation – the next phase

As we reported earlier, the key phase in the modernisation programme is now.

We are introducing new delivery methods throughout our 1,371 delivery offices and, in the next year, will complete this delivery transformation in more than 700 offices, over 50%.

This is a major and far-reaching exercise. Traditional methods involving postmen and women carrying the mail on foot or bicycle are being replaced by the use of 5,000 high-capacity trolleys and 11,300 two-person vans. Delivery rounds are being changed so that they will be more effective and efficient.

The pace of change in our mail centres will continue. We expect that around half of the mail centres could close by 2016-2017. We are focused on delivering all the benefits of the modernisation programme as quickly and effectively as possible, working closely with our people and with the CWU.

Many postmen and women are now using new equipment such as trolleys, replacing the need to carry mail by foot or bicycle.

World Class Mail

World Class Mail is revolutionising the way we work. Developed within Royal Mail, based on leading global practice and expert advice, World Class Mail is a unique and comprehensive system for improving safety, customer service, quality and productivity. A key element is engagement with our people to ensure they are fully involved in all aspects of our modernisation.

World Class Mail is already in operation in 24 mail centres and seven delivery sectors. This year will see the approach introduced in all our mail centres and an extension to many more delivery offices and collection hubs.

Root cause analysis of problem areas by employee teams is at the heart of World Class Mail. Safety is the first of its 10 improvement 'pillars'. At Greenford mail centre, the packet sorting conveyor area was the scene of six accidents in the year before World Class Mail was introduced and 50 working days were lost to injury. Since the programme was put in place, the area has been accident-free for 700 days – a remarkable achievement by the local team.

We were pleased when the World Class Manufacturing Association recognised the progress and achievements of our people last autumn in three mail centres – Gatwick, Cardiff and Belfast – by awarding them Bronze Awards at a ceremony in the Greenwich Maritime Museum in London.

Last October, teams at mail centres in Cardiff (pictured), Gatwick and Northern Ireland were presented with Awards by the World Class Manufacturing Association. They were recognised for their efforts to create safer and more productive places to work, in turn helping to improve quality of service.

3.140 Discussion should also include explanations of variations in expenditure from year to year.

3.141 Table 3.24.1 shows discussion of capital expenditure, distinguishing between 'sustaining' and 'expansionary' capital expenditure.

Table 3.24.1 – Capital expenditure

Xstrata plc – Annual Report – 31 December 2010

Financial review (extract)

Consolidated capital expenditure
Capital expenditure summary
(excludes deferred stripping expenditure)

$m	Year ended 31.12.10	Year ended 31.12.09
Alloys	126	114
Coal	568	424
Copper	572	498
Nickel	237	93
Zinc	316	133
Technology	2	2
Unallocated	2	1
Total sustaining	**1,823**	1,265
Attributable sustaining	*1,774*	*1,243*
Alloys	141	49
Coal	1,430	687
Copper	1,162	436
Iron Ore	67	23
Nickel	1,319	1,049
Zinc	177	114
Technology	–	1
Total expansionary	**4,296**	2,359
Attributable expansionary	*3,677*	*1,993*
Alloys	267	163
Coal	1,998	1,111
Copper	1,734	934
Iron Ore	67	23
Nickel	1,556	1,142
Zinc	493	247
Technology	2	3
Unallocated	2	1
Total	**6,119**	3,624
Attributable total	*5,451*	3,236

Total expansionary capital spending increased by 82% to $4.3 billion in 2010 as Xstrata approached peak spending at a number of major growth projects that will reach production within the next four years and underpin a 50% increase in volumes over 2009 levels by 2014. Investment was also accelerated to progress pre-feasibility and feasibility studies into the next tier of growth projects that will support significant further growth.

Capital expenditure at Xstrata Nickel's flagship Koniambo project in New Caledonia rose to $1.2 billion in 2010 and the project remains on schedule for commissioning in 2012.

Three new operations were commissioned in 2010: Nickel Rim South poly-metallic mine in Sudbury, Canada, the Goedgevonden thermal coal mine in South Africa, and Blakefield South underground coal mine in New South Wales.

Ten growth projects were approved during the year, including the Las Bambas and Antapaccay projects in Peru, which will require $4.2 billion and $1.5 billion respectively to completion, and the Ravensworth North and Ulan West coal projects in New South Wales at a capital cost of $1.4 billion and $1.3 billion respectively. At Antapaccay, early stage construction is already underway.

Construction continued to progress at Xstrata Copper's Lomas Bayas II project and full production is expected to start in 2012. At Ernest Henry mine in Queensland, construction work continued on the underground mine, and the magnetite facility base plant became operational at the end of 2010. In Peru, Antamina's expansion project to expand milling capacity to 130,000 tonnes started in the first quarter of 2010 and is expected to commence commissioning by the end of 2011.

The ATCOM East coal project in South Africa remains within budget and is on schedule to be commissioned during 2011, ramping up to full production in 2014 at an annual rate of four million tonnes per annum. The ATCOM East project is the second, after Goedgevonden, of three large-scale, lower-cost, open cut mine complexes that will eventually account for 90% of Xstrata Coal's South African production. The Mangoola greenfield project is now two thirds complete and on track to begin production in 2011, ramping up to full annual production of eight million tonnes of export and domestic coal.

In September 2010, the approval of a second phase expansion of the Lion ferrochrome smelter was announced and construction is due to commence in the first quarter of 2011. During the year, construction activities began on Project Tswelopele, a 600,000 tonnes per annum pelletizing and sintering plant that is on track to be fully operational in 2013. The development of the western and eastern declines at Eland continued and mining operations are expected to start in the first quarter and second quarter of 2011 respectively.

In May, development started on the Black Star Deeps project to extend the life of the open cut mine by four years. Following the completion of the feasibility study in the second quarter of 2010, work progressed on the Bracemac-McLeod zinc project in Canada. In October 2010, the AUD274 million George Fisher Underground zinc mine expansion was approved and will increase zinc concentrate production by 28% to 259,000 tonnes per annum by 2013.

3.142 Table 3.25 illustrates how investing in training for employees is part of the overall business model.

Table 3.25 Investing to implement business model

J Sainsbury plc – Annual Report — 19 March 2011

Our business model (extract)

Our business model

About Sainsbury's

J Sainsbury plc was founded in 1869 and today operates a total of 934 stores comprising 557 supermarkets and 377 convenience stores. It jointly owns Sainsbury's Bank with Lloyds Banking Group and has two property joint ventures with Land Securities Group PLC and The British Land Company PLC.

The Sainsbury's brand is built upon a heritage of providing customers with healthy, safe, fresh and tasty food. Quality and fair prices go hand-in-hand with a responsible approach

to business. Sainsbury's stores have a particular emphasis on fresh food and we strive to innovate continuously and improve products in line with our customer needs.

We now have 21 million customer transactions a week and have a market share of over 16 per cent. Our large stores offer around 30,000 products and we offer complementary non-food products and services in many of our stores. An internet-based home delivery shopping service is also available to over 93 per cent of UK households. We employ around 150,000 colleagues.

High level progress report on five areas of focus of business model

Our business model continued
Five areas of focus – progress highlights

Great food at fair prices

21m

Customer transactions on average every week, a million more than last year

- 21 million customer transactions on average every week, a million more than last year
- A 16.3 per cent market share in the UK, up by 0.2 per cent on last year
- Over 5,000 new or improved own-brand products launched, including the major re-launch of *Taste the Difference*
- Six food colleges opened as part of our *Great Food* programme. Up to 10,000 colleagues will receive training at them each year
- *Meat and Fish Retailer of the Year* and *Drinks Retailer of the Year*

Accelerating the growth of complementary non-food ranges and services

3x

Complementary non-food grew more than three times faster than food sales

- Non-food sales grew more than three times faster than food sales, with many areas of general merchandise growing in excess of 20 per cent
- TU clothing is now the seventh largest clothing brand in the UK by volume
- We re-launched Sainsbury's Energy in a new partnership with British Gas
- Sainsbury's Bank had a strong year, with pre-tax operating profit up over 50 per cent

Reaching more customers through additional channels

£1bn

Our convenience business now provides annual sales of over £1 billion

- Our convenience business now provides annual sales of over £1 billion and we opened a further 47 stores this year
- We were awarded *Convenience Retailer of the Year* at the annual Retail Industry Awards
- Our online groceries business continues to grow, with annual sales up over 20 per cent and weekly orders now over 130,000
- *Click and Collect*, allowing customers to order non-food items online and collect in-store, has been rolled out to over 160 stores this year

Growing supermarket space

15.9%

of gross new space added since March 2009

- We exceeded our two-year space growth target of 15 per cent, as we have grown gross space by 15.9 per cent since March 2009
- This year we opened 21 new stores, 24 extensions and 47 convenience stores
- We added a gross 1.5 million sq ft of space this year, equivalent to 8.5 per cent, and we expect to maintain this momentum into next year
- We were awarded *Community Retailer of the Year* at the annual Retail Industry Awards

Active property management

£10.5bn

Estimated market value of freehold property

- Estimated market value of freehold property increased to £10.5 billion
- Increase of £0.7 billion on last year, including £0.5 billion of property value created through our investment and development activity
- Generated £275 million proceeds from sale and leaseback of property with no further development potential, contributing to total property profits of £108 million

Our values make us different

Great food at fair prices

Accelerating the growth of complementary non-food ranges and services

J Sainsbury plc

Active property management

Reaching more customers through additional channels

Growing supermarket space

Operational excellence

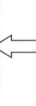

Six new Food Colleges

This year we opened six new food colleges across the country, to help us deliver the very best food and service to customers. The colleges offer training to colleagues working on the meat, fish, deli and hot food counters, as well as our cafés and we anticipate that over 10,000 colleagues will pass through the colleges each year. The food colleges follow on from the successful opening of Sainsbury's bakery college earlier in the year.

Sets investment in training in the context of its business model.

Taste the Difference re-launch

In September we re-launched our premium *Taste the Difference* range, a range of over 1,000 products, to give our tastiest food range ever. This was our biggest ever investment in own-brand, with over 700 new and improved products. The re-launch included a new 'Bistro' range which offers a selection of restaurant-quality starters, mains and desserts made using premium ingredients and the very best cooking methods. Sales of *Taste the Difference* were up by nearly ten per cent over Christmas.

this, we were awarded a BBC Radio 4 *Food and Farming Award* for our work in helping farmers reduce their carbon footprint. We offer British products at their best, when in season and when quality meets our customers' expectations. In Spring, we were number one in the UK for British asparagus and Jersey Royals. We are also number one for English pears and we sell almost one in four of all British apples when in season. We continued our direct-to-store initiative, with over 80 stores receiving strawberries or potatoes direct from local farmers. Nearly 80 per cent of our bakeries bake a selection of products from scratch and they only use British flour for this.

Our British seasonal fish sales were up over 50 per cent over the year and we now offer 100 per cent fresh fish (never frozen) on our counters; in addition we were the first UK supermarket to sell fresh dab as a way to reduce fish being discarded from the catch. We are also proud to be the UK's leading retailer of Marine Stewardship Certified (MSC) fish, with over 80 different sustainable MSC products. In recognition of our efforts, we were awarded *Seafood Retailer of the Year* at the 2010 Retail Industry Awards, a credit to our buying teams and a reflection of our commitment to do the right thing for our environment and sustainable sourcing.

Ethical issues remain important to our customers and, with over 12 per cent of our own-brand products coming from certified sustainable sources, we are meeting their needs. One pound in every four spent on Fairtrade in the UK is spent at a Sainsbury's store and, as more products have been added, our sales of Fairtrade products have reached over £280 million this year. Having been the first ever UK retailer to offer eggs from cage-free birds, all our fresh eggs now meet this standard and the RSPCA Freedom Food criteria. The RSPCA recognised our commitment to animal welfare with the *Most Progress* award at their annual Good Business Awards.

Six new Food Colleges

This year we opened six new food colleges across the country, to help us deliver the very best food and service to customers. The colleges offer training to colleagues working on the meat, fish, deli and hot food counters, as well as our cafés and we anticipate that over 10,000 colleagues will pass through the colleges each year. The food colleges follow on from the successful opening of Sainsbury's bakery college earlier in the year.

£1 in £4 of all Fairtrade sales in the UK are at Sainsbury's

£ £ £ £

It has been an outstanding year for the quality and value of our products and our high standards have been recognised by many other industry awards this year. In July, we won *Meat and Fish Retailer of the Year* at the Nantwich International Cheese Awards; we won over 100 awards at the Fish Awards; we won over 100 awards at the Nantwich International Cheese Awards; and we won nine Quality Food Awards, more than any other retailer. Great food is complemented by great wine and our new *House* range is now one of the UK's fastest-growing wine brands. We won *Drinks Retailer of the Year* at the Drinks Business Awards and enjoyed the most wins at both the International Wines and Spirits Competition and the Quality Drink Awards.

Our leadership position in offering great food, which is also sustainably and ethically sourced, remains key to our customers and we will continue to invest further in our offer as we strive to exceed the standards they expect of us.

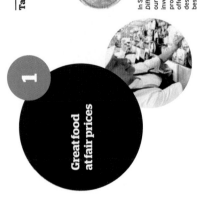

1 Great food at fair prices

Offering safe, healthy, fresh and tasty food is at the heart of what we do. A major area of development this year has been our *Great Food* programme, which aims to ensure we continue to have a market-leading food and wine offer. In particular, our investment in our food counters has made them a destination for many of our customers.

We refreshed the offer, from the range to the display, in 110 stores and have now introduced fresh pizza counters to nearly 140 stores. Over the coming year we will recruit and train more than 500 new counter and café colleagues to meet increased demand at the counters and to support the growth in our cafés. These recruits, as well as up to 10,000 colleagues already working on the meat, fish, deli, hot food counters and cafés, will receive training at one of the six food colleges we have opened across the UK. The colleges provide in-depth training from experts in areas like product knowledge and food preparation, helping us to offer the very best food and service to customers.

Customers remain very loyal to our own-brand products and we sell more proportionately than any of the major supermarkets. This gives us a significant competitive advantage and is an important way of offering our own-brand ranges this year, with over 5,000 new or improved products introduced, including a major re-launch of our *Taste the Difference* range prior to Christmas. This re-launch covered the entire range of over 1,000 products and was our largest ever one-off investment in own-brand. Our core own-brand range offers quality equal to or better than the leading brand but is at least 20 per cent cheaper. Over the next year we will be reviewing this 6,500 product range individually and benchmarking all aspects, including taste, nutrition and packaging, to ensure we offer the best products on the market. This will be our largest ever investment in our own-brand products.

We go to great lengths to source with integrity, and continue to support British agriculture. In recognition of

Resources

3.143 The OFR should include a description of the resources available to the entity and how they are managed. [RS (OFR) para 50]. It should set out the key strengths and resources, tangible and intangible, available to the business that will assist it in pursuing its objectives. This should include, in particular, resources that are not reflected in the balance sheet. Depending on the business' nature, these may include:

- Corporate reputation.

- Brand strength.

- Natural resources.

- Employees.

- Research and development.

- Intellectual capital.

- Licences, patents, copyright and trademarks.

- Market position.

[RS (OFR) para 51].

Other examples not specifically referred to in the standard, include:

- Customer/supplier relationships.

- Strength of proprietary business processes, such as distribution systems.

- Web sites and databases.

- Non-financial aspects of reputation, such as environmental reputation or strength of involvement in and identification with the community.

- Strength of geographical spread or product range.

3.144 As noted in the reporting statement, resources to be disclosed will depend on the nature of the business and the industry in which the company operates. The example in Table 3.26 shows how a company sees its brands as key assets and explains how it has developed them during the year.

Table 3.26 – Resources – brands

LVMH Group – Annual Report – 31 December 2010

Review of operations (extract)

Champagne and wines

In 2010, revenue generated by the Champagne and Wines business amounted to 1,664 million euros. Profit from recurring operations totaled 453 million euros.

Moët & Chandon consolidated its position as the world leader in champagne. The brand fully benefited from the recovery in demand in most of the major consumer countries and recorded remarkable growth in the emerging markets.

The creation of *Moët Ice Impérial*, the first champagne developed to be drunk over ice during the summer, was another illustration of the tradition of innovation and the pioneering spirit of Moët & Chandon. This new product offers a brand new experience and a radically new way to drink champagne. The introduction of the 2002 Vintage, the first since 1930 to have aged for seven years, achieving exceptional levels of maturity and harmony, was the year-end high point and illustrates the wine-making expertise of the brand.

Moët & Chandon expanded its presence and its visibility at international film festivals. The House also organized an extraordinary event at its vineyard during the harvest to celebrate its heritage and its expertise, an event attended by its international ambassador Scarlett Johansson.

Dom Pérignon, an iconic brand, showing strong growth, performed exceptionally well in the United States, Europe and Asia as retail inventories returned to normal levels. The brand organized dynamic events, including VIP dinners to highlight a history that dates back to 1668 at the Abbaye d'Hautvillers. The year 2010 was an exceptional year with the launch of four vintages (Vintage 2002, Rosé Vintage 2000, OEnothèque Vintage 1996 and OEnothèque Rosé Vintage 1990, the first of its kind), which were all received enthusiastically by the trade press. Another unique moment during the year was the tribute to Andy Warhol, the master of Pop Art, through a limited edition produced with the assistance of Central Saint Martin's College of Art and illustrated with an international advertising campaign.

Ruinart, whose strategy is geared primarily to the development of premium cuvées, recorded solid revenue growth in France and abroad. Several new product launches marked by exciting events illustrated the innovative values of the brand, like the *Extraits* box designed by India Mahdavi and the *Fil d'Or*, created by Patricia Urquiola. In the second half of the year, Ruinart launched the "Integrale" case holding its six vintages in France. True to its long -standing ties with the world of art, the brand continued to be present at major contemporary art exhibits and maintained its partnership with the magazine Connaissance des Arts.

Mercier, a brand which has geared its strategy primarily to the French market where it is highly appreciated, continued to expand its presence in its traditional restaurant segment through its original program "Les Lieux de Toujours".

Taking full advantage of the improved economic environment Veuve Clicquot grew substantially in all its markets. The sharp recovery seen in the major traditional countries went hand in hand with the appearance of solid prospects in emerging markets such as Brazil and Russia.

The performance of Veuve Clicquot is based on the constancy of its value strategy, the quality of its wines recognized by excellent ratings, and its tradition of daring and innovation, which was particularly illustrated in 2010 by the success of the *Fridge*, a designer case that suggests both "vintage" and the avant-garde.

Veuve Clicquot also relied on an international event platform that was set up and on a publicity campaign in the new media (internet sites and social networks, expanded relations with bloggers).The end of the year was marked by the happy discovery, reported by the international press, of the oldest bottles of Veuve Clicquot champagne known to date. The intact bottles, found on a wreck off the Alan Islands in the Baltic Sea, date from the mid-19th century and still have admirable organoleptic qualities.

Capitalizing on its fundamentals, Krug implemented a tasting program paying homage to the Grande Cuvée, its emblematic champagne which embodies the values of generosity, excellence and non-conformity. This initiative was highly successful worldwide. The Krug champagnes again earned the top international ratings. The brand focused on giving an opportunity to discover or rediscover its universe and the excellence of its champagnes to representatives from the general and trade press and to preferred consumers during trips to Reims and during an amazing gastronomical evening in Paris prepared by six famous chefs from around the world.

The excellence of the wines developed throughout the world by Estates & Wines has regularly been recognized by many international critics. These wines recorded strong growth in 2010 in all their markets, with a special mention for the Asia-Pacific and Latin American regions.

The Chandon sparkling wines achieved remarkable growth in their domestic markets, and consolidated their leadership position in the super premium category. After its successful launch in Japan and in Asia, the brand continued its internationalization strategy.

The still wine brands of Cloudy Bay (New Zealand) and Terrazas de los Andes (Argentina) recorded excellent results in all markets, as did Newton (California), Numanthia (Spain), Cheval des Andes (Argentina) and Cape Mentelle (Australia) in more selective markets.

Château d'Yquem offered the first sale of a classic vintage, the 2009, which was enthusiastically received by international experts and buyers, particularly in the Asian market. Out of a desire to place its brand within its era, Château d'Yquem created its own blog called "mYquem" and joined its fans in the social networks.

3.145 A further example is given in Table 3.27 where a company reports on key resources it must manage in order to deliver operational scale and capability. Table 3.27.1 identifies the factors contributing to the difference between the market capitalisation and the net asset value of another company.

Table 3.27 – Resources

Capita Group Plc – Annual Report and Accounts – 31 December 2010

4.2

Building scale and capacity and optimising our infrastructure

Aim: to have the right resources in place, both in terms of infrastructure and people, to satisfy clients that we have the operational scale and capability to deliver their requirements.

Progress: We have built up an extensive operational infrastructure and depth of capabilities which enable us to fully support our clients, provide flexible operating models and share economies of scale.

We continuously assess the needs of each business unit to ensure that we have the necessary people, infrastructure and resources for current and future development. Each month we review comprehensive operational management information through the MOB review process enabling us to manage our resources in a way that meets the needs of our clients and delivers our key financial targets. See page 33.

Wherever possible, we migrate and integrate systems, share resources and rationalise premises to optimise our infrastructure while maintaining and enhancing services. In 2010, we increased our focus on this and took significant steps forward, investing further in IT platforms in our life and pensions and registrar businesses and announcing the creation of a new business centre in Europe.

Sharing scale benefits

Our substantial scale and broad capability enable us to put forward compelling propositions to clients and are integral to us winning major integrated service transformation contracts.

The delivery of progressively larger contracts, with common processes and substantial numbers of transferring employees, fuels the growth of our operations and resources. As we increase scale, we are able to deliver more services and contracts through shared ICT platforms and operating structures, providing greater benefits to clients. They benefit not only from cost efficiencies but also from greater access to specialist skills and flexible service delivery models.

Our business centres, where we are able to run a broad range of shared services, form a central part of our service delivery infrastructure. At the end of 2010, we had 64 business centres onshore in the UK, nearshore in Ireland, the Channel Islands and Europe, and offshore in India.

Blended service delivery

Our infrastructure allows us to offer clients an onshore/nearshore/offshore blended delivery model structured to meet their individual needs. By combining onshore, nearshore and offshore resources we can deliver maximum service flexibility, quality and cost effectiveness. Our comprehensive security and quality assurance systems ensure consistent service quality across the entire infrastructure.

India

We established our offshore operations in India in 2004. We now have 3 sites in Mumbai, 1 site in Pune and 1 site in Bangalore. At the end of 2010, our Indian operations represented approximately 10% of our overall headcount. These operations play an important role in our business and long term growth strategy, providing high quality, cost effective English language based services.

Capita India is fully integrated into the Group and operates like any other Capita business with the same values, technical infrastructure and operating model. The sites share a combined management team to ensure they all benefit from their collective skills. We proactively recruit from the highly skilled graduate workforce that is available in these locations. Their skills, knowledge and excellent work ethic help us meet our objectives of delivering a first class service to our clients. Capita is widely regarded in India as a first class employer who will encourage and help employees grow and develop their careers. We therefore benefit from being able to attract and retain a highly skilled and professional workforce.

In addition to being the largest offshore operation for UK life and pensions administration, we continue to grow our BPO capability across other sectors such as general insurance, finance and accounting. Recently, we have expanded our service capability in India incorporating IT application development and testing, infrastructure consultancy and research and analytical services for UK based pharmaceutical companies.

"By combining onshore, nearshore and offshore resources we can deliver maximum service flexibility, quality and cost effectiveness."

Vic Gysin Joint Chief Operating Officer

Table 3.27.1 – Resources – brand value and other intangibles

SAP AG – Annual report – 31 December 2010

Management Report (extract)

Competitive Intangibles

The assets that are the basis for our current as well as future success do not appear on the Consolidated Statements of Financial Position. This is apparent from a comparison of the market capitalization of SAP AG, which was €46.7 billion at the end of the year (2009: €40.5 billion), with the equity on the Consolidated Statements of Financial Position, which was €9.8 billion (2009: €8.5 billion). The difference is mainly due to certain intangible assets that the applicable accounting standards do not allow to be recorded (at all or at fair value) on the Consolidated Statements of Financial Position. They include customer capital (our customer base and customer relations), employees and their knowledge and skills, our ecosystem of partners, software we developed ourselves, our ability to innovate, the brands we have built up – in particular, the SAP brand itself – and our organization. On December 31, 2010, SAP was the fourth most valuable company in Germany in terms of market capitalization. In 2010, the SAP brand ranked 26th on the Interbrand and *BusinessWeek* scoreboard of *100 Best Global Brands*, compared to 27th in the previous year. Our brand's ranking is now at an all-time high. Against other German brands, the SAP brand ranked third behind Mercedes-Benz and BMW, and globally against other IT brands ours ranked 10th. In 2009,Interbrand determined a value of US$12.8 billion (2009: US$12.1 billion) for the SAP brand.

Our investment in research and development, including R&D investment in the past, is also a significant element in our competitive intangibles.

Our customer capital continued to grow in 2010. We gained approximately 14,000 new customers in various market segments and strengthened our existing customer relationships. With the help of an independent service provider, IMAGIN AG, we regularly measure the satisfaction and loyalty of our customers. In 2010, overall customer satisfaction remained almost flat in comparison to the prior year, but our recommendation rate improved slightly. For more information about our new customers, see the *Customers* section. For more information about customer satisfaction, see our *Sustainability Report* at www.sapsustainabilityreport.com.

Employee-related and R&D activities increased the value of our employee base and our own software. For more information, see the *Employees* and *Research and Development sections*.

We also increased the value of our partner ecosystem by continuing to develop sales and development partnerships.

Principal risks and uncertainties

3.146   The OFR should include a description of the principal risks and uncertainties facing the entity, together with a commentary on the directors' approach to them. [RS (OFR) para 52]. The statutory business review to be included in the directors' report requires disclosure of the principal risks and uncertainties facing the company. [Sec 417]. The FRRP has expressed concern at the quality of these disclosures. See chapter 2 for more details.

3.147   The purpose of disclosing risks and risk management policies is to enable investors and other users to assess the sustainability of the entity's current performance. Future performance may be vulnerable to factors that the entity cannot control. Investors need to be aware of the risk appetite of management because their investment risk is linked to the risks being borne by the entity. In Table 3.27.2, PotashCorp describes its risk management policies. In Table 3.27.3, Fresnillo plc describes its risk appetite for each type of risk, followed by disclosure of the company's response to each risk. Only risk A is shown here, for illustration purposes.

Table 3.27.2 – Risk management

Potash Corporation of Saskatchewan – Financial Review Annual Report — 31 December 2010

Risk Management (extract)

Risk Management

Managing Risks to Our Fertilizer Enterprise

We must effectively manage all risks associated with our business goals and activities, which have been established to successfully execute our corporate strategy. After evaluating risks for their severity and likelihood to adversely affect the company, we prioritize them and determine the most appropriate responses among accept, control, share, transfer, diversify or avoid.

Global Risk Environment

The risks that can threaten our business are integrated, and affect each other. Only by understanding the inherent risks within each risk category can we design and implement mitigation activities so we can execute our strategies and meet our business goals within acceptable residual risk tolerances.

Six categories of risks have been identified within our global environment: market/business, distribution, operational, financial/information technology, regulatory and integrity/empowerment. However, damage to our reputation is the most severe risk faced by

PotashCorp, and it could ultimately impede our ability to execute our corporate strategy. To mitigate this risk, we strive continually to build goodwill through a commitment to sustainability, transparency, effective communication and corporate governance best practices.

Risk Methodology and Ranking Matrix

After identifying an inherent risk, we assess it against our risk ranking matrix as if no mitigation measures had been taken. Through the matrix, we weigh the severity and likelihood of such a potential event, and establish relative risk levels from A through E to guide our mitigation activities.

A Extreme: Initiate mitigation activities immediately to reduce risk. If such activities cannot sufficiently reduce risk level, consider discontinuation of the applicable business operation to avoid the risk.

B Major: Initiate mitigation activities at next available opportunity to reduce risk. If such activities cannot sufficiently reduce the risk level, board approval is required to confirm acceptance of this level of risk.

C Acceptable: Level of risk is acceptable within tolerances of the risk management policy. Additional risk mitigation activities may be considered if benefits significantly exceed cost.

D Low: Monitor risk according to risk management policy requirements, but no additional activities required.

E Negligible: Consider discontinuing any related mitigation activities so resources can be directed to higher-value activities, provided such discontinuance does not adversely affect any other risk areas.

We can lower risk by reducing the likelihood of the initiating event occurring or by reducing the significance of the consequence if it does occur.

Residual risk remains after mitigation and control measures are applied to an identified inherent risk. We endeavor to be fully aware of all potential inherent risks that could adversely affect PotashCorp, and to choose appropriately the levels of residual risk we accept.

PotashCorp Risk Management Ranking Methodology

Risk Ranking Matrix			SEVERITY OF CONSEQUENCE				
			1	2	3	4	5
			Negligible	Low	Acceptable	Major	Extreme
LIKELIHOOD OR FREQUENCY	5	**Probable** (0-6 months)	C	B	B	A	A
	4	**High** (6 months-2 years)	D	C	B	B	A
	3	**Medium** (2-10 years)	D	D	C	B	B
	2	**Low** (10-50 years)	E	D	D	C	B
	1	**Remote** (> 50 years)	E	E	D	D	C

Table 3.27.3 – Risk appetite

Fresnillo plc – Annual Report – 31 December 2011

Our Risk Management Framework (extract)

What we did in 2011	Benefits for our Stakeholders
Formalise the definition of risk appetite for our principal risks	
Risk appetite was defined by the Board of Directors through a series of workshops and dedicated time during the July and October Board meetings. During these sessions the Directors reviewed our goals and strategy from a risk perspective, the expectations of our stakeholderss and the current level of risk exposure for our principal risk areas. Risk appetite is not static, and going forward the Board of Directors will continue to monitor and reassess our principal risks and risk appetite to ensure it continues to be aligned with our goals and strategy.	Formalising the definition of risk appetite strengthens our risk governance structure within which opportunities can be pursued and the downside of risks mitigated by setting out which risks and how much risk we are willing to take in the pursuit of our goals.

Our approach for managing risk is underpinned by our understanding of our current risk exposures, risk appetite and how our risks are changing over time.

Risk	Risk rating	Risk appetite	Risk change during 2011	Description of risk change
A. Impact of global macroeconomic developments	High	High	↑	Considering the cyclical nature of metals prices the likelihood of a drop in the price of gold and silver has increased
B. Access to land	High	Medium	↑	More challenging negotiations for land in Mexico combined with an increase in requirement for land
C. Safety	High	Low	↑	Increased reliance on contractors, not all of whom are initially familiar or in compliance with our safety policies and procedures
D. Security	High	Low	↑	Increased state of insecurity in Mexico
E. Projects	High	Medium	—	We continue to mitigate project risk through our investment governance process and system of capital project controls
F. Human resources	Medium	Medium	↑	Greater competition for skilled personnel
G. Exploration	Medium	Medium	—	Continued investment in the exploration programme has stabilised this risk
H. Environmental incidents	Low	Low	↓	Mature environmental management programme continues to reduce the likelihood of a significant environmental incident
I. Potential actions by the government	Medium	Low	↑	Pressure for a mining tax in Mexico has increased. Mining taxes have recently been implemented in other Latin American countries (Chile and Peru), and Mexican legislators continue to take steps to move in this direction.

For those risks with a risk rating that is above our risk appetite, management takes action to reduce the level of risk. See Risk Response/Mitigation in the following table.

Our principal risks

Strategic objective	Risk description and context	Risk response/mitigation
A. Impact of Global Macroeconomic Developments		
1,2,3	There could be an adverse impact on our sales and profit, and potentially the economic viability of projects, from macroeconomic developments such as: – a decrease in gold and silver prices after a prolonged period of increase (primary driver of the risk) – adverse fluctuations in MXN/USD exchange rates or other foreign currencies – inflation and – a decrease in the price of by-products (zinc and lead)	**Prices of gold and silver**: we have full exposure to fluctuations and currently no hedging as per our investors' mandate **Prices of by-products and foreign exchange movements**, including currencies impacting equipment purchase commitments – we have hedging policies in place See Note 31 in the Financial Statements page 163 **Inflationary pressures**: we engage suppliers in long-term contracts to maintain our position as a low cost producer and control the impact of the rising cost of mining inputs See Suppliers page 24

3.148   It is important that companies distinguish their principal risks and uncertainties rather than listing all possible risks without highlighting to the reader which are the most important in assessing the potential success of the company's strategy.

3.149   In Table 3.28, Great Portland Estates plc sets out how it manages risk, discloses the principal risks and uncertainties it faces and links the commentary on each risk to its broader discussion of its business activities.

Table 3.28 – Management and disclosure of principal risks

Great Portland Estates plc – Annual Report – 31 March 2011

Risk management (extract)

Risk management (extract)

The successful management of risk is essential to enable the Group to deliver on its strategic priorities. Whilst the ultimate responsibility for risk management rests with the Board, the foundation of effective day-to-day management of risk is in the way we do business and the culture of our team. Our flat organisational structure, with close involvement of senior management in all significant decisions combined with our cautious and analytical approach, is designed to align the Group's interests with those of shareholders.

Board oversight

Board meetings
Audit Committee
Remuneration Committee

Operational Committees

Executive Committee – weekly

| Leasing co-ordination weekly | Investment weekly | Financial management weekly |
| Asset management weekly | Environmental policy bi-monthly | Corporate responsibility monthly |

Policies for highlighting and controlling risk

| Investment return benchmarks | Regular review of business plans | Development appraisal parameters |
| Debt leverage, covenant compliance and liquidity limits | Occupancy targets | Leasing objectives and tenant covenant testing |

Procedures and internal controls

| High level risk assessment framework | Extensive documentation to support decisions | Defined performance indicators with sensitivity analysis |
| Strict approval requirements | Formal policies and procedures consistently applied | External review of key controls |

People and culture

Focused market expertise	Integrity in business conduct	Conservative attitude to capital deployment
Open communication	Interests aligned with shareholders	Analytical rigour
Transparent disclosure with stakeholders	Qualified and experienced personnel with specific roles	

Business risk

Operating and financial review

The Group views effective risk management as integral to the delivery of superior returns to shareholders. Principal risks and uncertainties facing the business and the processes through which the Company aims to manage those risks are:

Risk and impact	Mitigation	Change From last year	Commentary

Market risk

Central London real estate market underperforms other UK property sectors leading to poor relative financial results	Research into the economy and the investment and occupational markets is evaluated as part of the Group's annual strategy process covering the key areas of investment, development and asset management and updated regularly throughout the year.		The central London real estate market has considerably out performed the wider UK Market during the year ended 31 March 2011, demonstrated by IPD's central TPR exceeding IPD's universe by 6.7 percentage points and the outlook continues to be favourable. Our market pages 20 to 23 ←
Economic recovery falters resulting in worse than expected performance of the business given decline in economic output	Regular economic updates received and scenario planning for different economic cycles. 46% of income from committed developments secured.		Whilst the economic environment appears to have stabilised and take up has increased markedly on last year, there remains the continued downward pressure from the Eurozone Sovereign debt crisis and the impact of the Government's austerity measures have yet to be seen. Our market pages 20 to 23 ←

Investment

Not sufficiently capitalising on market investment opportunities through difficulty in sourcing investment opportunities at attractive prices, poor investment decisions and mistimed recycling of capital	The Group has dedicated resources whose remit is to constantly research each of the sub-markets within central London seeking the right balance of investment and development opportunities suitable for current and anticipated market conditions. Detailed due diligence is undertaken on all acquisitions prior to purchase to ensure appropriate returns. Business plans are produced on an individual asset basis to ensure the appropriate choice of those buildings with limited relative potential performance.		With independent forecasts indicating that capital values are expected to rise over the near to medium term, limited disposals were made during the year. The Group has committed in excess of £370 million since its Rights Issue in May 2009 equating to nearly a quarter of the portfolio at 31 March 2011. With the market having risen from the low of 2009, the risk of missing compelling acquisitions has lessened. Our market pages 20 to 23 ← Case studies pages 8 to 11 ←

Asset management

Failure to maximise income from investment properties through poor management of voids, mispricing, low tenant retention, sub-optimal rent reviews, tenant failures and inappropriate refurbishments	The Group's in-house asset management and leasing teams proactively manage tenants to ensure changing needs are met with a focus on retaining income in light of vacant possession requirements for refurbishments and developments.		The Group continues to maintain a low void rate which was 2.7% at 31 March 2011. Tenant delinquencies were less than 1% of the rent roll for the year to 31 March 2011. The Group continues to actively manage the portfolio to maximise occupancy and drive rental growth. Asset management pages 26 and 27 ← Case study pages 12 and 13 ←

Development

Poor development returns relating to: – incorrect reading of the property cycle; – inappropriate location; – failure to gain viable planning consents; – level of development undertaken as a percentage of the portfolio; – level of speculative development; – contractor availability and insolvency risk; – quality of the completed buildings; and – poor development management	See market risk above. Prior to committing to a development the Group conducts a detailed Financial and Operational appraisal process which evaluates the expected returns from a development in light of likely risks. During the course of a development, the actual costs and estimated returns are regularly monitored to signpost prompt decisions on project management, leasing and ownership. 46% of income from committed developments secured. Due diligence is undertaken of the financial stability of demolition and main contractors prior to awarding of contracts. Working with agents, potential occupiers' needs and aspirations are identified during the planning application and design stages. All our major developments are subject to BREEAM ratings with a target to achieve a rating of "Very Good" on major refurbishments and "Excellent" on new build properties.		With forecasted supply of central London office space expected to be scarce in the near to medium term, the Group has embarked on a near-term development programme to capitalise on the expected resulting rental growth. The Group's exposure to development risk has increased accordingly. Development pages 28 and 29 ← Case study pages 14 and 15 ←

Risk and impact	Mitigation	Change From last year	Commentary
Financial risks			
Limited availability of further capital constrains the growth of the business	Cash flow and funding needs are regularly monitored to ensure sufficient undrawn facilities are in place. Funding maturities are managed across the short, medium and long term. The Group's funding measures are diversified across a range of bank and bond markets. Strict counterparty limits are operated on deposits.	↓	Since 31 March 2010, the Group has refinanced all of its 2012 debt maturities. Pro forma undrawn cash and committed credit facilities are £518 million. Our financial position pages 32 to 35 ← Note 16 forming part of the Group financial statements pages 74 to 77 →
Adverse interest rate movements reduce profitability	Formal policy to manage interest rate exposure by having a high proportion of debt with fixed or capped interest rates through derivatives.	→	With the strength of economic recovery still uncertain, the timing of interest rate rises remains unclear. Our financial position pages 32 to 35 ← Note 16 forming part of the Group financial statements pages 74 to 77 →
Inappropriate capital structure results in suboptimal NAV per share growth	Regular review of current and forecast debt levels.	→	The Group's existing capital structure is well placed to take advantage of opportunities as they arise and to deliver our near-term development programme. Our financial position pages 32 to 35 ←
People			
Correct level, mix and retention of people to execute our Business Plan. Strategic priorities not achieved because of inability to attract, develop, motivate and retain talented employees	Regular review is undertaken of the Group's resource requirements. The Company has a remuneration system that is strongly linked to performance and a formal appraisal system to provide regular assessment of individual performance and identification of training needs.	→	With increased levels of activity, the Group has strengthened and broadened its team and the process to appoint a new Finance Director is ongoing. At the 2010 AGM, shareholders approved a new Long Term Incentive Plan. Our people pages 38 to 42 ← Remuneration report pages 102 to 112 →
Regulatory			
Adverse regulatory risk including tax, planning, environmental legislation and EU directives increases cost base and reduces flexibility	Senior Group representatives spend considerable time, using experienced advisers as appropriate, to ensure compliance with current and potential future regulations. Lobbying property industry matters is undertaken by active participation of the Executive Directors through relevant industry bodies.	↑	During the year new Building Regulations came into effect requiring further reductions on carbon emissions whilst the risk to the Group from increasing regulation having unforeseen consequences and the impact of certain EU directives including the AIFM directive continues to be uncertain. Property industry representation page 47 → Corporate responsibility targets pages 48 to 51 →
Health and safety incidents Loss of or injury to employees, contractors or tenants and resultant reputational damage	The Company has dedicated Health & Safety personnel to oversee the Group's management systems which include regular risk assessments and annual audits to proactively address key Health & Safety areas including employee, contractor and tenant safety. On developments, the Group operates a pre-qualification process to ensure selection of competent consultants and contractors.	↑	The Group had no reportable accidents during the year, however, as a result of our near-term development programme we have increased exposure to health and safety incidents on our development sites. Corporate responsibility targets pages 52 and 53 →

3.150 Significant risks and uncertainties include both financial risks and non-financial risks. Indeed the two types are often indistinguishable because non-financial risk, such as the risk that a product may be faulty, may have serious financial consequences, such as the cost of withdrawing the product, penalties on long-term contracts, damage to the entity's reputation and so on. Other non-financial risks, which are increasingly referred to, reflect trends in consumer and social behaviour and potential regulatory actions. Examples include the health hazards of cigarettes, obesity risk and possible health risks from the use of mobile phones. Product risk is, in addition to many other risks, therefore, often significant for such businesses.

3.151 Entities should disclose the strategic, commercial, operational and financial risks where these may significantly affect the entity's strategies and development of the entity's value. [RS (OFR) para 53]. Specific risks facing entities will vary according to the nature of the business, but some risks, such as reputational risks, will be common to all. [RS (OFR) para 54]. Description of the principal risks should cover both exposures to negative consequences as well as potential opportunities. The directors' policy for managing principal risks should also be disclosed. [RS (OFR) para 55]. The OFR should cover the principal risks and uncertainties necessary to understand the business' objectives and strategy both where they constitute a significant external risk to the entity and where the entity's impact on other parties through its activities, products or services, affects its performance. Directors will need to consider the full range of business risks. [RS (OFR) para 56].

3.151.1 As highlighted by the FRC report, 'An update for directors of listed companies: Responding to increased country and currency risk in financial reports', for many entities, country and/or currency risks have recently become one of the principal risks they face. Of particular note are the risks arising from regime change in the Middle East, the funding pressures on certain European countries and curtailment of capital spending programmes. The outcome of these events remains uncertain. The austerity measures being widely adopted in Europe may result in significant changes to growth rates and demand for consumer products in those countries. In addition, entities may be affected significantly if one or more euro area countries are forced to exit the euro area. In Table 3.28.2, Vodafone plc describes its eurozone risk.

Table 3.28.2 – Eurozone risk

Vodafone plc – Annual Report – 31 March 2012

Principal risk factors and uncertainties (extract)

Eurozone risk

Country and currency risk

Recent conditions in the eurozone have resulted in a higher risk of disruption and business risk from high currency volatility and/or the potential of an exit of one or more countries from the euro.

As part of our response to these conditions we have reviewed our existing processes and policies, and in places, evolved them with the aim of both minimising the Group's economic exposure and to preserve our ability to operate in a range of potential conditions that may exist in the event of one or more of these future events.

Our ability to manage these risks needs to take appropriate account of our needs to deliver a high quality service to our customers, meet licence obligations and the significant capital investments we may have made and may need to continue to make in the markets most impacted.

Currency related risks

While our share price is denominated in sterling, the majority of our financial results are generated in other currencies. As a result the Group's operating profit is sensitive to either a relative strengthening or weakening of the major currencies in which it transacts.

The "Operating results" section of the annual report on pages 40 to 49 sets out a discussion and analysis of the relative contributions of the Group's Europe and AMAP regions and the major geographical markets in each, to the Group's service revenue and EBITDA performance. Our markets in Italy, Ireland, Greece, Portugal and Spain have been most directly impacted by the current market conditions and in order of contribution, represent 17% (Italy), 8% (Spain), 3% (Portugal) and 3% (Ireland and Greece combined) of the Group's EBITDA. An average 3% decline in the sterling equivalent of these combined geographical markets due to currency revaluation would reduce Group EBITDA by £0.1 billion. The Group's foreign currency earnings are diversified through its 45% equity interest in Verizon Wireless, which operates in the United States and generates its earnings in US dollars. Verizon Wireless, which is equity accounted, contributed 42% of the Group's adjusted operating profit for the year ended 31 March 2012.

The Group employs a number of mechanisms to manage elements of exchange rate risk at a transaction, translation and economic level. At the transaction level our policies require foreign exchange risks on transactions denominated in other currencies above certain de minimis levels to be hedged. Further, since the Company's sterling share price represents the value of its future multi-currency cash flows, principally in euro, US dollars and sterling, we aim to align the currency of our debt and interest charges in proportion to our expected future principal multi-currency cash flows, thereby providing an economic hedge in terms of reduced volatility in the sterling equivalent value of the Group and a partial hedge against income statement translation exposure, as interest costs will be denominated in foreign currencies.

In the event of a country's exit from the eurozone, this may necessitate changes in one or more of our entities' functional currency and potentially higher volatility of those entities' trading results when translated into sterling, potentially adding further currency risk.

A summary of this sensitivity of our operating results and our foreign exchange risk management policies is set out within "Financial risk management – Market risk – Foreign exchange management" within note 21 to the consolidated financial statements.

Operational planning

We have worked to develop operational plans to use as a basis for continuity planning across the Group in the event of significant exchange rate volatility and/or the withdrawal of one, or a small number of countries, from the euro. We have categorised "at risk" countries into three categories based on risk profile and identified three broad areas of operational risks for the Group where work has been focused, being:

Financial/investment risk: Our activities are focused on counterparty risk management and in particular the protection and availability of cash deposits and investments. Exposures in relation to liquid Group investments have been reviewed and actions have been taken to reduce counterparty limits with certain financial institutions and to convert a significant proportion of euro denominated holdings and deposits into sterling and US dollar investments. Existing Group policy requires cash sweep arrangements, to ensure no operating company has more than €5 million on deposit on any one day. Further, the Group has had in place for a number of years collateral support agreements with a significant number of its counterparties to pass collateral to the Group under certain circumstances. The Group has a net £980 million of collateral assets in its statement of financial position at 31 March 2012. Further information is provided within "Financial risk management – Credit risk" within note 21 to the consolidated financial statements.

Trading risks: We have investigated the structure of existing procurement contracts and we have started the process of amending certain contractual clauses to place the Group in a better position in the event of the exit of a country from the eurozone.

Business continuity risks: We have identified a number of key business continuity priorities which are focused on planning to allow migration to a more cash-based business model in the event banking systems are frozen, developing dual currency capability in contract customer billing systems or ensuring the ability to move these contract customers to prepaid methods of billing, and the consequential impacts to tariff structures. We have also put in place contingency plans with key suppliers that would assist us to continue to support our network infrastructure, retail operations and employees.

The Group continues to maintain appropriate levels of cash and short-term investments in many currencies and, with a carefully controlled group of counterparties, to minimise the risks to the ongoing access to that liquidity and therefore to the ability of the Group to settle debts as they become due. Further information is provided within "Financial risk management – Liquidity risk" within note 21 to the consolidated financial statements.

Risk of change in carrying amount of assets and liabilities

The main potential short-term financial statement impact of the current economic uncertainties is the potential impairment of non-financial and financial assets.

The Group has significant amounts of goodwill, other intangible assets and plant, property and equipment allocated to, or held by, companies operating in the eurozone. We have performed impairment testing for each country in Europe as at 31 March 2012 and identified aggregate impairment charges of £4.0 billion in relation to Vodafone Italy, Spain, Greece and Portugal. Further detail on this exercise together with the sensitivity of the results of this assessment to reasonably possible adverse assumptions is set out in note 10 to the consolidated financial statements.

Our operating companies in Italy, Ireland, Greece, Portugal and Spain have billed and unbilled trade receivables totalling £2.0 billion. IFRS contains specific requirements for impairment assessments of financial assets. We have a range of credit exposures and provisions for doubtful debts that are generally made by reference to consistently applied methodologies overlaid with judgements determined on a case-by-case basis reflecting the specific facts and circumstances of the receivable. Detailed disclosures made in relation to provisions against loans and receivables as well as disclosures about any loans and receivables that are past due at the end of the period, concentrations of risk and credit risk more generally as set out in "Financial risk management – Credit risk" within note 21 to the consolidated financial statements.

3.152 Table 3.28.3 illustrates a company reporting its risk discussion in the context of its overall business drivers. The company illustrates a clear flow of actions form business drivers, through risk and opportunities, and links to strategic objectives and key performance indicators. A concise diagram makes the information easy to absorb. The diagram cross references to a detailed analysis of the risks (not shown here).

Table 3.28.3 – Risks, business drivers and objectives

National Grid plc – Annual Report and accounts – 31 March 2010

Operating and Financial Review (extract)

Operating and Financial Review

Business drivers, principal risks and opportunities

Business drivers

There are many factors that influence the success of our business and the financial returns we obtain. We consider the factors described here to be our principal business drivers.

Price controls and rate plans

The prices we charge for use of our electricity and gas transmission and distribution networks are determined in accordance with regulatory approved price controls in the UK and rate plans in the US. These arrangements include incentive and/or penalty arrangements. The terms of these arrangements have a significant impact on our revenues.

Multi-year contracts

Revenues in our Long Island electricity distribution and generation operations are subject to long-term contracts with the Long Island Power Authority. In addition, revenues in our Grain LNG importation terminal are determined by long-term contractual arrangements with blue chip customers.

People

The skills and talents of our employees, along with succession planning and the development of future leaders, are critical to our success. We believe that business success will be delivered through the performance of all current and future employees, and enhanced by having a workforce that is diverse in its cultural, religious and community influences.

Principal risks and opportunities

There are a number of risks that might cause us to fail to achieve our vision or to deliver growth in shareholder value. We can mitigate many of these risks by acting appropriately in response to the factors driving our business. The principal risks are described here. For more detail on risks, see pages 91 to 93.

Regulatory settlements and long-term contracts

Our ability to obtain appropriate recovery of costs and rates of return on investment is of vital importance to the sustainability of our business. We have an opportunity to help shape the future of the regulatory environment, for example in our rate filings in the US. If we fail to take these opportunities, we risk failing to achieve satisfactory returns.

Financial performance

Financial performance and operating cash flows are the basis for funding our future capital investment programmes, for servicing our borrowings and paying dividends, and for increasing shareholder value. Failure to achieve satisfactory performance could affect our ability to deliver the returns we and our stakeholders expect.

Talent and skills

Harnessing and developing the skills and talent of our existing employees, and recruiting, retaining and developing the best new talent, will enable us to improve our capabilities. Failure to engage and develop our existing employees or to attract and retain talented employees could hamper our ability to deliver in the future.

Objectives

We have developed the Company strategy and objectives to address the key business drivers and risks, ensuring we manage the business appropriately so as to mitigate risks and optimise opportunities. For more detail on objectives, see pages 38 and 39.

Delivering strong, sustainable regulatory and long-term contracts with good returns

Building trust, transparency, and an inclusive and engaged workforce

Developing our talent, leadership skills and capabilities

Key performance indicators (KPIs)

We use a variety of performance measures to monitor progress against our objectives. Some of these are considered to be key performance indicators and are set out here. For more detail on performance, see pages 40 to 69.

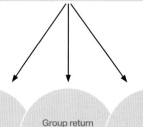

Adjusted earnings per share

Group return on equity

Total shareholder return

Employee engagement index

3.153 In Table 3.29, Taylor Wimpey plc links its risk discussion directly to its strategy and key performance indicators. Only four of the areas of risk are shown here for illustration purposes.

Table 3.29 Risk linked to strategy and KPIs

Taylor Wimpey plc – Annual report – 31 December 2010

Business review (extract)

Principal risks and uncertainties

As with any business, Taylor Wimpey faces a number of risks and uncertainties in the course of its day to day operations. By effectively identifying and managing these risks, we are able to improve our returns, thereby adding value for shareholders.

	Economic and market environment	Government regulations and planning policy	Compliance with financial and operational covenants	Land purchasing
Description of risk	Demand for our homes can be adversely affected by weakness in the wider economy. This includes factors such as unemployment levels, interest rates and the availability of credit, which are outside of the Group's control.	Governments issue a wide variety of requirements for new housing, particularly in the UK, covering areas such as design, quality, sustainability and product mix. The UK general election in 2010 resulted in a change of government and new planning regulations are being progressed through Parliament.	We completed a total refinancing in December 2010, which resulted in a standard set of financial and operational covenants for our sector. However, breach of our new covenants could, in certain circumstances, lead to a requirement to repay debt funding in its entirety.	Purchasing of land that is poor quality or mis-priced or purchasing land in insufficient quantity.
Relevance to strategy	The majority of the homes that we build are sold to individual purchasers who take on significant mortgages to finance their purchases. As such, customer demand is extremely sensitive to economic conditions.	In addition to our short term land portfolio we have a strategic land portfolio of 77,060 potential plots in the UK. Our ability to obtain the planning permission required to develop communities on this land is dependent on our ability to meet the relevant regulatory and planning requirements.	Our new financial arrangements no longer have specific limits on the level of land spend, but do set limits on our maximum level of gearing and specify a minimum amount of interest cover by reference to either operating cash or EBITDA. These requirements, while not expected to constrain the business under reasonably foreseeable market conditions, could be compromised under extreme market conditions.	Land is the major 'raw material' for the Group, but the availability of good quality land at an attractive price is currently scarce. Purchasing land of the appropriate quality on attractive terms will enhance the Group's ability to deliver strong profit growth as housing markets recover.
Potential impact on KPIs	The global economy has exhibited some volatility during 2010 arising from concerns regarding the sovereign debt of some countries. Credit availability and consumer confidence remain below normal levels. As a result, the level of effective demand for new homes continues to be significantly reduced, impacting both profitability and cash generation.	Inability to obtain suitable consents could impact on the number or type of homes that we are able to build. We could also be required to fund higher than anticipated levels of planning obligations, or incur additional costs to meet increased regulatory requirements. All of these would have a detrimental impact on the contribution per plot.	As our land portfolio is a relatively illiquid asset in adverse market conditions, any requirement to pay back debt at short notice under such conditions could lead to a requirement to sell land on unfavourable terms, or potentially cause the business to fail if sufficient funds cannot be raised.	Purchasing poor quality or mis-priced land would have a detrimental impact on our profitability. Purchasing insufficient land would reduce the Group's ability to manage its portfolio actively and lead to a shortfall in anticipated performance.
Mitigation	Our local teams select the locations and home designs that best meet the needs of the local community and customer demand. We continue to evaluate new outlet openings on the basis of local market conditions and regularly review the pricing and incentives that we offer. We also minimise the level of speculative build that we undertake.	We consult with the UK government on upcoming legislation, both directly and as a member of industry groups, to highlight potential issues. At a local level, our land specialists work closely with the relevant planning authorities, consult with local communities and structure purchase agreements to mitigate such risk.	We monitor our future and detailed cash requirements on a monthly basis, which takes into account land spend and projected site openings, together with headroom to cover contingencies and unforeseen requirements.	We operate an investment appraisal process for land purchases, which ensures that such projects are subject to appropriate review and authorisation, dependent on the proposed scale of expenditure.

3.154 Table 3.30 illustrates a company presenting a SWOT (strengths, weaknesses, opportunities and threats) analysis. MTU Aero Engines Holding AG includes this analysis in its 'Risk Report', where its risk management system and risks are described.

Table 3.30 – SWOT analysis

MTU Aero Engine Holding AG – Annual Report – 31 December 2010

Group Management Report (extract)

6.4 SWOT analysis

SWOT analysis of the MTU group

Corporate	Market
Strengths	**Opportunities**
Technological leadership – OEM: Excellence in engine modules: low-pressure turbines, high-pressure and IP compressors – MRO: Excellence in advanced repair techniques	Market environment of business units on a long-term growth trend
Balanced mix of production and after-market business, covering all stages from development and manufacturing to maintenance	Increasing technological complexity of future engines
Focus on high-profit-margin engine business	Good market opportunities for fuel-efficient engine designs (geared turbofan) in the event of steadily rising oil prices
Presence in fast-growing Asian market (MTU Maintenance Zhuhai)	Solid financing structure and technological leadership open the way to program investments
Long-term contracts in the OEM business, involvement in consortia and cooperative ventures	Growth of MRO in newly industrializing countries
Quality and on-time delivery form basis for reliable partnerships	Airline outsourcing in order to concentrate on core activities offers additional opportunities for MRO business
Proximity of MRO sales network to customers	Greater exploitation of synergies between areas of commercial business
Solid financing structure opens up opportunities for M&A activities and program investments	Positive changes in U.S. dollar exchange rate
Weaknesses	**Threats**
High dependency on U.S. dollar	Low, volatile profitability on the part of end customers (airlines); possible spending cuts in the event of an economic downturn
Cyclic business	Inherent risk of advanced technology development with regard to estimated schedules and costs
Small company by comparison with OEMs	Competition from low-cost PMA parts
	Entry of newly industrializing nations into the aerospace industry
	Restrained public spending may lead to defense budget cuts and structural reform of the German armed forces
	Difficulty of obtaining licenses in the MRO business
	Negative changes in U.S. dollar exchange rate

3.155   Table 3.30.1 is an example of a company presenting its risks diagrammatically to indicate the relationship between likelihood and impact. It also indicates how the risks have changed during the year.

Table 3.30.1 – Risk radar

Wartsila Corporation– Annual Report –31 December 2010

Corporate governance

Risks and Risk Management (Extract)

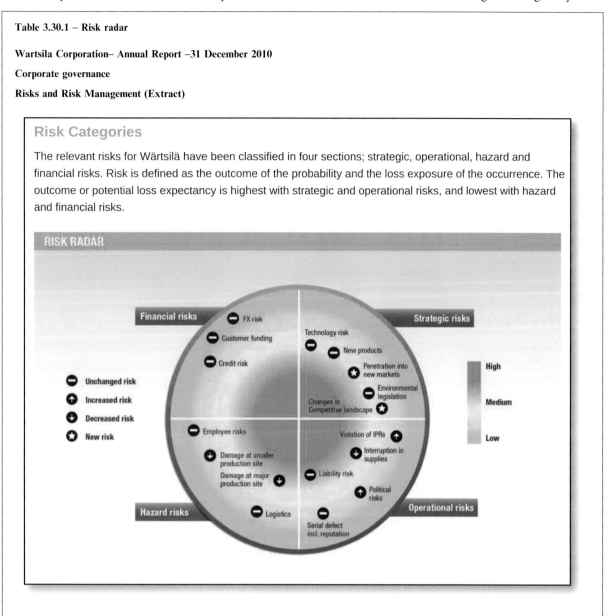

Risk Categories

The relevant risks for Wärtsilä have been classified in four sections; strategic, operational, hazard and financial risks. Risk is defined as the outcome of the probability and the loss exposure of the occurrence. The outcome or potential loss expectancy is highest with strategic and operational risks, and lowest with hazard and financial risks.

3.155.1   In Table 3.30.1.1, the risk diagram shows the relative likelihood and impact of each key risk. Not shown here, but included in the company's annual report immediately after this diagram, is an explanation of each risk, how it is being managed and how it has changed since the prior year. Each risk is cross referenced to a specific strategic priority and performance measure. The member of management responsible for managing each risk is also disclosed.

Table 3.30.1.1 – Likelihood and impact of risks

Afren plc – Annual Report and Accounts – 31 December 2011

Risk management process (extract)

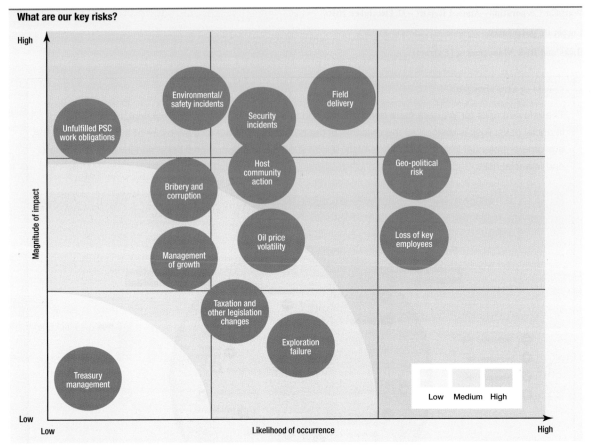

Risk Categories

The relevant risks for Wärtsilä have been classified in four sections; strategic, operational, hazard and financial risks. Risk is defined as the outcome of the probability and the loss exposure of the occurrence. The outcome or potential loss expectancy is highest with strategic and operational risks, and lowest with hazard and financial risks.

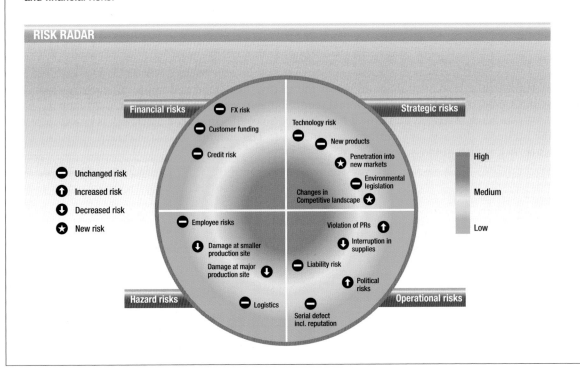

3.156 Management should disclose uncertainties as well as risks. These may include contingent liabilities relating to specific operational uncertainties, such as outstanding litigation; or market uncertainty, for example whether a new product will be successful. There are also inherent uncertainties that surround the preparation of the financial statements, which may require significant estimates and judgements. These may be referred to in the description of risk factors, but are more often dealt with in the description of critical accounting policies. Disclosure of critical accounting policies is addressed below under 'Accounting policies'. In addition, under IFRS, IAS 1 requires disclosure in the financial statements of significant judgements made by directors and of key sources of estimation uncertainty. [IAS 1 paras 113, 116].

3.157 As well as the recommendation in the reporting statement to disclose risks and uncertainties, including financial risks, IFRS 7, 'Financial instruments: Disclosures' and FRS 29 (its UK equivalent) require such disclosure for financial policies and risks. IFRS 7, 'Financial instruments: Disclosures', requires an entity to disclose information that enables users of its financial statements to evaluate the nature and extent of risks arising from financial instruments to which the entity is exposed at the end of the reporting period. [IFRS 7 para 31]. Potentially, the combination of IFRS 7's requirements and the reporting statement's recommendations could result in information being duplicated in an annual report. However, IFRS 7 recognises this issue and states that the information regarding the nature and risks arising from financial instruments must be given either in the financial statements, or incorporated by cross-reference from the financial statements to some other statement, such as a management commentary or risk report, that is available to users of the financial statements on the same terms as the financial statements and at the same time. [IFRS 7 para B6]. The Manual of Accounting – Financial instruments deals with these requirements.

Relationships

3.158 Information should be included in the OFR about significant relationships with stakeholders other than members, where they are likely to influence, directly or indirectly, the business performance and its value. This information should be given to the extent necessary to enable members to assess the entity's strategies and their potential to succeed. [RS (OFR) para 57].

3.159 Stakeholders other than members may include customers, suppliers, employees, contractors, lenders, creditors, regulators and tax authorities. They may also include the community in which the entity operates and society generally, as well as those entities with which the entity has strategic alliances. [RS (OFR) para 58].

3.160 The types of significant relationships that may be appropriate to disclose include:

- Customers – this may include management of customer service, details of customer losses or gains, in particular those on which the company has a degree of reliance, and new business developments.

- Suppliers – including management of procurement activities, ability to source appropriate suppliers, consideration of raw material availability and prices, vetting of supplier behaviour and policy regarding child labour, fair wages etc.

- Employees – including satisfaction surveys, recruitment and retention, training and development, diversity, health and safety, employee communications, productivity, human rights, ethical trading.

- Impact on society and communities – including environmental impact (for example, noise, pollution, waste), product safety, product responsibility, charitable donations and community projects.

- Lenders and creditors – for example, negotiations of credit facilities and other arrangements with lenders, impact of macro-economic factors on availability of credit.

- Regulators – for example licences to operate, pricing restrictions, tax negotiations, government discussions on legislation impacting the company.

- Strategic alliances – such as joint ventures, business partnerships, sub-contractors, franchises.

3.161 The reporting statement notes that in deciding what should be included in the OFR, directors will need to take a broad view in determining the extent to which the actions of stakeholders other than members may affect the entity's performance and value. [RS (OFR) para 58]. Each of the examples of relationships set out in the previous paragraph may impact the company more or less depending on its circumstances. The following paragraphs highlight just a few of these. Management should decide which are important to them and explain how managing those relationships contributes to the potential future success of their strategies.

3.162 Tables 3.30.2 and 3.30.3 are examples of the disclosure of key relationships.

Table 3.30.2 – Key relationships

Royal Mail Holdings Plc – Annual Report– 28 March 2010

Operating and Financial Review (extract)

Key Relationships
The Group has several key relationships that are critical to its day-to-day activities and its overall success.

People – The Company's people are the lifeblood of the organisation and brands. Without their continued support and dedication it will be impossible to function on a day-to-day basis and embrace the change within the Group's markets. Training, diversity, flexible resourcing and making the business a great place to work are some of the ways Royal Mail continues to improve this relationship.

Unions – The Communications Workers Union (CWU) represents non-managerial staff, with Unite the Union — Communication and Managers' Association (CMA) sector representing managerial staff. The Group's policy is to work with the CWU and CMA to engage staff in the development and execution of business decisions.

Pension trustees – The pension trustee board for the main Pension Plan comprises an independent chair plus 10 others including employees, union representatives, a pensioner and independent members. They take external professional advice from Sacker & Partners LLP (legal), Towers Watson Limited (actuary), KPMG LLP (auditors) and PricewaterhouseCoopers LLP (financial). They are responsible for obtaining regular actuarial valuations of the plan to satisfy the statutory funding objective, which involves reaching agreement with the Group on the statement of funding principles, the recovery plan and the schedule of contributions. There is a separate trustee board for the Senior Executives' Pension Plan which comprises the chair plus 5 individuals including employees, pensioners and an independent member. The Defined Contribution Plan's trustee board currently comprises 5 individuals including an independent chair, employees and an independent member.

Customers – The Group's businesses and brands are used or recognised by almost everyone in the UK – from the largest of companies to individuals. However, the 30 largest customers generate c.13% of Royal Mail Retail's turnover and consequently the business is reliant on a relatively small customer base. As competition increases, the Group will have to continue to simplify ways of doing business and design products around customers' needs. Customers are offered standard terms and conditions for the markets and countries in which the Group operates.

Subpostmasters – 97% of Post Offices are operated on a contractual basis by subpostmasters, franchisees or multiple partners. Post Office Limited provides operational, commercial and technical infrastructure and resources to underpin positive working relationships with these Post Office branches in order to ensure that high standards of consistent and compliant service are provided to customers wherever they are in the UK. As part of this general approach, Post Office Limited has constructive relationships with the National Federation of Subpostmasters (which acts as a representative body for subpostmasters), as well as with a number of national multiple retail organisations, which each operate significant numbers of Post Offices. In conducting its business and in determining future strategy Post Office Limited remains aware of the interests of subpostmasters and other agents, and it works despite an often challenging economic environment, to help promote the sustainability and success of these local businesses.

Suppliers – The Group has a wide range of suppliers, with its primary reliance on those relating to outsourcing of non-core services, such as IT support. It works in partnership with its suppliers to ensure the right products and services are delivered at the right time at competitive costs. A Group purchasing team monitors compliance to Group policy in awarding contracts or new business and adheres to agreed credit terms.

The consumer body: Consumer Focus – In October 2008, Postwatch merged with energywatch and the Welsh, Scottish and National Consumer Councils to form Consumer Focus. It is the statutory organisation campaigning for a fair deal for consumers in England, Wales, Scotland, and, for postal services, Northern Ireland. Consumer Focus wants to ensure postal consumers throughout the UK are receiving a fair deal. It has strong legislative powers including the right to investigate any consumer complaint if it is of wider interest, the right to open up information from providers, the power to conduct research and the ability to make an official super-complaint about failing services.

The Regulator: Postcomm – The independent regulator for the postal market, Postcomm, set up by the Postal Services Act 2000, is responsible for setting a framework for Royal Mail's prices – the Price Control, in the form of a cap on the average price of a basket of products. The price increases or reductions allowed by Postcomm through the Price Control have a very material impact on the likely levels of cash flow the Company can generate. Postcomm also investigates compliance with Licence conditions and has broad powers to reprimand publicly, or fine, Royal Mail if it finds it in breach of those conditions.

Shareholder – The Company is a plc 100% owned by the Government. The Shareholder Executive (within BIS) manages its relationship with the Company as a commercial shareholder. While management of the Group therefore lies with the Company's Board of Directors, the shareholder is kept advised through regular performance reviews and provision of information. Any new funding required by the Group (apart from short term borrowings of less than one year), can only be obtained from and approved by Government.

Table 3.30.3 – Key relationships

Takeda Pharmaceutical Company Limited– Annual Report and – 31 March 2010

Corporate Philosophy and Our Stakeholders

Our Stakeholders

Stakeholders comprise all parties that are influenced by, and/or have an influence on, corporate activities.
Currently, Takeda views its relationship with stakeholders as shown in the diagram on the facing page, as it pursues its activities.

		Main Method of Dialogue
Relationship with Medical Professionals and Patients	Through its pharmaceutical business, Takeda builds relationships of trust with medical professionals by providing high-quality pharmaceutical information services based on scientific evidence. Takeda's aim in this is to enable as many people as possible to be healthy. To allow us to develop a greater number of superior pharmaceutical products at a faster pace, and to better understand patient's needs, we believe it is also vital to build good relationships with patients through organizations such as patient support groups.	● Pharmaceutical information activities ● Provide information through Customer Relations and through our website, etc. ● Hold health courses, etc. ● Provide information through advertising
Relationship with Shareholders and Investors	In order to meet the expectations of shareholders and investors, Takeda will fulfill its economic responsibilities by maintaining a stable increase of the dividend payout ratio while pursuing sustainable growth. Takeda will also build better relationships with shareholders and investors by continuing to disclose information in a timely and appropriate manner through its annual report and website.	● Provide information through our Annual Report, website, and other media ● Shareholders meetings and investors' briefings ● Proactive IR activities ● Respond to CSR surveys by socially responsible investors
Relationship with Society	Takeda fully recognizes that the development of society globally is closely linked to the Company's own development. We will constantly consider how we as a corporate citizen should respond to the challenges facing global society and promote our initiatives accordingly. ■ Relationship with Public Organizations In the countries and regions where we conduct business, we will continue to contribute to those countries and associated regions, observing international rules and local laws, and cooperating with public organizations. ■ Relationship with Economic Organizations Takeda cooperates with the activities of economic organizations in regions where it conducts business, recognizing that such activities contribute to the sustainable growth of global society. ■ Relationship with Pharmaceutical Manufacturers' Associations Takeda's cooperation with pharmaceutical manufacturers' associations goes beyond problems facing pharmaceutical manufacturing at home in Japan. We also cooperate with pharmaceutical manufacturers' associations in the countries where we conduct business, to tackle global issues such as access to medicines and fighting disease in developing countries.	● Implement programs in cooperation with NGOs and NPOs ● Activities through involvement in economic and industry groups ● Hold CSR lectures for professional adults and students ● Exchange of views (dialogue) ● Volunteer activities
Relationship with Environment	Takeda is actively working in many ways to minimize the impact on the environment, including in relation to global warming, of the manufacturing process for pharmaceutical products. In addition, we are also taking steps to address biodiversity and water resource issues.	● Dialogue with local residents living near plants ● Disclosure of information through Annual Report and website, etc.
Relationship with Business Partners	Takeda considers partnerships with business partners to be vital to its efforts to develop superior-quality pharmaceutical products. We hope to grow together with our business partners, having gained their understanding of our aspiration to create pharmaceutical products of outstanding Takeda quality.	● Sincere purchasing based on Takeda Code of Compliance Standards and Takeda Basic Purchasing Policy ● Surveys of business partners ● Exchange of views, explanations, study sessions ● Inquiries desk
Relationship with Employees	Takeda aims to establish a work environment where all employees can be proud to work as members of the Takeda Group. We place a value on diversity, personality and individuality among staff, as well as human rights, and consider staff development to be the key driver for growth.	● Global Employee Survey ● Company intranet ● Consultation channel ● Labor-management cooperation ● Counseling ● Internal bulletins ● Hold "Takeda-ism Month" ● A range of skills development training

3.163 The example in Table 3.31 illustrates how customer relationships pose a key risk to the strategy of adidas AG. A major change in the customer base may have a significant effect on the business, because the extent and direction of operations may have to be materially curtailed or expanded and the entity's strategy may have to be modified to meet changed circumstances.

Table 3.31 Relationships – Customers

adidas AG — Annual Report – 31 December 2010

Risk and opportunity report (extract)

Customer risks

Customer risks arise from our dependence on key customers who have the ability to exert bargaining power and can therefore cause considerable margin pressure or cancel orders. These risks exist not only due to the relative size of some of our customers, but also as a result of our limited ability to influence how they conduct business. In addition, over recent years, several large customers have been expanding their own private brand and private label business, which can negatively impact our efforts to increase shelf space.

To limit these risks, we utilise a broad distribution strategy, which includes expanding our controlled space activities. This enables us to reduce negative consequences resulting from sales shortfalls that can occur with key customers. Specifically, no single customer of our Group accounted for more than 10% of Group sales in 2010.

When necessary, we also restrict or limit the distribution of our products to protect brand image or product margins. By differentiating our product offer to customers, we limit the risk of increased price competition on specific products which can result in margin erosion.

Furthermore, with our substantial marketing efforts we are aiming at building desirable brands which resonate with the tastes of our consumers and ultimately drive high sell-through rates for our customers, thus providing less incentive for our customers to engage private label initiatives.

In light of improving retail trends, we believe the risk of a strong reduction of business with one of our biggest retailers is unlikely. Nevertheless, due to increasing customer activity with regard to private brand and private label business, we now believe that on an aggregate level customer risks have increased and have a highly probable likelihood of occurrence on a continuous basis. The potential impact on the Group is regarded as major.

3.164 Table 3.33 illustrates management's efforts to manage relations with its employees to enable it to deliver its business strategy, including a table setting out its performance on employee-related targets.

Table 3.33 Relationships – Employees

Centrica plc – Annual Report and Accounts – 31 December 2010

Business review (extract)

Investing in our employees

Our business is complex and includes many highly technical functions. To undertake our activities safely and deliver a quality of service that matches and exceeds the expectations of our customers requires a highly skilled, motivated and diligent team. In 2010 we employed 34,969 skilled people who carry these responsibilities. Our retention rate was 89.9% compared with 92% in 2009. Retention is slightly down on last year although the improving economy was expected to make more of an impact on our ability to retain employees than it did.

Our 2010 annual employee survey, administered by an independent third party, had a high response rate of 81%. Due to specific changes occurring in British Gas Services to deliver greater flexibility to our customers, our British Gas engineers completed a separate survey. However we identified common themes and completed feedback and action planning process in the same way as for the main survey. The overall engagement score from the 2010 survey dropped two points from 66% to 64%. Given the scale of changes to the business experienced in 2010, this was expected. This score can be compared to an independent external benchmark which indicates that organisations with engagement scores above 60% consistently deliver better business results. We will be moving our engagement survey to a two-year cycle to provide sufficient time to respond to the findings and allow action plans to be better implemented and embedded. Our next full survey will take place in 2012.

We continue to invest in the skills and development of our employees. In 2010, we commenced a strategic review of our capability across the organisation aligned to our long-term strategic priorities. This has provided us with a picture of our future resource and capability needs and enabled us to shape our plans to ensure we have the right people, leadership and capabilities in place at the right time to deliver our business strategy.

For example we opened our British Gas Green Skills academy in Tredegar, Wales, an area of high unemployment. The academy aims to provide over 1,300 training days each year, including training for local long-term unemployed people and people employed by local small and medium enterprises.

We provide highly regarded opportunities for people entering the job market. In 2010, opportunities for 77 summer placements, 70 graduate recruits and 450 technical apprenticeships were provided across the Group.

As part of our performance cycle, employee progress is assessed and discussed with the employee throughout the year and in annual review meetings. Employees each have their own objectives that are aligned to our business strategy. Review meetings provide an opportunity to discuss development, training needs and career planning.

Employees receive regular communication and consultation through a wide variety of media. We increasingly use the intranet for training and communications but also invest in face-to-face events such as vision and values seminars. Company business and financial performance is communicated to all employees using online media, printed materials and face-to-face briefings with members of the Executive Committee.

We aim to have an inclusive and diverse workplace. We are committed to providing equal opportunities for all people. We will not tolerate discrimination against people with disabilities or any other group in recruitment, promotion, training, working conditions or dismissal, subject to health and safety considerations. If employees become disabled while in our employment we offer appropriate support, retraining, equipment and facilities to enable their employment to continue wherever possible.

We encourage greater representation of women and ethnic minorities. For the last eight years, we have undertaken an annual equal pay audit. As in previous years, the 2010 review found that Centrica's performance management and reward practices are not subject to gender bias and confirmed that our approach is aligned to FTSE 100 best practice.

Centrica continues to operate a 24/7 'Speak Up' programme that provides an opportunity for any employee to raise concerns regarding non-compliance with our business principles to an independent third party. In the period October 2009 to September 2010, 16 contacts were handled via the Speak Up programme and in a small number of cases, investigation has highlighted areas where further action has been initiated. We continue to promote awareness of the helpline throughout the year.

Our employees are at the heart of our business. During the year, we were pleased to be recognised for a number of employer awards, more details of which can be found at **www.centrica.com/awards**.

Aim	What we said we'd do in 2010	2010 performance	2009 performance	What we aim to do next
Foster a skilled, productive, motivated and diverse workforce	**Employee engagement[v]:** Achieve 67% employee engagement in the annual survey	64%	66%	Achieve a score of 67% and remain in the high performance category in 2012
	Diversity: Promote diversity and equal opportunities	29.4% female / 70.6% male	30% female / 70% male	Promote diversity in leadership roles and recruitment
		16% from ethnic minority groups	15.5% from ethnic minority groups	
	Attrition and retention: Retain 89% of our workforce in 2010	89.9% retention	92% retention	Retain 90% of our workforce in 2011
	Absence: Reduce absence to 7.5 days per full time employee (FTE)	6.8 days per FTE	7.7 days per FTE	Reduce absence to 6.6 days per FTE

3.165 There are many ways in which an entity's operations may affect the community in which it operates. How the entity interacts with society generally and those who are affected by its operations, can have a significant effect on its reputation and, consequently, on its business performance. The non-financial matters range widely, from the 'big issues', such as ethical trading, human rights and environment, to the smaller but valuable involvement in the community through, for example, donations and secondments of employees to charities and help given to aid organisations dealing with natural disasters. These are disclosed where they are material and relevant to the entity's business strategy. Table 3.34. illustrates one company's approach to the community and environment. Not included in the extract below is the separate report on the company's charitable trust which is included within the annual report. The annual report also includes a cross reference (not shown below) to the company's corporate responsibility website.

Table 3.34 Key relationships – Community and environment

Man Group plc – Annual Report – 31 March 2010

Business Review

Corporate responsibility (extract)

Community

Our engagement with and support of communities both local to Man's offices and further afield is a key differentiator in motivating our staff, attracting new talent and developing a positive culture. .Man's donation to the Man Group plc Charitable Trust and other charities via global offices is based on a formula which guarantees donations of no less than 0.5% of Group pre-tax profits.

This year has seen the launch of ManKind, our employee volunteering programme, where all UK employees receive two days paid leave per year to support either charities of their choice or one of the charities supported by the Trust and promoted in a quarterly programme. Employee volunteering levels are increasing, and we look forward to further engagement next year as ManKind gains momentum.

We partner with Arrival Education in theirs Success for Life programme developed toaddress issues facing young people. Through our management development and training programmes our senior managers are actively engaged in coaching students with the intention of preparing them for success in adulthood.

Our larger offices select an Employee Annual Charity, organising various fundraising activities that are matched by the Trust and global charitable committees. In the UK, employees are encouraged to participate in the Give As You Earn (GAYE) scheme that the Trust matches up to $150 per employee per month.

Environment

Our commitment to measuring and reducing our environmental impact remains a key part of our strategy, as is appropriate to the nature and scale of our office-based business.

In the UK from April 2010 Man will participate in the Carbon Reduction Commitment Energy Efficiency scheme. This is part of the government initiative to encourage companies to address their environmental impacts, specifically their greenhouse gas emissions that cause man-made climate change.

Using an Internet based application, our global non-financial data is consolidated and reported, including our use of utilities and air travel. During the year the Group has continued to enhance its infrastructure through significant investment in technology-driven initiatives that deliver greater efficiency. Our UK offices purchase 'green' electricity and benefit from a combined heat and power plant and an ice bank system. Our Swiss office utilises geothermal heating and cooling whilst the New York office benefits from the use of solar panels. Further progress has been made with the introduction of energy efficient IT infrastructure and video conference units. Whilst we recognise the need for air travel, and limit this where practical, we will continue to purchase Verified Emission Reduction credits to offset our emissions.

We have been a signatory to the Carbon Disclosure Project since 2006 and a member of the Dow Jones Sustainability Index since 2007, demonstrating our climate change commitment to the wider investment community. Man is also a member of the FTSE4Good Index.

3.166 Details should be given of receipts from and returns to shareholders in relation to their shareholdings. This should include a description of distributions, capital raising and repurchases of shares. The information should be given to the extent necessary to give an understanding of the business. [RS (OFR) para 59].

3.167 An entity's dividend policy can impact which investors are interested in the company, depending on whether they are looking for income growth or capital growth. An example disclosure of dividend policy is given in Table 3.35.

Table 3.35 – Relationships – shareholders

Deutsche Lufthansa AG – Annual Report – 31 December 2010

Financial strategy (extract)

↗ Dividend policy keeps the balance between sharing profit and preserving capital

Our dividend policy follows a clear logic and is embedded in our financial strategy: dividend payments are primarily oriented towards the Group's operating profit as reported under IFRS. After successful financial years we have distributed between 30 and 40 per cent of operating profit as a dividend in the past. However, this is subject to the ability to pay a dividend from the net profit for the year reported in the individual financial statements for Deutsche Lufthansa AG under HGB. The proposed amount of the dividend also considers the continued or successive achievement of our financial objectives. The continuity of this dividend policy means that our shareholders share in the success of the Lufthansa Group and we maintain the financial substance of the Company.

Dividend in €

2010	2009	2008	2007	2006
0.60	–	0.70	1.25	0.70

3.168 Significant share issues and repurchases affect members' interests as they may dilute those interests or require members to make further investment, for example in a rights issue. The reasons for such changes in capital may include:

- The need for additional finance for acquisitions or for organic expansion of the business.

- Changing the capital structure to one that the directors consider to be more appropriate to the business' needs by increasing capital and using the proceeds to reduce debt or by repurchasing shares and increasing debt.

- Returning capital as part of cash flow management.

Financial position

3.169 The OFR should include an analysis of the entity's financial position. [RS (OFR) para 60].

General

3.170 An entity's financial position – for example, plans for future capital expenditure and acquisitions and the robustness of its funding position to achieve those plans – is often contained in a separate section of the OFR. In larger entities with diversified operations, additional financial information may be given elsewhere, for example by dividing the OFR into sections covering each of the main business segments, which describe the operations and financial position of each segment. Even where that form of presentation is adopted, however, there is usually a separate financial review dealing with the group's overall financial position.

3.171 The analysis of financial position in the OFR, while based upon the financial statements, should supplement the disclosures required by accounting standards and comment on events that impacted the entity's financial position during the year. This is particularly relevant when a large part of the company operates in an area of economic instability. The analysis should also comment on future factors that are likely to affect the financial position going forward. The reporting statement refers specifically to supplementing disclosures required by FRS 25 (IAS 32),' Financial instruments – Presentation', or FRS 29 (IFRS 7),' Financial instruments: Disclosures'. [RS (OFR) para 61]. The use of derivatives and the requirement of the standards to fair value certain types of instrument means that there can be significant volatility in the reported results. Requirements to classify certain instruments and arrangements involving shares as debt, may also have significant effects on the balance sheet presentation. This is why particular emphasis is placed on the need to further explain the entity's policies and practices in the OFR. The guidance contained in the Manual of Accounting – Financial instruments may be useful when preparing disclosure in this area.

3.172 A number of the measures used to monitor the company's financial position may be directly taken from the financial statements, but directors often supplement these with other measures common to their industry to monitor their progress towards stated objectives. Such disclosure may reflect non-GAAP measures (see paras 3.61 to 3.65) and may include sensitivity analysis, for example in respect of financial instrument values where volatility can have a significant impact on the company's financial position.

3.173 The reporting statement also suggests that discussion should focus on future factors that are likely to affect the position going forward. [RS (OFR) para 61]. Forward-looking statements are discussed above from paragraph 3.39.

Accounting policies

3.174 The OFR should highlight the entity's critical accounting policies. The critical accounting policies are key to understanding the entity's performance and financial position. The focus should be on those that require the particular exercise of judgement in their application to which the results are most sensitive. Discussion of accounting policies should include changes in accounting policies during the year. [RS (OFR) para 62].

3.175 Often this disclosure is a lengthy list of detailed accounting policies – similar to those found in risk disclosures. However, the example above in Table 3.37 shows another approach by highlighting the key areas in which judgements that are made in applying accounting policies relate to the balance sheet. As with risks, emphasising those accounting policies that are truly key to the company's performance and position can make it easier for investors to understand the context in which those results are presented.

3.176 The accounting policies disclosed and discussed will vary from entity to entity and from industry to industry. Critical accounting policies may include the following:

- Revenue recognition – particularly in assessing revenue and profit to be recognised on long-term contracts and multiple component sales.
- Impairment – where choice of discount rates and other assumptions can have significant effects on calculations.
- Taxation – particularly where the entity has international operations and engages in significant tax planning activities.
- Provisions – certain types of provisions, particularly for long-term environmental obligations require significant judgements and estimates.
- Pensions – similar to provisions above, but pensions is an area where there is also additional volatility owing to the effects of stock market fluctuations.
- Intangible assets including goodwill and development expenditure – goodwill and intangibles may comprise a large element of an entity's net assets, particularly in certain industries, such as advertising and publishing. Significant estimates and judgements are often required in assessing recoverability of such intangibles.

3.177 Although the critical accounting policies should be outlined in the OFR, it may be appropriate to cross-refer to the detailed descriptions contained in the notes to the financial statements.

Capital structure and treasury policies

3.178 The OFR should discuss the entity's capital structure and should set out its treasury policies and objectives. [RS (OFR) paras 63, 65].

3.179 This could include:

■ Type of capital instruments used.

■ Balance between equity and debt.

■ Regulatory capital.

■ Maturity profile of debt.

■ Currency.

■ Interest rate structure.

3.180 The discussion should include comments on short- and long-term funding plans to support the directors' strategies to achieve the entity's objectives. In addition, the discussion should comment on why the entity has adopted its particular capital structure.

3.181 For many listed companies, this section of the OFR could be relatively complex. Discussion may include reference to inter-linking issues. For example, a discussion could:

■ Start with a description of the gearing and capital structure at the beginning of the year.

■ Observe that the gearing level was lower or higher than normal.

■ Discuss capital expenditure plans.

■ Explain that ten-year debt was raised to finance that expenditure.

■ Explain that long-term debt was raised because the investment was in long-term assets, but also acknowledge that:

    ■ The group was overly reliant on short-term debt.

    ■ The group wanted to take advantage of the historically low rate of interest on long-term debt.

Finally, this could lead to a discussion of the group's policy regarding fixed or floating rate finance. If interest rate swaps had been taken out as part of this policy, this fact could be explained.

3.182 In another example, a group might have overseas subsidiaries and may have changed the way in which these subsidiaries are financed. For example, the discussion could deal with the opening position, which might be that all funding was in sterling, and explain that the directors had decided during the year that, particularly in the light of their ambitions for overseas expansion, this gave rise to unduly high exchange rate exposure. The discussion could add that the directors had, therefore, decided to finance the overseas operations by a mixture of US dollar and euro borrowings. Alternatively, it might be explained that the group had retained its sterling borrowings, but taken out derivative contracts to hedge the overseas investments.

3.183 An example of disclosure relating to funding strategy is provided in Table 3.38.

Table 3.38 Funding strategy

Transnet Limited – Annual Report – 31 March 2010

Group chief executive's review (extract)

Funding strategy

Transnet has a robust, structured and well articulated funding strategy. Key imperatives for the strategy include: raising cost-effective funding ahead of demand; diversifying Transnet's funding sources, both in the domestic and international markets; and minimising market risk, foreign exchange risk and interest rate risk.

Given the increasingly volatile and uncertain credit markets during the year, the Company developed and implemented a pre-funding strategy. Stated differently, at any given point, Transnet will always 'pre-fund' or maintain a funding buffer of between R3 billion and R6 billion to mitigate the possible impact of the global liquidity risks caused by the recent economic crisis.

Because of the uncertain and volatile market conditions, Transnet elected to commence funding in the latter part of 2009 to avoid the pressure of funding in an area of possible liquidity shortage, which appeared imminent. It also initiated and utilised numerous funding platforms outside the norm to diversify and create additional avenues for funding both in the local and international arena.

The funding requirement for the year was R20 billion, including maturing debt. This was driven primarily by the need to fund the capital investment plan. During the year, Transnet raised the required R20 billion including pre-funding. Funding initiatives undertaken during the fiscal year under review are set out in the Chief Financial Officer's Review.

Transnet established its US$2 billion Global Medium Term Note (GMTN) programme, enabling the Company to issue bonds in the euro, dollar and pound sterling markets. Post-balance sheet, an international investor roadshow was conducted in Europe (UK and Germany) and the United States. This was in keeping with our strategy to diversify funding sources. However, due to the effect of the euro zone debt crisis on the credit markets, the Company deferred the issuance of any bonds to a later stage when markets have calmed down.

In addition, Transnet started negotiations with the African Development Bank (AfDB) for a substantial loan facility. Discussions are at an advanced stage, and a due diligence was conducted by the AfDB during the year.

Transnet has successfully created capacity by establishing and increasing available credit lines for ongoing funding and risk management. Further, the Company negotiated favourable credit terms in a market where lenders have tightened their credit terms.

In future, the commercial paper programme and long-term bonds, which are part of our R30 billion Domestic Medium Term Note (DMTN) programme, will continue to be the main sources of funding, although of course, in keeping with our strategy to diversify sources of cost-effective funding, we will also increasingly tap new sources such as the export credit agency, development finance institutions and international bonds under our GMTN programme. As in the past, Transnet will be responsible and strategic in the way it rolls out its funding strategy.

Also, critically important will be the continuation of Transnet's current self-funding method: that is borrowing on the strength of its financial position without reliance on Government subsidies or guarantees. A key part of this plan will be to vigilantly monitor adherence to the key financial metrics, such as cash interest cover, and maintaining and improving Transnet's positive standalone investment-grade credit rating.

targets for 2011

Key features of the funding strategy

Mitigate market risk.

Reduce weighted average cost of debt.

Diversify investor base and sources of funding.

Continue with the **pre-funding strategy**.

Raise **R17,2 billion** cost effectively.

Probable sources of funding

	Total R million
Commercial paper	2 209
Domestic bonds	4 000
Development finance institutions	5 000
Bank loans	2 000
International bonds	4 000
Total	**17 209**

Our key focus areas going forward – "Quantum Leap" (extract)

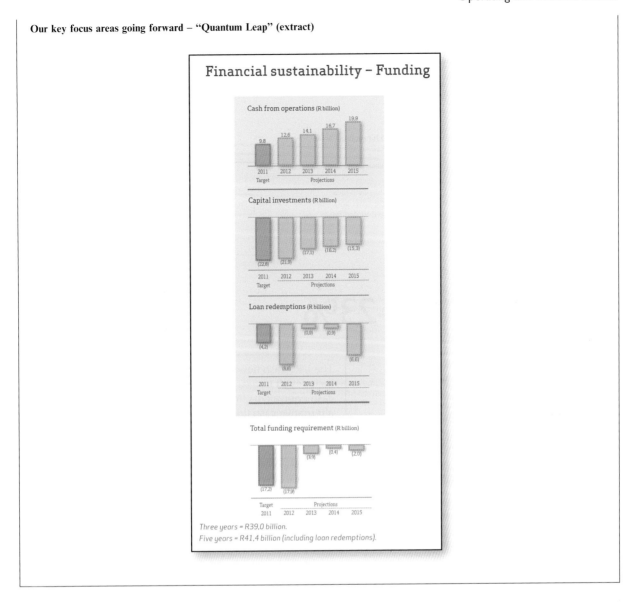

Cash flows

3.184   The OFR should discuss the cash inflows and outflows during the financial year, together with the entity's ability to generate cash, to meet known or probable cash requirements and to fund growth. [RS (OFR) para 68].

3.185   The discussion should supplement the information in the financial statements around operating, investing and financing cash flows. [RS (OFR) para 69]. Specific commentary should be given on cash flows by segment where this is different from profit by segment. [RS (OFR) para 70]. This would be relevant, for example, in a long-term contracting business where the agreed timing of billings and cash receipts is out of line with profit recognition.

3.186   The OFR should comment on any special factors that have influenced cash flows in the period and that may have a significant effect on future cash flows. This could include the existence and timing of commitments for capital expenditure and other known or probable cash requirements. [RS (OFR) para 69]. An example of the latter might be the need to repay a large tranche of debt at a particular date in the future. Unusual or non-recurring cash flows should be highlighted where material, such as proceeds of a sale and leaseback or the termination of an interest rate swap.

3.187   Where an entity has cash that is surplus to its future operating requirements and its current levels of distributions to members, the OFR should discuss the entity's plans for making use of the cash. [RS (OFR) para 69]. Table 3.35 above indicates an example of a company reporting on its use of surplus cash.

3.188   Cash flow is real; whether a company has more or less cash is not a matter of judgement. So, for many users of financial statements cash flow is a key measure of performance and entities often develop KPIs that relate to cash flow. Some measures focus on cash flow from operations after meeting the entity's obligations for interest, tax and dividends and after capital expenditure, which is sometimes termed 'free cash flow'. However, definitions of 'free cash flow' (a non-GAAP measure) often vary from entity to entity and should, therefore, be fully explained. An example of disclosure of free cash flow is provided in Table 3.40.

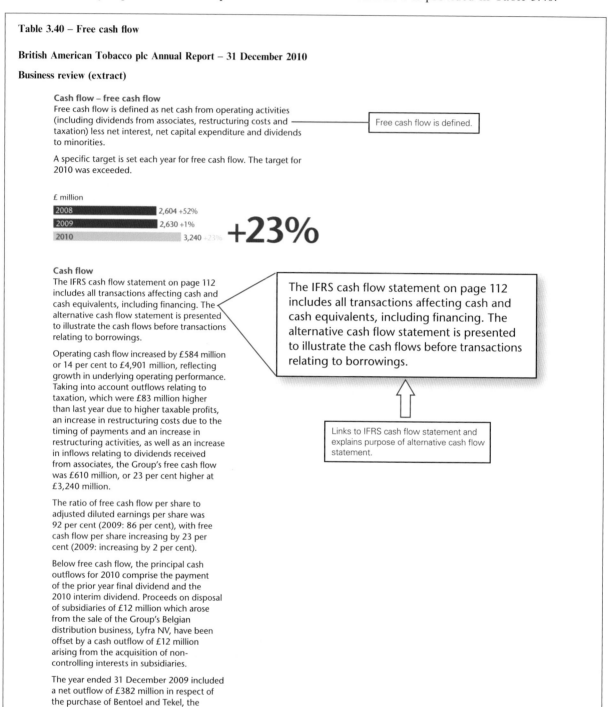

Table 3.40 – Free cash flow

British American Tobacco plc Annual Report – 31 December 2010

Business review (extract)

Cash flow – free cash flow

Free cash flow is defined as net cash from operating activities (including dividends from associates, restructuring costs and taxation) less net interest, net capital expenditure and dividends to minorities.

> Free cash flow is defined.

A specific target is set each year for free cash flow. The target for 2010 was exceeded.

£ million

2008 2,604 +52%
2009 2,630 +1%
2010 3,240 +23%

+23%

Cash flow

The IFRS cash flow statement on page 112 includes all transactions affecting cash and cash equivalents, including financing. The alternative cash flow statement is presented to illustrate the cash flows before transactions relating to borrowings.

> The IFRS cash flow statement on page 112 includes all transactions affecting cash and cash equivalents, including financing. The alternative cash flow statement is presented to illustrate the cash flows before transactions relating to borrowings.

> Links to IFRS cash flow statement and explains purpose of alternative cash flow statement.

Operating cash flow increased by £584 million or 14 per cent to £4,901 million, reflecting growth in underlying operating performance. Taking into account outflows relating to taxation, which were £83 million higher than last year due to higher taxable profits, an increase in restructuring costs due to the timing of payments and an increase in restructuring activities, as well as an increase in inflows relating to dividends received from associates, the Group's free cash flow was £610 million, or 23 per cent higher at £3,240 million.

The ratio of free cash flow per share to adjusted diluted earnings per share was 92 per cent (2009: 86 per cent), with free cash flow per share increasing by 23 per cent (2009: increasing by 2 per cent).

Below free cash flow, the principal cash outflows for 2010 comprise the payment of the prior year final dividend and the 2010 interim dividend. Proceeds on disposal of subsidiaries of £12 million which arose from the sale of the Group's Belgian distribution business, Lyfra NV, have been offset by a cash outflow of £12 million arising from the acquisition of non-controlling interests in subsidiaries.

The year ended 31 December 2009 included a net outflow of £382 million in respect of the purchase of Bentoel and Tekel, the proceeds from the ST trademark disposals and £2 million refunded from the original purchase consideration paid in 2008.

The other net flows principally relate to the impact of the level of shares purchased by the employee share ownership trusts and outflows in respect of certain derivative financial instruments.

The above flows resulted in net cash inflows of £1,070 million (2009: £433 million inflow). After taking account of exchange rate movements, net debt disposed and the change in accrued interest and other, total net debt was £7,841 million at 31 December 2010, down £1,001 million from £8,842 million on 31 December 2009.

Cash flow and net debt movements

	2010 £m	2009 £m
Adjusted profit from operations	4,984	4,461
Depreciation, amortisation and impairment	442	446
Other non-cash items in operating profit	59	25
Profit from operations before depreciation and impairment	5,485	4,932
Increase in working capital	(61)	(100)
Net capital expenditure	(523)	(515)
Gross capital expenditure	(584)	(554)
Sale of fixed assets	61	39
Operating cash flow	4,901	4,317
Net interest paid	(491)	(499)
Tax paid	(1,178)	(1,095)
Dividends paid to non-controlling interests	(234)	(234)
Restructuring costs	(219)	(187)
Dividends from associates	461	328
Free cash flow	3,240	2,630
Dividends paid to shareholders	(2,093)	(1,798)
Net investment activities	–	(196)
Purchases of subsidiaries and non-controlling interests	(12)	(383)
Disposal of subsidiaries and trademarks	12	187
Net flow from share schemes and other	(77)	(203)
Net cash flow	1,070	433
External movements on net debt		
Exchange rate effects*	(41)	672
Net debt disposed/(acquired)	11	(84)
Change in accrued interest and other	(39)	28
Change in net debt	1,001	1,049
Opening net debt	(8,842)	(9,891)
Closing net debt	(7,841)	(8,842)

*Including movements in respect of debt related derivatives

Liquidity

3.189 The OFR should discuss the entity's current and prospective liquidity. This should include, where relevant, a commentary on the level of borrowings, the seasonality of borrowing requirements (indicated by the peak level of borrowings during the period) and the maturity profile of borrowings and undrawn committed borrowing facilities. [RS (OFR) para 73].

3.190 The discussion should cover the entity's ability to fund its current and future operations and stated strategies. [RS (OFR) para 72]. This is consistent with the increased emphasis on the need for a forward-looking orientation.

3.191 An example of disclosure of current and future liquidity is shown in Table 3.41, including explanations of the impact of the seasonality of its business.

3.192 Beyond information on liquidity, our research has shown that investors also want a clear picture of a company's debt position in order to understand management's plans for servicing it and any risks associated with it. Companies have to give information about how they are funded, but this can be scattered throughout the annual report – both in the OFR and in the financial statements. In addition, some of the information relating to debt is not provided in the annual report at all – investors get the information outside the regulatory model. In Table 3.41 ITV plc presents its debt maturity profile diagrammatically to accompany the narrative commentary.

Table 3.41 Maturity profile of debt

ITV plc – Annual Report – 31 December 2010

Financial and performance review (extract)

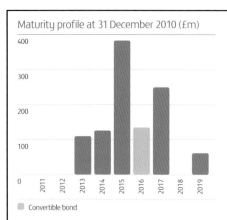

Maturity profile at 31 December 2010 (£m)

Convertible bond

Funding

ITV is aware of the perceived inefficiency of holding £860 million of cash and cash equivalents and over £1 billion of gross debt, but it is important to note the speed at which the net debt has reduced over the past two years. The extent of decline of the television advertising market in 2008 and 2009, and then the subsequent recovery in 2010, was unexpected. This recovery, combined with tight cash control, has allowed net debt to reduce significantly over two years from £730 million at 31 December 2008 to £188 million at 31 December 2010. In addition to net debt of £188 million at 31 December 2010, the Group also has an IAS 19 Pension Deficit of £313 million.

In 2010 ITV bought back €63 million (£54 million) nominal of the 2011 bonds, £42 million nominal of 2015 bonds and repaid the £50 million May 2013 loan. As at 31 December 2010, ITV's net sterling position after the impact of cross currency swaps against the remaining €54 million 2011 Eurobond is a receivable of £16 million. This receivable has arisen due to large positive swap values arising from favourable currency movements; when ITV exchanged or bought back these series of bonds it was more efficient to enter into new swaps to protect this position rather than terminate existing swaps.

In October 2010 ITV increased the size of its undrawn, covenant free bilateral bank facility secured on advertising receivables from £75 million to £125 million and the maturity of this facility was extended from March 2013 to September 2015. This facility remains undrawn. ITV is financed using debt instruments with a range of maturities. Borrowings at 31 December 2010 (net of currency hedges and secured gilts) are repayable as follows:

Amount repayable	£m	Maturity
€54 million Eurobond*	(16)	October 2011
£110 million Eurobond	110	March 2013
€188 million Eurobond*	126	June 2014
£383 million Eurobond	383	October 2015
£135 million Convertible bond	135	November 2016
£250 million Eurobond	250	January 2017
£200 million bank loan**	62	March 2019
Finance leases	61	Various
Total repayable	**1,111**	

* Net of cross currency swaps.
**Net of £138 million (nominal) Gilts secured against the loan.

At 31 December 2010 ITV had £860 million of cash and cash equivalents. This figure includes £89 million of cash equivalents whose use is restricted to finance lease commitments and unfunded pension commitments. Cash and cash equivalents also include £47 million held principally in overseas and part owned subsidiaries.

As explained above, steps have been taken to repurchase some of the more expensive debt. The remaining debt now held is not expensive given our credit rating (at an average gross cost of debt of 7%), is an appropriate mix of medium to long-term debt and has no financial covenants. As ITV drives forward the Transformation Plan it is also important that some flexibility is maintained to invest in the business.

© 2012 PricewaterhouseCoopers LLP. All rights reserved.

3.193 The problem of determining a company's credit risk profile is even greater if it has a number of subsidiaries. In this case, investors need a clear debt profile of the group and its individual business units, as well as an understanding of any restrictions on the transfer of funds between business units. Such internal sources of liquidity should be discussed. If there are restrictions on the group's ability to transfer funds from one part of the group to meet the obligations of another part of the group – for example as a result of exchange controls or tax consequences of transfers – this should be discussed. This applies where the restrictions *"...represent, or might foreseeably come to represent..."* a significant restraint on the group. [RS (OFR) para 73]. The restrictions could be in the form of legal barriers, such as exchange controls, that preclude or limit repatriation of profits, or they could be commercial obstacles, such as where funds could be repatriated, but unduly high rates of withholding or other taxes would have to be paid.

3.194 Investors' view of debt does not stop at financial instruments or borrowings. They want to know about other debt-like liabilities. These could include revenues paid in advance by customers, operating leases, pensions, or other liabilities such as decommissioning costs that could trigger major cash outflows in the future.

3.195 We suggest that companies should include an analysis of net debt that incorporates financial debt, operating debt in off-balance sheet leases and other debt-like liabilities. Although not a requirement, investors have indicated that they value such disclosure. Investors believe all instruments that the company views as debt should be incorporated in this statement, including instruments that accounting standards classify as equity. By the same token, instruments classified by accounting standards as debt, but which the company sees as equity, should be excluded. A comprehensive maturity table of all components, analysis by currency and by subsidiary and details of any collateral or other restrictions are also highly desirable to investors.

3.196 Net debt analyses are common amongst UK companies – most often within the notes to the financial statements. Table 3.42 shows a company that has included a separate 'analysis of net debt' after its 'consolidated cash flow statement' and cross-references to other financial statement notes for further details of maturities etc.

Table 3.42 – Analysis of net debt

Home Retail Group plc – Annual Report & Financial Statements – 26 February 2011

Consolidated Cash Flow Statement (extract)

Analysis of net cash/(debt)

At 26 February 2011

Non-GAAP measures	Notes	26 February 2011 £m	27 February 2010 £m
Financing net cash:			
Cash and cash equivalents	20	**159.3**	364.0
Current asset investments	19	**100.0**	50.0
Total financing net cash		**259.3**	414.0
Operating net debt:			
Off balance sheet operating leases		**(2,874.1)**	(3,148.1)
Total operating net debt		**(2,874.1)**	(3,148.1)
Total net debt		**(2,614.8)**	(2,734.1)
Adjusted for:			
Off balance sheet operating leases		**2,874.1**	3,148.1
Current asset investments	19	**(100.0)**	(50.0)
Total cash and cash equivalents reflected in balance sheet		**159.3**	364.0

The Group uses the term 'total net debt' to highlight the Group's aggregate net indebtedness to banks and other financial institutions together with debt-like liabilities, notably operating leases. The capitalised value of these leases is £2,874.1m (2010: £3,148.1m), based upon discounting the current rentals at the estimated current long-term cost of borrowing of 4.1% (2010: 4.1%).

Current asset investments comprise term cash deposits invested for initial terms of between six and nine months, which mature after the balance sheet date. The analysis of net cash/(debt) forms part of the notes to the financial statements.

3.197 Our research has also shown that investors consider a net debt reconciliation to be a particularly useful disclosure. A net debt reconciliation is intended to show how an entity's indebtedness has changed over a period as a result of cash flows and other non-cash movements. A net debt reconciliation allows investors to see how business financing has changed over the year. It is a way of identifying whether an entity that, for example, seems to have had a significant increase in cash has, for example, achieved this only by taking on a corresponding increase in debt. It can also highlight:

■ Debt acquired or disposed of in business combinations;

■ Foreign exchange movements arising on debt; and

■ Information that is not always obvious elsewhere in the statements.

3.198 In providing a net debt reconciliation, companies should explain clearly what they mean by 'net debt', preferably with an accompanying analysis. Table 3.42.1 is an example of a net debt reconciliation.

Table 3.42.1 – Net debt reconciliation

GlaxoSmithKline plc – 31 December 2010

Business review (extract)

Financial position and resources (extract)

Net debt

	2010 £m	2009 £m
Cash, cash equivalents and liquid investments	**6,241**	6,813
Borrowings – repayable within one year	**(291)**	(1,471)
Borrowings – repayable after one year	**(14,809)**	(14,786)
Net debt	**(8,859)**	(9,444)

Net debt decreased by £585 million due to the free cash flow generated by the company exceeding the amounts paid in dividends to shareholders and invested in new businesses.

Movements in net debt

	2010 £m	2009 £m
Net debt at beginning of year	**(9,444)**	(10,173)
(Decrease)/increase in cash and bank overdrafts	**(642)**	1,054
Cash inflow from liquid investments	**(91)**	(87)
Net increase in long-term loans	**–**	(1,358)
Net repayment of short-term loans	**1,290**	102
Debt of subsidiary undertakings acquired	**(20)**	(9)
Exchange movements	**61**	1,041
Other movements	**(13)**	(14)
Net debt at end of year	**(8,859)**	(9,444)

3.199 In Table 3.43, Diageo plc gives information on contractual obligations. Post employment benefits are not included in the table, but the narrative explains their position.

Table 3.43 Contractual obligations

Diageo plc -Annual Report – 30 June 2010

Business review (extract)

Contractual obligations

	Less than 1 year £ million	1-3 years £ million	3-5 years £ million	Payments due by period More than 5 years £ million	Total £ million
As at 30 June 2010					
Long term debt obligations	439	2,124	2,666	3,205	8,434
Interest obligations	461	829	600	1,335	3,225
Credit support obligations	80	–	–	–	80
Operating leases	95	147	108	322	672
Finance leases	8	16	12	80	116
Deferred consideration payable	3	25	–	–	28
Purchase obligations	776	585	142	17	1,520
Provisions and other non-current payables	134	113	52	138	437
	1,996	3,839	3,580	5,097	14,512

Long term debt obligations comprise the principal amount of borrowings (excluding foreign currency swaps) with an original maturity of greater than one year. Interest obligations comprise interest payable on these borrowings. Where interest payments are on a floating rate basis, rates of each cash flow until maturity of the instruments are calculated based on the forward yield curve at the last business day of the year ended 30 June 2010. Credit support obligations represent liabilities to counterparty banks in respect of cash received as collateral under credit support agreements. Purchase obligations include various long term purchase contracts entered into for the supply of certain raw materials, principally bulk whisky, grapes, cans and glass bottles. The contracts are used to guarantee supply of raw materials over the long term and to enable more accurate predictions of future costs. Provisions and other non-current payables exclude £14 million in respect of vacant properties and £75 million for onerous contracts, which are included in operating leases and purchase obligations, respectively.

Potential income tax exposures included within corporate tax payable of £391 million (2009 – £532 million) and deferred tax liabilities are not included in the table above, as the ultimate timing of settlement cannot be reasonably estimated.

Post employment benefit liabilities are also not included in the table above. The group makes service-based cash contributions to the UK Pension Scheme which in the year ending 30 June 2011, are expected to be approximately £50 million. The company has agreed a deficit funding plan with the trustee of the UK Scheme based on the trustee's actuarial valuation at 31 March 2009 under which annual income of approximately £25 million will be generated by the new funding structure for the UK Pension Scheme, commencing in the year ended 30 June 2011. The company also agreed to make conditional contributions of up to £338 million if an equivalent reduction in deficit is not achieved over the 10 year term of the funding plan. In addition, Diageo has provisionally agreed a deficit funding arrangement in respect of the Guinness Ireland Group Pension Scheme (the Irish Scheme) which is expected to result in additional annual contributions to the Irish Scheme of €21 million (£17 million) for the next 18 years. The company also provisionally agreed to make conditional contributions of up to €188 million (£154 million) if an equivalent reduction in deficit is not achieved over the next 18 years. Annual contributions to the GrandMet Irish Pension Fund of €6 million (£5 million) have been agreed with the Irish trustee for the next seven years. Contributions to other plans in the year ending 30 June 2011 are expected to be approximately £128 million.

Capital commitments at 30 June 2010 are excluded from the table above.

3.200 Another example of disclosure of current and future liquidity is shown in Table 3.43.1. This example also gives details of cash flows and of funding, such as operating leases that are not treated as debt.

3.201 Management should disclose when borrowing covenants are in place that restrict the use of financing arrangements or credit facilities and *"...negotiations with the lenders on the operation of these covenants are taking place or are expected to take place"*. The reporting statement also states that *"where a breach of a covenant has occurred or is expected to occur, the OFR should give details of the measures taken or proposed to remedy the situation"*. [RS (OFR) para 74]. In Table 3.43A, a company discloses its financial covenants.

Table 3.43.1 – Financial covenants

Great Portland Estates plc – Annual Report -31 March 2011

Notes to the financial statements (extract)

The Group meets its day-to-day working capital requirements through the utilisation of its revolving credit facilities. The availability of these facilities depends on the Group complying with a number of key financial covenants; these covenants and the Group's compliance with these covenants are set out in the table below:

Key covenants	Covenant	March 2010 Actuals
Group		
Net debt/net equity	≤1.25x	0.26x
Inner borrowing	≥1.66x	5.43x
Interest cover	≥1.30x	3.55x
Joint venture – GCP		
Loan to value	≤70%	45.6%

The Group has undrawn credit facilities of £417 million and has substantial headroom above all of its key covenants. As a result the directors consider the Group to have adequate liquidity to be able to fund the ongoing operations of the business.

3.202 The meaning of the second quote in paragraph 3.201 is clear, although there is some judgement involved in addressing whether a breach of covenant is expected to occur. But the meaning of the first quote is quite clear. It recommends disclosure when negotiations are being held, perhaps to change the covenants, in a situation where there is neither a breach nor any expectation of a breach. An example might be where a covenant is being renegotiated, not because of financial difficulty, but following the introduction of a new accounting standard that alters the ratios without any change in the underlying economic position.

3.203 Take an example where an entity's year end borrowings were £450,000, peak borrowings were £550,000 and its facilities were £500,000, that is, it had temporarily exceeded its borrowing facilities and breached its covenants. The reporting statement's recommendation in such circumstances is for the entity to give details about *"...measures taken or proposed to remedy the situation"*. This could lead to awkward disclosures if the company and its bankers have not agreed what the remedial measures might be. Disclosure in these circumstances is of course exactly what the reporting statement is aiming for and exactly what investors would welcome. An example of disclosure of a breach of covenant is given in Table 3.43.2.

Table 3.43.2 – Breach of covenant

Thomas Coffey limited – 30 June 2010

Directors Report (extract)

Notes to the financial statements (extract)

Note 1 Significant accounting policies (extract)

GOING CONCERN

As at 30 June 2010, the consolidated entity was in breach of its borrowing covenants with respect to its banking facilities. Subsequent to year end the consolidated entity received a waiver from the financier and amended covenants are to apply during the year ending 30 June 2011. Further details regarding the breach of the borrowing covenants, waiver and amended covenants are detailed in the note 1 of the financial statements.

Accordingly, no adjustments have been made to the financial report relating to the recoverability and classification of recorded asset amounts and classification of liabilities that might be necessary should the consolidated entity not continue as a going concern.

Going concern

As at 30 June 2010, the consolidated entity was in breach of its borrowing covenants with respect to its banking facilities. As a result, the consolidated entity classified $12.5m of borrowings for which the facility expires in excess of 12 months from the reporting date as current liabilities on the statement of financial position, reflecting at that time the lender had the right to call these funds immediately. As a result the consolidated entity had a net current asset deficiency of $10,106,000.

Subsequent to the 30 June 2010 the consolidated entity's financier agreed to a borrowing covenant waiver as at 30 June 2010 and amended the covenants to apply during the year ending 30 June 2011.

The ongoing viability of the consolidated entity and its ability to continue as a going concern and meet its debts and commitments as they fall due are mainly dependent upon the consolidated entity being successful in:

1. receiving the continuing support of its financiers; and

2. achieving forecast operational performance and generate sufficient future cash flows to meet its business objectives and financial obligations.

The directors believe that the consolidated entity will be successful in the above matters and, accordingly, have prepared the financial report on a going concern basis. At this time, the directors are of the opinion that no asset is likely to be realised for an amount less than the amount at which it is recorded in the financial report at 30 June 2010. This is mainly due to the following factors:

1. the directors expect the consolidated entity will achieve positive operating cash flows;

2. since the 30th June 2010, the consolidated entity's banker has provided a waiver for the 30 June covenant breaches and amended the financial covenants to apply during the year ending 30 June 2011. (refer to note 19 for further details of the amended facility). The directors expect the consolidated entity to comply with these covenants;

3. the directors have announced that a number of capital raising initiatives are also being considered;

4. if required the consolidated entity will sell non-core assets in line with the strategic direction of the consolidated entity.

In addition and as a result of the loss for the year and the classification of borrowings as current the consolidated entity has not met financial requirements under certain licensing regulatory criteria at year end. Steps are being taken to ensure the licenses are maintained and renewed.

Accordingly, no adjustments have been made to the financial report relating to the recoverability and classification of recorded asset amounts and classification of liabilities that might be necessary should the consolidated entity not continue as a going concern.

3.204 FRS 18, 'Accounting policies', and IAS 1, 'Presentation of financial statements', require disclosure (by all companies) of any material uncertainties, of which directors are aware, that may cast significant doubt on the entity's ability to continue as a going concern. [FRS 18 para 61; IAS 1 para 23]. In addition, IFRS 7 requires disclosures of any defaults and breaches of principal, interest, sinking fund or redemption provisions on loans payable and of any other breaches of loan agreements where the breaches can permit the lender to demand repayment (except where the breaches have remedied before the balance sheet date). [IFRS 7 paras 18, 19]. The Manual of Accounting – Financial instruments deals with these requirements.

3.205 Management should discuss any seasonality in its liquidity position. If the level of borrowings at the year end is not representative of the normal level during the year, this should be disclosed. If the level of cash is unrepresentative of the year as a whole this should also be disclosed.

Going concern

3.206 The FSA's Listing Rules require a listed company to make a statement that it is a going concern, as part of its corporate governance disclosures. [LR 9.8.6R (3)]. Often the required statement is made in the OFR, usually in the financial review section.

3.207 Guidance on the form of going concern statement that companies might use was published in November 1994 in a document entitled 'Going concern and financial reporting — guidance for directors of listed companies registered in the UK'. An example of disclosure given in the document was:

> *"After making enquiries, the directors have a reasonable expectation that the company has adequate resources to continue in operational existence for the foreseeable future. For this reason, they continue to adopt the going concern basis in preparing the accounts."*

3.208 Most going concern statements do no more than reproduce with minor variations the suggested wording of the guidance. Table 3.43.2 shows an example that points out that in the business' particular circumstances, there are a number of fundamental uncertainties in relation to going concern

Key performance indicators

3.209 To the extent necessary to meet the requirements set out in paragraph 3.110 above, the OFR should disclose the key performance indicators (KPIs), both financial and non-financial, used by the directors to assess progress against their stated objectives. [RS (OFR) para 38].

3.210 Key performance indicators are those the directors judge are effective in measuring the entity's development, performance or position. They are quantified measurements that reflect the entity's critical success factors and disclose progress towards achieving a particular objective or objectives. [RS (OFR) para 3]. The explanation of the entity's performance measures will be part of the company's broader discussion of its performance. See further from paragraph 3.118.

What is key?

3.211 The reporting statement does not prescribe specific KPIs that entities should disclose. However, comparability will be enhanced if the KPIs are accepted and widely used, either within an industry sector or more generally. [RS (OFR) para 40]. The performance indicators that are key to a particular company are those that the directors use to manage the business.

3.212 A challenge is whether the KPIs currently presented to the board are those that allow them to assess progress against stated strategies, and when reported externally, allow readers to make a similar assessment. If not, is this because the information is simply not available or because it is not yet escalated to the board but may instead be assessed by management of individual business units?

3.213 In addition, the KPIs will, to a degree, be conditioned by the industry in which a company operates. Comparability will be enhanced if the KPIs are accepted and widely used, either within an industry sector or more generally. [RS (OFR) para 40]. However, management should not feel compelled to create KPIs to match those reported by their peers. The overriding need is for the KPIs to be relevant to that particular company. Management should explain its choice in the context of the chosen strategies and objectives and provide sufficient detail on measurement methods to allow readers to make comparisons to other companies' choices where they want to.

How many KPIs?

3.214   Where multiple performance measures are disclosed, management should explain which are key to managing the business. The choice of which ones are key is unique to each company and its strategy; it is impossible to specify how many KPIs a company should have. However, in practice, companies typically report between four and ten measures.

How flexible is the choice of KPIs?

3.215   Management should reflect on whether the KPIs chosen continue to be relevant over time. Strategies and objectives develop over time, sometimes making it inappropriate to continue reporting the same KPIs as in previous periods. Equally, more information may become available to management, facilitating reporting of new KPIs that provide a deeper understanding of the business, or changing how an existing KPI is calculated.

Does reliability matter?

3.216   Management may sometimes be concerned about the reliability of some of the information reported on KPIs, particularly as they are encouraged to move beyond the more traditional financial KPIs that are usually the output of established systems and controls processes and routine audit. There is no specific narrative reporting requirement for KPIs to be reliable, but the nature of the information should be clear to the users of narrative reports.

3.217   In order to address this issue and provide readers with useful information, it is more important that the limitations of the data and any assumptions made in providing it are clearly explained. Readers can then judge the reliability for themselves and make any necessary adjustments in their own analysis. Where data has been specifically assured by independent third parties, identifying this may also assist the reader.

Reporting KPIs – a model for effective communication

3.218   The reporting statement does not prescribe either the types or the methods of calculating KPIs. However, to ensure that the KPIs can be understood by readers and properly used by them to assess the strategies adopted by the entity and the potential for those strategies to succeed, it sets out a model for effective communication of KPIs, recommending certain disclosures to be given for each KPI reported in the OFR, as follows:

- The KPI definition and its calculation method. Given the rapidly increasing use of industry-specific terminology, clear definitions of performance indicators add greatly to the reader's understanding of exactly what is being measured and allows comparisons between companies within an industry. An explanation of a metric's components and how it is calculated should be included, given the absence of standards for the measurement of many industry-specific indicators and with many companies also applying their own indicators.

- The KPI's purpose. Management should explain why it believes a performance indicator is relevant. This may be because it measures progress towards achieving a specific strategic objective.

- The source of underlying data and, where relevant, assumptions. To enable readers to make their own assessment of the reliability of the information, management should identify the sources of the data used in calculating performance indicators and any limitations on that data. Any assumptions made in measuring performance should be explained so that readers can reach an informed view of judgements made by management.

- Quantification or commentary on future targets. Some performance indicators are best suited to a quantification of future targets. Expectations and aims for other indicators may be better explained in commentary. Either way, a forward-looking orientation is essential for readers to assess the potential for strategies to succeed and to give them a basis against which to assess future performance.

- Where information from the financial statements has been adjusted for inclusion in the OFR, that fact and a reconciliation should be provided. Performance indicators may be financial or non-financial. Where the amounts measured are financial, but are not 'traditional' measures required by accounting standards (that is, GAAP measures), it is good practice to explain any differences. A reconciliation should, therefore, be provided between accounting measures and non-GAAP measures.

- Corresponding amounts, where available, should be given for the previous year. Measurement of performance in isolation over a single period does not provide the reader with useful information. An indication of how performance has changed over time is much more valuable in assessing the success of management's strategies. It is also beneficial to explain to the reader what a particular trend in the data means (for example, an increasing measure is not always a sign of strength) and to explain management's actions to address or maintain such trends.

- Any changes to KPIs and their measurement used compared to previous years should be identified and explained, including significant changes in the underlying accounting policies adopted in the financial statements.

[RS (OFR) paras 75, 76, 77].

3.219 The following information is also useful to investors and management when considering reporting around KPIs:

- Link to strategy: the primary reason for including performance indicators in corporate reporting is to enable readers to assess the strategies adopted by the company and their potential to succeed. KPIs presented in isolation from strategies and objectives, or *vice versa*, cannot fulfil this requirement and will fail to provide the reader with the level of understanding they need.

- Segmental: Management should consider how KPIs are collated and reported internally; whether they make sense when aggregated and reported at a group level, or would be more usefully reported at business segment level. Corporate reporting users may want more detailed segmental information to assess progress towards specific segmental strategic aims. Performance indicators that are relevant to a specific segment's industry or strategy should, therefore, be provided in addition to those with a more group-wide focus.

- Benchmarking: Performance benchmarked against a relevant peer group, with an explanation of why these peers were chosen, is valuable to users. It provides a clear indication of who management believes the company's competitors to be, as well as setting the company's own performance in the context of a well defined peer group.

3.220 The implementation guidance contains 23 examples of types of KPI. Each of the examples in the guidance follows the disclosure recommendations described above. But the layout shown in the examples is not prescriptive and directors should decide how best to present the information, perhaps by presenting some of the details in footnotes or in a separate section of the OFR.

3.221 The following examples, in Tables 3.44, 3.45 and 3.46, show how three companies have aligned their KPIs with specific group strategies and objectives and to illustrate a variety of content aspects. Note also that the disclosure of risks provided by the first two companies (see Tables 3.29 and 3.28.3) reflects on the link with KPIs.

Table 3.44 – Key performance indicators

Taylor Wimpey plc – Annual report – 31 December 2010

Business Review (extracts)

Strategy

Vision and goal

Taylor Wimpey is a focused community developer. We aim to be the developer of choice for customers, employees, shareholders and communities.

Our Group strategy

We create value through active management of our land portfolio and deliver this value through building high quality communities that meet the needs of local residents and our customers.

Long term objectives

- Provide growth in earnings per share, in light of market conditions.
- Deliver a return on capital employed above the level of our cost of funding.
- Return the Group to an investment-grade credit rating.
- Attract and retain the highest calibre of employees and strive to be a company that people want to work for.

Short term priorities

- Enhance the Group's profitability in both of our main markets through:
  - Focusing on sales price increases rather than volume growth.
  - Continued focus on operating efficiency.
  - Maintaining a tight control on overhead costs.
- Active management of our land portfolio.
- Evaluate proposals for our North American business.
- Maximise the potential of our employees through training and development programmes.

Group key performance indicators

Our Group KPIs provide a measure of our performance against our strategy

Adjusted earnings/(loss) per share

0.6p
for 2010

Objective
We seek to provide growth in earnings per share in light of market conditions.

Definition
The basic earnings per share from continuing operations based upon the profit attributable to ordinary shareholders before exceptional items divided by the average number of shares in issue during the year.

Why is it key to our strategy?
The generation of earnings is essential to deliver share price growth and dividends to shareholders and to fund future growth in the business. This measure is also commonly used by stock market analysts in assessing the value of companies.

Return on average capital employed

8.2%
for 2010

Objective
We aim to deliver a return on capital employed above the level of our cost of funding.

Definition
Profit on ordinary activities before finance costs, exceptional items and amortisation of brands but including share of results of joint ventures, divided by the average of opening and closing tangible net worth.

Why is it key to our strategy?
Developing communities is a capital-intensive business due to the need to fund our landbank, so it is essential to ensure that this capital is used as effectively as possible.

Tangible net assets per share

56.9p
for 2010

Objective
To deliver growth in tangible net assets per share as market conditions allow.

Definition
The net asset value of the Group, as reported on the consolidated Balance Sheet, less goodwill and other intangible assets, divided by the number of shares in issue at the period end.

Why is it key to our strategy?
The Group must meet its financial covenants in order to retain access to its debt funding.

Please note this key performance indicator has been amended following the Group's refinancing in December 2010, which removed the requirement to meet the cash flow covenant test as set out in the previous financing arrangement.

Employee turnover

9%
for 2010

Objective
We endeavour to attract and retain the highest calibre of employees and strive to be a company that people want to work for.

Definition
The number of employees leaving the Group (excluding redundancies) expressed as a percentage of the average number of employees across the Group during the year.

Why is it key to our strategy?
Having high quality teams in place is essential to developing communities and delivering high quality homes that our customers want to live in, on time and to budget.

Table 3.45 — Key performance indicators

National Grid plc – Annual Report and Accounts

Operating and Financial Review (extract)

Key performance indicators (KPIs)

Financial KPIs

Company strategy and objectives	Financial KPIs	Definitions
Sustainable growth and superior financial performance	Adjusted earnings per share	Adjusted earnings* divided by the weighted average number of shares
	Total shareholder return	Growth in share price assuming dividends are reinvested
Delivering strong, sustainable regulatory and long-term contracts with good returns	Group return on equity	Adjusted earnings* with certain regulatory based adjustments divided by equity
Becoming more efficient through transforming our operating model and increasingly aligning our processes	Regulated controllable operating costs	Regulated controllable operating costs as a proportion of regulated assets

Our performance and the progress we have made against our strategic aims and against the objectives we have set ourselves are described below and on the following pages. Commentary on our overall financial results can be found on pages 38 to 45, and information on the performance and financial results of each line of business is set out on pages 46 to 73.

We measure the achievement of our objectives both through the use of qualitative assessments and through the monitoring of quantitative indicators. To provide a full and rounded view of our business, we use non-financial as well as financial measures. Although all these measures are important, some are considered to be of more significance than others, and these more significant measures are designated as KPIs. Our financial and non-financial KPIs are highlighted here. KPIs are used as our primary measures of whether we are achieving our principal strategic aims of sustainable growth and superior financial performance. We also use KPIs to measure our performance against our objectives; the relationships between the objectives and the KPIs is explained above.

Adjusted earnings per share*+†

Total shareholder return

Group return on equity^

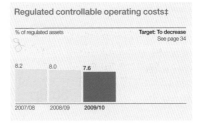

Regulated controllable operating costs‡

* Adjusted earnings excludes exceptional items, remeasurements and stranded cost recoveries
\+ 2007/08 data includes continuing operations acquired with KeySpan for the period from 24 August 2007 to 31 March 2008 or as at 31 March 2008
^ 2007/08 results include KeySpan operations on a pro forma financial performance basis assuming the acquisition occurred on 1 April 2007
† Comparative data has been restated for the impact of the scrip dividend issues
‡ Comparative data has been restated to present information on a consistent basis with the current year

Non-financial KPIs

Company objectives	Non-financial KPIs	Definitions
Modernising and extending our transmission and distribution networks	Network reliability targets	Various definitions appropriate to the relevant line of business
Driving improvements in our safety, customer and operational performance	Customer satisfaction	Our position in customer satisfaction surveys
	Employee lost time injury frequency rate	Number of employee lost time injuries per 100,000 hours worked on a 12 month basis
Building trust, transparency and an inclusive and engaged workforce	Employee engagement index	Employee engagement index calculated using responses to our annual employee survey
Positively shaping the energy and climate change agenda with our stakeholders in both regions	Greenhouse gas emissions	Percentage reduction in greenhouse gas emissions against our 1990 baseline

Network reliability targets

	Performance					Measure	Target
	05/06	06/07	07/08	08/09	**09/10**		09/10
Electricity transmission – UK	99.9999	99.9999	99.9999	99.9999	**99.9999**	%	99.9999
Gas transmission – UK	100	100	100	100	**100**	%	100
Gas distribution – UK	99.999	99.999	99.999	99.9999	**99.999**	%	99.999
Electricity transmission – US	348	259	437	266	**147**	MWh losses	<253
Electricity distribution – US	141	121	110	114	**114**	Mins of outage	<122

See pages 50, 58 and 66 for additional details on network reliability

Customer satisfaction

	Performance		Measure	Target
	08/09	**09/10**		
Gas Distribution – UK	4th quartile	**Not yet available**	Quartile ranking	To improve
Gas Distribution – US: Residential	4th quartile	**3rd quartile**	Quartile ranking	To improve
Gas Distribution – US: Commercial	3rd quartile	**2nd quartile**	Quartile ranking	To improve
Electricity Distribution & Generation: Residential	4th quartile	**4th quartile**	Quartile ranking	To improve
Electricity Distribution & Generation: Commercial	4th quartile	**3rd quartile**	Quartile ranking	To improve

Employee lost time injury frequency rate

Per 100,000 hours worked

Target: Zero
See page 31

0.28	0.24	0.30	0.25	0.15
2005/06	2006/07	2007/08	2008/09	**2009/10**

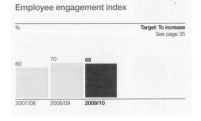

Employee engagement index

%

Target: To increase
See page 35

60	70	68
2007/08	2008/09	**2009/10**

Greenhouse gas emissions~#

% reduction against 1990 baseline

Target: 45% reduction by 2020 and 80% reduction by 2050
See page 36

2005/06	2006/07	2007/08	2008/09	**2009/10**
26	35	38	42	55

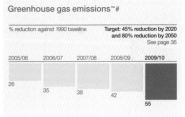

~ 2007/08 restated due to improved baseline data relating to KeySpan. Previously published figure excluding KeySpan was 30%
# Our greenhouse gas emissions for 2009/10 are not fully verified at the date of this Report. Fully verified data will be published on our website in July 2010

Table 3.46 — Industry-specific key performance indicators

InterContinental Hotels Group PLC — Annual Report and Financial Statements — 31 December 2011

Business review (extract)

How we win – Delivering Great Hotels Guests Love

Strategic priorities	KPIs	Current status and 2011 development	2012 priorities
Preferred brands To operate a portfolio of preferred brands attractive to both owners and guests that have clear market positions and differentiation in the eyes of the guest.	(14.7)% / 6.2% (2010) / 6.2% (2011) — 2009 Global RevPAR growth/(decline) Comparable hotels, constant $	• Near completion of the Holiday Inn relaunch; • launched global repositioning programme for our Crowne Plaza brand; • developed two new brands to further capture opportunities in North America and China; and • grew our industry-leading loyalty programme to 63 million members.	• Build upon the success of the Holiday Inn relaunch with the repositioning of Crowne Plaza; • continue development of our brand portfolio with further signings of our newer brands in expanding markets; and • increase IHG business from Priority Club Rewards' members.
Talented people Creating hotels that are well run, with brands brought to life by people who are proud of the work they do.	Survey non-comparable (2009) / 76% (2010) / 78% (2011) Employee engagement scores	• Training delivered to all senior managers on brand leadership; • training delivered to 60 per cent of franchised hotels to deliver our branded guest experience; • jointly hosted our global recognition event – 'Celebrate Service' week – with the IHG Owners Association, with over 3,000 hotels and offices participating; and • supported 49 employees from 22 countries to manage the athletes' accommodation and placed 10 people in LOCOG head office roles, as part of our London 2012 Olympic and Paralympic sponsorship.	• Strengthen brand capabilities, including cascading brand training to all our leaders; • strengthen IHG's employment brand, particularly through the use of new media to make the Group an employer of choice; • develop our talent pipeline to meet our commercial goals; and • continue to develop compelling people offer to our franchisees.
Best-in-class delivery To generate higher returns for owners and IHG through increased revenue share, improved operating efficiency and growing margins.	16.8 (2009) / 18.7 (2010) / 20.2 (2011) Total gross revenue Actual $bn 68% (2009) / 68% (2010) / 69% (2011) System contribution to revenue (reservations channels and Priority Club Rewards' members direct to hotels) As percentage of rooms revenue	• Strengthened revenue streams from mobile booking channels; • established strategic industry partnerships to develop roomkey.com; • strengthened coverage of our global sales force; and • grew our industry-leading loyalty programme, contributing over $6.9bn to global system rooms revenue.	• Optimise revenue from third-party, partner and IHG websites; • strengthen global sales force effectiveness; and • ensure IHG's industry-leading system of delivering demand and revenue to hotels retains competitive advantage.
Responsible business To take a proactive stance and seek creative solutions through innovation and collaboration on environment and community issues, and to drive increased value for IHG, owners, guests and the communities in which we operate.	911 (2009) / 1,122 (2010) / 1,772 (2011) Hotels signed-up to 'Green Engage' Hotels, cumulative Pilot stage (2009) / 4,800 (2010) / 5,608 (2011) Pupils enrolled with 'IHG Academy' Students enrolled	• Exceeded our 'Green Engage' programme target to enrol 1,700 hotels; • 'IHG Academy' programme expanded to every IHG operating region and student participation up by 17 per cent; and • led a Cornell University study on developing an industry standard for carbon measurement.	• Enrol 50 per cent of IHG hotels in 'Green Engage' by the end of 2012; • achieve energy savings of six per cent to 10 per cent in our owned and managed estate by end of 2012 (on a per available room night basis); • continue to drive carbon strategy work to develop an industry standard for measuring carbon emission reduction; • create new opportunities for communities by growing the 'IHG Academy' to more countries and increasing the student base; and • continue to use social media to drive stakeholder engagement.

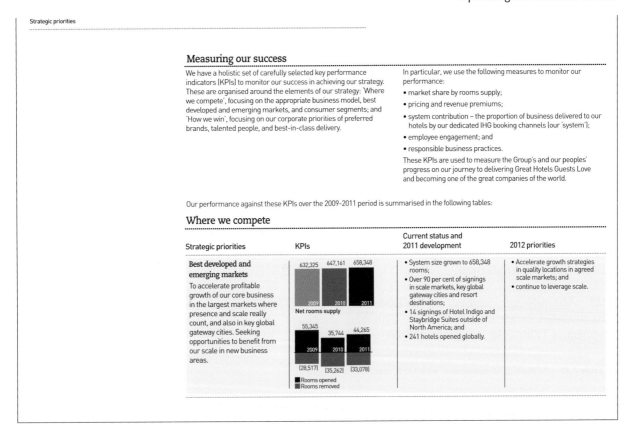

Strategic priorities

Other performance indicators

3.222   Disclosure may also be given of other quantified measures that management use to monitor trends and factors and that can provide further context to their narrative reporting. However, if they are not considered by management to be KPIs and/or are outside the entity's control, the level of information about each one should be less than for a KPI.

3.223   The reporting statement includes less stringent disclosure recommendations for other performance indicators that are not KPIs. It states that where quantified measures other than KPIs are included, the OFR should disclose:

■   The definition and calculation method.

■   Where available, corresponding amounts for the previous financial year.

[RS (OFR) para 78].

'Seriously prejudicial'

3.224   The reporting statement recommends that disclosure should not be made in the OFR of information about impending developments or about matters in the course of negotiation if the disclosure would, in the directors' opinion, be seriously prejudicial to the entity's interests. [RS (OFR) para 79].

3.225   The reporting statement notes that this is consistent with existing practice in informing the markets on such matters. This is a reference to the UK Listing and Prospectus Rules, which contain exemptions from disclosure of information that would be seriously detrimental to a company. [PR 2.5.2].

3.226   Instances where non-disclosure is justified tend to include those where the omission is unlikely to mislead investors with regard to facts and circumstances that are essential for an informed assessment. This means that for information to be excluded on 'seriously prejudicial' grounds, the omission itself should not give rise to a misleading impression.

3.227   Situations where non-disclosure on seriously prejudicial grounds might apply are likely to be rare. They include those where a company's position might be seriously prejudiced in relation to disputes with other parties on the subject matter of a provision, contingent liability or contingent asset. FRS 12 and IAS 37,

'Provisions, contingent liabilities and contingent assets', contain an exemption from disclosure of some of the information otherwise required by those standards but require disclosure of the general nature of the dispute, together with the fact that the information has not been disclosed and the reason why. [FRS 12 para 97; IAS 37 para 92].

3.228 Although not mentioned in the reporting statement, disclosure of the fact that information on a particular matter has not been disclosed and the reasons for non-disclosure may be useful to shareholders, where such disclosure would not itself be prejudicial. For example, an entity may have let it be known that it would welcome offers for a particular segment of its business that it wishes to dispose of. It may be in negotiation with several parties who may be unaware of each other's interest. The company might disclose in the OFR that the segment is for sale, but it may consider that it would be seriously prejudicial to disclose that it is negotiating with more than one party. Non-disclosure of that information would be unlikely to mislead investors. It might instead (voluntarily) state that details of the negotiations have not been disclosed, but the outcome will be announced when the negotiations have been concluded.

Statement of compliance

3.229 Although not required, the OFR should, as good practice, include a statement as to whether it has been prepared in accordance with the reporting statement. [RS (OFR) para 80]. An example of such a statement is Table 3.46.

Table 3.46 – Statement of compliance with OFR reporting statement

Xstrata plc – Annual Report and Accounts – 31 December 2010

Cautionary note regarding forward-looking statements (extract)

The Business review section of this report, comprising the Business, Strategy, Financial and Operating reviews, has been prepared in accordance with the Accounting Standards Board Reporting Statement on Operating and Financial Reviews (January 2006), as applicable best practice guidance for UK companies required to prepare a business review.

International developments

3.230 The IASB has published a practice statement on management commentary (MC). The practice statement sets out a non-binding framework for preparing and presenting management commentary. MC provides an opportunity for management to outline how an entity's financial position, financial performance and cash flows relate to management's objectives and its strategies for achieving those objectives.

3.231 The practice statement follows developments in narrative reporting in a variety of jurisdictions and other recent work by the IASB on the objective and qualitative characteristics of financial reporting. The IASB is developing a Conceptual Framework for Financial Reporting that will replace the Framework for the Preparation and Presentation of Financial Statements; two chapters of the Conceptual Framework have been published so far.

3.232 Many of the principles and disclosures in the practice statement are consistent with those of the ASB's reporting statement on the OFR. For example, the principles for preparing an MC are to:

■ Provide management's view of the entity's performance, position and development.

■ Supplement and complement information presented in the financial statements.

■ Have an orientation to the future.

3.233 The practice statement states that a decision-useful MC includes information that is essential to an understanding of:

■ The nature of the business.

■ Management's objectives and strategies for meeting those objectives.

■ The entity's most significant resources, risks and relationships.

■ Results of operations and prospects.

■ Critical performance measures and indicators that management uses to evaluate the entity's performance against stated objectives.

3.234 The practice statement acknowledges that management commentary is already an important part of communication with the market. The practice statement presents a broad framework for MC reporting and management will need to decide how best to apply this reporting framework to the business' particular circumstances.

Chapter 4

Corporate governance

Corporate governance

History and development of corporate governance in the UK

Introduction

4.1 In 1992 the Cadbury Committee defined corporate governance in its report 'The financial aspects of corporate governance' as *"the system by which companies are directed and controlled. Boards of directors are responsible for the governance of their companies. The shareholders' role in governance is to appoint the directors and the auditors and to satisfy themselves that an appropriate governance structure is in place. The responsibilities of the board include setting the company's strategic aims, providing the leadership to put them into effect, supervising the management of the business and reporting to shareholders on their stewardship. The board's actions are subject to laws, regulations and the shareholders in general meeting"*. [CR]. In 2010, the latest version of the UK Corporate Governance Code still quotes this as the classic definition of the context of the Code.

4.1.1 In the preface to its Corporate Governance Principles published in 2004, the OECD provided the following comment on what corporate governance involves and achieves:

> *"Corporate governance involves a set of relationships between a company's management, its board, its shareholders and other stakeholders. Corporate governance also provides the structure through which the objectives of the company are set, and the means of attaining those objectives and monitoring performance are determined. Good corporate governance should provide proper incentives for the board and management to pursue objectives that are in the interests of the company and its shareholders and should facilitate effective monitoring. The presence of an effective corporate governance system, within an individual company and across an economy as a whole, helps to provide a degree of confidence that is necessary for the proper functioning of a market economy. As a result the cost of capital is lower and firms are encouraged to use resources more efficiently thereby underpinning growth."* [OECD Principles of Corporate Governance, 2004].

4.2 Most UK companies have a single 'unitary' board of directors. Corporate governance in the UK corporate sector is, therefore, primarily concerned with:

- The procedures adopted by the board and its committees to discharge its duties (for example, membership of the board; frequency of, and procedures at, board meetings; the role of non-executive directors; constitution and terms of reference of audit and remuneration committees; and the role of the company secretary).

- The board's accountability to shareholders and other stakeholders (for example, annual reporting; use of AGMs; and shareholder voting rights).

- The manner in which the board controls the company or group (for example, management structures; group legal structure; and internal control philosophy and practice).

4.3 Corporate governance potentially covers a very wide range of issues and disciplines from company secretarial and legal, through to business strategy and risk management, executive and non-executive management, investor relations, and accounting and information systems.

4.4 Governance went higher up the corporate agenda in the early 1990s partly in response to a series of scandals, fuelled by the recession. Business failures heightened concerns about effective governance and led amongst other things to the development of corporate governance disclosures. More recently, corporate governance has again been in the spotlight following the perceived failures of companies in the banking sector during the economic downturn which began in 2008.

4.5 The importance of corporate governance disclosures is that, provided the information can be relied upon, they should help determine a company's value and be useful to stakeholders wishing to assess their risk exposure before deciding whether to commit resources to, or withdraw resources from, a company. Company failures have highlighted the need for stakeholders to obtain assurance on governance. They have also heightened the need for directors to be able to give such assurance if they are to continue to attract funds.

4.6 Some governance issues have generated significant political and public interest, because they strike at the root of the objectives of companies – none more so than the accountability of boards to shareholders in relation to executive pay.

4.7 Improvements in governance disclosures over the last few years have meant that UK public companies are among the most accountable of organisations. In addition to publishing their results and having their financial statements audited, public companies are required to disclose detailed information about their operations, relationships, remuneration and governance.

The development of corporate governance disclosures

4.8 The response to the scandals and failures of the late 1980s was a series of committees, reports and recommendations. The first of these was the Committee on the Financial Aspects of Corporate Governance, generally referred to as the Cadbury Committee, after its chairman Sir Adrian Cadbury. Its report was issued in December 1992 and, as a result, major changes occurred in the way in which governance was viewed by companies as well as in the disclosures that they give.

4.9 Whilst board remuneration was one of a number of issues addressed by Cadbury, it was not the main focus. Nonetheless, the level of board remuneration continued to attract a high profile, particularly in relation to levels of pay in privatised utilities. In response to this a separate group was set up to study the matter and the result was 'Directors' remuneration: report of a study group chaired by Sir Richard Greenbury'. This is known as the Greenbury report and was published in July 1995. The Greenbury report led to additional disclosure requirements being included in the Listing Rules. Remuneration disclosures are discussed in chapter 5.

4.10 One of Cadbury's recommendations was that a successor body should be set up to review progress and it identified a number of issues which that body might consider. The successor body, 'The Committee on Corporate Governance' (the 'Hampel committee') was set up in November 1995 under the chairmanship of Sir Ronald Hampel.

4.11 The final version of the Hampel report was published in January 1998. The recommendations aimed to ensure a balance between business prosperity and accountability.

4.12 Following the completion of its report, the Hampel Committee co-operated with the London Stock Exchange in producing 'The Combined Code – Principles of Good Corporate Governance and Code of Best Practice' in June 1998. The Combined Code (1998) embraced the Cadbury and Greenbury Reports, and took into account the Hampel Committee's Report and changes made by the London Stock Exchange, with the committee's agreement, following consultation.

4.13 The original Combined Code, published in June 1998, contained both principles and detailed provisions and was in two parts, part 1, 'Principles of good governance' and part 2, 'Code of best practice'. Each part of the Combined Code (1998) was split into two sections. Section 1 contained the corporate governance principles and Combined Code provisions applicable to companies incorporated in the UK. Section 2 contained the principles and Combined Code provisions applicable to institutional shareholders with regard to their voting, dialogue with the company and evaluation of governance arrangements.

4.14 The Combined Code (1998) was appended to the Listing Rules (although it did not form part of those rules) and a new listing rule required companies to include a two part disclosure statement in their annual report describing how they had applied the principles of the Combined Code (1998), whether or not they had complied with its detailed provisions throughout the accounting period and details of any non-compliance. Although the changes to the Listing Rules in June 1998 only addressed the principles and Combined Code (1998) provisions in section 1 (that is for companies), the Hampel Committee regarded section 2 as an integral part of the recommendations and it encouraged institutional investors to make voluntary disclosure to their clients and the public based on these recommendations.

4.15 Also during 1998 the government announced a new initiative to modernise company law, known as the Company Law Review, which was completed in July 2001. In 2002 the government issued a White Paper outlining potential new legislation covering various matters including a statutory statement outlining directors' duties. The government did not advocate legislating for corporate governance requirements and disclosures, but supported the best practice approach of having a code for companies and investors to follow. Following the White Paper, the Companies Act 2006 received Royal Assent in November 2006. The Companies Act 2006 represents a major overhaul of company law, with all provisions coming into force by 1 October 2009.

4.15.1 Part 43 of the Companies Act 2006 (secs 1269 and 1273) includes provisions on corporate governance. These give powers to a 'competent authority' to implement European transparency obligations and, therefore, it is the Financial Services Authority that has created the UK corporate governance rules, through the Disclosure Rules & Transparency Rules ('DTR') and the Listing Rules (which require companies to report against the UK Corporate Governance Code).

4.16 In February 2002 the government announced that Sir Derek Higgs was to carry out a review of the role and effectiveness of non-executive directors. This review was in part building on the work of the company law review that noted a growing body of evidence from the USA suggesting that companies with a strong contingent of non-executives produced superior performance. Therefore, this review was focused on improving UK performance by progressive strengthening of the quality and role of non-executive directors. The terms of reference of the review noted that this had already begun in the decade following the introduction of the Cadbury Code. The government sought recommendations from Higgs as to how to further strengthen the quality, independence and effectiveness of non-executive directors in the UK.

4.17 Another strong influence on the review was the timing of its launch, since it took place when company accounting scandals and collapses, predominantly taking place in the USA, were shocking investors and the public. Shortly after Higgs' review was announced, the government also formed a co-ordinating group to consider the implications of the US scandals for the arrangements for financial reporting and auditing in the UK. This group requested the Financial Reporting Council ('FRC') to set up a working group to consider whether the remit of audit committees under the existing Combined Code (1998) needed to change. The working group was chaired by Sir Robert Smith and worked closely with Higgs. The group's output was known as the Smith Guidance. The group suggested new provisions for the Combined Code (1998) around the role and responsibilities of audit committees. These were incorporated into the revised draft Combined Code published as part of the Higgs Report in January 2003. The Smith Guidance was later revised in 2008 and further discussion of this can be found in paragraph 4.293.1 onwards.

4.18 The FRC approved the new Combined Code on Corporate Governance on 23 July 2003, hereafter referred to as the Combined Code (2003). The format of the Combined Code (2003) was slightly different to the original, containing both main and supporting principles with the provisions. The division into two sections, companies and institutional shareholders, remained the same.

4.19 The Combined Code (2003) applied for reporting years beginning on or after 1 November 2003. Initially the Financial Services Authority ('FSA') replaced the Combined Code (1998) that was annexed to the Listing Rules with the Combined Code (2003). Since 1 July 2005, the Combined Code (2003) has not been appended to the Listing Rules (although it remains linked to them), because it was recognised as being the responsibility of the FRC, rather than the UK Listing Authority.

4.20 The FRC performed an informal review of the implementation of the Combined Code (2003) during 2004 and a formal review in 2005. In its review, the FRC found no appetite for major change to the Combined Code (2003). The Code was reported to have bedded down well and to have had a positive impact on the quality of corporate governance amongst listed companies. This outcome resulted in the FRC proposing only a few minor modifications to the Code in early 2006, concluding that major change was unnecessary. Following a period of consultation on these minor modifications, the FRC issued a revised Combined Code on Corporate Governance, hereafter referred to as the Combined Code (2006), in June 2006.

4.21 In 2007, the FRC performed a further review of the Combined Code. The review's main objective was to assess whether the Code was *"appropriately enabling UK listed companies to be led in a way which facilitates entrepreneurial success and the management of risk"*. The results of the consultation were published in November 2007 and concluded that the Combined Code continued to be broadly beneficial to the governance of UK listed companies, without undermining boards' entrepreneurial leadership.

4.21.1 Following the 2007 review of the Combined Code and a further consultation, the FRC issued a revised Combined Code on Corporate Governance, hereafter referred to as the Combined Code (2008). There were two changes from the 2006 Code: (i) removal of the restriction on an individual chairing more than one FTSE 100 company and (ii) a relaxation for smaller companies outside the FTSE 350 allowing the company chairman to be a member, but not chair, of the audit committee provided that he/she was considered independent on appointment. The Combined Code (2008) was applicable for accounting periods beginning on or after 29 June 2008.

4.22 In June 2008 the FSA revised the Listing Rules by introducing its Corporate Governance Rules to implement the recent EU Company Law 4th and 8th Directives requiring companies to have an audit committee (or similar body) and to publish a corporate governance statement. The FSA Corporate Governance Rules (chapter 7 of the Disclosure Rules and Transparency Rules (DTR)) are also applicable for accounting periods beginning on or after 29 June 2008. Furthermore, the corporate governance compliance statement requirement of the Listing Rules was restricted to compliance with the main principles of the Code only and not the supporting principles as previously required (the requirement to explain departures from the Code's provisions remains).

4.23 In 2010, the FSA's Listing Regime was restructured into two new segments (premium and standard listed companies) with the objective of providing more clarity about the regime for market participants. The new listings regime changed the applicability of the FSA Corporate Governance Rules with effect from 6 April 2010. The FSA rules are discussed further from paragraph 4.43.

4.24 As noted earlier, the 2008 financial crisis triggered widespread reappraisal of the governance systems which might have helped to alleviate it. In the UK, Sir David Walker was appointed by the UK government in 2009 to review the governance of banks and other financial industry entities (BOFIs), and the FRC brought forward its regular review of the Combined Code so that corporate governance for other sectors could be assessed at the same time. The final report by Sir David Walker, published in November 2009, includes 39 recommendations. The FSA was given responsibility for implementing those recommendations specific to BOFIs. The recommendations that apply to all listed companies were implemented by the FRC as part of its review of the Combined Code. The Walker report is further discussed from paragraph 4.28.4.

4.25 The 2009-10 FRC review of the Combined Code resulted in publication of the revised UK Corporate Governance Code on 28 May 2010, hereafter referred to as the UK Corporate Governance Code (2010) (or UKCGC). This new edition of the Code applies to all premium listed companies for financial years beginning on or after 29 June 2010, including overseas companies. As a result of changes to the FSA's Listing Regime, overseas companies with a premium listing need to report against the Code for financial years beginning after 31 December 2009. Therefore, the change of name makes the Code's status as the UK's recognised corporate governance standard clearer to overseas investors and companies. See paragraph 4.77 for further information on the changes for overseas companies.

4.26 The overriding view emerging from the 2009-10 FRC review as a whole was that the governance code is effective and that the 'comply or explain' approach is sufficiently flexible to embrace different companies' circumstances. However, the FRC also concluded that much more attention needs to be paid to following the spirit of the Code as well as its letter and that the quality of corporate governance ultimately depends on board behaviour not process.

4.27 The FRC, therefore, made structural and wording changes, aimed at changing the 'tone' of the Code by giving more prominence to factors that underpin an effective board, such as the pivotal role of the chairman in leading the board, the responsibility of the non-executive directors to provide constructive challenge, the directors' expected time commitment, the board's composition and the board's responsibility for risk. Additionally, there are strengthened provisions on director development and two new provisions for FTSE 350 companies: externally facilitated performance reviews of boards at least every three years and annual re-election of all directors. The main changes in the UKCGC are further discussed from paragraph 4.221 onwards.

4.28 The FRC hopes that these changes will promote greater clarity and understanding with regard to the tasks of an effective board and that communication with shareholders will be more effective as a result. The FRC has also taken responsibility for a Stewardship Code for institutional investors to enhance shareholder engagement following Sir David Walker's recommendations. This resulted in the FRC publishing the first UK Stewardship Code in July 2010, effective immediately. The previous Section 2 'Institutional Investors' of the Combined Code (2008), therefore, ceased to apply. The purpose of the Stewardship Code is to improve the quality of corporate governance through promoting better dialogue between shareholders and company boards, and more transparency about the way in which investors oversee the companies they own. The FRC is encouraging all institutional investors to report publicly on the extent to which they follow the UK Stewardship Code. Paragraph 4.343 onwards deals further with the UK Stewardship Code.

4.28.1   Following the release of the UK Corporate Governance Code, a number of the FRC's guidance documents have been subject to review. In December 2009, the FRC commissioned the Institute of Chartered Secretaries and Administrators ('ICSA') to develop new guidance to replace the Higgs guidance issued in 2006. The FRC published the resulting 'Guidance on board effectiveness' in March 2011. The purpose of the new guidance is *"to help boards of UK companies avoid some of the problems that contributed to significant value destruction during the recent financial crisis"*. [Guidance on board effectiveness, March 2011]. The guidance is designed to stimulate boards' thinking on how they can carry out their role most effectively and, therefore, addresses sections A and B of the UK Corporate Governance Code on leadership and effectiveness of the board.

4.28.2   In July 2010, the FRC launched a consultation on proposed revisions to the FRC guidance on audit committees (formerly known as the 'Smith' guidance). This consultation was carried out in parallel with the APB's consultation on revisions to ethical standards for auditors, focussing on non-audit services. The updated guidance was released in December 2010 and included changes to guidance around the policy on appointing the external auditor to carry out non-audit services as well as enhancing disclosure around how objectivity and independence of the external auditor is safeguarded.

4.28.3   The FRC announced in December 2010 its intention to defer a review of the Turnbull Guidance on Internal Control. Paragraphs 4.305.6.1 onwards deal with the Turnbull Guidance in more detail. The FRC explained that it wanted to explore how companies were responding to Main Principle C.2 in the UK Corporate Governance Code, which asks boards to be responsible for determining the nature and extent of the significant risks they were willing to take in achieving their strategic objectives. The FRC held a series of meetings with companies, investors and advisers in 2011 to discuss the issues, and conclusions from these meetings will inform a review of the Turnbull guidance as a whole.

The Walker review

4.28.4   Sir David Walker was appointed in 2009 by the UK government to lead a review of corporate governance in banks and other financial industry entities (BOFIs). The terms of reference of the Walker Review included considering:

■   The effectiveness of risk management at board level, including the incentives in remuneration policy to manage risk effectively.

■   Board balance in banks, in terms of skills, experience and independence.

■   Effectiveness of board practices and performance of committees.

■   Institutional investor engagement.

■   Degree of consistency of UK with international practice and how to promulgate best practice.

4.28.5   The final Walker Report, published in November 2009, highlighted five key themes and included 39 recommendations. The five key themes are summarised below:

■   Both the UK unitary board structure and the FRC Combined Code remain fit for purpose. Combined with tougher capital and liquidity requirements and a tougher regulatory stance on the part of the FSA, the 'comply or explain' approach to guidance and provisions under the Combined Code provides the surest route to better corporate governance practice, with some additional BOFI-specific elements to be taken forward through the FSA.

■   The principal deficiencies in BOFI boards related much more to patterns of behaviour than to organisation. The most critical need is for an environment in which effective challenge of the executive is expected and achieved in the boardroom before decisions are taken on major risk and strategic issues.

■   Given that the overriding strategic objective of a BOFI is the successful management of financial risk, board-level engagement in the high-level risk oversight should be materially increased with particular attention to monitoring risk and discussion leading to decisions on the entity's risk appetite and tolerance.

■   There is a need for fund managers and other major shareholders to engage more productively with their investee companies.

■   Substantial enhancement is needed in board level oversight of remuneration policies, in particular in respect of variable pay and in associated disclosures. The remit and responsibility of board remuneration committees should be extended beyond board members to cover the remuneration structure and levels for all senior employees whose role puts them in a position of significant influence over the entity's risk profile.

4.28.6 Walker made 39 recommendations. The key recommendations for BOFIs included:

- To enhance risk management, have a separate risk committee and strengthen the chief risk officer's role.

- The chairman to face annual re-election and the chairman of the remuneration committee to face re-election if the remuneration report gets less than 75% approval of the shareholders.

- Non-executives to spend substantially more time on the job. An induction process to be introduced for all non-executive directors and regular training. Non-executive directors to face tougher scrutiny under the FSA authorisation process.

- On remuneration, to defer incentive payments to align reward with sustainable performance and consider clawback provisions to reclaim amounts in cases of misstatement or misconduct.

- New remuneration disclosure of 'high end' remuneration on a banded basis for those earning over £1 million.

- A Stewardship Code for institutional investors under the FRC.

4.28.7 The implementation process was the responsibility of the FSA for those recommendations specific to banks and other financial industry entities. The recommendations that apply to all listed companies were implemented by the FRC as part of its review of the Combined Code (2008). The FRC has published the first UK Stewardship Code; see paragraph 4.343.

4.28.8 See 'Future corporate governance developments' from paragraph 4.354 onwards for further discussion of the development of corporate governance.

Corporate governance concepts

4.29 The concepts of the Hampel Report that led to the original Combined Code (1998) are still applicable to the UK Corporate Governance Code issued in 2010. The key concepts are discussed below.

Avoidance of 'box ticking'

4.30 Hampel argued for flexibility when considering corporate governance standards and a proper regard for the individual circumstances of the companies concerned. Too often companies' experience of Cadbury and Greenbury was as sets of prescriptive rules with shareholders and their advisors following a 'box ticking' approach focusing only on whether a rule had been complied with rather than considering the particular circumstances involved.

4.31 In Hampel's view this 'box ticking' approach did not take account of the diversity of circumstances and experience among different companies and within the same company. Although Hampel agreed with Cadbury that there are guidelines that are appropriate in most cases, Hampel considered that there will often be valid reasons for exceptions and companies should not be penalised for this. A focus by those considering corporate governance arrangements on 'box ticking' draws attention away from the diligent pursuit of corporate governance objectives and becomes an objective in itself. Compliance with every Code recommendation does not guarantee that a business will not fail. It is possible for a company to arrange matters so that the letter of every governance rule is complied with, but not the substance.

'Comply or explain'

4.32 As noted above, it was recognised that not all listed companies would be able to comply with all the provisions of the Combined Code, given their different circumstances, and that there would be valid reasons for such non-compliance. Therefore the 'comply or explain' mechanism was adopted so that if the company had not complied with the Code's provisions during the year it could provide an explanation in respect of those provisions with which it did not comply. This mechanism allows companies to demonstrate proper consideration of the Code without forcing them to adopt a 'box ticking' approach to compliance and is a key characteristic of a code-based (as opposed to legislation-based) governance framework.

4.33 Listing Rule 9.8.6 requires a premium listed company to give a two-part compliance statement in its annual financial report; first to explain how it has *applied* the Code's main principles and, secondly, how it has *complied* with its provisions. This is supported by companies, investors and regulators in the UK and has increasingly been adopted as a model in other financial markets.

4.33.1 Although it is a cornerstone of the UK corporate governance framework, 'comply or explain' comes under regular scrutiny, particularly when corporate governance arrangements have arguably failed. It is significant that the FRC in its response to the April 2011 European Green Paper 'The EU Corporate Governance Framework' took pains to emphasise the importance of comply or explain, describing it as essential in promoting best practice in corporate governance. The FRC warned that *"replacing principles with a series of prescriptive regulations could stifle enterprise at a time when European economies are seeking to promote economic growth"*. See paragraph 4.359 for further details.

Shareholder/stakeholder engagement

4.34 Hampel recognised that the board's relationship with the company's shareholders is different to that with other stakeholders. The board of directors is responsible for relations with stakeholders but, because the shareholders elect the directors, the board is accountable to the shareholders. Although the directors' primary responsibility is to the shareholders, both present and future, different types of companies will have different relationships with stakeholders and the objective of enhancement of long-term shareholder value can only be met by directors developing and sustaining their relationship with stakeholders.

4.35 The Hampel Committee considered that if companies do not let their investors know what they are doing and how, the investors will look elsewhere for information on whether or not the board is managing the company's affairs well. As there is a risk that investors will draw erroneous conclusions, and as it is the investors who influence the company's market value, it is in the directors' interests to be open and transparent. The theme of the directors having a dialogue with investors based on mutual understanding of objectives appeared in the Higgs Report and was carried through into the Combined Code (2003).

4.36 This underlying philosophy is responsible for the inclusion of a section in all four Combined Codes (1998, 2003, 2006 and 2008) on institutional shareholders. Transparency and openness are less effective if the communication is a one-way process. Investors have duties and responsibilities too. Included in section 2 of each Combined Code are three main principles relating to institutional shareholders. These cover dialogue with companies, evaluation of governance disclosures and shareholder voting. In 2010 this section was replaced by the first UK Stewardship Code for institutional investors published by the FRC, which is discussed from paragraph 4.343.

[The next paragraph is 4.43.]

FSA corporate governance rules

Revised FSA Corporate Governance Rules — impact of Disclosure Rules and Transparency Rules

4.43 On 27 June 2008, the FSA released revisions to the Listing Rules and the DTR to implement amendments to the EU 4th and 8th Company Law Directives and chapter 7 of the DTR became the FSA Corporate Governance Rules. The revised requirements are effective for accounting periods beginning on or after 29 June 2008 and are discussed further below.

4.44 The advent of the Disclosure Rules and Transparency Rules (DTR)/FSA Corporate Governance Rules adds another set of rules governing parts of the front end of the annual report to the principles and provisions of the UK Corporate Governance Code (UKCGC), the Listing Rules (LR), and the legislative requirements of the Companies Act 2006 (CA 2006) and its accompanying regulations and instruments. Key elements of the DTR/FSA Corporate Governance Rules are set out from paragraph 4.46.

4.45 The table below summarises the corporate governance requirements under the Codes, Listing Rules and DTR for each type of listed company. The UKCGC applies to financial years starting on or after 29 June 2010.

Corporate governance

	UK premium	UK standard	Overseas premium	Overseas standard
Listing Rule 9.8.6 (5) and (6) (Compliance statement)	✓	✗	✓	✗
The UKCGC ('comply or explain')	✓	✗	✓ (for financial years beginning after 31/12/09)	✗
Listing Rule 9.8.6 (3) (Going concern statement)	✓	✗	✗ (though UKGCG provision C.1.3 requires similar going concern disclosures)	✗
FSA Corporate Governance Rules				
● DTR 7.1 Audit Committee	✓	✓	✗	✗
● DTR 7.2 Corporate Governance Statement	✓	✓	✓	✓
Auditors' Report (LR 9.8.10) (9 Code provisions)	✓	✗	✓ (though APB guidance relates only to UK companies)	✗

AIM companies are not required to comply with the DTR (see para 4.90 onwards), but may voluntarily elect to do so.

Corporate governance reporting requirements for companies with only listed debt

4.45.1   In most cases neither the reporting requirements of the UK Corporate Governance Code nor of DTR 7.2 apply to companies that have only listed debt (that is, no equity listing).

4.45.2   Although Listing Rule 9.8.6 refers to 'listed companies', LR 9.1.1 states at the start of the Continuing Obligations chapter of the Listing Rules that: *"This chapter applies to a company that has a premium listing of equity shares"*.

4.45.3   Although DTR 7.2 refers to 'issuers' in general (which would include issuers of debt) and might therefore mean that a corporate governance statement is still needed, DTR 1B.1.6 states that: *"The rules in DTR 7.2.2 R, 7.2.3 R and 7.2.7 R do not apply to an issuer which has not issued shares which are admitted to trading unless it has issued shares which are traded on an multilateral trading facility ('MTF')"*.

Requirement to have an audit committee (DTR 7.1)

4.46   The DTR requires certain companies (see para 4.47) to have an audit committee (or a body performing equivalent functions). At least one member must be independent and at least one member (who may, but need not be, the same person) must have competence in accounting and/or auditing. [DTR 7.1.1R].

As a minimum the relevant body must:

■   Monitor the financial reporting process.

■   Monitor the effectiveness of the internal control, internal audit where applicable and risk management systems.

■   Monitor the statutory audit of the annual and consolidated financial statements.

■   Review and monitor the independence of the statutory auditor and, in particular, the provision of additional services. [DTR 7.1.3R].

The FSA has indicated that there are a number of overlaps between the UKCGC and the DTR. These have been summarised in paragraph 4.59.

4.47 DTR 7.1 applies to UK incorporated companies with transferable securities admitted to trading on either the London Stock Exchange or the PLUS-listed markets and that are required to appoint a statutory auditor. There are exemptions to this requirement for:

- A listed company whose parent is subject to this rule (or an equivalent rule of any EEA State).

- An issuer whose sole business is to act as the issuer of asset-backed securities, provided that the issuer makes a public statement explaining why it is not appropriate to have an audit committee.

- A credit institution whose shares are not admitted to trading if the total nominal value of its listed debt securities is less than €100 million and the company has not prepared a prospectus in accordance with section 85 of the Financial Services and Markets Act 2000.

4.48 The FSA has applied DTR 7.1 only to UK incorporated issuers, not to overseas issuers.

Requirement to present a corporate governance statement (DTR 7.2)

4.49 For accounting periods beginning on or after 29 June 2008, companies (see para 4.51) are required to present a corporate governance statement in one of the following ways. It may be included: as part of the directors' report (or incorporated by reference into the directors' report); separately issued to accompany the annual report and financial statements; or made available on the company's web site, but with cross-references from the directors' report. Where a company chooses to present its corporate governance statement separately there are new Companies Act requirements in respect of the approval, signing and filing of the separate governance statement. These requirements are discussed further in paragraph 4.334.

4.50 It should be noted that the Listing Rules (LR 9.8.9) require the corporate governance statement to be included in the company's annual report; in effect this currently prevents the statement being presented separately from the annual report in the UK. The FRC consulted on this issue to consider whether to change the Code and allow companies a choice of whether to place the corporate governance statement on the company website or in the annual report, but did not resolve the point when it published the final UKCGC in 2010.

4.51 DTR 7.2 applies to all companies with shares admitted to trading on the London Stock Exchange or PLUS-listed markets or traded on a multi-lateral trading facility. [DTR 1B.1.5, 1B.1.6]. In this respect, it is different from DTR 7.1, which applies only to UK incorporated issuers under the FSA Corporate Governance Rules.

4.52 The DTR contains a number of disclosures that must be given in the corporate governance statement. Many of those requirements are also dealt with elsewhere in UK legislation or guidance. The requirements are listed below, together with any overlap with other legislation or guidance.

4.53 The corporate governance statement must contain a reference to:

- Any corporate governance code to which the company is subject.

- Any corporate governance code which the company may have voluntarily decided to apply.

- All relevant information about the corporate governance practices applied beyond the requirements under national law.

- Where any corporate governance code that is applied (either mandatorily or voluntarily) is publicly available.

- An explanation of any departure from any corporate governance code applied. (This overlaps with the 'comply or explain' rule in LR 9.8.6 R(5) – see further para 4.70).

[DTR 7.2.2R, 7.2.3R].

4.54 In addition, the corporate governance statement must contain:

- A description of the main features of the company's internal control and risk management systems in relation to the financial reporting process. [DTR 7.2.5R]. (See para 4.56)

- The information required to be included in the directors' report by paragraphs 13(2)(c), (d), (f), (h) and (i) of Schedule 7 to the Large and Medium-sized Companies and Groups (Accounts and Reports) Regulations 2008, resulting from the EU Takeover Directive. [DTR 7.2.6R]. (These requirements are discussed further in chapter 2.) Whilst these disclosures now need to be made in both the corporate governance statement *and* the directors' report, the disclosure may continue to be given once and appropriate cross-reference made.

■ A description of the composition and operation of the company's administrative, management and supervisory bodies and their committees. [DTR 7.2.7R].

4.55 The FSA has indicated that compliance with provisions A.1.1, A.1.2, B.2.4, D.2.1 and C.3.3 of UKCGC will ensure compliance with DTR 7.2.7R. See the summary table of overlapping provisions in paragraph 4.59 for more details.

4.56 Over and above the recommendations of the UKCGC, there is a requirement in DTR 7.2.5R for a *description* of the main features of the company's internal control and risk management systems *in relation to the financial reporting process*. The FRC has indicated that while this requirement in DTR 7.2.5R differs from the recommendation in the UKCGC provision C.2.1, the FRC envisages that both the Code and the DTR can be satisfied by a single internal control statement.

4.57 For a group, there is also a requirement to include a *description* of the main features of the group's internal control and risk management systems *in relation to the process for preparing consolidated financial statements*. [DTR 7.2.10R].

Table 4.1 – Description of internal control over financial reporting (DTR 7.2.5R)

Stagecoach plc – Annual Report and Financial Statements – 30 April 2012

Corporate governance report (extract)

5.13 Process for preparing consolidated financial statements

The Group has established internal control and risk management systems in relation to the process for preparing consolidated financial statements. The key features of these internal control and risk management systems are:

● The Risk Assurance function and management conducts various checks on internal financial controls periodically.

● Management regularly monitors and considers developments in accounting regulations and best practice in financial reporting, and where appropriate, reflects developments in the consolidated financial statements. Appropriate briefings and/or training are provided to keyfinance personnel on relevant developments in accounting and financialreporting. The Audit Committee is also kept appraised of such developments.

● A written certificate is provided annually by the management of each business unit confirming that the internal financial controls have been reviewed and highlighting any departures from the controls system that the Group has determined to be appropriate practice.

● The financial statements of each business unit are subject to review by a local finance manager prior to being submitted to the Group Finance function.

● The financial statements of each business unit are subject to review by the Group Finance function for unusual items, unexplained trends and completeness. Any unexplained items are referred back to localmanagement to explain.

● The Group Finance function compares the financial statements of each business unit to the management accounts received during the year and obtains explanations for any material differences.

● The Group's consolidation, which consolidates the results of each business unit and makes appropriate adjustments, is subject to various levels of review by the Group Finance function.

● The draft consolidated financial statements are reviewed by an individual independent from those individuals who were responsible for preparing the financial statements. The review includes checking internal consistency, consistency with other statements, consistency with internal accounting records and arithmetical accuracy.

● The Audit Committee and the Board review the draft consolidated financial statements. The Audit Committee receives reports from management and the external auditors on significant judgements, changes in accounting policies, changes in accounting estimates and other pertinent matters relating to the consolidated financial statements.

● The financial statements of all material business units are subject to external audit.

Interaction between the DTR and the UK Corporate Governance Code

4.58 Although many of the DTR requirements overlap with provisions of the UKCGC, the FRC has indicated that, where a company chooses to 'explain' rather than 'comply' with any of the overlapping provisions, it will need to ensure that it, nonetheless, meets the requirements in the DTR. It is possible to comply with UKCGC provision C.2.1 but still be in breach of DTR 7.2.5R and, therefore, the Listing Rules. Conversely, if a smaller listed company has only one independent non-executive director on the audit committee, the company will need to explain a departure from UKCGC provision C.3.1, but it will have complied with DTR 7.1.1R. In this case, non-compliance with the UKCGC does not necessarily mean a breach of the DTR.

4.59 The table below shows the overlapping provisions between the DTR and the UKCGC:

DTR	UKCGC
DTR 7.1.1R: Minimum requirements on composition of the audit committee or equivalent body.	Provision C.3.1: Recommended composition of the audit committee.
DTR 7.1.3R: Minimum functions of the audit committee or equivalent body.	Provision C.3.2: Recommended minimum terms of reference for the audit committee.
DTR 7.1.5R: Disclosure of composition and function of audit committee (or equivalent) in the annual report. DTR 7.1.7G states that compliance with Code provisions A.1.2, C.3.1, C.3.2 and C.3.3 will result in compliance with DTR 7.1.1R to DTR 7.1.5R.	Provision A.1.2: The annual report should identify members of the board and board committees. Provision C.3.1 and C.3.2: See above. Provision C.3.3: The annual report should describe the work of the audit committee (also see further recommendations in the FRC Guidance on audit committees).
DTR 7.2.5R: The corporate governance statement must include a description of the main features of the company's internal control and risk management systems in relation to the financial reporting process. While this requirement differs from the UKCGC requirement, it is envisaged that both could be met by a single internal control statement. See paragraph 4.56.	Provision C.2.1: The Board must report that a review of the effectiveness of the risk management and internal control systems has been carried out. Further recommendations on the content of the internal control statement are set out in the Turnbull Guidance. NB 'risk management' was a new requirement brought in with the UKCGC Provision C.2.1 in 2010.
DTR 7.2.7R: The corporate governance statement must include a description of the composition and operation of the administrative, management and supervisory bodies and their committees. DTR 7.2.8G states that compliance with UKCGC provisions A.1.1, A.1.2, B.2.1, C.3.3 and D.2.1 will result in compliance with DTR 7.2.7R.	This requirement overlaps with a number of different provisions of the Code: A.1.1: the annual report should include a statement of how the board operates. A.1.2: the annual report should identify members of the board and board committees. B.2.4: the annual report should describe the work of the nomination committee. C.3.3: the annual report should describe the work of the audit committee. D.2.1: a description of the work of the remuneration committee should be made available. [Note: in order to comply with DTR 7.2.7R this information will need to be included in the corporate governance statement.]

Governance reporting

UK premium listed companies — Listing Rules — two-part statement

4.60 A premium listed company is required to include in its annual report and accounts a two-part statement on corporate governance. The first part of the statement requires the company to make a statement explaining how it has applied the main principles. This statement is to provide sufficient information to enable the company's shareholders to evaluate how the principles have been applied. [LR 9.8.6R(5)].

4.61 In practice, few companies list out every main principle and discuss specifically how each has been applied. However, it should be possible to deduce this from the content of the corporate governance statement as a whole.

[The next paragraph is 4.63.]

Statement 1 — Applying the main principles (UKCGC)

4.63 The main principles in the UKCGC are included in the following table. These must all be applied by a listed company to comply with the Code. The supporting principles and specific Code provisions are discussed later in this chapter, and are designed to assist the preparer in addressing each of the main principles. The table below also shows the paragraph number where they are discussed in more detail.

Section	Area	Main principle
A Leadership	A.1 The role of the board	Every company should be headed by an effective board which is collectively responsible for the long-term success of the company. (See para 4.237.)
	A.2 Division of responsibilities	There should be a clear division of responsibilities at the head of the company between the running of the board and the executive responsibility for the running of the company's business. No one individual should have unfettered powers of decision. (See para 4.237.)
	A.3 The chairman	The chairman is responsible for leadership of the board and ensuring its effectiveness on all aspects of its role. (See para 4.237.)
	A.4 Non-executive directors	As part of their role as members of a unitary board, non-executive directors should constructively challenge and help develop proposals on strategy. (See para 4.237.)
B Effectiveness	B.1 The composition of the board	The board and its committees should have the appropriate balance of skills, experience, independence and knowledge of the company to enable them to discharge their respective duties and responsibilities effectively. (See para 4.262.)
	B.2 Appointments to the board	There should be a formal, rigorous and transparent procedure for the appointment of new directors to the board. (See para 4.274.)
	B.3 Commitment	All directors should be able to allocate sufficient time to the company to discharge their responsibilities effectively. (See para 4.274.)
	B.4 Development	All directors should receive induction on joining the board and should regularly update and refresh their skills and knowledge. (See para 4.280.1.)
	B.5 Information and support	The board should be supplied in a timely manner with information in a form and of a quality appropriate to enable it to discharge its duties. (See para 4.237.)
	B.6 Evaluation	The board should undertake a formal and rigorous annual evaluation of its own performance and that of its committees and individual directors. (See para 4.251.)
	B.7 Re-election	All directors should be submitted for re-election at regular intervals, subject to continued satisfactory performance. (See para 4.246.)
C Accountability	C.1 Financial and business reporting	The board should present a balanced and understandable assessment of the company's position and prospects. (See para 4.306.)
	C.2 Risk management and internal control	The board is responsible for determining the nature and extent of the significant risks it is willing to take in achieving its strategic objectives. The board should maintain sound risk management and internal control systems. (See para 4.305.15.1.)
	C.3 Audit committee and auditors	The board should establish formal and transparent arrangements for considering how they should apply the corporate reporting and risk management and internal control principles and for maintaining an appropriate relationship with the company's auditor. (See para 4.287.)
D Remuneration	D.1 The level and components of remuneration	Levels of remuneration should be sufficient to attract, retain and motivate directors of the quality required to run the company successfully, but a company should avoid paying more than is necessary for this purpose. A significant proportion of executive directors' remuneration should be structured so as to link rewards to corporate and individual performance. (See para 4.294.)

	D.2 Procedure	There should be a formal and transparent procedure for developing policy on executive remuneration and for fixing the remuneration packages of individual directors. No director should be involved in deciding his or her own remuneration. (See para 4.294.)
E Relations with shareholders	E.1 Dialogue with shareholders	There should be a dialogue with shareholders based on the mutual understanding of objectives. The board as a whole has responsibility for ensuring that a satisfactory dialogue with shareholders takes place. (See para 4.316.)
	E.2 Constructive use of the AGM	The board should use the AGM to communicate with investors and to encourage their participation. (See para 4.321.)

Statement 2 — compliance throughout the period

4.64   In the second part of the corporate governance statement required by the Listing Rules, premium listed companies have to report whether or not the company has complied throughout the accounting period with the provisions set out in the Code. Where a company has not complied with the UKCGC provisions, or has only complied with some of these provisions or (in the case of provisions whose requirements are of a continuing nature) has complied for only part of an accounting period, the compliance statement must identify the Code provisions with which the company has not complied, for what part of the period such non-compliance continued (where relevant) and give reasons for any non-compliance. [LR 9.8.6 R(6)].

4.65   There is no requirement in the UKCGC specifying where the statement of compliance should be located within the annual report. Such statements are commonly included within the corporate governance report, or within the directors' report itself. Occasionally, the issue is dealt with or referred to within the chairman's statement. It is not appropriate to include the statement within the audited financial statements. See paragraph 4.49 for discussion of the impact of the Companies Act 2006 on these requirements.

4.66   For a company that complies with the provisions of the UKCGC in their entirety, it is reasonable to assume that, in doing so, they have applied the main principles.

4.67   Where an explanation of non-compliance with one or more of the Code's provisions is given in respect of one particular main principle, it will be necessary to consider explaining how the company has, nonetheless, applied that particular main principle.

[The next paragraph is 4.69.]

4.69   In support of the compliance statement, boards or audit committees may expect to see a paper that sets out how the company complies with each aspect of the UKCGC, supported by relevant documentation. It is helpful for the board or audit committee to minute its approval of such a paper.

Statements of non-compliance with Code provisions

4.70   Any element of non-compliance with Code provisions for any part of the period must be identified, giving reasons. The specific aspect of the Code must be identified. This does not mean that the paragraph number in the Code must be used, although some companies might do so. It would not be adequate simply to list the paragraph numbers of the Code, because the reader would have to refer elsewhere to discover the significance of the statement.

4.71   Statements of non-compliance might become quite lengthy where there are a significant number of departures from the Code's recommendations.

4.72   The shortest way to make a statement of non-compliance is to provide a list of areas of non-compliance with individual provisions or overall reasons for non-compliance. However, such a minimalist approach will be very negative, because it focuses on the areas of non-compliance. It is preferable to give a more balanced statement which gives information on compliance and/or on areas where the company is moving towards compliance or has decided that compliance will not best suit the circumstances of the company and, therefore, a departure from the UKCGC provisions is appropriate.

4.73   There could be valid reasons why some of the provisions have not been followed or some alternative procedures may have been adopted. As long as the company explains and has reasonable justification for any non-compliance with specific aspects and governance is effective in practice, then in the spirit of transparency, it is hoped that the market will react in a positive way.

4.73.1 In February 2012 the FRC issued a paper entitled 'What constitutes an explanation under comply-or-explain?' in response to questions raised by the European Commission about the operation of comply-or-explain, with the aim of ensuring that the explanations provided are as full as is necessary to meet shareholder expectations. The information in the introductory section of the UK Corporate Governance Code on 'Comply-or-explain' will be updated in the 2012 edition of the Code to state that: *"In providing an explanation, the company should aim to illustrate how its actual practices are consistent with the principle to which the particular provision relates, contribute to good governance and promote delivery of business objectives. It should set out the background, provide a clear rationale for the action it is taking, and describe any mitigating actions taken to address any additional risk and maintain conformity with the relevant principle. The explanation should indicate whether the deviation from the Code's provisions is limited in time and, if so, when the company intends to return to conformity with the Code's provisions".*

4.74 As discussed in paragraph 4.58, it is necessary to bear in mind that, for accounting years beginning on or after 29 June 2008, where a company is explaining a departure from any of the Code's provisions that overlap with that disclosure requirement of the DTR, then this departure from the Code may result in a breach of the DTR.

4.75 It is recommended that shareholders and others monitoring compliance with the UKCGC should do so with flexibility, common sense and with regard to the individual company's circumstances, for example, in a newly listed company in its first year of reporting compliance with the Code. As all Premium Listed companies must now apply the Code, those that are incorporated overseas and are therefore accustomed to other governance frameworks may take time to adjust their arrangements. This may result in a need to explain more departures from the Code than is the case with other companies and — for those provisions of an ongoing nature where arrangements were put in place during the year — the periods of non-compliance and compliance. We recommend that this is done clearly in the governance reporting, with areas of non-compliance at the end of the period being identified separately. Strictly speaking, all instances of non-compliance for provisions of an ongoing nature should be included in the compliance statement required under Listing Rule 9.8.6 (6), but we believe that it is adequate for them to be mentioned in the narrative statement under LR 9.8.6 (5) provided that the non-compliance is clearly described and the compliance statement identifies those provisions that have still not been complied with at the end of the period.

4.75.1 Effective shareholder engagement is one of the areas that recent corporate governance reviews have focussed on and viewed as being of critical importance. In general it is argued that, on the one hand, there need to be sufficient institutional investors willing and able to engage actively with the companies in which they invest and, on the other hand, that companies must be willing to welcome communication with investors as an opportunity to obtain external views on their performance. Further discussion of the corporate governance reviews and developments in respect of the UK Stewardship Code can be found in paragraph 4.343.

UK standard listed companies

4.76 UK standard listed companies are required to comply with both DTR 7.1, 'Audit Committees', and DTR 7.2, 'Corporate governance'. UK standard listed companies are not, however, required to report under the UKCGC. See paragraphs 4.43 to 4.57 for details of the DTR requirements.

Overseas companies — standard and premium listed companies

4.77 As discussed above, from 6 April 2010, the Listing Rules were amended to reclassify listed entities from having either 'primary' or 'secondary' listings to 'premium' or 'standard'. One effect of the changes in the Listing regulations is that overseas companies, which did not previously have to comply with the Combined Code, are now required under the Listing Rules to report against the UKCGC if they have a premium listing.

4.78 Whilst only premium listed companies (both UK and overseas) are required to comply with the UKCGC, all listed companies, whether standard or premium, are required to comply with the DTR requirements in respect of corporate governance (DTR 7.2).

4.79 Where a standard listed overseas company applies any corporate governance code, even on a voluntary basis, DTR 7.2.2R and 7.2.3R require it effectively to 'comply or explain' against that code. This could significantly increase the scope of its governance disclosures in some cases.

4.80 The FSA has not applied Listing Rule 9.8.6 (3), which requires "*a statement made by the directors that the business is a going concern*" to overseas incorporated premium listed companies (and Listing Rule 9.8.6 (3) does not apply to any standard listed company). However, provision C.1.3 of the UKCGC, states that "*the directors should report in annual and half-yearly financial statements that the business is a going concern...*" so any failure to do this would need to be explained under Listing Rule 9.8.6 (6) by an overseas premium listed company.

Other aspects of reporting and compliance

Good practice reporting

4.81 A number of UK listed companies have gone above and beyond the disclosure recommendations of the Combined Code (2008) and UKCGC in their corporate governance statement. PricewaterhouseCoopers' compendium, 'Corporate governance: Best practice reporting' last issued in January 2010, features a wide range of good practice disclosures from the corporate governance statements published in annual reports. It provides examples of good practice disclosure in terms of both format and content and may be used as a practical guide to preparing corporate governance statements. Companies should, however, ensure that their statements reflect their own particular circumstances and are specific to the company and its activities during the year or period under review. Many of these examples given in the January 2010 publication remain appropriate where Code provisions remain unchanged in the UKCGC. However, we have incorporated some recent good practice examples within this chapter.

Structure of front end, quality of reporting and compliance

4.82 To improve the quality of their reporting, companies often want to bring together all the required disclosures relating to a topic in one place. This approach is also specifically advocated by the regulators: for instance, the October 2009 FRC publication, 'Going concern and liquidity risk: guidance for directors of UK companies', advocates bringing together in one place in the annual report the various disclosures around going concern.

4.83 The challenge for this approach is that the various pieces of legislation and guidance often specify where certain information must be given – usually in the directors' report or in the governance statement. For instance, the disclosure requirements of DTR 7.2.5R on internal control over the financial reporting process must be dealt with in the governance statement and the disclosures on risk management and internal control required by the 2005 Turnbull guidance are also normally included in the governance statement, but the principal risk disclosures required by section 417(3)(b) of the Companies Act 2006 must be in the directors' report.

4.84 To address this, many companies follow the principle of DTR 7.2.1R and include the corporate governance statement within the directors' report: in practice, they frequently include in the annual report a section entitled, 'Report of the directors' (or similar) which has, as subsections within it, the governance statement, remuneration report, and the technical requirements of the directors' report. It should be noted that this approach may also allow the directors to take advantage of the 'safe harbour' provisions of section 463 of 2006 Act in relation to the other statements included within the report of the directors.

Use of cross-references and 'incorporation by reference'

4.85 Where the governance statement is included within the directors' report (or the 'report of the directors'), it will often be necessary to provide cross-references to other parts of the directors' report to ensure regulatory requirements are met.

4.86 Where it is not a subsection of the directors' report, companies may 'incorporate by reference' the governance statement within the directors' report. In this situation, the mechanism used to link the two should be more formally worded than a simple cross-reference and should include a phrase such as "*the governance statement is incorporated by reference into*" or "*the governance statement forms part of*" the directors' report. Whether this mechanism would bring with it the safe harbour protections is a legal matter on which companies may wish to take advice.

4.87 Companies may also incorporate by reference into the governance statement parts of other components of the front end of the annual report. For instance, the risk management and internal control disclosures may be given in the business review, but certain parts may relate to the Turnbull guidance and allow the company to comply with the related Code provision on internal control. These specific parts may be incorporated by reference into the governance statement.

Differences for smaller and FTSE 350 listed companies

4.88   The UK Corporate Governance Code provides a small number of concessions specific to smaller listed companies (those below the FTSE 350 for all of the preceding year):

- The board, the audit committee and the remuneration committee should have at least two independent non-executive directors. [B.1.2, C.3.1, D.2.1].

- The company chairman may be a member of, but not chair, the audit committee so long as he or she was considered independent on appointment as chairman. This appointment would be in addition to the existing independent non-executive members of the committee.

4.89   The UKCGC also introduced two new Code provisions that apply only to FTSE 350 companies:

- Evaluation of the board of FTSE 350 companies should be externally facilitated at least every three years. A statement should be made available of whether an external facilitator has any other connection with the company. [UKCGC B.6.2].

- All directors of FTSE 350 companies should be subject to annual election by shareholders. All other directors should be subject to election by shareholders at the first annual general meeting after their appointment, and to re-election thereafter at intervals of no more than three years. Non-executive directors who have served longer than nine years should be subject to annual re-election. The names of directors submitted for election or re-election should be accompanied by sufficient biographical details and any other relevant information to enable shareholders to take an informed decision on their election. [UKCGC B.7.1].

Non-listed organisations and AIM

4.90   Where non-listed organisations choose voluntarily to report on compliance with the UKCGC, we recommend that they report fully as though they were listed. We, therefore, advise against phrases such as: "*We comply with all aspects of the UK Corporate Governance Code relevant to the organisation*".

4.91   This form of disclosure on its own provides the reader with no indication of what aspects of the Code the organisation has considered relevant and, therefore, is of no real value.

4.92   Although non-listed organisations are encouraged to aim at meeting the UKCGC's recommendations, this has been rare to date outside of public interest entities and financial services institutions.

4.93   Companies that are considering the possibility of a listing will need to consider establishing appropriate governance procedures well in advance of coming to the market. In particular, they should review and, if necessary, improve their systems of internal control. In seeking a listing, companies are expected to make a statement of 'support' for the principles of the relevant Code. It is also usual to describe the steps the company has taken to comply in the areas of non-executive directors, audit, remuneration and nomination committees (describing their composition and principal functions), even if they have only recently been appointed or established. The sponsors will also normally expect to see significant moves toward compliance in other areas. In their first period following listing, the UK Listing Authority has generally permitted new registrants to make a statement of compliance for the period from the date of listing only, rather than for the full accounting period. Nevertheless, it will be important to be well prepared, because certain procedures can take some time to implement.

4.94   Companies that are considering registering on AIM should also consider establishing appropriate governance procedures. Although AIM companies are not required to follow the recommendations in the Code it is considered best practice, with the focus being on applying the 'comply or explain' principle to key areas such as board composition, audit and remuneration committees, board effectiveness and internal control. AIM companies are not required to comply with the DTR (see para 4.45) but may voluntarily elect to do so.

4.95   In September 2010, the Quoted Companies Alliance (QCA), which is a not-for-profit organisation that works with small and mid-cap quoted companies in the UK, published 'Corporate Governance Guidelines for Smaller Quoted Companies'. Although these guidelines seek to help small and mid-cap companies apply the UKCGC, they could also be applied by AIM and PLUS quoted companies.

Other codes

4.96 A number of other codes have been issued, often adapting the UKCGC or its predecessors for particular industries or situations. For instance, the Association of Investment Companies (AIC) published the 'AIC Code of Corporate Governance' in October 2010 to provide *"boards of our Member companies with a framework of best practice in respect of the governance of investment companies. The AIC Code addresses the governance issues relevant to investment companies and enables boards to satisfy any requirements they may have under the UK Corporate Governance Code"*. [AIC Code of Corporate governance, 2010]. The AIC Code has been endorsed by the FRC and includes an appendix with suggested text for a preamble to an investment company's corporate governance report when applying the AIC Code.

4.97 HM Treasury has issued its own code of governance; the focus of 'Corporate Governance in central government departments: Code of good practice 2011' for ministerial departments of central government.

4.98 As a third example, Higher Education bodies are bound by the HEFCE Financial Memorandum (July 2010/19) as a condition of accepting funding from HEFCE. This states in Annex B paragraph 31 (the Audit Code of Practice) that HEFCE's position is that governing bodies and audit committees should conduct themselves in line with the Committee of University Chairs' Guide for Members of Higher Education Governing Bodies in the UK (which incorporates the Governance Code of Practice and General Principles), and that where they believe they differ in any material respects then this should be explained and made public. Higher Education bodies must therefore effectively comply or explain against an industry-based code.

[The next paragraph is 4.220.]

The UK Corporate Governance Code (2010)

Introduction

4.220 In June 2010 the Financial Reporting Council (FRC) published the revised UK Corporate Governance Code ('UKCGC') to replace the 2008 Combined Code. This edition of the Code applies to all premium listed companies for financial years beginning on or after 29 June 2010, including overseas companies. Note that the 2010 edition will itself be superseded by a revised version for years beginning on or after 1 October 2012. See paragraph 4.357.6 onwards for details.

Main changes from the Combined Code (2008)

4.221 The overriding view emerging from the FRC consultation during 2009-2010 as a whole was that the governance code is effective and that the 'comply or explain' approach is sufficiently flexible to embrace different companies' circumstances. However the FRC also concluded that much more attention needs to be paid to following the spirit of the Code as well as its letter and that the quality of corporate governance ultimately depends on board behaviour not process. The new Code therefore puts greater emphasis on the leadership and effectiveness of boards, and on the board's responsibility for the management of risk. It also recognises that there needs to be better communication and engagement with shareholders.

4.222 In general, the new Code includes points of re-emphasis and re-focus rather than fundamental change. The main changes are summarised below:

For FTSE 350 companies only

- Annual re-election of all directors to increase accountability to shareholders.

- Externally facilitated performance reviews of boards at least every three years to help enhance the board's performance and awareness of its strengths and weaknesses.

For all listed companies

- To encourage boards to be well balanced and avoid 'group think', there are new principles on the composition and selection of the board, including the need to appoint members on merit, against objective criteria, and with due regard for the benefits of diversity, including gender diversity.

- To promote proper debate in the boardroom, there are new principles on the leadership of the chairman, the responsibility of the non-executive directors to provide constructive challenge, and the time commitment expected of all directors.

- To help enhance the board's performance and awareness of its strengths and weaknesses, the chairman should hold regular development reviews with each director.

- To increase accountability to shareholders, chairmen are encouraged to report personally on how the principles relating to the leadership and effectiveness of the board have been applied.

- To improve risk management, the board should be responsible for determining the nature and extent of the significant risks it is willing to take (and there must be specific reporting on the company's business model in the annual report).

- Performance-related pay should be aligned to the company's long-term interests and its risk policies and systems.

- There are significant structural changes: the section on directors is divided into two sections 'Leadership' and 'Effectiveness' and the preamble is updated to form a new introductory section reinforcing important messages about the way the Code should be viewed and applied.

4.223 The FRC has confirmed separately how a 'FTSE 350 company' will be defined for the purposes of the Code provisions on re-election of directors and board performance evaluations. The definition is the converse of that for a 'smaller company' elsewhere in the Code: that is, it is a company that is within the FTSE 350 throughout the year immediately prior to the reporting year.

4.224 The FRC hopes that these changes will promote greater clarity and understanding with regard to the tasks of an effective board and that communication with shareholders will be more effective as a result. In addition, the FRC also took responsibility for a code for institutional investors to enhance shareholder engagement. This resulted in the FRC publishing the first UK Stewardship Code in July 2010, effective immediately. See paragraph 4.343 onwards for a discussion of the UK Stewardship Code.

4.225 The FRC has amended the Code to adopt those recommendations from the Walker review that it believes apply to all listed companies. In particular, there are revised principles on the roles of the chairman and non-executive directors, the composition of the board, the commitment expected of directors and the board's responsibility for risk. The new provisions on annual re-election and performance evaluation are also consistent with Walker. Examples of Walker recommendations that have not been applied outside the banking sector include having a board risk committee and risk officer and stipulating a minimum time commitment for non-executive directors.

4.226 More commentary on the changes in the UK Corporate Governance Code is included under each area of governance in the sections that follow.

Reporting under the Code and 'comply or explain'

4.227 The Listing Rules continue to require a two-part compliance statement:

- one statement explaining how the main principles have been applied; and

- a second on whether the company has complied with the related provisions, or explaining why this is not the case. For requirements under the DTR, compliance is mandatory.

The descriptions together should give shareholders a clear and comprehensive picture of a company's governance arrangements in relation to the Code. See from paragraph 4.60 for a discussion on compliance statements.

4.228 Current good practice corporate governance reporting in terms of 'comply or explain' statements show:

- Companies getting behind the principles-based environment provided by the Code.

- A commitment to transparent reporting, tailored to the circumstances of the business. This aids effective engagement between investors and boards.

4.229 One of the main themes of the FRC review was that there needs to be better communication and engagement with shareholders. The FRC believes there is a need for boards to make communications with shareholders more confident and persuasive, and it encourages board chairmen, and the chairmen of the main board committees, to see the corporate governance statement as an opportunity to demonstrate to current and potential investors why they can have confidence in the board. The FRC hopes particularly that chairmen will choose to report personally in their annual statements how the principles of the Code relating to the role and effectiveness of the board have been applied.

Overview of the contents of the UK Corporate Governance Code (2010)

4.230 The UK Corporate Governance Code (2010) structure is as follows:

- Preamble covering: Governance and the Code; Preface; Comply or Explain

- The main principles of the Code

- Section A – Leadership

- Section B – Effectiveness

- Section C – Accountability

- Section D – Remuneration

- Section E – Relations with shareholders

4.231 Sections A to E contain the main principles and provisions to be reported against in the two-part compliance statement as required by the Listing Rules (discussed further in para 4.60).

Schedules forming part of the UK Corporate Governance Code

4.232 In the UKCGC three schedules provide further information:

- Schedule A – The design of performance-related remuneration for executive directors

- Schedule B – Disclosure of corporate governance arrangements

- Schedule C – Engagement principles for institutional shareholders

4.233 Schedule B summarises the disclosure requirements of corporate governance arrangements including the FSA Listing Rules and Disclosure Rules and Transparency Rules. Disclosure requirements are discussed from paragraph 4.49. Schedule B also summarises the information that should be 'made available' (which may be met by placing it on the company's web site) and the information that should be set out to shareholders in relation to election/re-election of directors and appointment /re-appointment of an external auditor.

4.233.1 Schedule C ceased to apply on 2 July 2010 when the UK Stewardship Code for institutional investors came into effect. The UK Stewardship Code is discussed from paragraph 4.343.

Structure of sections that follow

4.234 Key areas of governance covered by the UKCGC are set out below. For each area, the following information is provided, where applicable:

- The main and supporting principles.

- Specific disclosure requirements.

- Other related provisions.

- Trends in good practice disclosures, in some cases addressing themes of the 2009/10 governance reviews. Such disclosures, while not mandatory, may help to avoid a 'box-ticking' approach to governance reporting.

- Details of any other guidance that should be considered when dealing with the relevant area.

Disclosures required under DTR 7 are not included below other than for comparative purposes against Code disclosures. See paragraphs 4.43 to 4.57 for details of these.

The board and its committees

Introduction

4.235 The UKCGC's principles on leadership cover the role of the board, division of responsibilities and responsibilities of the chairman and non-executive directors.

4.236 One of the main topics of discussion in the corporate governance reviews during 2009/10 concerned the role and activity of the board and whether there was sufficient oversight from the non-executive directors. Questions were raised such as:

- Was the board effective in its decision making?

- Was sufficient attention paid to risk management or was this an area that was delegated to the audit committee?

- What did the board spend their time discussing at their board meetings?

- What role were the non-executive directors expected to fill and did they spend enough time getting to know the business?

Personal behaviours by directors underpin this area. The FRC, therefore, made structural changes to the Combined Code (2008) by splitting the previous section 'Directors' into two separate sections ('Leadership' and 'Effectiveness') and revising the principles and provisions within them. This was to give more prominence to the factors that underpin an effective board.

Principles

4.237 The main principles that should be applied in relation to the board are as follows:

- Every company should be headed by an effective board which is collectively responsible for the long-term success of the company. [UKCGC Main principle A.1].

- There should be a clear division of responsibilities at the head of the company between the running of the board and the executive responsibility for the running of the company's business. No one individual should have unfettered powers of decision. [UKCGC Main principle A.2].

- The chairman is responsible for leadership of the board and ensuring its effectiveness on all aspects of its role. [UKCGC Main principle A.3].

- As part of their role as members of a unitary board, non-executive directors should constructively challenge and help develop proposals on strategy. [UKCGC Main principle A.4].

- The board should be supplied in a timely manner with information in a form and of a quality appropriate to enable it to discharge its duties. [UKCGC Main principle B.5].

4.238 The supporting principles relevant to the board go on to explain that:

- The board's role is to provide entrepreneurial leadership of the company within a framework of prudent and effective controls that enables risk to be assessed and managed. The board should set the company's strategic aims, ensure that the necessary financial and human resources are in place for the company to meet its objectives and review management performance. The board should set the company's values and standards and ensure that its obligations to its shareholders and others are understood and met. [UKCGC Supporting principle A.1].

- All directors must act in what they consider to be the company's best interests, consistent with their statutory duties. [UKCGC Supporting principle A.1].

- The chairman is responsible for setting the board's agenda and ensuring that adequate time is available for discussion of all agenda items, in particular strategic issues. The chairman should also promote a culture of openness and debate by facilitating the effective contribution of non-executive directors in particular and ensuring constructive relations between executive and non-executive directors. [UKCGC Supporting principle A.3].

- The chairman is responsible for ensuring that the directors receive accurate, timely and clear information. The chairman should ensure effective communication with shareholders. [UKCGC Supporting principle A.3].

- Non-executive directors should scrutinise the management's performance in meeting agreed goals and objectives and monitor the reporting of performance. They should satisfy themselves on the integrity of financial information and that financial controls and systems of risk management are robust and defensible. They are responsible for determining appropriate levels of remuneration of executive directors and have a prime role in appointing and, where necessary, removing executive directors, and in succession planning. [UKCGC Supporting principle A.4].

- The chairman is responsible for ensuring that the directors receive accurate, timely and clear information. Management has an obligation to provide such information, but directors should seek clarification or amplification where necessary. [UKCGC Supporting principle B.5].

- Under the direction of the chairman, the company secretary's responsibilities include ensuring good information flows within the board and its committees and between senior management and non-executive directors, as well as facilitating induction and assisting with professional development as required. [UKCGC Supporting principle B.5].

- The company secretary should be responsible for advising the board through the chairman on all governance matters. [UKCGC Supporting principle B.5].

Disclosure requirements

4.239 Disclosures in relation to the board that are required within the annual report are as follows:

- A statement should be made about how the board operates, including a high level statement of which types of decisions are to be taken by the board and which are to be delegated to management. [UKCGC A.1.1].

- UKCGC provision A.1.2 requires that the annual report should identify:

    - The chairman.

    - The deputy chairman (where applicable).

    - The chief executive.

    - The senior independent director.

    - The chairmen and members of each of the nomination, audit and remuneration committees.

    This provision also requires that the annual report includes the number of meetings of the board and each committee and individual attendance by directors.

4.240 There are a number of Code provisions that overlap with the requirements of the DTR, as noted in paragraph 4.59. The DTR confirms that if a company provides the information specified by UKCGC A.1.1, A.1.2, B.2.4, C.3.1, C.3.2, C.3.3 and D.2.1 it will satisfy the relevant requirements of DTR 7.1.5 R and 7.2.7 R.

Other related provisions

4.241 The following provisions are not disclosure provisions. However, it is envisaged that compliance with these detailed provisions will mean that the main principle has been applied.

- The board should meet sufficiently regularly to discharge its duties effectively. There should be a formal schedule of matters specifically reserved for its decision. [UKCGC A.1.1].

- The roles of chairman and chief executive should not be exercised by the same individual. The division of responsibilities between the chairman and chief executive should be clearly established, set out in writing and agreed by the board. [UKCGC A.2.1].

- The company should arrange appropriate insurance cover in respect of legal action against its directors. [UKCGC A.1.3].

- Where directors have concerns which cannot be resolved about the running of the company or a proposed action, they should ensure that their concerns are recorded in the board minutes. On resignation, a non-executive director should provide a written statement to the chairman, for circulation to the board, if they have any such concerns. [UKCGC A.4.3].

- The terms of reference of the nomination, audit and remuneration committees, including each committee's role and authority delegated to it by the board, should be made available. This can be met by making the information available on the company's website. [UKCGC B.2.1, C.3.3, D.2.1].

- All directors, especially non-executive directors, should have access to independent professional advice at the company's expense, where they judge it necessary to discharge their responsibilities as directors. Committees should be provided with sufficient resources to undertake their duties. [UKCGC B.5.1].

- All directors should have access to the advice and services of the company secretary, who is responsible to the board for ensuring that board procedures are complied with. Both the appointment and removal of the company secretary should be a matter for the board as a whole. [UKCGC B.5.2].

Good practice disclosures

4.242 Current disclosures in this area tend to focus on the division of responsibilities between chairman and chief executive, with good practice examples showing clear explanations of the responsibilities of the respective roles, in a manner tailored to the circumstances of the business. As the role of the chairman has been brought under a new main principle, it would be helpful for disclosures to highlight the chairman's pivotal role in defining the board's 'culture' and ensuring its effectiveness. As noted above, the FRC is encouraging chairmen to report personally in their annual reports how the Code's principles relating to the board's role and effectiveness have been applied. Most companies now include at least a brief introduction to the governance report from the chairman and many have the chairman emphasise the company's key governance messages. A number have also taken up the suggestion to personalise the committee reporting.

Table 4.2 – Personal reporting by the Chairman

Berendsen plc – Report and Accounts — 31 December 2011

Chairman's overview (extract)

What good governance means to Berendsen

At Berendsen, we do not view corporate governance as an isolated exercise in compliance but as a core and vital discipline that complements our desire continually to improve upon the long-term growth and success of the group on behalf of shareholders. Good governance is an evolving process and our aim is to consistently be at the forefront of corporate governance best practice in order to deliver effectively on the company's strategic objectives. During 2011 we were pleased that once again our focus on good governance was recognised with Berendsen being shortlisted for the Investor Relations Society 2011 Best Practice Awards for 'Best Communication of Governance and Risk in the Annual Report'. At Berendsen, we believe that effective governance is realised through leadership and collaboration resulting in consistently focused and sensible business decisions.

As Chairman, my primary responsibility is to ensure that the board has the right mix of skills, knowledge and experience so that it works effectively as a team, supporting management to formulate and execute the corporate strategy, whilst encouraging the nonexecutive directors to bring fresh perspectives to the table and, where appropriate, to hold management to account. In this way the Berendsen board comprises a team of experienced individuals with the complementary skills and talents to carry out their duties to the best of their abilities, which we hope engenders the trust and respect of all stakeholders.

New business line organisation structure

During 2011, the board has liaised with executive management to ensure that our governance systems are appropriate for our new business line structure which is effective from 1st January 2012. This has included updating the group's vision and values and the group's delegated authorities, ensuring that responsibility and accountability for all business areas are agreed and communicated and that the risk management systems and group's key policies and procedures have been reviewed and updated. The board has met the entire executive board three times during 2011 and has also received presentations, in August from Christian Ellegaard on Sales Effectiveness, in October from Chris Thrush (the newly appointed Group Director, Human Resources) on Management Development and Succession, and in December from Steve Finch on Procurement.

Board achievements during 2011

The key responsibilities of the Berendsen board are to set the strategy, monitor what management are doing, hold them accountable for performance against agreed targets and challenge their thinking to ensure that they remain focused on achieving our strategic aims and objectives.

2011 has been a very busy and exciting year for the group. The board has been committed to ensuring that the key recommendations from our 2010 strategic review are implemented and that we have the right incentive schemes to motivate (and arguably, as importantly, retain) key management. This involved an additional board meeting in March 2011 and liaison with our major shareholders in respect of changes to management shortterm incentive arrangements.

In order to gain a better understanding of our business strategy and also to meet local management, two board meetings were held outside the UK, in May in Norway and in September in Poland. This provided the board with an excellent insight into the challenges facing these businesses.

Board evaluation

We have recently completed our first external board evaluation, which was conducted by Dr Tracy Long of Boardroom Review. The findings were presented at our board meeting on 21st February 2012 and the key actions agreed by the board are detailed on page 55.

Shareholder engagement

As Chairman, I am responsible for ensuring that there is ongoing and effective communication between the board and its shareholders. During 2011, I have kept in contact with our major shareholders and in December arranged a dinner where all our major shareholders had the opportunity to meet the non-executive directors. Feedback received from shareholders was that this was a very useful event and we will arrange a similar dinner during the last quarter of 2012.

Appointment of new Chairman

As announced on 7th December 2011, I have decided to retire after this year's Annual General Meeting. Iain Ferguson has been appointed to replace me and I am sure he will be a worthy successor. I wish him every success in his new role.

Christopher Kemball
Chairman

4.243 Other good practice trends in this area include:

- Providing insight into the organisation's underlying culture and purpose, which underpins the governance arrangements.

- Explaining how appropriate board behaviours and dynamics are encouraged, acknowledging behavioural aspects of a successful board.

- Describing the actual activities undertaken by the board as well as matters reserved for it; this is a recurring feature of good practice reporting on governance – listing out the responsibilities of the board or its committees does not represent best practice in any area.

- Giving a breakdown of the time spent on particular parts of the board or committee's role – for example, strategy, performance, risk. This can be done using diagrams and comparatives are also helpful.

Other guidance

4.244 Both Walker and the FRC review recognise the chairman's crucial role in setting the 'tone at the top' for the rest of the board, including determining the board agenda and ensuring sufficient time for issues to be debated between executives and non-executives. The FRC, therefore:

- brought the existing material on the chairman's role from main principle A.2 of the Combined Code (2008) under a new main principle A.3;

- amended the supporting principle to include that the chairman is responsible for ensuring that adequate time is available for discussion of all agenda items, in particular strategic issues; and

- stated that the chairman should promote a culture of openness and debate.

4.245 FRC guidance on the chairman's role was included in the 'Good Practice Suggestions from the Higgs Report' (the 'Higgs Guidance') issued in June 2006. Following consultation by the Institute of Chartered Secretaries and Administrators, the updated guidance was published by the FRC in March 2011, renamed 'Guidance on board effectiveness'.

4.245.1 The FRC Guidance on Board Effectiveness aims to assist companies in applying the sections of the Code that deal with leadership and board effectiveness. As with the FRC's separate guidance notes on audit committees and internal control, it *"is not intended to be prescriptive. It does not set out the 'right way' to apply the Code. Rather it is intended to stimulate boards' thinking on how they can carry out their role most effectively".*

[The next paragraph is 4.245.3]

4.245.3 The new guidance reflects the changes made to the Code in 2010 and now focuses on board behaviours rather than process. It covers areas such as: the roles of the chairman, senior independent director, other directors and the company secretary, decision-making policies and processes; board composition and succession planning; and performance evaluation.

4.245.4 The guidance explains that the board's role is to provide company's entrepreneurial leadership and lists out a number of behaviours/cultures it should follow to be effective. These include:

- Providing direction for management.

- Demonstrating ethical leadership, displaying behaviours consistent with the culture and values it has defined for the organisation.

- Creating a performance culture that drives value creation without exposing the company to excessive risk of value destruction.

- Making well-informed and high-quality decisions based on a clear line of sight into the business.

- Creating the right framework for helping directors meet their statutory responsibilities.

- Being accountable, particularly to those that provide the company's capital.

- Thinking carefully about governance arrangements and embracing evaluation of their effectiveness.

[Guidance on board effectiveness, FRC, March 2011].

4.245.5 The Guidance on Board Effectiveness also discusses the chairman's role and suggests the role should include:

- Demonstrating ethical leadership.

- Setting a board agenda which is primarily focused on strategy, performance, value creation and accountability, and ensuring that issues relevant to these areas are reserved for board decision.

- Making certain that the board determines the nature, and extent of the significant risks the company is willing to embrace in implementing its strategy, and that there are no 'no-go' areas that prevent directors from operating effective oversight in this area.

- Regularly considering succession planning and the board's composition.

- Developing productive working relationships with all executive directors, and the CEO in particular, providing support and advice while respecting executive responsibility.

- Ensuring effective communication with shareholders and other stakeholders and, in particular, that all directors are made aware of the views of those who provide the company's capital.

[Guidance on board effectiveness, FRC, March 2011].

Re-election of directors

Principles

4.246 The main principle that should be applied in relation to the re-election of directors is as follows:

- All directors should be submitted for re-election at regular intervals, subject to continued satisfactory performance. [UKCGC Main principle B.7].

Disclosure requirements

4.247 None for the annual report, but see provisions B.7.1 and B.7.2 below.

Other related provisions

4.248   The following detailed provisions should be implemented:

■   All directors of FTSE 350 companies should be subject to annual election by shareholders. All other directors should be subject to election by shareholders at the first annual general meeting after their appointment, and to re-election thereafter at intervals of no more than three years. Non-executive directors who have served longer than nine years should be subject to annual re-election. [UKCGC B.7.1].

■   The board should set out to shareholders in the papers why they believe an individual should be elected as a non-executive director. When proposing re-election, the chairman should confirm to shareholders that, following formal performance evaluation, the individual's performance continues to be effective and to demonstrate commitment to the role. [UKCGC B.7.2].

Other guidance

4.249   To enhance accountability to, and the influence of, shareholders the Walker review recommended the annual re-election of the board chairman and the re-election of the remuneration committee chair if the remuneration report fails to secure 75% support. The FRC extended these Walker recommendations by introducing a new provision requiring re-election for all directors of FTSE 350 companies on the basis that it is appropriate for shareholders to have an annual opportunity to express their views on the performance of all the directors. The FRC recognises the concern that smaller companies with a more concentrated shareholder base might be exposed to disagreements between their major shareholders and, therefore, has limited the new provision to FTSE 350 companies. The FRC also note in the preface to the 2010 Code that: "... *companies are free to explain rather than comply if they believe that their existing arrangements ensure proper accountability and underpin board effectiveness, or that a transitional period is needed before they introduce annual re-election. The boards of smaller companies are also encouraged to consider their policy on director re-election.*"

4.250   Although the FRC believed that there was widespread support from the investor community for annual re-election of all directors during the consultation process on the new Code, initial indications were that some institutional investors would not insist upon the change on the grounds that it may create instability. Despite this, most FTSE 100 companies adopted annual re-election in the last year of compliance with the Combined Code (2008), that is, before they were required to under the UK Corporate Governance Code.

Performance evaluation

Principles

4.251   The main principle that should be applied in relation to evaluation of the board is as follows:

■   The board should undertake a formal and rigorous annual evaluation of its own performance and that of its committees and individual directors. [UKCGC Main principle B.6].

4.252   The supporting principles set out that:

■   The chairman should act on the results of the performance evaluation by recognising the strengths and addressing the weaknesses of the board and, where appropriate, proposing new members be appointed to the board or seeking the resignation of directors. [UKCGC Supporting principle B.6].

■   Individual evaluation should aim to show whether each director continues to contribute effectively and to demonstrate commitment to the role (including commitment of time for board and committee meetings and any other duties). [UKCGC Supporting principle B.6].

Disclosure requirements

4.253   Disclosures relevant to performance evaluation are as follows:

■   The board should state in the annual report how performance evaluation of the board, its committees and its individual directors has been conducted. [UKCGC B.6.1].

■   Where an external facilitator is used to evaluate the board, a statement should be made as to whether the facilitator has any other connection with the company. This statement may be made on the company's website. [UKCGC B.6.2].

Corporate governance

Other related provisions

4.254 The following related detailed provisions should be addressed:

- All FTSE 350 companies should engage an external party to evaluate the board's performance at least every three years. [UKCGC B.6.2].

- The chairman should hold meetings with the non-executive directors without the executive directors present. The non-executive directors, led by the senior independent director, should be responsible for the chairman's performance evaluation, taking into account the views of executive directors. [UKCGC A.4.2, B.6.3].

Good practice disclosures

4.255 Existing good practice disclosures include:

- Giving details of the outcome of the evaluation and any follow up action proposed; although the Code provision relates only to *how* the evaluation was conducted, discussing the outcomes indicates commitment to improvement and transparency.

- Following up on progress against recommendations carried forward from previous years.

- Indicating what use the company makes, or plans to make in future, of externally facilitated performance reviews; where one has not been done in the year describe where the company is in the recommended three-year cycle.

Table 4.3 – Board evaluation outcomes, actions and progress

GlaxoSmithKline plc – Annual Report for shareholders – 31 December 2011

Corporate governance (extract)

Board evaluation

The Board carries out an evaluation of its performance and the performance of its Committees every year. The evaluation is normally carried out by the Senior Independent Director, but every third year, the evaluation is conducted by an external facilitator. In 2008, Dr Tracy Long of Boardroom Review carried out the evaluation and she also conducted the 2011 evaluation. Dr Long has no other connection with the company.

The action points from previous Board evaluations are set out in the table below:

Date	Action	Progress
2008	Utilise Board and Committee time more effectively and facilitate further contribution by Non-Executive Directors.	Board and Committee papers are reviewed for appropriateness and timeliness of circulation has improved. Meetings have been structured to create more time for debate.
	Enhance continuous education process for Non-Executive Directors.	Non-Executive Directors are encouraged to attend a range of internal management meetings and to visit Group sites.
	Provide greater visibility to executive talent and management succession planning process.	An annual presentation is made to the Board on executive talent and succession plans. Opportunities for emerging talent to meet with the Board are included in the annual Board and Committee programmes.
2009	Increase Board time devoted to strategic discussion and the indicators of success in the delivery of the R&D pipeline.	The Board has increased its focus on R&D activities and was pleased with progress on R&D during the year. Separately, in February 2011, the Remuneration Committee granted incentive awards linked to R&D new product performance.
	Devote more time to focused consideration of the company's key risks on an ongoing basis.	The Board sought assistance from the Audit & Risk Committee (ARC) to more fully understand the Group's key risks and continued to consider regular reports from the ARC in 2011.
	Provide the Board with more regular updates and insights into the newly enhanced management succession planning process.	The Board was pleased with the operation by the Nominations Committee of the enhanced succession planning process. This resulted in the appointment of the Chief Financial Officer Designate and further positive progress has been made on the recruitment of new Board members to refresh the Board with the appointment of Stacey Cartwright and Judy Lewent as Non-Executive Directors.
2010	Allocate more time on a regular basis for strategic issues and the significant challenges facing the industry to further enhance returns to shareholders.	Board agendas have been revised to create more time for strategic discussion and debate. Fundamental reviews of key issues have been introduced to ensure focused consideration of our strategic priorities.
	Further enhance information flow by providing Board members with a wider variety of external perspectives on the company and the industry.	Board members are provided with external reports and reviews of the industry and the company to further inform their deliberations.
	Assess the extent to which the new R&D policies implemented in recent years have added value.	The Board programme has been enhanced by the inclusion of deep dive discussions on aspects of R&D, such as the R&D commercial interface and diseases of the developing world.
	Continue to support executive management on ethical leadership within the Group.	The Group's compliance function has been reviewed and enhanced to provide further support to management in driving ethical leadership across the Group.

2011 Board evaluation

The Board evaluation process included a one-to-one interview with each Director and the Company Secretary. The topics discussed, which had been circulated to the Directors in advance, included a variety of aspects associated with Board effectiveness, including Board and Committee information flows, handling of strategic issues, collective effectiveness and exploration of ways to further improve the way in which the Board operates.

The key conclusions of the 2011 evaluation were presented to, and discussed by, the Board.

Consistent with Dr Long's findings in 2008, the review concluded that the Board was highly effective in the way in approached its work, developed its relationships and used its time. The CEO and Executive management were welcoming of the Non-Executive Directors, the quality of debate was high and there was strong leadership by the Chairman and Committee Chairmen. The use of Board dinners and the Board calendar and agendas were more effective than when previously reviewed in 2008. The quality of papers and presentations had further improved.

The challenge, given the environment within which the company operated, was to build on the Board's contribution and impact.

The Board agreed the following recommendations with a view to further increasing its ability to add value:

(i) The external landscape

- The Board agenda should dedicate time throughout the year for the consideration of major external influences, including competitive business models, market developments, and GSK's relative strengths and weakness to help expand the Board's knowledge.

- The Board would look to increase its understanding and knowledge through individual Non-Executive Director and Board site visits.

- Given the size of the Board, it was important that Non-Executive Directors, assisted by the Company Secretary, continued to engage both formally and informally with the company, drawing on relevant personal experience inside and outside of Board meetings, and attending relevant internal executive meetings and industry events to keep abreast of current developments.

- Management should demonstrate to the Board how they are embedding the culture of risk awareness within Emerging Markets and how emerging risks are captured within the Assurance process.

(ii) Board contribution and composition

- The Board had a opportunity to build on relevant skills and competencies for the future as its composition was due to change over the next two years. It would be helpful for the Board to plan its composition over the next five to six years, to optimise its effectiveness.

- The Directors had identified two significant gaps in the Board's current composition: global CEO experience and knowledge of, and experience in, Emerging Markets. These aspects will be addressed in the recruitment of new Board members by the Nominations Committee.

A summary of the conclusions of the Committee evaluations is included in each Committee's report.

The Non-Executive Directors, led by the Senior Independent Director, met separately, without the Chairman being present, to discuss the Chairman's performance. They considered that his leadership, performance and overall contribution were of a high standard.

In addition, the Chairman met with all the Non-Executive Directors independently of the Executive Directors.

Other guidance

4.256 Performance evaluation can be an effective way of assessing the board's performance and bringing issues to light where remedial action should be taken. The FRC followed Walker by including a new provision requiring FTSE 350 companies to perform an externally facilitated evaluation every three years, although it acknowledges that in the short to medium term there will continue to be concerns about the availability of board evaluation services and for that reason has limited the new provision to FTSE 350 companies only. The FRC will also consider whether there are any steps it should take to raise standards among service providers.

4.256.1 The updated FRC Guidance on board effectiveness issued in March 2011 includes guidance on evaluating the performance of the board and directors. The guidance includes a list of areas which may be considered as part of any internal or external evaluation process, including the mix of skills, experience, knowledge and diversity on the board. The list is not exhaustive, but aims to give guidance on the types of considerations to expect. The guidance also suggests that the outcome of the evaluation should be shared with the whole board and should be used to help design induction and development programmes. A 'review loop' may also be useful for the company to consider how effective the board evaluation process has been.

Forms of performance evaluation

4.257 The most common forms of board evaluation are paper questionnaires and interviews. An externally facilitated evaluation will generally involve one-to-one interviews with each member of the Board and, possibly, senior management or other third parties who interact with the Board. Interviews may be complemented by the completion of questionnaires or may be based around high level questions. An internal board evaluation will most commonly involve the completion of a questionnaire or checklist, which will be facilitated by the chairman. However, in some cases, board evaluation is simply an informal discussion of the board's strengths and weaknesses and its achievements and shortcomings. Companies may also consider a similar approach for committee reviews.

4.258 A formal externally facilitated board evaluation will usually include one-to-one interviews, completion of questionnaires (with examples to support responses), desk-top review of board papers and constitution and observation of board and/or committee meetings. For individual director (and chairman) performance evaluation, peer evaluation questionnaires are often used which require individual directors to assess their performance and the performance of their peers on a number of different criteria.

4.259 The UKCGC requires companies to report how their performance evaluation has been conducted. Currently, most companies include a short piece in their corporate governance statement, confirming that a board evaluation has taken place and, in some cases, explaining the methodology and highlighting some of the findings.

[The next paragraph is 4.261.]

Board balance and independence

Introduction

4.261 One focus of the recent governance reviews was the importance of having an appropriate balance of skills, experience, independence and knowledge amongst the directors. The FRC has made this the main principle to replace the former one on the balance of executive and non-executive directors to emphasise that the over-riding consideration for assessing board composition is that the board is fit for purpose rather than independence criteria.

Principles

4.262 The main principle that should be applied in relation to board balance and independence is as follows:

■ The board and its committees should have the appropriate balance of skills, experience, independence and knowledge of the company to enable them to discharge their respective duties and responsibilities effectively. [UKCGC Main principle B.1].

4.263 The supporting principles relevant to board composition are:

- The board should be of sufficient size that the requirements of the business can be met and that changes to the board's composition and that of its committees can be managed without undue disruption, and should not be so large as to be unwieldy. [UKCGC Supporting principle B.1].

- The board should include an appropriate combination of executive and non-executive directors (and, in particular, independent non-executive directors) such that no individual or small group of individuals can dominate the board's decision taking. [UKCGC Supporting principle B.1].

- The value of ensuring that committee membership is refreshed and that undue reliance is not placed on particular individuals should be taken into account in deciding chairmanship and membership of committees. [UKCGC Supporting principle B.1].

- No one other than the committee chairman and members is entitled to be present at a meeting of the nomination, audit or remuneration committee, but others may attend at the invitation of the committee. [UKCGC Supporting principle B.1].

Disclosure requirements

4.264 Disclosures in relation to board balance and independence that are required within the annual report are:

- The annual report should identify each non-executive director that the board considers to be independent. If the board considers a director to be independent, but circumstances or relationships exist that may appear relevant to that decision, disclosure should be made of the reasons for determining that director to be independent. [UKCGC B.1.1].

Other related provisions

4.265 The following are the detailed provisions related to the principles above:

- Circumstances that could appear to affect a director's independence will include:
  - employment with the company or group within the last five years;
  - a material business relationship within the last three years between the company and the director, or a body of which he/she is a partner shareholder, director or senior employee;
  - any entitlement to remuneration from the company other than a director's fee or participation in the company's share option or a performance-related pay scheme or membership of the company's pension scheme;
  - close family ties between the director and any of the company's advisers, directors or senior employees;
  - a cross-directorship or significant links with other directors through involvement in other companies or bodies;
  - representing a significant shareholder; or
  - more than nine years' service on the board.

  [UKCGC B.1.1].

- At least half the board, excluding the chairman, should comprise independent non-executive directors. A smaller company (that is, a company below the FTSE 350 throughout the year immediately prior to the reporting year) should have at least two independent non-executive directors. [UKCGC B.1.2].

- An independent non-executive director should be appointed by the board as the senior independent director. This director should provide a sounding board for the chairman and serve as an intermediary for the other directors. This director should also be available to shareholders if they have concerns that contact through the normal channels of chairman, chief executive or finance director has failed to resolve or for which such contact is inappropriate. [UKCGC A.4.1].

- A chief executive should not go on to be chairman of the same company. If exceptionally a board decides that a chief executive should become chairman, the board should consult major shareholders in advance and should set out its reasons to shareholders at the time of the appointment and in the next annual report. [UKCGC A.3.1].

- The chairman should on appointment meet the independence criteria set out in B.1.1. [UKCGC A.3.1].

- The board should establish both an audit committee and a remuneration committee of at least three, or in the case of smaller companies (that is, those below the FTSE 350 throughout the year immediately prior to the reporting year) two independent non-executive directors. [UKCGC C.3.1, D.2.1].

- The company chairman may also be a member of, but not chair, the remuneration committee if he or she was considered independent on appointment as chairman. [UKCGC D.2.1].

- For smaller companies, the company chairman may be a member of, but not chair, the audit committee if he or she was considered independent on appointment as chairman. This is in addition to the independent non-executive directors. [UKCGC C.3.1].

4.266 Although the main principle is now wider than independence, provision B.1.2 still requires that at least half the board (excluding the chairman) should comprise independent non-executive directors. Thus a board that comprises a chairman, three executive directors and three independent non-executive directors would comply with this provision as at least half the board excluding the chairman (that is, three independent directors out of six directors) are independent.

4.267 This provision does not apply to smaller companies (defined as those companies categorised as falling outside of the FTSE 350 throughout the year immediately prior to the reporting year), which instead should have at least two independent non-executive directors. These recommendations can be difficult for smaller companies to comply with, given the practical difficulty of attracting and retaining high quality independent non-executives.

Good practice disclosures

4.268 Good practice disclosures in this area include:

- Clear information on the tenure of directors; diagrams including all the directors are helpful in understanding the balance of the board.

- A description of succession planning to ensure ongoing balance is appropriate.

- An indication of future plans for succession for non-executives serving more than nine years (which remains relevant despite the new provision for FTSE 350 directors to be subject to annual re-election), and also for those directors that have served between six and nine years (who are also subject to a particularly rigorous review of their commitment and performance under provision B.2.3).

- A description of the criteria used for independence judgements, not simply a conclusion that the director is independent.

Table 4.4 – Explanation of independence of non-executive directors

Standard Chartered PLC – Annual Report – 31 December 2011

Corporate governance (extract)

Our Board (extract)

Assessment of Director Independence

The Board is satisfied that all of our non-executive directors are independent. Rudy Markham has been on the Board for 11 years and as a result, his continued independence has been the subject of particular scrutiny. The Nomination Committee considered this point in detail. Rudy continues to demonstrate excellent stewardship as Senior Independent Director and Chairman of the Audit Committee. His continuity of service and commitment provides an in-depth knowledge and understanding of the Group that is invaluable to the Board, the Audit Committee, Risk Committee, Governance Committee and the Nomination Committee. In 2010 three new independent non-executive directors were appointed, thus ensuring regular refreshing of the Board. As a result, it was felt that there would be a positive benefit to having non-executive directors with a deep and long-standing knowledge of the Group, such as Rudy, continuing on our Board and as Chairman of our Audit Committee.

Rudy continues to demonstrate the attributes of an independent non-executive director and there is no evidence that his tenure has had any impact on his independence. He continues to bring to the role the same rigorous enquiry and intellectual challenge that the Board has come to expect. Through his continued tenure, Rudy's familiarity with the business has only further enhanced his contribution to the Board rather than weakened it in any way. He probes and validates the assertions made by the Group's executive management through his regular visits to the Group's overseas offices, obtaining feedback from key staff and senior leadership teams throughout the year. For example, during 2011, Rudy held over 20 separate meetings during his visits to six of the Group's markets.

The Committee has also considered the fact that Rudy is a non-executive director on the board of AstraZeneca PLC whilst Simon Lowth is an executive director at the same company. We do not believe that this creates a cross-directorship which in any way impacts upon the independence of either director.

Other guidance

4.269   The corporate governance reviews following the financial crisis questioned the role and activity of the board and whether there was sufficient oversight from the non-executive directors. The FRC, therefore, aimed in the new Code to emphasise the responsibility of non-executives and encourage appropriate behaviours by bringing the existing material on the role of the non-executives from supporting principle A.1 of the Combined Code (2008) under a new main principle A.4 stating that non-executives should constructively challenge and help develop proposals on strategy. In addition, the FRC adopted the Walker recommendation to expand the role of the Senior Independent Director (SID) to provide a sounding board for the chairman and serve as intermediary for other directors.

4.270   The recommendation that a senior independent non-executive director should be identified in the annual report provides an additional route for concerns to be conveyed to the board and/or an early warning system.

4.270.1   FRC guidance on the role of the non-executive director is included in the FRC's 'Guidance on board effectiveness' issued in March 2011. The non-executive director should:

■   Devote sufficient time to any induction process as well as ongoing development and refreshing of his/her knowledge.

■   Make sufficient time available to be able to discharge his/her responsibilities.

■   Uphold standards of integrity and probity, and assist the chairman and executive directors in instilling the appropriate culture, values and behaviours in the board room and beyond.

■   Insist on receiving high quality information sufficiently in advance of board meetings, to enable thorough consideration of the issues.

■   Take into account the views of shareholders and other stakeholders.

[Guidance on board effectiveness, FRC, March 2011].

4.271   Good practice disclosures in this area may include:

■   Personal statements or examples from non-executive directors to demonstrate commitment to good board behaviours and constructive challenge of the executives.

■   Clear explanation of why the senior independent director is suitable for the role including any explanations around independence.

[The next paragraph is 4.273.]

Appointments to the board

Introduction

4.273   One of the areas of focus in recent governance reviews was whether non-executive directors spend enough time to fulfil their role, and it is clearly important that they can make the necessary commitment prior to appointment. The Walker recommendations discuss minimum time commitments: 30 to 36 days for a non-executive director in a major bank and, for a chairman of a major bank, around two-thirds of their time. The FRC has steered away from stipulating a minimum time commitment for non-executive directors, but a theme from previous supporting principle A.4 of the Combined Code (2008) has been elevated to new main principle B.3, emphasising the importance of this area.

Diversity

4.273.1   Under the UKCGC, the FRC encourages boards to avoid 'group think' by considering diversity when making board appointments. The FRC, therefore, amended supporting principle B.2 by explicitly providing that due regard must be had to the benefits of diversity on the board, including gender, when searching for board candidates and making appointments. In February 2011, Lord Davies published his report 'Women on boards'. He recommended the following disclosures for listed companies, to which investors should pay close attention when considering company reporting and board appointments:

- FTSE 350 companies should announce by September 2011 their targets for female board representation by 2013 and 2015. FTSE 100 boards should aim for a minimum of 25% female representation by 2015 and he expects that many will achieve a higher number.

- Listed companies should disclose annually the proportion of women on their board, in senior executive positions and female employees in the whole organisation. The FRC has noted that BIS will consult on this disclosure.

- The FRC should amend the UKCGC to require listed companies to establish a policy concerning boardroom diversity. A summary of the policy and progress made should be disclosed annually, with the first disclosures being made in the 2012 corporate governance statements.

- Companies should report on the matters in the above three recommendations in their 2012 corporate governance statements whether or not the underlying regulatory changes are in place. In addition, chairmen will be encouraged to sign a charter supporting the recommendations.

- The nomination committee report should provide meaningful information about how the company's appointment process addresses diversity, including a description of the search and nominations process.

4.273.2 Following the Davies Report the FRC published a consultation paper seeking views on the recommendation to make changes to the UKCGC. It subsequently announced in October 2011 that the Code will be amended in 2012 to add a provision requiring companies to publish their policy on boardroom diversity and report against it annually, as recommended by Lord Davies. A supporting principle will also be added recommending that diversity of the board, including gender, should be one of the factors to be considered when evaluating its effectiveness. The revised version of the Code will apply to financial years beginning on or after 1 October 2012 but the FRC strongly encourages all companies to voluntarily apply and report on the intended additions to the Code with immediate effect.

Principles

4.274 The main principles that should be applied in relation to appointments to the board are as follows:

- There should be a formal, rigorous and transparent procedure for the appointment of new directors to the board. [UKCGC Main principle B.2].

- All directors should be able to allocate sufficient time to the company to discharge their responsibilities effectively. [UKCGC Main principle B.3].

4.275 The supporting principles relevant to appointments to the board state that:

- The search for board candidates should be conducted, and appointments made, on merit, against objective criteria and with due regard for the benefits of diversity on the board, including gender. [UKCGC Supporting principle B.2].

- The board should satisfy itself that plans are in place for orderly succession for appointments to the board and to senior management, so as to maintain an appropriate balance of skills and experience within the company and on the board and to ensure progressive refreshing of the board. [UKCGC Supporting principle B.2].

Disclosure requirements

4.276 Disclosures should be made of the chairman's other significant commitments before his/her appointment. Any changes to these should be reported to the board as they arise and their impact explained in the annual report. [UKCGC B.3.1].

Other related provisions

4.277 The following detailed provisions should be addressed:

- There should be a nomination committee that should lead the process for board appointments and make recommendations to the board. [UKCGC B.2.1].

- The nomination committee should have a majority of independent non-executive directors. The chairman or an independent non-executive director should chair the committee. The chairman should not chair the nomination committee when it is dealing with the appointment of a successor to the chairmanship. [UKCGC B.2.1].

- Non-executive directors should be appointed for specified terms subject to re-election and to statutory provisions relating to the removal of a director. Any term beyond six years for a non-executive director should be subject to particularly rigorous review, and should take into account the need for progressive refreshing of the board. [UKCGC B.2.3].

- The nomination committee should prepare a job specification for the appointment of a chairman, including an assessment of the time commitment expected, recognising the need for availability in the event of crises. [UKCGC B.3.1].

- The terms and conditions of appointment of non-executive directors should be made available for inspection (at the company's registered office during business hours and at the AGM for 15 minutes before the meeting and during the meeting). This information may be made available on the company's website. [UKCGC B.3.2].

- Letters of appointment should set out the expected time commitment. Non-executive directors should undertake that they will have sufficient time to meet what is expected of them. Their other significant commitments should be disclosed to the board before appointment, and upon subsequent changes. [UKCGC B.3.2].

- The board should not agree to a full time executive director taking on more than one non-executive directorship in a FTSE 100 company nor the chairmanship of such a company. [UKCGC B.3.3].

Good practice disclosures

4.278 Current good practice reporting in this includes:

- Explanation proportionate to the company's circumstances around the commitments of directors and the chairman; where there is a potential challenge, this should be dealt with transparently.

- Appropriate insight on the subject of diversity; different aspects of diversity are particularly relevant for specific companies and age, nationality and other factors may be equally as important as gender. Companies often stress that their principal concern remains selecting the right candidate for the role.

Table 4.5 – Diversity disclosures

Johnson Matthey Plc – Annual Report and Accounts – 31 March 2012

Corporate governance report (extract)

Appointments to the Board and its Committees

The board, through the Nomination Committee, follows a formal, rigorous and transparent procedure for the selection and appointment of new directors to the board. The processes are similar for the appointment of executive and of non-executive directors.

The Nomination Committee leads the process for board appointments and makes recommendations to the board. Further information on the Nomination Committee and its work is set out in the Nomination Committee Report.

In considering board composition, the Nomination Committee assesses the range and balance of skills, experience, knowledge and independence on the board, identifies any gaps or issues, and considers any need to refresh the board. If it is determined in light of such evaluation that it is necessary to appoint a new non-executive director, the Committee prepares a description of the role and of the capabilities required for the appointment and sets objective selection criteria accordingly. In doing so it has regard for the benefits of diversity on the board, including gender diversity. This is discussed more fully under 'Boardroom Diversity' below.

The Committee considers any proposed recruitment in the context of the company's strategic priorities, plans and objectives as well as the prevailing business environment. The Committee also takes into account succession plans in place (and this is discussed further under 'Succession Planning' below). The Committee seeks prospective board members who can make positive contributions to the board and its committees, including the capability to challenge on such matters on strategy. This is balanced with the desire to maintain board cohesiveness.

The Committee uses external search consultancies to assist in the appointment process. Appointments are ultimately made on merit against the agreed selection criteria.

The board recognises the importance of developing internal talent for board appointments as well as recruiting externally. In this regard, the company has in place various mentoring arrangements and various types and levels of management development programmes.

The board also recognises the importance of recruiting non-executive directors with the necessary technical skills and knowledge relevant to the work of its committees and who have the potential to take over as committee chairmen.

Statement on Board Diversity

In response to the Davies Report, on 28th November 2011 the board published the following statement on board diversity. It is set out in the Investor Relations / Corporate Governance section of the company's website.

"The board of Johnson Matthey has followed the important debate around the recommendations of Lord Davies' review on Women on Boards and the question of boardroom diversity. We do not think quotas, for the proportion of women on the board or otherwise, are appropriate for a number of reasons. We believe all appointments should be made on merit rather than through positive discrimination. We are clear, however, that maintaining an appropriate balance around our board table through a diverse mix of skills, experience, knowledge and background is of paramount importance. Gender diversity is a significant element of this.

At present the board has one woman member in a board of nine. When we next make an appointment to the board, our brief to search consultants in the selection process as regards external candidates will be to review candidates from a variety of backgrounds and perspectives. The consultants will be asked to work to a specification which will include the strong desirability of producing a long-list of possible candidates which fully reflects the benefits of diversity, including gender diversity. Any appointment of an internal candidate, while similarly based on merit, will also take into account the benefits of diversity, including gender diversity.

Looking beyond the board to our wider workforce, we recognise the importance of diversity, including gender diversity, and the benefits this can bring to our organisation. With regard to gender diversity specifically, Johnson Matthey faces challenges similar to those faced by other organisations in the chemical, technology and manufacturing sectors. To address these, we have policies and processes in place which are designed to support gender diversity in employee recruitment, development and promotion and we are committed to ensuring that women have an equal chance with men of developing their careers within our business. Finally, we encourage gender diversity at the early career stage by working outside Johnson Matthey to encourage women to enter scientific and industrial fields."

Gender Diversity Statistics

	Number	Proportion
The board	1 woman on the board as at the date of publication of this annual report	11% of board membership
Senior management	32 women out of 196 total as at 31st March 2012	16% of senior management
Graduate intake	–	30% of graduate intake
The group	2,205 women employees as at 31st March 2012	22% of group employees

The company has taken, and continues to take, several steps to promote diversity, including gender diversity, at senior management level and in the boardroom. The basis of these measures is in developing policies and processes that prevent bias in relation to recruitment and promotion, but the key to progress is in actively promoting diversity, ensuring that other positive measures are taken. These include requesting balanced shortlists when recruiting, looking at diversity mix in company events and conferences, actively discussing diversity in succession planning, promoting industrial and scientific careers to young women and developing family friendly and flexible employment policies. There are challenges to overcome, particularly in respect of gender diversity, given the sector within which the group operates but the group is making good progress.

Boardroom Diversity Policy

Following the publication of the Davies Report, in October 2011 the FRC confirmed its intention to include revisions in the next version of the amended Code to be published in 2012 in order to accommodate the Davies Report recommendation in respect of diversity policy. These revisions will require companies to include in the section of the annual report describing the work of the nomination committee a description of the board's policy on diversity, including gender, any measurable objectives that it has set for implementing the policy and progress on achieving the objectives. The changes will formally apply to companies with a financial year commencing on or after 1st October 2012, and so for Johnson Matthey's year ending 31st March 2014.

The board is in the process of reviewing the broad question of diversity within the group and is considering a policy for diversity.

Board Evaluation Process

The FRC also announced in October 2011 that a new supporting principle would be included in the Code to the effect that evaluation of the board should consider the balance of skills, experience, independence and knowledge of the company on the board, its diversity, including gender, how the board works together as a unit and other factors relevant to its effectiveness. Again, this change will be incorporated in an updated version of the Code to be published in 2012. The board is following this principle in its board and committee evaluation process which is underway as at the date of publication of this annual report. Further information is set out under '2011/12 Evaluation Process'.

Appointments to the Board

As described under 'Appointments to the Board and its Committees', the search for board candidates is conducted, and appointments made, on merit, against objective selection criteria having due regard for the benefits of diversity on the board, including gender. Further information on diversity in the context of board appointments is contained in the Nomination Committee Report.

Nomination Committee Report (extract)

Boardroom Diversity

The search for board candidates is conducted, and appointments made, on merit, against objective selection criteria having due regard, amongst other things, to the benefits of diversity on the board, including gender. Diversity is considered by the Nomination Committee on behalf of the board in considering board composition and in its process for making board appointments, including in setting selection criteria. This is referred to further in the board's statement on board diversity dated 28th November 2011 which is published in the Investor Relations / Corporate Governance section of the company's website and is set out in the Corporate Governance Report.

In respect of the proposed recruitment of a new non-executive director, at its meeting on 29th March 2012 the Committee considered a specification which set out certain essential characteristics for the role, while stating the desirability of diversity.

Induction, training and ongoing professional development

Introduction

4.279 Another point of focus of the 2009/10 governance reviews was the extent of the induction, training and ongoing professional development of non-executive directors. If the non-executive directors are expected to challenge constructively and question sensibly, they need to have sufficient knowledge and understanding of the business and its issues. The FRC therefore split a previous main principle into two main principles 'Development' and 'Information and support' to recognise that they are two separate activities of an effective board. Within the development section the FRC also included:

■ A new provision that the chairman should regularly review and agree with each director their training and development needs.

■ A new supporting principle recognising the importance of directors acquiring appropriate knowledge of the company. This recognises that non-executive directors would be better able to provide constructive challenge if they spent more time in the operational parts to gain a better understanding of its activities and challenges.

Principles

4.280 The main principle that should be applied is as follows:

■ All directors should receive induction on joining the board and should regularly update and refresh their skills and knowledge. [UKCGC Main principle B.4].

The related supporting principles are:

■ The chairman should ensure that the directors continually update their skills and the knowledge and familiarity with the company required to fulfil their role both on the board and on board committees. The company should provide the necessary resources for developing and updating its directors' knowledge and capabilities. [UKCGC Supporting principle B.4].

■ To function effectively, all directors need appropriate knowledge of the company and access to its operations and staff. [UKCGC Supporting principle B.4].

4.280.1 The following detailed provisions should be addressed:

■ The chairman should ensure that new directors receive a full, formal and tailored induction on joining the board. As part of this, directors should avail themselves of opportunities to meet major shareholders. [UKCGC B.4.1].

■ The chairman should regularly review and agree with each director their training and development needs. [UKCGC B.4.2].

Good practice disclosures

4.281 Companies may wish to explain as part of good practice disclosures:

■ The specific arrangements for tailored induction and ongoing professional development for directors. Some companies provide a précis of the programme provided for specific directors.

■ Opportunities provided for non-executives to understand the business more fully. Examples of site visits or meetings with people around the business can bring this reporting to life.

■ How executive directors take on non-executive roles to enhance their experience and development.

Other guidance

4.281.1   The Higgs Guidance issued in June 2006 included an induction checklist for non-executive directors. The updated FRC guidance on board effectiveness does not include such tools, but does refer readers to the Institute of Chartered Secretaries website. Directors may wish to refer to the guidance note issued in May 2011 'ICSA guidance on joining the right board: due diligence for prospective directors', which gives questions individuals should consider before taking up a board position.

4.282   The Walker Review recommended a dedicated support for non-executives of banks and financial institutions on any matter relevant to the business. The FRC did not change the existing Code provisions, so that the arrangement above continues to apply.

Report of the nomination committee

Introduction

4.282.1   The nomination committee is responsible for board composition, new appointments and succession planning; it therefore fulfils a vital role in creating an effective board.

Disclosure requirements

4.283   Disclosures in relation to the nomination committee that are required within the annual report are as follows:

■   A separate section of the annual report should describe the work of the nomination committee, including the process it has used in relation to board appointments. An explanation should be given if neither an external search consultancy nor open advertising has been used in the appointment of a chairman or a non-executive director. [CC B.2.4].

The above disclosure provision overlaps with the DTR and the guidance in DTR 7.2.8G confirms that, if a company provides the information specified by CC B.2.4 above, it will satisfy the requirements of DTR 7.2.7R in respect of this committee.

Other related provisions

4.284   The following are the relevant detailed provisions:

■   The nomination committee should lead the process for board appointments and make recommendations to the board. The majority of the committee should be independent non-executive directors. The chair of the nomination committee should be either the chairman or an independent non-executive director. The chairman should not chair the committee when dealing with the appointment of a successor to the chairmanship. [UKCGC B.2.1].

■   The nomination committee should evaluate the balance of skills, knowledge and experience on the board. In the light of this evaluation, the committee should prepare a description of the role and capabilities required for a particular appointment. [UKCGC B.2.2].

[The next paragraph is 4.286.]

Good practice disclosures

4.286   Current good practice disclosures and practices on nomination committees include:

■   A description of the skills and experience criteria for new board appointments; these should show due regard for diversity.

■   The setting up of a specialised nomination committee for key appointments, such as chairman.

Audit committee and auditors

Introduction

4.286.1 The following section relates to audit committee reporting under the 2010 UK Corporate Governance Code. The FRC's proposals for revisions to that Code (and the Guidance on audit committees) for years beginning on or after 1 October 2012 would significantly expand the role and reporting requirements of audit committees. See paragraph 4.357.6 onwards for more details of the FRC's proposals.

Principles

4.287 The main principle that should be applied in relation to the audit committee is as follows:

- The board should establish formal and transparent arrangements for considering how they should apply the corporate reporting and risk management and internal control principles and for maintaining an appropriate relationship with the company's auditors. [UKCGC Main principle C.3].

Disclosure requirements

4.288 Disclosures in relation to audit committees arising from both the UKCGC and the FRC guidance on audit committees ('ACG'), formerly known as the 'Smith Guidance', have been summarised below. The FRC guidance is discussed further from paragraph 4.293.1 onwards.

- The terms of reference of the audit committee, including its role and the authority delegated to it by the board, should be made available. A separate section in the annual report should describe the work of the committee in discharging its responsibilities. [ACG para 5.1; UKCGC C.3.3].

- The audit committee section should include:

  - A summary of the role of the audit committee.

  - The names and qualifications of all members of the audit committee during the period.

  - The number of audit committee meetings.

  - A report on the way the audit committee has discharged its responsibilities.

  [ACG para 5.2].

- Where there is no internal audit function, the reasons for its absence should be explained. [ACG para 4.10; UKCGC C.3.5].

- The audit committee should have primary responsibility for making a recommendation to the board on the appointment, reappointment and removal of the external auditors. If the board does not accept the audit committee's recommendation, the annual report should include a statement from the audit committee explaining its recommendation and the reasons why the board has taken a different position. [ACG para 4.18; UKCGC C.3.6].

- The audit committee section of the annual report should explain to shareholders how it reached its recommendation to the board on the appointment, reappointment or removal of the external auditors. This explanation should normally include supporting information on tendering frequency, the tenure of the incumbent auditor, and any contractual obligations that acted to restrict the audit committee's choice of external auditors. [ACG para 4.23].

- If the auditor provides non-audit services, it should be explained how the auditor's objectivity and independence is safeguarded. [ACG para 4.37; UKCGC C.3.7].

The above disclosure provisions overlap with the DTR and the guidance in DTR 7.1.7G confirms that, if a company provides the information specified by CC A.1.2, C.3.1, C.3.2 and C.3.3 above, it will satisfy the requirements of DTR 7.1.1R to 7.1.5R in respect of this committee.

Other related provisions

4.289 The following detailed provisions and guidance are relevant to this area:

- The audit committee should consist of at least three, or in the case of smaller companies, (that is, those below the FTSE 350 throughout the year immediately prior to the reporting year), two independent non-executive directors. In smaller companies the company chairman may be a member of, but not chair, the committee in addition to the independent non-executive directors, provided he or she was considered independent on appointment as chairman. The board should satisfy itself that at least one member of the audit committee has recent and relevant financial experience. [UKCGC C.3.1; ACG paras 2.1 and 2.3]. See paragraph 4.291 for further discussion of 'recent and relevant' financial experience.

- The audit committee should have written terms of reference setting out its responsibilities that should include:

  - monitoring the integrity of the company's financial statements, and announcements relating to the company's financial performance and reviewing significant financial reporting judgements contained in them;

  - reviewing the company's financial and non-financial internal controls and risk management systems (to the extent that these are not delegated to another committee made up of independent non-executive directors);

  - monitoring and reviewing the effectiveness of the company's internal audit function;

  - making recommendations to the board relating to the appointment, re-appointment and removal of the external auditor and approving the remuneration and terms of engagement of the external auditor;

  - reviewing and monitoring the external auditor's and effectiveness of the audit process;

  - developing and implementing a policy on the engagement of the external auditor to supply non-audit services and reporting to the board, identifying matters in where action or improvement is needed.

  [UKCGC C.3.2; ACG para 2.2].

- The audit committee should monitor and review the effectiveness of the internal audit activities. Where there is no internal audit function, the audit committee should consider annually whether there is a need for one and make a recommendation to the board. [UKCGC C.3.5; ACG para 4.10].

- The audit committee should review arrangements by which staff of the company may, in confidence, raise concerns about possible improprieties in matters of financial reporting or other matters. It should ensure the proportionate and independent investigation of such matters and follow-up action. [UKCGC C.3.4].

Good practice disclosures

4.289.1   Current good practice reporting on audit committees may include:

- Specific examples of audit committee activities in the year and how these addressed developments in the business.

- Details of the qualifications and experience of audit committee members to confirm their suitability and recent and relevant financial experience.

Other guidance

4.290   In banks and other financial industry entities the role of a separate risk committee and the need for a chief risk officer have been key areas of discussion and Walker has specific recommendations around these. The FRC has not extended these recommendations to all listed entities. The board retains responsibilities for elements of risk and control and the main principle on audit committees has been reworded to reflect the committee's role in risk management. Otherwise there have been no changes to this part of the UK Corporate Governance Code. Further guidance is included in the FRC guidance on challenges for Audit Committees arising from current economic conditions, discussed from paragraph 4.293.7. In addition there are DTR requirements on audit committees, which are discussed in paragraph 4.46.

Provision C.3.1 'Recent and relevant' financial experience

4.291 Some companies feel that identifying one individual as having recent and relevant financial experience may increase that individual's exposure to liability and as a result choose not to identify one individual, but rather explain that audit committee members collectively have recent and relevant financial experience. If this is the case, it is a departure from the Code and requires an explanation. The FSA Rules, which are discussed further in paragraph 4.46, also provide that at least one member of the audit committee (or the equivalent body) must have competence in accounting and/or auditing.

[The next paragraph is 4.293.]

DTR overlap summary

4.293 Refer to paragraph 4.59 for an explanation of the overlapping provisions between the UKCGC and the DTR requirements on audit committees.

FRC guidance on audit committees (formerly the 'Smith Guidance')

4.293.1 The Smith Guidance, originally published in 2003, was designed to assist company boards in making suitable arrangements for their audit committees and to assist directors serving on audit committees in carrying out their role. While this guidance does not form part of the Code, so that companies do not have to comply or explain against it, it is intended to assist them when implementing the relevant provisions of the Code.

4.293.2 In March 2008, the FRC announced the launch of a consultation on the Smith Guidance following the release of recommendations by the FRC Market Participants Group report on promoting choice in the audit market. The new guidance was published in October 2008 and the main changes to the guidance were:

- Recommended disclosure in the annual report of how the audit committee reached its recommendation to the board on the appointment, re-appointment or removal of the external auditor, including supporting information on tendering frequency, the tenure of the incumbent auditor and any contractual obligations that acted to restrict the audit committee's choice of external auditor.

- Encouragement to audit committees to consider the need to include the risk of the withdrawal of their auditor from the market in their risk assessment process.

- Amendments to the information that audit committees should seek from the external audit firm about the independence of its staff, its policies for maintaining staff independence and monitoring compliance with relevant requirements (including the rotation requirements for partners and staff) and its safeguards in relation to provision of non-audit services. These changes simply ensure consistency with the existing APB Ethical Standards for auditors.

- Introduction of the suggestion that it may be appropriate for the audit committee of a group to consider using audit firms from more than one network of firms, with additional guidance on considerations relevant to such a decision, including the option of joint audits.

- A suggestion that the audit committee, as well as obtaining a report on the audit firm's own internal quality control procedures, gives consideration to the audit firm's annual transparency report, where available.

4.293.3 In July 2010, a new consultation paper on the Smith Guidance was issued. The paper acknowledged a perception amongst investors that confidence in the audit can be reduced where non-audit services are provided by the auditor and emphasised the need to address this perception issue through improved transparency and disclosure of non-audit services provided, and governance around the decision as to whether a company's auditors should be engaged to provide such services.

4.293.3.1 The updated guidance, named 'FRC Guidance on Audit Committees' was published in December 2010 to take account of changes made at the same time to the APB Ethical Standards in relation to non-audit services. Like the Ethical Standards, the guidance is effective from April 2011. The most significant updates relate to the following parts of the guidance:

- *Governance around the policy on appointing the external auditor to carry out non-audit services* – the policy should specify the types of non-audit services:

- for which the use of the external auditor is pre-approved (that is, approval has been given in advance as a matter of policy, rather than the specific approval of an engagement being sought before it is contracted);

- for which specific approval from the audit committee is required before they are contracted; and

- from which the external auditor is specifically excluded. [ACG December 2010 para 4.30].

- *Guidance on types of non-audit services that it may be appropriate to pre-approve* – the guidance clarifies that pre-approval of the use of the external auditor may be appropriate where the threats to auditor independence are considered low, for example if the engagement is:

  - routine in nature and the fee is not significant in the context of the audit fee; or

  - for an audit related service. [ACG December 2010 para 4.31]. The APB Ethical Standards give a number of examples of audit relates services which include reporting required by law or regulation to be provided by the auditor, reviews of interim financial information, reporting on regulatory returns, reporting on internal financial controls when required by law.

- *Enhanced disclosure of how auditor objectivity and independence is safeguarded where the auditor provides non-audit services* – the guidance suggests the following disclosures:

  - describe the committee's work in discharging its responsibilities;

  - set out the audit committee's policy on the engagement of the external auditor to supply non-audit services in sufficient detail to describe each of the elements in paragraph 4.30, or cross-refer to where this information can be found on the company's website;

  - set out, or cross-refer to, the fees paid to the auditor for audit services, audit related services, and other non-audit services; and

  - if the auditor provides non-audit services, other than audit related services, explain for each significant engagement, or category of engagement:

    - what the services are;

    - why the audit committee concluded that it was in the company's interests to purchase them from the external auditor (rather than another supplier); and

    - how auditor objectivity and independence has been safeguarded. [ACG December 2010 para 4.38].

4.293.4   There is specific additional guidance on audit engagement partner rotation and using the external auditor to undertake aspects of the internal audit function.

4.293.5   This guidance may change again as a result of the FRC's planned review of the Turnbull guidance. This is due to the overlap between these two sets of guidance on the Audit Committee's role in relation to risk management and internal controls.

4.293.6   Audit committees should also consider the FRC Audit Quality Framework published in February 2008, which is designed to support effective communication between auditors, audit committees, investors and other stakeholders on audit quality. The Framework is intended to be complementary to existing regulations and guidelines and to assist audit committees in undertaking annual assessments of the effectiveness of external audits.

Challenges for audit committees arising from the current economic crisis

4.293.7   In November 2008, the FRC issued guidance entitled 'Challenges for audit committees arising from current economic conditions', to assist audit committees in meeting their responsibilities relating to financial statements in difficult economic conditions. This guidance was updated in November 2009 and 2010 because the FRC believed that, although the current economic outlook appeared to be less depressed than in 2008, significant economic risks remained and would present challenges for many audit committees during the next reporting season.

4.293.8   The updated guidance does not establish any new requirements, nor does it alter the role of an audit committee, which is outlined in the UK Corporate Governance Code; but it offers a number of questions that committee members may wish to consider when fulfilling their responsibility to "*monitor the integrity of the* *financial statements of the company and any formal announcements relating to the company's financial performance, reviewing significant financial reporting judgements contained in them*". [UKCGC.3.2].

4.293.9 In the 2009 update, the FRC specifically highlighted that past experience showed insolvencies increased after the technical end of recessions as companies ran out of working capital. Such conditions could increase the risk that annual reports and accounts misreport facts and circumstances and contain unidentified errors and omissions.

4.293.10 The 2010 update reflected that the financial crisis had moved on, with the focus of concern moving from the banking sector to government deficits, creating additional pressure for companies that rely on government spending.

4.293.11 The key areas in both the 2008 and 2009 guidance that audit committees may wish to consider are:

■ Year end planning – prompt action by audit committees will better enable them to ensure that they, and the company, have sufficient resources and expertise in place to ensure the financial statements' integrity, particularly with regard to areas of difficult year end judgements.

■ Liquidity and going concern – when market conditions mean that many companies face difficulties servicing debt or securing financing, audit committees may wish to examine in more detail the rigour of the analysis supporting the use of the going concern assumption, as well as the integrity of the disclosures about going concern in the financial statements and other market communications. In some cases, detailed consideration will need to be given as to whether there are, or are not, material uncertainties leading to significant doubt about whether the business is a going concern.

■ Reliance on assumptions – in times of market volatility, audit committees are likely to want to better understand the assumptions that support cash flow and other forecasts on which asset valuations and impairment assessments rely. They will need to ensure that a wide range of reasonably possible outcomes are considered when performing sensitivity analysis on estimates.

■ Significant judgements – in times of uncertainty, audit committees are likely to want to be assured that key judgments are supported by a greater degree of rigour and analysis than in more normal circumstances.

4.293.12 The key areas in the 2010 guidance suggests that audit committees may wish to consider are:

■ Risks, uncertainties and cash flow forecasts – this message is consistent with the FRRP, which issued a press notice in February 2011 explaining that companies tend to present a list of all possible risks in their annual report, rather than focusing on the 'principal risks'. Disclosures often lack company specific detail to enable the risks, and therefore their exposure, to be properly understood by the reader.

■ Enhancing the contribution of audit – the guidance explains the important role played by the audit committee in creating an environment where the audit team can challenge material assumptions and estimates effectively.

Remuneration Committee

Principles

4.294 The main principles that should be applied in relation to remuneration are as follows:

■ Levels of remuneration should be sufficient to attract, retain and motivate directors of the quality required to run the company successfully, but a company should avoid paying more than is necessary for this purpose. A significant proportion of executive directors' remuneration should be structured so as to link rewards to corporate and individual performance. [UKCGC Main principle D.1].

■ There should be a formal and transparent procedure for developing policy on executive remuneration and for fixing the remuneration packages of individual directors. No director should be involved in deciding his or her own remuneration. [UKCGC Main principle D.2].

4.295 The supporting principles relevant to remuneration are as follows:

■ The performance-related elements of executive directors' remuneration should be stretching and designed to promote the long-term success of the company. [UKCGC Supporting principle D.1].

- The remuneration committee should judge where to position their company relative to other companies. But they should use such comparisons with caution in view of the risk of an upward ratchet of remuneration levels with no corresponding improvement in performance. [UKCGC Supporting principle D.1].

- They should also be sensitive to pay and employment conditions elsewhere in the group, especially when determining annual salary increases. [UKCGC Supporting principle D.1].

- The remuneration committee should consult the chairman and/or chief executive about their proposals relating to the remuneration of other executive directors. The remuneration committee should also be responsible for appointing any consultants in respect of executive director remuneration. Where executive directors or senior management are involved in advising or supporting the remuneration committee, care should be taken to recognise and avoid conflicts of interest. [UKCGC Supporting principle D.2].

- The chairman of the board should ensure that the company maintains contact as required with its principal shareholders about remuneration. [UKCGC Supporting principle D.2].

Disclosure requirements

4.296   Disclosures in relation to the remuneration committee that are required within the annual report are as follows:

- The remuneration report should include a description where an executive director serves as a non-executive director elsewhere, whether or not the director will retain such earnings and, if so, what the remuneration is. [UKCGC D.1.2].

- The remuneration report should include a description of the work of the remuneration committee. Where remuneration consultants are appointed, a statement should be made available of whether they have any other connection with the company. [UKCGC D.2.1].

The second disclosure provision overlaps with the DTR and the guidance in DTR 7.2.8G confirms that, if a company provides the information specified by UKCGC D.2.1 above, it will satisfy the relevant requirements of DTR 7.2.7R in respect of this committee as long as this information is given within the corporate governance statement itself.

Other related provisions

The level and components of remuneration

4.297   The following detailed provisions in relation to the level and components of remuneration should be complied with, or explanations given:

- In designing schemes of performance-related remuneration for executive directors, the remuneration committee should follow the provisions in Schedule A to the Code. [UKCGC D.1.1].

- Levels of remuneration for non-executive directors should reflect the time commitment and responsibilities of the role. Remuneration for non-executive directors should not include share options or other performance-related elements. If, exceptionally, options are granted, shareholder approval should be sought in advance and any shares acquired by exercise of the options should be held until at least one year after the non-executive director leaves the board. Holding of share options could be relevant to determining a non-executive director's independence (as set out in provision B.1.1). [UKCGC D.1.3].

- The remuneration committee should carefully consider what compensation commitments (including pension contributions and all other elements) their directors' terms of appointment would entail in the event of early termination. The aim should be to avoid rewarding poor performance. They should take a robust line on reducing compensation to reflect departing directors' obligations to mitigate loss. [UKCGC D.1.4].

- Notice or contract periods should be set at one year or less. If it is necessary to offer longer notice or contract periods to new directors recruited from outside, such periods should reduce to one year or less after the initial period. [UKCGC D.1.5].

Procedure

4.298 The Code includes specific provisions regarding the procedures relating to remuneration.

- The remuneration committee should have delegated responsibility for setting remuneration for all executive directors and the chairman, including pension rights and any compensation payments. The committee should also recommend and monitor the level and structure of remuneration for senior management. The definition of 'senior management' for this purpose should be determined by the board, but should normally include the first layer of management below board level. [UKCGC D.2.2].

- The board itself or, where required by the Articles of Association, the shareholders should determine the remuneration of the non-executive directors within the limits set in the Articles of Association. Where permitted by the Articles, the board may however delegate this responsibility to a committee, which might include the chief executive. [UKCGC D.2.3].

- Shareholders should be invited specifically to approve all new long-term incentive schemes (as defined in the Listing Rules) and significant changes to existing schemes, save in the circumstances permitted by the Listing Rules. [UKCGC D.2.4].

Good practice disclosure

4.298.1 The UKCGC principles and best practice provisions concerning directors' remuneration are considered in more detail in chapter 5.

Other guidance

4.299 Performance-related pay was much discussed during the 2009/10 governance reviews. Walker made several recommendations in this area and the FRC implemented the following in the new Code:

- performance-related remuneration to be stretching and designed to promote the company's long term success (supporting principle and provision);

- incentives to be compatible with risk policies and systems (provision); and

- consideration to be given for the company to claw-back variable components of remuneration in exceptional circumstances (provision). [UKCGC Sch A]

Provision D.1.3 has also been strengthened to clarify that all forms of performance-related remuneration are discouraged for non-executives, not just share options. No changes were made to the remuneration 'procedure' part of the Code.

Internal control

Introduction

4.301 The UKCGC recommends that the directors should at least annually review the effectiveness of all material controls, including operational, financial and compliance controls and risk management systems. Guidance was issued to directors in 1999 to assist them in complying with the internal control provision in the Combined Code (1998), known as the Turnbull guidance. In 2005, following a consultation process, the Turnbull guidance was updated. The Turnbull guidance (2005) supersedes and replaces the Turnbull guidance (1999).

4.302 The purpose of the review of controls effectiveness is to ensure that there is a strong control framework through which the organisation can both protect and increase shareholder value. For many companies this may be the most onerous aspect of the UKCGC and will require the active involvement of senior management.

[The next paragraph is 4.305.]

4.305 The importance of internal control to good governance is well recognised and the UKCGC recommends that all companies, regardless of their size, consider the need for an internal audit function annually. [UKCGC C.3.5]. Modern internal audit should be focussed on all aspects of internal control including business risk assessment and response, financial management, safeguarding assets and compliance

4043

with laws and regulations. In addition, internal audit can add value to the organisation as well as providing assurance on the control environment.

4.305.1 The requirement in provision C.2.1 (below) for boards to review the effectiveness of all material controls also affects the company's auditors, who are currently required by the Listing Rules to review the directors' statement of compliance with that provision of the Combined Code. [LR 9.8.10R(2)(b)].

Reporting on internal control

4.305.2 The UKCGC states that:

"The board should, at least annually, conduct a review of the effectiveness of the company's risk management and internal control systems and should report to shareholders that they have done so. The review should cover all material controls, including financial, operational and compliance controls and risk management systems." [UKCGC C.2.1].

4.305.3 The recommendation for directors to review the effectiveness of all material controls goes further than the original Cadbury Code recommendation to review financial control and requires the active involvement of senior management.

4.305.4 For many companies that had already accepted that in practice it is difficult to distinguish financial from other controls, this wider risk and control review may already have been well established. For others, when this provision was introduced, compliance with the UKCGC may have required a significant extension of the work previously done to review and report on internal financial control. Past experience shows that the review of internal financial control was one of the more onerous requirements of Cadbury. It was also one of the more fruitful where undertaken effectively.

4.305.5 The remit for the review to cover risk management and operational, financial and compliance controls provides an ideal opportunity to review the effectiveness of the existing processes, taking into account developments in risk management thinking that have occurred in recent years. High level integrated risk management approaches that take account of strategy, organisation and people as well as business processes have, for some time, been seen by leading corporations as offering clear potential for enhancing shareholder value.

4.305.6 Companies with a listing in the US are required to provide an internal control report containing an assessment by management of the effectiveness of controls and financial reporting procedures under the Sarbanes-Oxley Act.

Turnbull guidance (2005) for directors

4.305.6.1 The Turnbull guidance specifically outlines broad principles rather than boxes to be ticked, requiring directors to use their judgement to decide whether or not they have complied. Listed companies are expected to embrace the spirit of the guidance, rather than just follow the letter of it. The aim is to help companies to achieve their own business objectives. This challenges boards to develop an approach that fits the operating style of their organisation and builds upon any practices already in place. The Turnbull guidance deliberately does not attempt to set out prescriptive procedures that will fit all companies, as the 'right' procedures will be those that support the individual businesses.

4.305.7 The framework of the Turnbull guidance is that companies adopt a risk-based approach to setting and managing their internal control processes. Throughout the guidance the importance of an embedded ongoing process of identifying and responding to risk is emphasised. This integrated approach will need to include procedures to:

- Establish business objectives.
- Identify the key risks associated with these.
- Agree on the risk profiles to be adopted and the control processes to address the accepted risks.
- Set up a system to implement the decisions, which will include regular feedback.
- Ensure that the company's implementation of the Turnbull guidance and the related disclosures are aligned with their risk register and other disclosures around risk in the annual report.

4.305.8 The internal control system to be implemented should encompass all the policies and procedures that, taken together, facilitate the effectiveness and efficiency of a company's operations and enable it to respond to significant business, operational, financial, compliance and other risks. The internal control system is a crucial element in managing risks which, if not operating effectively, may adversely affect the fulfilment of business objectives.

4.305.9 The main issues to address are that:

- The identification and management of risks needs to be linked to the achievement of business objectives and enhancing shareholder value.

- There should be a risk based approach to internal control including evaluation of the likelihood and impact of risks becoming a reality.

- Business, operational and compliance risks must be addressed as well as financial risks.

- Risk assessment must be embedded within ongoing operations.

- The board should receive regular reports during the year on internal control and risk (not just annually).

- The principal results of risk identification, evaluation and management review should be reported up to, and reviewed at, board level.

4.305.10 The appendix to the Turnbull guidance includes questions to consider and related examples that will assist companies when implementing the guidance.

The board's role

4.305.11 The role of the board is crucial under the Turnbull guidance. The onus is on the board to sponsor and take ownership of internal control. Specifically, it is important that the board defines the process to be adopted for its ongoing review of the effectiveness of internal control. There needs to be regular reporting to the board during the year and the board must set out both the scope and frequency of the reports it wishes to receive during the year.

4.305.12 The Turnbull guidance includes a preface highlighting to boards the importance of having a continuous process to review and update the system of internal controls. In addition, it encourages boards to take the opportunity to explain the specific risk and control issues facing the company, how the company maintains a framework of internal controls to address these issues and how the board has reviewed the effectiveness of that framework. The board should exercise the standard of care generally applicable to directors in the exercise of their duties when forming a view on the effectiveness of the internal control.

4.305.13 The board reports may cover particular business or risk areas rather than the whole system. They will, however, need to provide a balanced assessment of the significant risks relevant to the particular area and the effectiveness of the procedures put in place to manage those risks. Any significant control failings or weaknesses identified should be discussed in the reports, as the board will need to be aware of these and their implications, including the need for actions to rectify them. The board should confirm that necessary action has been (or is being) taken to remedy any significant failings or weaknesses identified from its review of the effectiveness of the internal control system. The board will also be interested in the financial or business impact that these failings have had or could have had and the actions being taken.

4.305.14 By setting out a requirement for full and open reporting, and defining the scope of such reports, the board should be able to build a picture of the internal control system and its operation during the year. The board should be comfortable that it is aware of the significant risks and how these have been identified, evaluated and managed; it has been able to assess the effectiveness of managing these risks, notably by considering how significant failings or weaknesses have occurred, been reported and rectified; and it has put in place any additional monitoring that may be required.

4.305.15 Such regular reporting may be made to a board committee rather than the full board, but the board is still required to take responsibility and ownership of the overall issue. In addition to the regular reviews, the board also needs to undertake a separate assessment each year to enable it to make the public statements required by the Turnbull guidance. This annual assessment will cover the issues raised during the regular reporting process and any other issues necessary to ensure all significant aspects of the internal control process have been covered. In particular, the annual assessment should consider any changes in the company's risk profiles; the company's ability and effectiveness in responding to such changes; the scope and results of ongoing monitoring of the internal controls including the significance and response to any failings or weaknesses identified; and the extent and frequency of reports to the board and how comprehensive a picture has been obtained through this process.

Principles

4.305.15.1   The main principle that should be applied in relation to internal control is as follows:

■   The board is responsible for determining the nature and extent of the significant risks it is willing to take in achieving its strategic objectives. The board should maintain sound risk management and internal control systems. [UKCGC Main principle C.2].

Disclosure requirements

4.305.16   Disclosures in relation to internal controls that are required within the annual report are as follows:

■   The board should, at least annually, conduct a review of the effectiveness of the company's risk management and internal control systems and should report to shareholders that they have done so. The review should cover all material controls, including financial, operational and compliance controls. [UKCGC C.2.1].

4.305.17   As a reminder, the DTR also requires the following additional disclosures (see para 4.56):

■   The corporate governance statement must include a description of the main features of the company's internal control and risk management systems in relation to the financial reporting process. [DTR 7.2.5 R].

■   Where the issuer is required to prepare a group directors' report, it should include a description of the main features of the group's internal control and risk management systems in relation to the process of preparing consolidated financial statements. [DTR 7.2.10 R].

The DTR requirements differ from the UKCGC; however, the FRC envisages that both could be met by a single internal control statement.

4.305.18   Another of the themes of the 2009/10 corporate governance reviews was in relation to boards taking greater responsibility for assessing the company's risk profile, tolerance of risk and oversight of risk management systems. The FRC, therefore, enhanced the relevant main principle by adding that the *"... board is responsible for determining the nature and extent of the significant risks it is willing to take in achieving its strategic objectives"*. In the financial sector, this is usually referred to as a company's 'risk appetite'. In the accompanying provision it has also been made explicit that the annual effectiveness review over internal control should include the risk management system.

4.305.19   The main guidance to assist directors in complying with the annual effectiveness review provision is the Turnbull guidance. The disclosures required by Turnbull are discussed from paragraph 4.305.20 below.

Disclosures required under Turnbull

4.305.20   The Turnbull guidance proposes the inclusion in the annual report and financial statements of a statement by the board on internal control. The recommended content is simple disclosure with the intention of avoiding boilerplate descriptions of high level controls, which had become somewhat common previously.

4.305.21   The Turnbull guidance states that *"the annual report and accounts should include such meaningful, high-level information as the board considers necessary to assist shareholders' understanding of the main features of the company's risk management processes and system of internal control, and should not give a misleading impression"*.

4.305.22   Regarding the application of principle C.2 of the UKCGC, the board should disclose that there is an ongoing process for identifying, evaluating and managing the significant risks faced by the company, that this process has been in place for the year under review, and up to the date of approval of the annual report, that it is regularly reviewed by the board and accords with the Turnbull guidance (2005). This is the minimum disclosure acceptable, but additional information can be given, particularly if it would assist in understanding the company's risk management processes and system of internal control. Some companies, therefore, may take this as an opportunity to describe their significant risks (including opportunities) and how these are managed.

4.305.23 There should be a specific acknowledgement that the board is responsible for the company's system of internal control and for reviewing its effectiveness. The board should confirm that it has reviewed the effectiveness of controls during the year. It should also explain that such a system is designed to manage rather than eliminate the risk of failure to achieve business objectives and can only provide reasonable, and not absolute, assurance against material misstatement or loss.

4.305.24 In relation to provision C.2.1 of the UKCGC, the board needs to summarise the process undertaken in the (at least) annual review of the effectiveness of the internal control system. In addition, if any significant problems have been noted in the annual report (for example, in the chairman's statement) the process applied to deal with any material internal control aspects of these need to be identified. This is an area of disclosure that needs to be specifically addressed by boards prior to approving the annual report.

4.305.25 The board should confirm that necessary actions have been or are being taken to remedy any significant failings or weaknesses identified from that review. The Turnbull Review Group's published deliberations indicated that it considered requiring companies to provide details of material or significant changes made to the internal control system as a result of the board's annual review of effectiveness. However, the Review Group recognised that if this was imposed on companies, then in effect it would be asking them to disclose any material weaknesses, with consequences for market perceptions. It was precisely in order to avoid any such concerns that the Review Group acknowledged that this may result in boilerplate disclosures, but at least it would provide investors with some additional assurance that the outcome of the annual review process was action-oriented.

4.305.26 Where a board cannot make one or more of the disclosures listed in the Turnbull guidance, it should state this fact and provide an explanation. The Listing Rules require the board to disclose if it has failed to conduct a review of the effectiveness of the company's system of internal control.

Application of Turnbull guidance to groups

4.305.27 The Turnbull guidance refers throughout to the 'company'. It states, however, that this should be taken to mean the group of which the reporting company is the parent company. The disclosures made and the reviews of internal control should be in relation to the group as a whole. This may not be possible for some joint ventures or associates. If those have not been dealt with as part of the group when undertaking internal control reviews, this fact should be disclosed by the board in the annual report.

Good practice disclosure

4.305.28 Good reporting practices in this area would include:

■ A tailored description of the company's internal control and risk management framework. The use of diagrams adds clarity and allows complex concepts to be presented effectively.

■ A discussion of how 'risk appetite' has been set; the reworded principle C.2 focuses on 'risk appetite' without using the specific term. In the narrative disclosures of how the main principles of the Code have been applied, it is therefore particularly important to focus on this aspect of risk, which is the key link between risk and strategy and very much a board responsibility.

■ Clear linkage between business and industry risks and the system of internal control. An example of how reporting could be improved in this respect is governance of the supply chain, which is fundamental to the operation of companies and is frequently partially outsourced or dependent on joint ventures or associates. This brings with it a number of governance challenges that are rarely addressed in the annual report. Good practice reporting would detail how a decision to outsource or place reliance in a third party was seen by the board as consistent with the company's risk appetite. It could also address the question of what the board has done to make sure it is clear where the responsibilities of the company stop and start — avoiding the risk of 'falling between stools'.

■ How the board engineers 'risk resilience' into the company, including resilience against 'black swans', or unforeseen risk events.

■ How risk is measured and reported to the board and how governance is applied to it.

Other guidance

4.305.29   The FRC announced in December 2010 its intentions to defer the review of the Turnbull Guidance on Internal Control. The FRC explained that it wanted to explore how companies were responding to Main Principle C.2 in the UKCGC, which asks boards to be responsible for determining the nature and extent of the significant risks they are willing to take in achieving their strategic objectives. The FRC held a series of meetings with companies, investors and advisers in 2011 to discuss the issues, and conclusions from these meetings will inform a review of the Turnbull guidance as a whole.

Financial reporting

Principles

4.306   The main principle that should be applied in relation to financial reporting is as follows:

■   The board should present a balanced and understandable assessment of the company's position and prospects. [UKCGC Main principle C.1].

4.307   The supporting principle relevant to financial reporting states that the board's responsibility to present a balanced and understandable assessment extends to interim and other price-sensitive public reports and reports to regulators as well as to information required to be presented by statutory requirements. [UKCGC Supporting principle C.1].

Disclosure requirements

4.308   Disclosures in relation to financial reporting that are required within the annual report are as follows:

■   There should be a statement from the directors explaining their responsibility for preparing the financial statements. [UKCGC C.1.1].

■   The directors should include in the annual report an explanation of the basis on which the company generates or preserves value over the longer term (the business model) and the strategy for delivering the objectives of the company. [UKCGC C.1.2].

■   The directors should report in annual and half-yearly financial statements that the business is a going concern, with supporting assumptions or qualifications as necessary. [UKCGC C.1.3].

Good practice disclosures

4.308.1   Current good practice reporting on financial reporting may include:

■   Discussion of the key judgements and estimates that were dealt with by the audit committee and auditors in the process of preparing and auditing the financial statements; this is currently best practice but such disclosures are likely to be incorporated into section C of the Code in the revised edition to apply from 1 October 2012. See paragraph 4.357.6 onwards for more information.

Table 4.6 – Audit committee reporting of key judgements and estimates

Barclays PLC – Annual Report – 31 December 2011

Corporate governance (extract)

Board Audit Committee Chairman's Report (extract)

I describe below the key issues we considered during 2011:

Financial Reporting and Significant Financial Judgements
Given continuing global economic uncertainty and market concerns over the financial health of the sector, our role in monitoring significant financial reporting issues is key in ensuring that trust in the financial services sector and Barclays is maintained. We seek support from the external auditor to assess whether suitable accounting policies have been adopted and whether management has made appropriate estimates and judgements. The main issues we reviewed in 2011 are set out below:

– We regularly reviewed the Group's investment in BlackRock, Inc. and whether it should be impaired. Key in our decision-making was whether the diminution in value could be considered to be significant or prolonged. We closely monitored the BlackRock, Inc. share price throughout the year and agreed with management's conclusion at the time of our third quarter interim management statement that the decline in value was such that the investment should be impaired. The impairment has been recognised in the full year results for 2011.

– We monitored the goodwill held for our business in Spain throughout 2011. We agreed with management's assessment that the goodwill associated with our business in Spain should be written off during the fourth quarter.

– The credit impairment charge during 2011 was significantly better than prior year across each of the businesses. We examined the impairment charge carefully to satisfy ourselves that this was appropriate.

– Management decided in late 2010 that it no longer intended to hold the Protium loan for the long term given its low return on regulatory capital. Consequently, and as part of finalising the year-end 2010 results, we agreed with management's recommendation that the value of the loan should be reduced to the fair value of the underlying assets. This resulted in an impairment charge for the year ended 31 December 2010. During the second quarter of 2011, management decided to restructure the loan and the proposal to purchase the outstanding financial interest in Protium in order to facilitiate earlier repayment of the loan was agreed by Board Finance Committee (a specifically authorised sub-committee of the Board). This resulted in Barclays controlling Protium's operating and financial policies and consolidating Protium. The Committee agreed with the accounting treatment.

– Given the continuing economic and political uncertainty in the Eurozone, we reviewed both our exposures to the selected Eurozone countries of Ireland, Italy, Portugal, Spain and Greece and the form of our disclosure of these exposures in our financial reporting during 2011. Our exposures have been reduced during 2011.

– We considered the impact of own credit and other one-off items that could be treated as adjusting items to the adjusted Profit Before Tax measure and worked with management to ensure that equal prominence was given to both the statutory and adjusted results.

– As part of reviewing the results for 2011, we considered the recognition and valuation of deferred tax assets in the US and Spain and agreed with management's judgement that the deferred tax assets were appropriately supported by the forecasted profit. We also considered the appropriateness of tax risk provisions made.

– We also reviewed the appropriateness of the judgements made by management in valuing certain portfolios and asset classes and were satisfied that these judgements were appropriate.

– Following the dismissal in May 2011 of judicial review proceedings brought by the British Bankers' Association in relation to the assessment and redress of Payment Protection Insurance (PPI) claims, we reviewed management's assumptions in arriving at a provision of £1bn against future redress and administration of PPI claims. We were content that the provision was adequate, although it will be considered further against actual claims experience.

– We reviewed the year-end and half-year disclosures in respect of legal proceedings and competition and regulatory matters, particularly in the light of developments in the Lehman litigation.

Other guidance

4.309 The 2009/10 corporate governance reviews emphasised the need for boards to take greater responsibility for risk management. Concerns were also expressed about the quality of risk reporting. The FRC has, therefore, included a new provision in the UKCGC that the business review section of the annual report should include an explanation of the business model and strategy for delivering the company's objectives. The FRC has also amended the provision on going concern disclosures to clarify that these disclosures should be made both in half-yearly and annual financial statements. Paragraph 4.309.3 onwards discusses the FRC guidance on going concern and liquidity risk that suggests means of applying this provision. The Listing Rules also require a statement on going concern (see para 4.309.2).

Reporting on going concern

4.309.1 The UKCGC states that *"the directors should report in their annual and half year financial statements that the business is a going concern, with supporting assumptions or qualifications as necessary"*. [UKCGC C.1.3].

4.309.2 A going concern statement became a separate requirement of the Listing Rules effective for accounting periods beginning on or after 31 December 1995 and this requirement remains in the Listing Rules. [LR 9.8.6R(3)]. See paragraph 4.80 for the position regarding overseas companies in this respect.

FRC guidance – Going concern and liquidity risk: guidance for directors of UK companies 2009

4.309.3 In November 2008 the FRC published guidance for directors entitled 'An update for directors of listed companies: going concern and liquidity risk' ('FRC guidance'), to assist directors of listed companies preparing and approving annual reports in a difficult economic environment.

4.309.4 Subsequently, in October 2009, the FRC published updated guidance on going concern for directors of UK companies, which brings together in one place the requirements of company law, accounting standards and the Listing Rules on going concern and liquidity risk for small, medium and large UK companies.

4.309.5 The guidance provides a framework to assist directors, audit committees and finance teams, of all sizes of company, in determining whether it is appropriate to adopt the going concern basis for preparing financial statements (both annual and half-yearly) and in making balanced, proportionate and clear disclosures. The FRC guidance for directors is effective for accounting periods ending on or after 31 December 2009.

4.309.6 The FRC guidance is principles-based, with supporting detailed information bringing together the requirements of company law, accounting standards and the Listing Rules on going concern, and providing further information on their application. The three principles are:

---

1 Assessing going concern
Directors should make and document a rigorous assessment of whether the company is a going concern when preparing annual and half-yearly financial statements. The process carried out by the directors should be proportionate in nature and depth depending upon the size, level of financial risk and complexity of the company and its operations.

2 The review period
Directors should consider all available information about the future when concluding whether the company is a going concern at the date they approve the financial statements. Their review should usually cover a period of at least twelve months from the date of approval of the annual and the half-yearly financial statements.

3 Disclosures
Directors should make balanced, proportionate and clear disclosures about going concern for the financial statements to give a true and fair view. Directors should disclose if the period that they have reviewed is less than twelve months from the date of approval of the annual and the half-yearly financial statements and explain their justification for limiting their review period. [FRC Going concern and liquidity risk: guidance for directors of UK companies 2009].

4.309.7 The FRC's guidance on going concern also considers what companies should discuss in their half-yearly financial statements. The half-yearly financial statements should focus on new activities, events and circumstances that have not been reported previously and suggests that additional disclosure may be needed where new events and circumstances have arisen, for example where borrowings are renegotiated and assets and business are sold or closed. Directors will need to exercise judgement in determining the disclosures about going concern and liquidity risk in the half-yearly financial statements.

4.309.7.1 The principles should be applied by directors of all companies when preparing annual and half-yearly financial statements, but do not apply when preparing interim management statements in accordance with the Disclosure and Transparency Rule (DTR) 4.3.

4.309.8 The appendices to the guidance provide examples of going concern disclosures for small companies; for companies other than small companies (including subsidiary companies of large private or listed groups) and key questions for boards to consider.

4.309.9 The form of disclosure depends on the directors' conclusions having undertaken procedures in relation to going concern. There are three basic conclusions:

■ no material uncertainties exist that lead to significant doubt concerning the entity's ability to continue in operational existence for the foreseeable future;

■ material uncertainties exist that may cast significant doubt over the company's ability to continue in operation but, nonetheless, the directors consider it appropriate to use the going concern basis in preparing the financial statements; or

■ the going concern basis of accounting is not appropriate.

4.309.10 Where no uncertainties (material or otherwise) exist over the company's ability to continue as a going concern, the Going Concern and Financial Reporting (GCFR) guidance published in November 1994 suggests the appropriate form of words to be:

"After making enquiries, the directors have a reasonable expectation that the company has adequate resources to continue in operational existence for the foreseeable future. For this reason, they continue to adopt the going concern basis in preparing the accounts. " [GCFR para 49].

4.309.11 This form of disclosure has historically been adopted by most companies, although a significant number of blue chip companies, especially in the financial services sector, have chosen to give rather more detail in the current uncertain economic conditions. Principle 3 of the FRC guidance set out in paragraph 4.309.6 above should lead to this basic statement being expanded to explain more about the enquiries made by the directors and the basis for their 'reasonable expectation'.

4.309.12 The GCFR guidance recommends that the disclosure should be located in an operating and financial review (OFR) recognising that the OFR provides a context for a going concern statement. Despite this, it is quite common for the going concern statement to be included within the corporate governance statement or the business review with a separate sub-heading. An example of a going concern statement is set out in the table below.

Table 4.7 – Going concern reporting

Electrocomponents plc – Annual report – 31 March 2012

Going concern
The Group's activities, strategy and performance are explained in the Chairman's report on pages 2 to 3, the Group Chief Executive's review on pages 4 to 9 and the Business review on pages 18 to 29.

Further detail on the financial performance, financial position and cash flows of the Group is provided in the Business review on pages 18 to 29.

Note 19 on pages 80 to 87 of the consolidated financial statements provides details of the Group's debt maturity profile, capital management policy, hedging activities and financial instruments and its exposures to interest rate and foreign currency risks.

The Group is cash generative as evidenced in its cash flow performance with free cash flow representing 62% of profit after tax for the year ended 31 March 2012. Management reviews its actual and forecast cash flows each month to ensure that sufficient facilities are in place to meet the Group's requirements.

At 31 March 2012, the Group's net debt was £154.2m with total committed debt and loan facilities of £300.6m and undrawn committed facilities of £128.3m.

The Group's main sources of finance are a syndicated multicurrency facility from seven banks for US$75m, £120m and €50m maturing in November 2015 and US$150m of Private Placement notes, split US$65m maturing June 2015 and US$85m maturing

---

June 2017. The syndicated bank facility was put in place during the course of this year with comparable covenants to the previous one.

Compliance with the Group's bank covenants is monitored monthly and sensitivity analyses are periodically applied to forecasts to assess their impact on covenants and net debt. At 31 March 2012 there was significant headroom between the Group's financial position and its banking covenants; it is expected that such covenants will continue to be complied with for the foreseeable future.

The Group has sufficient financial resources, a large and geographically spread customer base and strong supplier relationships. Therefore, the Directors believe that the Group is well placed to manage its business risks successfully.

The Directors, having made appropriate enquiries, have a reasonable expectation that the Group has adequate resources to continue in operational existence for the foreseeable future. For this reason the Directors believe that it is appropriate to continue to adopt the going concern basis in preparing the Group's accounts. The Directors confirm that this statement has been prepared in accordance with Going Concern and Liquidity Risk: Guidance of UK Companies 2009, published by the Financial Reporting Council in October 2009.

4.309.13 If the directors conclude that the company is unlikely to continue in operational existence for the foreseeable future, a non-going concern basis will be required in preparing the financial statements and this will require disclosure. Directors will generally wish to take legal advice before making such a disclosure, in particular in relation to whether the directors may be liable for wrongful trading.

4.309.14 The FRC launched an inquiry under Lord Sharman into going concern and liquidity risk assessments to identify lessons for companies and auditors during 2011. See paragraph 4.357.9 onwards for more detail of the outcome of the Sharman inquiry.

4.309.15 Further discussion of going concern matters is included in chapter 3.

Directors' responsibility statements

4.310 Refer to chapter 2 for a discussion on directors' responsibility statements.

Business model

4.311 The FRC refers to paragraphs 30 to 32 of the ASB's reporting statement on the OFR for guidance as to the matters that should be considered in an explanation of a business model. These paragraphs are discussed in 'The business' nature, objectives and strategies' section of chapter two. The FRC has made it clear that companies reporting in line with the ASB's reporting statement will have met the requirements of UKCGC C.1.2 (see chapter 3).

4.312 The relevant paragraphs of the ASB's reporting statement are as follows:

- The OFR should include a description of the business and the external environment in which it operates as context for the directors' discussion and analysis of performance and financial position.

- A description of the business is recommended in order to provide members with an understanding of the industry in which the entity operates, its main products, services, customers, business processes and distribution methods, the structure of the business, and its economic model, including an overview of the main operating facilities and their location.

- Every entity is affected by its external environment. Depending on the nature of the business, the OFR should include discussion of matters such as the entity's major markets and competitive position within those markets and the significant features of the legal, regulatory, macro-economic and social environment that influence the business. For example, an entity may disclose the fact that it has significant operations in a number of countries, which could have an impact on the future development and performance of the business. [RS (OFR) paras 30 to 32].

[The next paragraph is 4.314.]

Communication

4.314 One of the themes of recent governance reviews has been that there needs to be appropriate two-way communication between the board and its investors if the 'comply or explain' mechanism of the Code is to work effectively. Too often, both companies and shareholders have reported frustration over the quality of 'engagement'. Companies criticise investors for taking a box-ticking approach to monitoring their investees, while shareholders criticise companies for preferring presentations to dialogue.

4.315 As recommended in the Walker Report the FRC has issued a Stewardship Code for institutional investors, which came into effect in July 2010. As a result section E of the Combined Code ceased to be applicable. See from paragraph 4.343 for discussion of UK Stewardship Code. Section D of the Combined Code on the company side continues to be applicable and is carried forward, with amendment, in section E of the UKCGC.

Dialogue with institutional shareholders

Principles

4.316 The main principle that should be applied in relation to dialogue with institutional shareholders is as follows:

- There should be a dialogue with shareholders based on the mutual understanding of objectives. The board as a whole has responsibility for ensuring that a satisfactory dialogue with shareholders takes place. [UKCGC E.1].

4.317 The supporting principles relevant to this dialogue include the following:

- Whilst recognising that most shareholder contact is with the chief executive and finance director, the chairman (and the senior independent director and other directors as appropriate) should maintain sufficient contact with major shareholders to understand their issues and concerns. [UKCGC Supporting principle E.1].

- The board should keep in touch with shareholder opinion in whatever ways are most practical and efficient. [UKCGC Supporting principle E.1].

Disclosure requirements

4.318 Disclosures in relation to this dialogue that are required within the annual report are as follows:

- Disclosure should be made of the steps that the board has taken to ensure that the members of the board, and in particular the non-executive directors, develop an understanding of the views of the major shareholders (for example through direct face-to-face contact, analysts' or brokers' briefings and surveys of shareholder opinion) about their company. [UKCGC E.1.2].

Other related provisions

4.319 The following provisions are not disclosure provisions. However it is envisaged that compliance with these detailed provisions will mean that the main principle has been applied.

- The chairman should ensure that the views of shareholders are communicated to the board as a whole. [UKCGC E.1.1].

- The chairman should discuss governance and strategy with major shareholders. Non-executive directors should be offered the opportunity to attend meetings with major shareholders and should expect to attend them if requested by major shareholders. The senior independent director should also attend sufficient meetings with a range of major shareholders to listen to their views. [UKCGC E.1.1].

Good practice disclosure

4.320 Current good practice and transparent reporting in this area may include the following:

- The use of an independent third party to assist the board in obtaining investor views; this demonstrates commitment and encourages openness.

- Company-specific disclosure about two-way communication and investor relations process.

- Recognition in practice and in the annual report of the importance of the whole investor base, including non-institutional investors, where applicable; diagrams breaking down the current investor base by size of holding, type organisation, geography and so on can be helpful to potential investors.

- Effective use of technology to enhance shareholder communications, such as reference to websites where investor relations information is held.

Constructive use of the AGM

Principles

4.321   The main principle that should be applied in relation to constructive use of the AGM is as follows:

■   The board should use the AGM to communicate with investors and to encourage their participation. [UKCGC Main principle E.2].

Other related provisions

4.322   There are no disclosure provisions associated with constructive use of the AGM. However, the following detailed provisions should be implemented by the company:

■   The chairman should arrange for the chairmen of the audit, remuneration and nomination committees to be available to answer questions at the AGM and for all directors to attend. [UKCGC E.2.3].

■   The company should propose a separate resolution on each substantially separate issue and should in particular propose a resolution at the AGM relating to the report and accounts. For each resolution, proxy appointment forms should provide shareholders with the option to direct their proxy to vote either for or against the resolution or to withhold their vote. The proxy form and any announcement of the results of a vote should make clear that a 'vote withheld' is not a vote in law and will not be counted in the calculation of the proportion of the votes for and against the resolution. [UKCGC E.2.1].

■   The company should ensure that all valid proxy appointments received for general meetings are properly recorded and counted. For each resolution, after a vote has been taken, except where taken on a poll, the company should ensure that the following information is given at the meeting and made available as soon as reasonably practicable on the company's website:

   ■   the number of shares in respect of which proxy appointments have been validly made; and

   ■   the number of votes (i) for, and (ii) against the resolution, and (iii) the number of shares in respect of which the vote was directed to be withheld.

   [UKCGC E.2.2].

■   The company should arrange for the Notice of the AGM and related papers to be sent to shareholders at least 20 working days before the meeting. [UKCGC E.2.4].

4.323   The AGM is the main formal opportunity for dialogue and communication between the company and its shareholders. From the company's point of view, the AGM provides a forum for the board to inform its shareholders about what the company does and how well it has performed during the year. For investors, it provides a forum to learn more about the business and ask questions of the directors, (particularly the chairmen of the audit, remuneration and nomination committees) and to use their votes responsibly.

Good practice disclosure

4.324   Current good practice reporting in this area may explain that the company:

■   Ensures shareholders are aware of meeting protocol, such as by referring to a separate Notice of Meeting booklet.

■   Appoints an independent assessor to scrutinise the AGM to strengthen reporting and enhance transparency.

[The next paragraph is 4.326]

Auditor review of compliance with the UK Corporate Governance Code

Listing Rules requirement

4.326   The Listing Rules include reference to the Code and explain auditor responsibilities in relation to it. The Listing Rules were amended with effect from August 2010 to include reference to the new name of the Code. The Listing Rules' transitional provisions (FSA 2010/39) state that: "*References to provisions in the*

UK Corporate Governance Code are to be read as references to the equivalent provisions in the Combined Code for accounting periods beginning before 29 June 2010".

4.327 There is no other change in the auditor responsibilities as a result of the introduction of the UKCGC.

4.328 The Listing Rules state that auditors should review companies' disclosures in relation to nine provisions of the UK Corporate Governance Code. This excludes provision C.1.3, relating to going concern, because this provision is covered by Listing Rule 9.8.6R(3). The provisions covered by the auditors' review requirement are stated in Listing Rule 9.8.10R(2) and are as follows:

- The directors should explain in the annual report their responsibility for preparing the financial statements and there should be a statement by the auditors about their reporting responsibilities. [UKCGC C.1.1].

- The board should, at least annually, conduct a review of the effectiveness of the company's risk management and internal control systems and should report to shareholders that they have done so. The review should cover all material controls, including financial, operational and compliance controls. [UKCGC C.2.1].

- The board should establish an audit committee of at least three, or in the case of smaller companies two, independent non-executive directors. In smaller companies the company chairman may be a member of, but not chair, the committee in addition to the independent non-executive directors, provided he or she was considered independent on appointment as chairman. The board should satisfy itself that at least one member of the audit committee has recent and relevant financial experience. [UKCGC C.3.1].

- The main role and responsibilities of the audit committee should be set out in written terms of reference and should include:

    - To monitor the integrity of the company's financial statements and any formal announcements relating to the company's financial performance, reviewing significant financial reporting judgements contained in them.

    - To review the company's internal financial controls and, unless expressly addressed by a separate board risk committee composed of independent directors, or by the board itself, to review the company's internal control and risk management systems.

    - To monitor and review the effectiveness of the company's internal audit function.

    - To make recommendations to the board, for it to put to the shareholders for their approval in general meeting, in relation to the appointment, re-appointment and removal of the external auditor and to approve the remuneration and terms of engagement of the external auditor.

    - To review and monitor the external auditor's independence and objectivity and the effectiveness of the audit process, taking into consideration relevant UK professional and regulatory requirements.

    - To develop and implement policy on the engagement of the external auditor to supply non-audit services, taking into account relevant ethical guidance regarding the provision of non-audit services by the external audit firm.

    - To report to the board, identifying any matters in respect of which it considers that action or improvement is needed and making recommendations as to the steps to be taken.

    [UKCGC C.3.2].

- The terms of reference of the audit committee, including its role and the authority delegated to it by the board, should be made available. A separate section of the annual report should describe the work of the committee in discharging those responsibilities. [UKCGC C.3.3].

- The audit committee should review arrangements by which the company's staff may, in confidence, raise concerns about possible improprieties in matters of financial reporting or other matters. The audit committee's objective should be to ensure that arrangements are in place for the proportionate and independent investigation of such matters and for appropriate follow-up action. [UKCGC C.3.4].

- The audit committee should monitor and review the effectiveness of the internal audit activities. Where there is no internal audit function, the audit committee should consider annually whether there is a need for an internal audit function and make a recommendation to the board, and the reasons for the absence of such a function should be explained in the relevant section of the annual report. [UKCGC C.3.5].

- The audit committee should have primary responsibility for making a recommendation on the appointment, re-appointment and removal of the external auditors. If the board does not accept the audit committee's recommendation, it should include in the annual report, and in any papers recommending appointment or re-appointment, a statement from the audit committee explaining the recommendation and should set out reasons why the board has taken a different position. [UKCGC C.3.6].

- The annual report should explain to shareholders how, if the auditor provides non-audit services, auditor objectivity and independence is safeguarded. [UKCGC C.3.7].

4.329 In addition to the review requirement under the Listing Rules, the scope of the auditor's report on the financial statements must cover certain disclosure requirements concerning directors' remuneration. These include the disclosures required by Listing Rules 9.8.11R(1), (2), (3) and (4) (see further chapter 5). The auditor must state in the audit report if in his or her opinion the company has not complied with the disclosures specified above and, where this information has not been given, must include in the report, so far as he/she is reasonably able to do so, a statement giving the required information. [LR 9.8.12R].

APB guidance on auditors' review

4.330 Detailed guidance on how to perform the auditors' review in relation to companies' reporting under the Combined Code was issued by the APB in Bulletin 2006/05, 'The Combined Code on corporate governance: requirements of auditors under the Listing Rules of the Financial Services Authority and the Irish Stock Exchange'. This sets out specific procedures to be followed in relation to each relevant provision. The auditors' responsibilities in respect of the directors' statement on going concern are set out in APB Bulletin 2009/04, 'Developments in corporate governance affecting the responsibilities of auditors of UK companies'.

4.331 The guidance in APB Bulletin 2006/05 also covers the auditors' review responsibilities in relation to the directors' statement on internal control.

4.332 There is no requirement, in either the UK Corporate Governance Code or the Listing Rules for publication of an auditors' report on corporate governance. In 1999 the APB concluded that such a report could be seriously misleading for readers. They were of the view that the narrow scope of the auditors' review and the introduction of a statement of auditors' responsibilities meant that it was no longer appropriate for auditors' reports on the directors' compliance statement to be published in the annual report. This position resulted in the discontinuance of published auditors' reports on corporate governance matters in the annual reports of listed companies.

4.333 Instead of a separate report on corporate governance matters, auditors of premium listed UK companies now report in an 'Other matters' section of the report on the annual report and financial statements that they have reviewed the nine provisions of the UK Corporate Governance Code specified and the going concern statement. The review of the nine provisions and the going concern statement is applicable to all premium listed companies including overseas companies, but the APB guidance applies to UK companies only.

Impact of DTR on the company and auditors' reporting on governance

4.334 As discussed in paragraph 4.49, the DTR requires certain companies to present a corporate governance statement, which may be included as part of the directors' report. Alternatively, it can be separately issued to accompany the annual report or may be made available on the company's web site, but with cross-references in the directors' report. Where the company publishes a separate corporate governance statement, there are new requirements for the auditors under the Companies Act 2006, which were introduced by SI 2009/1581, 'The Companies Act 2006 (Accounts, Reports and Audit) Regulations 2009'. This SI amends Parts 15 and 16 of the Companies Act 2006 to deal with the approval, signing and filing of the corporate governance statement where companies choose to present such a statement separately, rather than including it in the directors' report and includes additional duties for the auditors. The auditor is required to give an opinion on whether certain information in the corporate governance statement is consistent with the financial statements. Where the company chooses to present a separate corporate governance statement, the auditor has to give a separate opinion in the audit report.

Approval, signing and filing of separate corporate governance statement

4.335 When the corporate governance statement is included as part of the directors' report it will be approved on behalf of the board and filed with the Registrar of Companies as part of the directors' report. For companies presenting a separate corporate governance statement, the SI is effectively putting into law the same provisions regarding approval, signing and filing that would apply had the corporate governance statement been included within the directors' report.

4.336 A new section 419A has been inserted after section 419 of the Companies Act 2006 (approval and signing of directors' report), which requires that any separate corporate governance statement must be approved by the board of directors and signed on behalf of the board by a director or the company secretary.

4.337 Sections 446 and 447 of the Companies Act 2006 have been amended to provide that the directors of a quoted or an unquoted company must deliver to the Registrar of Companies a copy of any separate corporate governance statement, in addition to the company's annual financial statements, the directors' remuneration report (for quoted companies only) and the directors' report. The separate corporate governance statement must state the name of the person who signed it on behalf of the board under section 419A and must be signed on behalf of the board by a director or the company secretary. They must also deliver a copy of the auditors' report on any separate corporate governance statement.

Auditors' report and auditors' duties on separate corporate governance statement

4.338 There are different requirements of auditors depending on which option a company exercises for the publication of its corporate governance statement.

4.339 (Under DTR 7.2.1 R) – If the corporate governance statement is included as part of the directors' report, the audit requirement is that of existing section 496 of the Companies Act 2006. That is, the auditors are required to state in their report on the company's annual financial statements whether, in their opinion, the information given in the directors' report for the financial year for which the financial statements are prepared is consistent with those accounts.

4.340 (Under DTR 7.2.9 R) – A new section 497A has been inserted after section 497 of the Companies Act 2006, which provides that if the corporate governance statement is not included within the directors' report, the auditor must state in their report whether, in their opinion, the information given in the corporate governance statement in compliance with rules 7.2.5 and 7.2.6 of the FSA's Disclosure Rules and Transparency Rules (Corporate Governance Rules) regarding internal control and risk management systems and certain disclosures on share capital structures is consistent with the annual financial statements for the year. For the other information in the corporate governance statement, the auditor must check that the information has been included.

4.341 A new section 498A has been inserted after section 498 of the Companies Act 2006 (duties of auditor), which provides that, where a company is required to prepare a corporate governance statement, and has neither included such a statement as part of its directors' report nor prepared a separate corporate governance statement, the auditors must state that fact in their report.

4.342 The APB recommends that prior to the release of the annual report, the auditor communicates, and discusses, with the directors the scope and factual findings of their review.

The UK Stewardship Code

4.343 The FRC agreed to take on responsibility for oversight of a code to enhance shareholder engagement following Sir David Walker's recommendations. The FRC subsequently published the first Stewardship Code for institutional investors in July 2010, following a consultation process. The purpose of the Code is to improve the quality of corporate governance through promoting better dialogue between shareholders and company boards, and more transparency about the way in which investors oversee the companies they own.

Who should apply the Code

4.344 The Code is addressed in the first instance to firms who manage assets on behalf of institutional shareholders such as pension funds, insurance companies, investment trusts and other collective investment vehicles. The FSA made it mandatory for all UK-authorised asset managers to produce a statement of commitment to the Stewardship Code or explain why it is not appropriate to their business model from 6 December 2010.

4.345 The responsibility for monitoring company performance does not rest with fund managers alone. The FRC, therefore, strongly encourages all institutional investors to publicly report if and how they have complied with the Code. Pension funds and other owners may not wish to become directly involved in engagement, but they can make a significant contribution by, for example, mandating their fund managers to do so on their behalf.

4.346 Principle 1 of the Code (see Content of the UK Stewardship Code below) states that institutional investors that make use of proxy voting and other advisory services should disclose how they are used. The FRC encourages those service providers in turn to disclose how they carry out the wishes of their clients by applying the principles of the Code that are relevant to their activities.

4.347 The FRC also hopes that investors based outside the UK will commit to the Code. It is recognised that, in practice, local institutions usually take the lead in engagement.

Comply or explain

4.348 Like the UK Corporate Governance Code, the UK Stewardship Code is to be applied on a 'comply or explain' basis. In reporting terms this currently entails providing a statement on the institutional investor's website containing:

- a description of how the principles of the Code have been applied; and
- disclosure of the specific information listed under Principles 1, 5, 6 and 7; or
- an explanation if these elements of the Code have not been complied with.

Content of the UK Stewardship Code

4.349 The UK Stewardship Code is based on the Institutional Shareholders' Committee (ISC) Code and consists of the following seven principles and further guidance on each of them.

The principles are as follows. Institutional investors should:

1. Publicly disclose their policy on how they will discharge their stewardship responsibilities.
2. Have a robust policy on managing conflicts of interest in relation to stewardship and this policy should be publicly disclosed.
3. Monitor their investee companies.
4. Establish clear guidelines on when and how they will escalate their activities as a method of protecting and enhancing shareholder value.
5. Be willing to act collectively with other investors where appropriate.
6. Have a clear policy on voting and disclosure of voting activity.
7. Report periodically on their stewardship and voting activities.

4.350 The amendments made to the ISC Code to arrive at the UK Stewardship Code are intended to incorporate guidance to institutional investors previously contained in Section E of the 2008 Combined Code, and to align this Code with the guidance on engagement provided to companies in the new UK Corporate Governance Code. Specifically, the guidance on Principle 3 (on the monitoring of companies) has been amended to encourage investors to:

- meet the chairman of investee companies, and other board members where appropriate, as part of their ongoing monitoring and not only when they have concerns;
- attend the General Meetings of companies in which they have a major holding, where appropriate and practicable; and
- consider carefully explanations given by investee companies for departure from the UK Corporate Governance Code, and advise the company where they do not accept its position.

Reporting to clients

4.351 Under the Stewardship Code, investment firms and other agents should report regularly to their clients on how they have discharged their responsibilities. The Code also recommends that investors who sign up to it should consider obtaining an independent audit opinion on their engagement and voting processes and that the existence of such assurance reports should be publicly disclosed. The most relevant existing reporting standard is the Audit and Assurance Faculty (AAF) 01/06 guidance, produced by the ICAEW.

[The next paragraph is 4.353.]

Monitoring

4.353 The FRC maintains on its website a list of those institutions that have published a statement on their compliance or otherwise with the Stewardship Code.

Proposed revisions to the Stewardship Code

4.353.1 See paragraph 4.357.7 for details of proposed amendments to the Stewardship Code that would apply for years beginning on or after 1 October 2012.

Future corporate governance developments

Department for Business, Innovation and Skills (BIS)

4.354 During 2010, the Department for Business, Innovation and Skills (BIS) issued two calls for evidence relating to corporate governance as part of its 'Plan for growth' agenda.

4.355 Following consideration of the responses to the call for evidence 'A long-term focus for corporate Britain', business secretary Vince Cable stated that *"equity investment needs to be recalibrated to support the long-term interests of companies and underlying beneficiaries such as pension fund members"*. The government, therefore, appointed Professor John Kay in June 2011 to carry out a review into investment in UK equity markets and its impact on the long-term performance and governance of UK quoted companies. The Kay Review looked at the whole investor chain including pension funds, pension advisers and fund managers. The final report was published in July 2012, setting out seventeen recommendations addressed to government, regulatory authorities and the key players in the investment chain. The business secretary is to consider the report and respond later in 2012.

4.356 The Future of Narrative Reporting – Following an initial call for evidence which ran from August to October 2010, the government is developing plans to materially simplify narrative reporting for quoted companies *"... to provide clear and relevant information to investors about strategy, performance and risk in a simpler and more concise report, with supporting information provided on the company's website"*. BIS proposes splitting the directors' report into two separate documents: a strategic report and an annual directors' statement. The strategic report would have a forward-looking slant and would contain key information about the performance and strategy of the business, including environmental and other corporate social responsibility issues. The annual directors' statement would be designed to be viewed mainly online and is likely to be in a prescribed format to enable greater ease of comparison between the reports of different companies.

4.357 The main focus for BIS in recent times has been directors' pay. Following a consultation in March 2012 on shareholder voting rights, the government announced in June 2012 a significant reform of the framework for directors' remuneration. The government's stated aim is to:

- give shareholders binding votes (at AGMs) on pay policy and exit payments, so they can hold companies to account and prevent rewards for failure; and

- boost transparency so that what people are paid is easily understood and the link between pay and performance is clearly drawn.

4.357.1 The binding vote on the 'policy report' will be held annually unless companies choose to leave their remuneration policy unchanged, in which case it will be compulsory at least every three years. An annual advisory vote on the amounts paid (that is, the 'implementation report') will continue as before but companies will have to report a single figure for the total pay directors received for the year. This figure will cover all rewards received by directors, including bonuses and long term incentives. Companies will also have to report details of whether they met performance measures and a comparison between company performance and chief executives' pay.

4.357.2 The government intends all of these reforms to be enacted by October 2013. A consultation paper on the proposed revisions to the remuneration reporting regulations was launched in June 2012 – these would be enacted through the replacement of the current regulations in SI 2008/41. The changes to shareholder voting procedures are included in the Enterprise and Regulatory Reform Bill. Once the government's legislation on voting and reporting on executive remuneration has been finalised, the FRC will consult on two proposals that the government has asked it to consider: to extend the Code's existing provisions on claw-back arrangements; and to limit the practice of executive directors sitting on the remuneration committees of other companies. It will also seek views on whether companies should engage with shareholders and report to the market in the event that they fail to obtain at least a substantial majority in support of a resolution on remuneration.

Parliamentary inquiries

4.357.3 Two parliamentary inquiries into corporate governance in the financial sector have also been announced in 2012. The first was the Commons Treasury Select Committee inquiry into corporate governance in systemically important financial institutions, which published its terms of reference in April 2012. This was followed in July 2012 by the announcement of an inquiry into banking standards by a Joint Committee of both Houses of Parliament, *"…building on the Treasury Select Committee's work and drawing on the conclusions of UK and international regulatory and competition investigations into the LIBOR rate-setting process, consider what lessons are to be learnt from them in relation to transparency, conflicts of interest, culture and the professional standards of the banking industry"*. It is the government's intention that the Joint Committee's report should be published before the end of 2012 in order that its recommendations can be reflected in the Banking Reform Bill.

The FRC

Cutting clutter

4.357.4 The FRC plans to liaise with BIS in order to simplify narrative reporting. In April 2011, the ASB published 'Cutting clutter: Combating clutter in annual reports'. This report defines clutter as including (a) immaterial disclosures that inhibit the ability to identify and understand relevant information and (b) explanatory information that remains unchanged from year to year. It identifies some of the causes of clutter and provides those preparing annual reports with a number of 'disclosure aids' for reducing clutter, including one that seeks to declutter the corporate governance report.

4.357.5 The report also identifies three calls for action to combat some of the barriers to cutting clutter, including the ASB continuing to engage with stakeholders and regulators to ensure that their legitimate information needs can be met without adding clutter to annual reports.

Revised UK Corporate Governance Code

4.357.6 In April 2012 the FRC launched consultations on changes arising from its 2011 initiative 'Effective Company Stewardship – Enhancing Corporate Reporting and Audit'; a number of the themes of this initiative had also been followed up in 'Developments in corporate governance 2011: The impact and implementation of the UK Corporate Governance and Stewardship Codes', which was published by the FRC in December 2011.

4.357.7 On 28 September 2012 the FRC published a feedback statement in relation to its April consultation on changes to the UK Corporate Governance Code and the FRC's Guidance on Audit Committees, and new editions of the Code and Guidance. The new editions of the UK Corporate Governance Code and the 'Guidance on Audit Committees' will apply to all premium listed companies other than as indicated below for reporting periods beginning on or after 1 October 2012. The revised International Standards on Auditing (UK and Ireland) 260, 700 and 720A, which set out enhancements to auditor reporting in relation to the new disclosures expected of the board and audit committee, will apply from the same date. The paragraphs that follow summarise the amendments that have been made.

4.357.8 The amendments made concerning audit tendering are as follows:

■ As proposed in the consultation paper, the Code now states that: *"FTSE 350 companies should put the external audit contract out to tender at least every ten years"*. [2012 Code C.3.7].

■ The FRC has published on its website non-binding transitional arrangements that would spread the tenders for the FTSE 350 over the ten years to 2022 if companies were to go out to tender at the earliest recommended time. However, it is important to bear in mind that all the provisions of the Code are to be applied on a comply-or-explain basis, so tendering can be deferred and, equally importantly, the incumbent auditors can be reappointed after a tender process. The guidance on audit committees has been specifically amended to make this clear, stating that the purpose of tendering is *"to enable the audit committee to compare the quality and effectiveness of the services provided by the incumbent auditor with those of other audit firms"*. [2012 Guidance on audit committees para 4.23].

■ The consultation paper proposed that audit tenders should be conducted on an 'open book' basis. This has been amended in the published Guidance to *"all tendering firms have such access as is necessary to information and individuals during the duration of the tendering process"*. [2012 Guidance on audit committees para 4.21]. The FRC has also indicated that it will consider issuing further guidance on audit tendering.

■ As part of the audit committee's explanation of its approach to the appointment or reappointment of auditors, disclosure of the length of tenure of the current audit firm and when a tender was last conducted is now included in the Code itself rather than in the guidance. [2012 Code C.3.8].

4.357.8.1 With regard to the directors' statement that the annual report is 'fair, balanced and understandable', the following amendments have been made:

■ The directors should now *"state that they consider the annual report and accounts, taken as a whole, is fair, balanced and understandable and provides the information necessary for shareholders to assess the company's performance, business model and strategy"*. [2012 Code C.1.1].

■ When requested by the board, the audit committee *"should provide advice"* on this but the original proposal to amend the expected terms of reference of all audit committees to include this responsibility has not been included in the published Code. [2012 Code C.3.4].

■ The guidance makes it clear that consistency is an important factor: *" …any review undertaken by the committee would need to assess whether the narrative in the front of the report was consistent with the accounting information in the back, so as to ensure that there were no surprises hidden in the accounts"*. [2012 Guidance on audit committees para 4.6].

4.357.8.2 Related changes to the auditing standards concerning the directors' statement are summarised below:

■ Under ISA (UK&I) 700 the auditor will be required to report, in the report on the financial statements, if the board's statement that the annual report is fair, balanced and understandable…is inconsistent with the knowledge acquired by the auditor in the course of performing the audit.

■ Under ISA (UK&I) 260 the auditor will be required to communicate to the audit committee the information that the auditor believes will be relevant to the board and (where applicable) the audit committee in relation to their responsibilities under Code provision C.1.1 and C.2.1 (provision C.1.1 includes the statement by the directors that the annual report is fair, balanced and understandable, and provision C.2.1 relates to the board's annual review of the effectiveness of the company's risk management and internal control systems).

■ This would include, without expressing an opinion on the effectiveness of the system of internal control as a whole, and based solely on the audit procedures performed in the audit of the financial statements, the auditor's *views* on 'the effectiveness of the entity's system of internal control relevant to risks that may affect financial reporting; and other risks arising from the entity's business model and the effectiveness of related internal controls to the extent, if any, that the auditor has obtained an understanding of such matters' (which would most likely be under ISA (UK&I) 315 as part of risk assessment). The application material in ISA (UK&I) 260 notes that 'views on effectiveness can go beyond identifying [significant] deficiencies' under ISA (UK&I) 265, and provides a list of potential areas on which views may be expressed.

4.357.8.3 The impact on audit committee reporting is explained below:

- As proposed in the consultation paper, the Code now states that the audit committee should include in its section of the annual report *"the significant issues that it considered in relation to the financial statements and how these issues were addressed"*.

- The guidance includes some more information on what might constitute a 'significant issue': *"The committee will need to exercise judgement in deciding which of the issues it considered in relation to the financial statements are significant, but should include at least those matters that have informed the board's assessment of whether the company is a going concern"*. [2012 Guidance on audit committees para 5.3].

- The guidance also allows some judgement in the disclosures provided – the audit committee *"would not be expected to disclose information which, in its opinion, would be prejudicial to the interests of the company (for example, because it related to impending developments or matters in the course of negotiation)"*. [2012 Guidance on audit committees para 5.4].

- The provision on audit committee reporting also now recommends *"an explanation of how [the committee] has assessed the effectiveness of the external audit process"*. [2012 Code C.3.8].

4.357.8.3 *Related changes to the auditing standards concerning audit committee reporting are summarised below:*

- Under ISA (UK&I) 700 the auditor will be required by auditing standards to report, in the report on the financial statements, if the section of the annual report describing the work of the audit committee does not appropriately address the matters communicated by the auditor to the audit committee.

- Under ISA (UK&I) 260 the auditor will be required to communicate to the audit committee the information that the auditor believes will be relevant to the board and the audit committee in order to understand the rationale and the evidence relied upon when making significant professional judgments in the course of the audit and reaching an opinion on the financial statements.

4.357.8.4 Other changes include the following:

- As announced in October 2011, specific disclosures on diversity have been introduced – the nomination committee report *"should include a description of the board's policy on diversity, including gender, any measurable objectives that it has set for implementing the policy, and progress on achieving the objectives"* and diversity should form part of the board evaluation process.

- The FRC's advice on what constitutes an appropriate explanation under comply-or-explain has been updated, and there are additional recommendations around the identification of external advisers including executive search consultants, external facilitators of board evaluations and remuneration consultants.

4.357.9 The FRC has also issued a revised version of the UK Stewardship Code ('the Code') for institutional investors, which was first published in 2010. The changes are limited in scope but include:

- Clarification of the respective responsibilities of asset managers and asset owners for stewardship, and for stewardship activities that they have chosen to outsource (the focus on the how outsourced stewardship activities are consistent with the company's approach is new since the April 2012 consultation document).

- Investors are to explain more clearly how they manage conflicts of interest, the circumstances in which they will take part in collective engagement, and the use they make of proxy voting agencies.

- Asset managers are encouraged to have the processes that support their stewardship activities independently verified, to provide greater assurance to their clients (principle 7 of the Code says they should do so).

The changes are designed to give companies and savers a better understanding of how signatories to the Code are exercising their stewardship responsibilities.

4.357.10 The Preface to the Stewardship Code has also been restructured to follow the pattern of the UK Corporate Governance Code.

4.357.11 With these revisions the FRC addresses some of the issues identified around the initial version of the Stewardship Code, some of which date back to the time of the Code's launch in July 2010 and some of which were identified in the FRC's 'Developments in corporate governance' report in December 2011. The

FRC's view is that the Stewardship Code is still in its infancy and that it will take time for its full impact to be felt.

The Sharman inquiry

4.357.12 The FRC has also been responsible for an inquiry into going concern and liquidity risk assessments to identify lessons for companies and auditors. The panel of inquiry, chaired by Lord Sharman issued its final report in June 2012. The recommendations in this report will need to be addressed by the FRC and go through further due process before any changes to codes or standards.

4.357.13 The key recommendations of the final report include:

- Enhanced and more joined-up narrative disclosure in company annual reports on business strategy and liquidity and solvency risks.

- Companies should perform stress tests of both liquidity and solvency.

- An explicit statement in the auditor's report about whether the auditor has anything to add to the narrative disclosures made by the directors about the process of assessing going concern and its outcome.

- The panel has been responsive to stakeholder comment on the previous draft proposals and has retained the ability of auditors to include an emphasis of matter in cases of material uncertainty.

4.357.14 There is no specific headline recommendation on banks and going concern, but there is extensive commentary in the report on this area, which has attracted considerable attention. The report notes the dilemma between the objectives of ensuring financial stability and market transparency. It states (para 29) *"….the FRC would need to consider making clear that liquidity support from central banks may be a normal funding source for a bank and therefore reliance on such support if reasonably assured, does not mean that the bank is not a going concern or that material uncertainty disclosures or an emphasis of matter paragraph are required".*

4.357.15 The FRC will be revising 'Going concern and liquidity risk: Guidance to Directors', which is intended to assist directors in applying section C.1.3 of the UK Corporate Governance Code, to take account of the recommendations of the Sharman inquiry into Going Concern. The aim is to consult on revised interim guidance by December 2012.

Review of the Turnbull Guidance

4.357.16 In its paper, 'Effective company stewardship: Next steps' and its report, 'Boards and risk: A summary of discussions with companies, investors and advisers', published on 1 September 2011 the FRC stated its intention to update the Turnbull guidance. The FRC confirmed this intention in the feedback statement revised with the 2012 Code, and intends to consult on the revised guidance by December 2012.

The role of Europe

4.358 Many countries across the EU have established their own corporate governance practices and many have their own equivalents of the UK Corporate Governance Code. Some of these Codes were inspired by the UK's ground-breaking Cadbury and Hampel reforms and contain similar principles, including 'comply or explain'. Compliance with these national Codes is often voluntary except where, as in the UK, the requirements have been incorporated in local listing rules.

4.358.1 The implementation of European Directives in the UK has a direct impact on UK governance requirements, as the Disclosure Rules and Transparency Rules demonstrate (see para 4.43 onwards). The current activities of the EC relating to governance, which are associated with the G20 agenda for reform in the financial services sector, may well have a very significant impact on UK governance requirements in the future. The impact would be unlikely to be restricted to the financial sector.

European Commission activities

Green papers on corporate governance

4.359 The European Commission (EC) continues to consider corporate governance following the recent financial crisis and has issued two Green Papers. The following is an update of the status of EC activities related to governance that would be likely to affect the UK framework.

4.360 The first Green Paper Corporate Governance in Financial Institutions and Remuneration Policies closed for comment in September 2010. The EC's proposals on bank governance resulting from this consultation are incorporated in its proposed Capital Requirements Directive IV (CRD IV), which is intended to translate Basel III into draft European legislation. CRD IV applies to banks and investment firms and is subject to consent from European Parliament and the Council of the EU. The EC intends for member states to apply CRD IV from 1 January 2013. The provisions on bank governance cover:

- the attributes, knowledge and skills of the board; directors' time commitment, with proposed limitations of the number of directorships: directors can either combine one executive directorship with two NED positions or combine four NED positions;

- board diversity (gender, age, geographical, educational and professional diversity) to be taken into account as one of the selection criteria for board appointments (firms will be required to provide the European Banking Authority (EBA) with information in relation to diversity practices, which the EBA will use to benchmark diversity practices at EU level in the future);

- increasing the effectiveness of risk oversight by boards, improving the status of the risk management function and ensuring effective monitoring by supervisors of risk governance; and

- remuneration policies, including linking pay to risk, rules around variable pay and the role of the remuneration committee.

4.361 A second Green Paper The EU Corporate Governance Framework, dealing with all listed companies, consulted on possible ways forward to improve existing corporate governance mechanisms. This Green Paper focused on three areas: boards of directors, shareholder engagement and the 'comply or explain' approach. The period for comment closed in July 2011. Analysis of the commission's summary of responses, published in November 2011, shows strong support for the current practice of 'comply or explain' and for a flexible approach to corporate governance. While many respondents called for improvements in the quality of information provided, most saw no need for additional regulation at EU level to supplement or strengthen national rules and governance codes. There was little support for the idea that EU corporate governance regimes should take into account the size of listed companies, arguing that comply or explain already offers sufficient flexibility to cover all company sizes.

4.362 The Commission is reflecting further and has announced that any follow-up actions relating to the second Green Paper will be part of its Action Plan on European Company Law and Corporate Governance (Action Plan) expected to be launched in October 2012. This Action Plan is expected to include measures intended to address several underlying reasons for the lack of appropriate shareholder engagement, such as the short-termism of the financial markets, problems arising from the principal-agent relationship between investors and their asset managers, conflicts of interests, the role of proxy agents and difficulties with shareholder co-operation.

Audit reform proposals

4.363 In November 2011 the Commission released proposals intended to reform the European Public Interest Entity (PIE) audit market, relationships with audit clients and the scope of services provided by the audit firm. The proposals include:

- a requirement for virtually all PIEs to have an audit committee and criteria for its members;

- expansion of the audit report;

- increased reporting requirements to audit committees;

- mandatory audit firm rotation;

- mandatory tendering processes;

- audit-only firms for the very largest firms by revenue; and

- prohibition of certain non-audit services by audit firms to audit clients including, for example, financial due diligence and tax compliance services.

4.364 As they currently stand, the proposals could have a significant impact on both PIEs and audit firms, both within and outside the EU. The proposed legislation is radical in terms of its scope and measures.

4.365 If the current proposals were to become law, the oversight role of the audit committee would be increased in some respects, but adversely affected in a number of ways. For example, mandatory audit firm rotation would limit their choice of audit firms and other restrictions would limit their ability to procure services from the best provider. There would also be additional requirements for reporting both by audit committees and auditors, such as additional public disclosure by the audit committee in relation to the appointment of auditors and conduct of the audit, detailed requirements for the content of the auditor's report and wider access to the auditor's report to the audit committee.

Chapter 5

Disclosure of directors' remuneration

Disclosure of directors' remuneration

Disclosure of directors' remuneration

Introduction

5.1 Directors' remuneration is one of the most sensitive and closely regulated aspects of financial reporting. Generally, directors are well rewarded and it is inevitable that, given their stewardship role, comparisons are made by investors and others between the company's performance and the level of the directors' remuneration.

5.2 The legal rules relating to disclosure of directors' remuneration are contained in the Companies Act 2006 and its statutory instruments: The 'Small Companies and Groups (Accounts and Directors' Report) Regulations 2008' (SI 2008/409) and the 'Large and Medium-sized Companies and Groups (Accounts and Reports) Regulations 2008' (SI 2008/410). The rules fall broadly into three main sections: those that apply to all companies, those that apply only to unquoted companies and those that apply to quoted companies. AIM companies have to give more information than other unquoted companies in relation to share option gains and long-term incentives received in shares. In addition, AIM companies are required to provide additional details of remuneration for each director. The scope of the requirements is dealt with from paragraph 5.6 onwards.

5.3 Under UK company law, remuneration should be disclosed when it is paid to or receivable by a director in respect of qualifying services to the company and/or its subsidiaries. Generally, disclosure is required in respect of:

■ The aggregate amount of remuneration (including salary, fees, bonuses and benefits in kind).

■ Share options.

■ Long-term incentive schemes.

■ Pension schemes.

■ Compensation for loss of office.

■ Sums paid to or receivable by third parties for making available directors' services.

These disclosure requirements are covered in detail in this chapter.

5.4 Directors' remuneration disclosures made by quoted companies are extensive. They include information on policy and details of remuneration given for each individual director. The legal requirements for quoted companies substantially reproduce the requirements in the Listing Rules relating to disclosure of directors' remuneration, but they also contain additional disclosures over and above those in the Listing Rules. In addition, there are some differences between the legal requirements and those of the Listing Rules, which are discussed later in the chapter.

5.4.1 The UK Corporate Governance Code, issued by the FRC, contains principles and provisions relating to directors' remuneration. UK listed entities are required by the Listing Rules to disclose how they have applied the principles of the code and confirm that they have complied with its provisions – or provide an explanation where they have not done so. The UK Corporate Governance Code is discussed further in chapter 4.

5.5 In addition, for companies preparing their financial statements under IFRS, IAS 24, 'Related party disclosures', requires disclosure of 'key management personnel compensation' in the notes to the financial statements.

Scope of the requirements

5.6 Disclosure of directors' remuneration is governed by:

■ The Companies Act 2006.

■ The Listing Rules of the FSA.

■ The UK Corporate Governance Code.

5.6.1 In addition, as noted in paragraph 5.5 above, for companies that are preparing their financial statements in accordance with IFRS, IAS 24 requires disclosure of 'key management personnel compensation' in the notes to the financial statements. The requirements of IAS 24 differ from those contained in both the law and the Listing Rules. The requirements are considered in chapter 29 of the Manual of Accounting – IFRS for the UK.

5.6.1.1 In addition to the requirements set out above in paragraphs 5.6 and 5.6.1, various organisations such as the National Association of Pension Funds (NAPF), the Association of British Insurers (ABI) and RiskMetrics Group have published good practice guidance on remuneration. Further details are provided from paragraph 5.223.1 below.

5.6.2 The definition of quoted company for the purposes of disclosure is:

'…a company whose equity share capital –

(a) has been included in the official list in accordance with the provisions of Part VI of the Financial Services and Markets Act 2000; or

(b) is officially listed in an EEA State; or

(c) is admitted to dealing on either the New York Stock Exchange or the exchange known as Nasdaq;

and in paragraph (a) 'the official list' shall have the meaning given it by section 103(1) of the Financial Services and Markets Act 2000.'

[CA06 Sec 385(2)].

5.6.2.1 The 2006 Act clarifies that *"a company is a quoted company in relation to a financial year if it is a quoted company immediately before the end of the accounting reference period by reference to which that financial year was determined"*. [CA06 Sec 385(1)]. Our view is that, if a company is quoted at the year end, then any disclosures required by the law or accounting standards that are applicable to quoted companies must be given. In this respect, a delisting is regarded as a non-adjusting post balance sheet event.

5.6.3 'Company' means a company formed and registered under any Companies Act since 1929. The definition of quoted company applies only to UK companies. [CA06 Sec 1(1)]. Quoted, as defined above, effectively means listed on the London Stock Exchange or officially listed in the European Economic Area (which includes EU Member States plus Iceland, Norway and Liechtenstein) or admitted to dealing on the New York Stock Exchange or on Nasdaq. For the purpose of this definition, therefore, companies listed on AIM are not included.

5.6.4 The requirements of Schedule 8 to SI 2008/410 substantially reproduce the requirements of Listing Rule 9.8.8R relating to disclosure of directors' remuneration, although there are some differences. The requirements of LR 9.8.8R are set out in Section IV below, but as its requirements are generally similar to Schedule 8 to SI 2008/410, these are not discussed in detail in this chapter. However, because there are some differences between the requirements of the Listing Rules and those of the 2006 Act, the disclosures can be complicated. An illustrative example is given in the directors' remuneration report for IFRS GAAP plc (see separate publication containing illustrative financial statements). Other Listing Rules relating to directors' remuneration that are not covered by Schedule 8 to SI 2008/410 are also dealt with in section IV below. Annex 1 sets out the principles and provisions of the UK Corporate Governance Code that relate to directors' remuneration.

5.6.5 Where a company is not quoted, but has debt or fixed income shares listed in the UK, it does not have to comply with the requirements of Schedule 8 to SI 2008/410. Such an entity has to comply with the disclosures relating to directors' remuneration contained in Schedule 5 to SI 2008/410. Although such a company has to comply with the Listing Rules, it is not required to comply with the requirements concerning directors' remuneration in LR 9.8.8R (see Annex 2).

5.6.6 Where a company is quoted on an overseas exchange, but has debt or fixed income shares listed in the UK, it has to comply with the directors' remuneration requirements contained in part 1 of Schedule 5 and in Schedule 8 to SI 2008/410. In addition, such an entity is exempt from the Listing Rule requirement concerning the disclosure of directors' remuneration in LR 9.8.8R (see Annex 2). [LR 9.8.6R].

5.7 AIM companies do not fall within the definition of quoted companies.

> **Example – AIM companies and directors' remuneration**
>
> Are AIM companies required to present a directors' remuneration report in accordance with Schedule 8 to SI 2008/410?
>
> No. The requirement in Section 420(1) of the Companies Act 2006 is that quoted companies should prepare a directors' remuneration report compliant with Schedule 8 to SI 2008/410. The definition of a quoted company is given in paragraph 5.6.3 above.
>
> A company with equity shares listed on AIM does not fall within the definition of a quoted company, so is not required to prepare a directors' remuneration report compliant with Schedule 8 to SI 2008/410.
>
> However, AIM companies, whilst largely treated as unquoted companies, have to give more information than other unquoted companies in relation to share option gains and long-term incentives received in shares. In addition, AIM companies are required to provide details of certain remuneration by individual director. The requirements for AIM-listed companies are dealt with from paragraph 5.118.

5.8 The disclosure of directors' remuneration can be considered under a number of headings and sub-headings:

- Section I – All companies.
  - General Rules.
  - Directors' and auditors' duties.
  - Payment for directors' services.
  - Disclosure in which year.
  - Other matters.
- Aggregate remuneration and other benefits.
  - Aggregate remuneration.
  - Benefits in kind.
  - Gains made on exercise of share options and amounts received or receivable under long-term incentive schemes.
  - Pension contributions.
- Section II – Unquoted companies (including AIM companies).
  - Highest paid director's emoluments and other benefits.
  - Excess retirement benefits of directors and past directors.
  - Compensation for loss of office.
  - Sums paid to third parties in respect of directors' services.
  - Companies Act 2006 disclosure requirements.
  - AIM Rules disclosure requirements.
- Section III – AIM companies.
  - Companies Act 2006 disclosure requirements.
  - AIM Rules disclosure requirements.
- Section IV – Quoted companies (excluding companies listed on AIM).
  - Remuneration report.
  - Information not subject to audit.
    - Composition of remuneration committee and advisors.
    - Statement of policy on directors' remuneration.

- ■ Performance graph.

- ■ Service contracts.

- ■ Compensation for past directors.

- ■ Appendix – UK Corporate Governance Codes (2008) and (2010).

■ Information subject to audit.

- ■ Individual directors' emoluments and compensation.

- ■ Share options.

- ■ Long-term incentive schemes.

- ■ Pensions.

- ■ Excess retirement benefits of directors and past directors.

- ■ Compensation for past directors.

- ■ Sums paid to third parties in respect of directors' services.

- ■ Approval of remuneration report.

■ Section V – Audit requirements.

■ Section VI – Group situations.

Each of these is considered in turn below and Annex 2 to the chapter includes a directors' remuneration decision tree, which shows for different companies the parts of the 2006 Act that apply and whether the Listing Rules need to be followed.

Section I — All companies

General rules — all companies

Directors' and auditors' duties

5.9 A company's directors have a duty to give information about their remuneration (including pensions, compensation for loss of office and sums paid to third parties) to the company so that the information discussed below can be disclosed in the financial statements. This requirement also applies to a person who has been a director of the company within the preceding five years. Any director failing to give notice of the required information to the company is liable to a fine. [CA06 Sec 412(5),(6)].

5.10 If the required information is not disclosed in the financial statements or if information subject to audit that is required to be included in the directors' remuneration report of a quoted company is not disclosed in that report, the auditors have a duty to include the information (so far as they are reasonably able to do so) in their audit report. [CA06 Sec 498(4)].

Payment for directors' services

5.11 The remuneration to be disclosed should include all amounts paid to a director for his services as a director of the company and any subsidiary, or for managing the company and its subsidiaries while a director. [SI 2008/409 3 Sch 12(1); SI 2008/410 5 Sch 15(1); SI 2008/410 8 Sch 17(1)]. All payments should be included, whether those payments are made by the company, or by a subsidiary undertaking of the company or by any other person, unless the director has to account in turn to another group company, or to members under section 219 of the 2006 Act (directors' duty to make disclosure on company takeover and consequences of non-compliance), for the receipt of the remuneration. [SI 2008/409 3 Sch 5(2); SI 2008/410 5 Sch 8(1); SI 2008/410 8 Sch 19(2)]. This also applies to payments by way of compensation for loss of office.

Example – Director paid by non-group company

Mr Smith spends part of his time as an executive director of company A and part of his time as an employee of company B, which is controlled by him. Company B pays Mr Smith's salary and it invoices company A for an amount to cover that part of the time that Mr Smith spends working for company A. Although Mr Smith is paid by company B (and not by company A of which he is a director), the amount that he receives from company B is partially in respect of his services as a director of company A.

Consequently, Mr Smith should disclose to company A, and company A should disclose in its financial statements as remuneration, the proportion of his salary that relates to his services as a director of company A. This figure may or may not be the same as the amount that company B has invoiced company A. This will depend on whether the invoiced amount is intended to cover an amount that is either more or less than the actual cost of the director's services to company A.

5.12   There is also nothing in the Companies Act 2006 to suggest that the director must receive payments personally in order that they should be subject to disclosure as remuneration. Amounts paid to or receivable by a director, including amounts paid in respect of compensation for loss of office, will include amounts paid to or receivable by a person connected with, or a body corporate controlled by that director (but such amounts should not be counted twice). [SI 2008/409 3 Sch 5(3); SI 2008/410 5 Sch 7(3); SI 2008/410 8 Sch 19(3)]. The definitions of connected persons and body corporate controlled by a director are set out in sections 252 to 255 of the 2006 Act. [SI 2008/410 5 Sch 15(2); SI 2008/410 8 Sch 17(4)]. Consequently, even where a director sets up another company specifically to receive remuneration, that remuneration will be deemed to be remuneration received by him if that company is controlled by him.

5.13   Furthermore, if the company has nominated (either directly or indirectly) the director to be a director of another company, that other company is treated as if it were a subsidiary undertaking for the purposes of determining the amounts to be disclosed for directors' remuneration, compensation for loss of office and payments to third parties for directors' services. Accordingly, the director's remuneration and compensation for loss of office should include any amount he receives as a director of that other company (whether or not that other company is a subsidiary of the company). [SI 2008/409 3 Sch 11; SI 2008/410 5 Sch 14; SI 2008/410 8 Sch 16(1), 17(1)]. Any sums that the other company pays to third parties in respect of his services should be disclosed as sums paid to third parties.

Example – Nominated director of an associate

Company A has nominated one of its directors to the board of its associate, company B. Company B pays £20,000 per year to the director in respect of his services to that company. Does this £20,000 have to be disclosed as directors' remuneration in company A's financial statements?

The Companies Act 2006 requires disclosure of remuneration received by a director of a company for qualifying services, which includes services as a director of the company or its subsidiaries. This might appear to exclude services to associates, but paragraph 14 of Schedule 5 to SI 2008/410 (and paragraph 11 of Schedule 3 to SI 2008/409 for small companies), or for quoted companies paragraph 17(1) of Schedule 5 to SI 2008/410, states that reference to a subsidiary undertaking, in relation to a person who whilst a director of the company is also a director of any other undertaking by virtue of the company's nomination, includes that other undertaking whether or not it is in fact a subsidiary undertaking.

This means that because the director has been nominated by company A as a director of the associate, the associate is deemed for the purposes of directors' remuneration disclosure to be a subsidiary. The director is performing qualifying services for company A by being its representative on company B's board. Therefore, in this situation, the director must disclose to company A, as remuneration, the amount of £20,000 that he receives from company B. Company A will need to disclose, as directors' remuneration, the aggregate of the amount paid to the director in respect of his services as director of company A and the amount of £20,000 he receives from company B.

If, on the other hand, the amount of £20,000 is paid to company A (that is, as a sum to be accounted for to the company, see para 5.11) and not to the director personally, then this amount need not be included as directors' remuneration in company A's financial statements. However, company B will need to disclose the payment of £20,000 in its own financial statements as a sum paid to a third party in respect of the director's services.

Note that the answer would be the same if company B was not related to company A, but company A had nominated one of its directors to company B's board.

5.13.1   Further practical guidance in relation to group situations is provided in section VI, from paragraph 5.233 below.

Disclosure in which year

5.14 A director's remuneration that should be disclosed in the financial statements for a particular year is the remuneration receivable by the director in respect of that year, regardless of when it is paid to the director. [SI 2008/409 3 Sch 5(4); SI 2008/410 5 Sch 7(4); SI 2008/410 8 Sch 20(1)]. For example, if a bonus is receivable by a director in respect of services performed in year one, but is not paid to the director until year two, it is disclosable as that director's remuneration in year one.

5.15 In the case of remuneration that is receivable by a director in respect of a period that extends beyond the financial year, for example, a long-term incentive scheme covering a period of three years, where the only condition is for the director to remain in service, disclosure should be made in year three (but see para 5.20 below). [SI 2008/409 3 Sch 5(4); SI 2008/410 5 Sch 7(4); SI 2008/410 8 Sch 20(1)]. Whilst not explicitly stated, the implication of this is that where remuneration is receivable in respect of a period, be that a period of one year or more than one year, it should be disclosed when due, that is, in the year in which it becomes receivable, regardless of when it is paid.

[The next paragraph is 5.19.]

5.19 Where remuneration is not receivable in respect of a period, whether of a single financial year or a period of over one financial year, it should be disclosed in the financial statements of the period in which it is paid. This might apply, for instance, when a single *ex gratia* payment is made to a director that is unrelated to a financial year or other period. An example might be a payment made as compensation for a reduction in the length of a director's service contract.

5.20 One problem that sometimes arises in respect of long-term incentive schemes is where the performance period lasts three years, but a director must then remain with the company for a further period, say six months, before he becomes entitled to receive any amounts under the scheme. The question that arises in such a case is whether the amounts due under the scheme are receivable in respect of the three-year performance period and are, therefore, disclosable in the third year of the scheme, or whether they are receivable only after a further six months, when the additional service period has been completed, in which case they would be disclosable in the fourth year.

5.21 The answer to the question may depend on the particular terms of the scheme and on when the remuneration becomes a firm entitlement. If, for instance, the additional service period has no real effect in practice, and the director would receive the remuneration whether or not he stayed for the extra six months, this would imply that the substance was that the remuneration was effectively a firm entitlement in respect of the three-year performance period and should be disclosed in the third year. If, however, the additional service period was of real significance, for instance if the director would get nothing if he were to leave the company within that additional period, then it is probable that the remuneration should be disclosed in the fourth year.

5.22 In practice, there is some variation on the way that companies apply the rules to the situation described in paragraphs 5.20 and 5.21 above, with some companies preferring to disclose when all performance conditions have been satisfied, even when there is a further service period. For quoted companies, where the problem mainly arises, Schedule 8 to SI 2008/410 requires disclosure of full details of long-term incentive schemes, which means that, whichever approach is taken, there is still full disclosure of the benefits arising, or the benefits that have arisen, under such schemes during the period for which they operate. This is discussed further in paragraph 5.185.

5.23 The above rules apply to remuneration generally and also extend to compensation for loss of office.

Other matters

5.24 Under the 2006 Act, a company is permitted to end its financial year on the same day in the week rather than on the same date, if it wishes to (see further chapter 8). Therefore, a financial year (and, consequently, the financial statements) may cover a period slightly longer than one year. In this situation, the amounts disclosed for directors' remuneration are those in respect of the longer period, as explained in the following example.

Example – Remuneration for a 53 week period

A company has a 53 week financial year this year. Can the disclosure of directors' remuneration be given for a 52 week (365 day) period, rather than for 53 weeks?

For unquoted companies, paragraph 7(4) of Schedule 5 to SI 2008/410 (or paragraph 5(4) of Schedule 3 to SI 2008/409 for small companies) and for quoted companies paragraph 20(1) of Schedule 8 to SI 2008/410) require that the amounts of remuneration to be shown for any financial year are the sums receivable in respect of that year (whenever paid).

Section 390(3) of the Companies Act 2006 states that *"subsequent financial years begin with the day immediately following the end of the company's previous financial year and end with the last day of its next accounting reference period or such other date, not more than seven days before or after the end of that period, as the directors may determine"*. Therefore, the company's financial year is 53 weeks and so the amounts to be disclosed must be for the 53 weeks of the financial year.

As an analogy, if the company prepares statutory accounts for a short period (for example, nine months), the amounts to be disclosed under the Act is the remuneration for that period (that is, nine months).

5.24.1   Where a director is appointed during the year, only the remuneration while he is a director of the company is disclosable as director's remuneration, as explained in the example in paragraph 5.167.

5.24.2   If it is necessary to apportion remuneration and compensation for loss of office paid to a director between the matters in respect of which it has been paid or is receivable, the directors may apportion it in any way that they consider appropriate. [SI 2008/409 3 Sch 5(6); SI 2008/410 5 Sch 7(6); SI 2008/410 8 Sch 21].

5.25   In certain situations, directors' remuneration might not be included in the notes to the financial statements (or in the directors' remuneration report, in the case of a quoted company) for a period because either the director is liable to account for it to the company or to another group company, or because it is considered to be an expense allowance not chargeable to UK income tax. Where this is so, and these reasons are subsequently found not to be justified, the remuneration must be disclosed in a note to the first financial statements (or in the first directors' remuneration report, in the case of a quoted company) in which it is practicable for this to be done, and the remuneration must be identified separately. This also applies to compensation for loss of office. [SI 2008/409 3 Sch 5(5); SI 2008/410 5 Sch 7(5); SI 2008/410 8 Sch 20(2)].

Aggregate remuneration and other benefits — all companies

Aggregate remuneration and other benefits

5.26   The Act requires the following information to be disclosed in the notes to the annual financial statements:

- The aggregate amount of emoluments paid to or receivable by directors in respect of qualifying services. [SI 2008/409 3 Sch 1(1)(a); SI 2008/410 5 Sch 1(1)(a)].

- The aggregate of the amount of gains made by directors on the exercise of share options (but see para 5.28 below). [SI 2008/410 5 Sch 1(1)(b)].

- The aggregate of the following:

  - the amount of money paid to or receivable by directors under long-term incentive schemes in respect of qualifying services; and

  - the net value of assets (other than money and share options) received or receivable by directors under such schemes in respect of such services (but see para 5.28 below).

  [SI 2008/409 3 Sch 1(1)(b); SI 2008/410 5 Sch 1(1)(c)].

- The aggregate value of any company contributions paid, or treated as paid, to a pension scheme in respect of directors' qualifying services, being contributions by reference to which the rate or amount of any money purchase benefits that may become payable will be calculated. [SI 2008/410 5 Sch 1(1)(d)].

- In the case of each of the following:

  - money purchase schemes; and

  - defined benefit schemes.

The number of directors (if any) to whom retirement benefits are accruing under such schemes in respect of qualifying services. [SI 2008/409 3 Sch 2; SI 2008/410 5 Sch 1(2)].

5.27 The above requirements relate to *all* companies other than small companies reporting under SI 2008/409 (see further the Manual of Accounting – UK GAAP) with the following additional exception. Companies which are not quoted (see para 5.6.3) and are not listed on AIM do not have to disclose either the aggregate of the amount of gains made by the directors on the exercise of share options or the net value of shares received or receivable under long-term incentive schemes in respect of qualifying services. Instead, such companies must disclose:

■ the number of directors who exercised share options; and

■ the number of directors in respect of whose qualifying services shares were received or receivable under long-term incentive schemes.

[SI 2008/410 5 Sch 1(3)].

[The next paragraph is 5.31.]

5.31 Each of the elements of the disclosure described above is discussed in turn in the following paragraphs.

Aggregate remuneration

All companies

5.32 All companies (that is, quoted, and unquoted, including AIM) have to disclose aggregate remuneration paid to or receivable by directors in respect of qualifying services.

5.33 Qualifying services means:

■ Services as a director of the company.

■ Services as a director of any subsidiary undertaking of the company, during the time in which a person is a director of the company.

■ Services in connection with the management of the affairs of either the company or any subsidiary undertaking of the company, during the time in which a person is a director of the company.

[SI 2008/409 3 Sch 12(1); SI 2008/410 5 Sch 15(1)].

5.34 In addition, qualifying services includes services, while a director of the company, as a director of any other undertaking of which he is a director by virtue of the company's nomination (direct or indirect). [SI 2008/409 3 Sch 11(1); SI 2008/410 5 Sch 14(1)]. See further paragraph 5.13 above.

5.35 If an undertaking is a subsidiary undertaking at the time the service is rendered by the directors, it should be included even where the undertaking is no longer a subsidiary at the reporting date. [SI 2008/409 3 Sch 11(2); SI 2008/410 5 Sch 14(2)].

5.36 For this purpose, 'remuneration' paid to or receivable by a director includes not only his salary, but also the following:

■ Fees and bonuses.

■ Any expense allowances (to the extent that they are chargeable to UK income tax).

■ The estimated money value of any other benefits received otherwise than in cash (but see para 5.37 below).

■ Remuneration in respect of a person accepting office as director.

[SI 2008/409 3 Sch 7; SI 2008/410 5 Sch 9(1), 15(3)].

5.37 In this context, the term 'remuneration' does not include the value of share options granted to or exercised by directors. It does not include any company pension contributions paid on behalf of directors (although it does include contributions that directors themselves pay by way of a compulsory deduction from salary) nor any benefits to which directors are entitled under any pension scheme. Also excluded from the definition are money or other assets paid to or receivable by directors under long-term incentive schemes. [SI 2008/409 3 Sch 12(2); SI 2008/410 5 Sch 9(2)].

5.38 The reason for excluding those elements from the disclosure of aggregate remuneration is, quite simply, that they are picked up by separate disclosure requirements that are discussed below.

5.39 The term 'paid to or receivable by' is discussed from paragraph 5.14 above.

5.40 Whether the director receives remuneration for services as a director of the company or in connection with the management of its affairs is a question of fact. It should be presumed that all payments made to a director, except for reimbursement of expenses, will generally fall within one of these categories, unless it can clearly be demonstrated otherwise. However, an exception could be where payments have been made to a director in a self-employed or professional capacity. Consider the following example:

> **Example – Director paid on a self-employed basis**
>
> A director of a company is paid for technical services supplied on a 'self-employed persons' basis. How should this be disclosed?
>
> Provided that it can be clearly established that the fees are genuinely for technical services and that they are not connected with management services (which they might be if the director were a technical director), then the amounts paid need not be disclosed as remuneration. However, the transaction may need to be disclosed as a related party transaction (see the Manual of Accounting – UK GAAP or the Manual of Accounting – IFRS for the UK). In practice, however, it is often difficult to make such a precise distinction and the remuneration for other services is often included with directors' remuneration.

5.41 When considering directors' remuneration, there is no need to distinguish between a director's service contract and a contract for services that a director has with the company. Remuneration received in either capacity will fall to be disclosed in the company's financial statements as directors' remuneration. However, a director's service contract makes him essentially an employee of the company and, therefore, such remuneration will have to be included in staff costs. On the other hand, a contract for services puts the director in essentially the same position as a third party hired to do a particular job. Amounts invoiced to the company should be recognised as an expense, but should not be classified as 'staff costs'.

Benefits in kind

5.42 The estimated money value of a benefit in kind that must be included in directors' remuneration should be taken as the market value of the facility that is provided for the director's private benefit, less any contribution the director pays. The amount used to assess the taxable benefit should be used *only* where it is an approximation of the market value of the benefit. However, in practice the value of the taxable benefit is often a good starting point for considering the value that should be placed on the amounts for accounting disclosure purposes.

5.43 Where there is a tax concession such that part of a benefit is not taxable even though it is a benefit for the director (as opposed to a valid business expense), the value of the taxable benefit will not be an appropriate starting point. If there is a benefit to the director, the total amount receivable by a director is disclosable as a benefit in kind. The fact that the tax rules allow some of this benefit to be tax-free (for instance, certain relocation allowances) does not change the position.

5.44 Benefits in kind may include: provision of accommodation at below market rates; provision of a car or health benefit. Gains on exercise of share options and amounts or assets receivable under long term incentive schemes are dealt with separately (see para 5.47 below).

Example – Premium paid for director's life assurance cover

A company pays a premium to an insurance company to purchase life assurance cover for a director. This life cover is in addition to the life cover provided by the pension scheme and is an entirely separate arrangement. The beneficiary would be the next of kin of the director. How should this be disclosed for the purpose of directors' remuneration?

The premium should be included as a benefit in kind in arriving at the aggregate directors' remuneration and will be included in the aggregate of remuneration to be disclosed (for all companies) under paragraphs 1(1) and 7 of Schedule 3 to SI 2008/409 and paragraphs 1(1) and 9(1) of Schedule 5 to SI 2008/410. If the company is quoted the benefit would also be disclosed in the total of benefits received by the director, which is required to be shown separately in the table of individual directors' remuneration in the directors' remuneration report, together with the nature of the benefit (see further para 5.164). [SI 2008/410 8 Sch 7(1), 7(3)].

5.44.1   Where a company pays a director's tax liability on benefits, the amount disclosed in respect of benefits should be grossed up for the tax paid, that is, the amount disclosed should reflect the gross amount payable in cash to leave the director in the same position had the company not paid the tax on his behalf. For example, if the benefit received is £100,000 and the director is taxed at 40% (that is, the director would expect to receive a net amount of £60,000, even though this would be disclosed as £100,000 in the remuneration disclosure). However, where the company pays the tax, such that the benefit received is actually a net amount of £100,000, then the gross amount the director would receive is 100,000/(1-0.4) = £167,000 and hence it is the £167,000 that should be disclosed as part of the director's remuneration.

5.45   Whilst separate disclosure of benefits in kind is not required by SI 2008/409 or SI 2008/410, some companies do so. As noted in the example in paragraph 5.44 above, for quoted companies separate disclosure of benefits by individual director is required (see para 5.164 onwards).

5.46   Remuneration in respect of a person accepting office as director (see the last point in para 5.36) requires disclosure of incentive payments (so-called 'golden hellos') that are made by companies to attract people to join the board of directors.

Gains on share options and amounts receivable under long-term incentive schemes

Quoted and AIM companies

5.47   For quoted (see para 5.6.3) and AIM companies, separate totals for the aggregate of gains made by directors on exercising share options and for the aggregate of amounts of money and the net value of other assets received or receivable under long-term incentive schemes must be disclosed. [SI 2008/410 5 Sch 1(1)(b), (c)]. This disclosure requirement would be met if the information can be readily ascertained from other information provided – see further paragraph 5.72. An example of disclosure of gains made on the exercise of share options is given in Table 5.1.

Table 5.1 – Gains made on the exercise of share options and amounts receivable under long-term incentive plans

ARM Holdings plc – Annual Report & Accounts – 31 December 2011

Notes to the financial statements (extract)

3 Key management compensation and directors' emoluments (extract)

Directors' emoluments
The aggregate emoluments of the directors of the Company are set out below:

	2011 £'000	2010 £'000
Aggregate emoluments in respect of qualifying services	5,526	4,632
Aggregate Group pension contributions to money purchase schemes	182	226
Aggregate gains on exercise of share options	1,096	6,178
Aggregate amounts receivable under the Long Term Incentive Plan	24,195	5,133
	30,999	**16,169**

Detailed disclosures of directors' emoluments are shown on page 92. Details of directors' interests in share options and awards are shown on pages 87 to 91 which form part of the financial statements.

5.48   The amount of the gain on exercising share options (quoted and AIM companies only) is the difference between market price of the shares on the day of exercise and the price actually paid for the shares. [SI 2008/410 8 Sch 17(1)].

Example – Market price of shares

A quoted company (see para 5.6.3 for definition) is disclosing gains on exercise of directors' share options in accordance with the Companies Act disclosure rules. In the rules the gain is defined as the difference between the market price of the shares on the day the option was exercised and the exercise price. A company wishes to know what price it should take as market price, as there was considerable price movement on the day in question, for instance can the definition in taxes legislation be used?

We consider that the mid-market price is the price that should be used. By way of support for this the FSA Listing Rules define market value as the middle market quotation for a share as derived from the Daily Official List of the London Stock Exchange. [LR 9.5.10R (2)]. It seems to us this is a straight forward and sensible interpretation of the term 'market value' in the absence of a more precise definition in the Companies Act. The definition of market value in taxes legislation is not relevant to this disclosure issue.

5.49   Share options granted in respect of a person's accepting office as a director are to be treated as share options granted in respect of that person's services as a director. [SI 2008/410 5 Sch 15(3)]. Accordingly, the exercise of such options requires disclosure by quoted and AIM companies of the amount of the gain made in accordance with the requirement in paragraph 5.47 above.

Unquoted companies excluding companies listed on AIM

5.50   Unquoted companies, excluding companies listed on AIM, are not required to include the amount of gains made by directors on the exercise of share options. Nor do they have to include the value of any shares received or receivable under long-term incentive schemes. Instead they should give the aggregate amount of money and net value of other assets (excluding shares) received and receivable under long-term incentive schemes and disclose separately:

■   The number of directors who exercised share options.

■   The number of directors in respect of whose qualifying services shares were received or receivable under long-term incentive schemes.

[SI 2008/410 5 Sch 1(3)].

This does not apply to small companies reporting under SI 2008/409.

Example – Exercise of share options by director of unquoted company

A director of an unquoted subsidiary of a quoted company (see para 5.6.3 for definition) has share options convertible into shares of the parent company. The director has exercised some of these options in the year. Do the gains on the exercise (which can be measured because the parent is quoted) need to be disclosed in the subsidiary's financial statements in the directors' remuneration note under the disclosure rules set out in Schedule 5 to SI 2008/410?

No. The Act's disclosure rules for unquoted companies (unless they are AIM companies) specifically exclude gains on the exercise of share options, even if they can be measured. Instead, the subsidiary should disclose the number of directors who exercised share options. [SI 2008/410 5 Sch 1(3)]. A share option is defined as the right to acquire shares; 'shares' in this context includes shares in any group company. [SI 2008/410 5 Sch 12].

Similarly, for an unquoted company (unless it is an AIM company), disclosure of the highest-paid director's remuneration does not include an amount for gains on exercise of share options, but the fact that the highest-paid director exercised options must be disclosed. [SI 2008/410 5 Sch 2(3)(a)].

5.51   The accounting implications under IFRS 2 and FRS 20, of share options in a group situation are dealt with in the Manual of Accounting – IFRS for the UK and the Manual of Accounting – UK GAAP.

5.52   In addition, for companies reporting under IFRS, IAS 24, requires disclosure of remuneration (in total and split into five categories) for key management personnel in respect of services provided to the entity. One of the categories is share-based payment and would include the share options, because the remuneration includes *"all forms of consideration paid, payable or provided by the entity, or on behalf of the entity in exchange for services rendered to the entity"*. The options are provided by the quoted parent to the director of the subsidiary in return for his services to the subsidiary. Therefore, in so far as it relates to directors and key managers, amounts charged in the subsidiary's financial statements under IFRS 2 would be disclosed in the subsidiary's financial statements as part of key management personnel compensation under the category 'share-based payment'. (If the subsidiary is a UK GAAP reporter, this disclosure would not be required as it is not required by FRS 8.)

Definitions

5.53 Share options are defined as the right to acquire shares. [SI 2008/409 3 Sch 9; SI 2008/410 5 Sch 12(b)]. We interpret this to include the right to acquire shares through subscription, by way of gift, by purchasing shares from an ESOP or indeed any other form of acquisition. It should be noted that there is a difference between the definition in Schedule 3 to SI 2008/409 and Schedule 5 to SI 2008/410 of share options for the purpose of disclosure of aggregate gains and the definition in Schedule 8 to SI 2008/410 for the purpose of disclosure of individual directors' share options in the directors' remuneration report. See further paragraph 5.178.

5.54 A long-term incentive scheme is defined as *"an agreement or arrangement (a) under which money or other assets may become receivable by a director, and (b) which includes one or more qualifying conditions with respect to service or performance which cannot be fulfilled within a single financial year"*. [SI 2008/409 3 Sch 8(1); SI 2008/410 5 Sch 11(1)]. The definition specifically excludes:

■ Bonuses the amount of which is determined by reference to service or performance within a single financial year.

■ Compensation for loss of office, payments for breach of contract and other termination payments.

■ Retirement benefits.

[SI 2008/409 3 Sch 8(2); SI 2008/410 5 Sch 11(2)].

5.55 Amounts received or receivable means amounts that become due to directors during the financial year. For example, if a long-term incentive scheme runs for three years and amounts or other assets become due to the directors at the end of the third year, they are disclosable in that year, even if they are not actually paid over to or received by the directors until the following year (see from para 5.14 above). (For long term incentive schemes, the disclosures required for an unquoted company are different from the disclosures required in tabular form for a quoted company. See further paragraph 5.188.1.)

5.56 Other assets received or receivable under long-term incentive schemes may include all sorts of non-cash items, for example, diamonds, gold, wine or works of art. Most commonly, however, such assets will be in the form of shares. Shares are defined as shares (whether allotted or not) in the company, or any undertaking which is a group undertaking in relation to the company and it includes share warrants. [SI 2008/409 3 Sch 9(a); SI 2008/410 5 Sch 12(a)]. A share warrant is a warrant that states that the bearer of the warrant is entitled to the shares specified in it. The phrase *'any undertaking which is a group undertaking in relation to the company'* would, we believe, include the parent undertaking and fellow subsidiary undertakings as well as subsidiary undertakings of the company. The 'value' of the shares received or receivable is defined elsewhere in the Act as the market price of the shares on the day the shares are received or receivable. [SI 2008/410 8 Sch 17(1)].

5.57 The net value of other assets received or receivable by a director under a long-term incentive scheme means the value after deducting any money paid or other value given by the director. [SI 2008/409 3 Sch 12(1); SI 2008/410 5 Sch 15(1)].

Pension contributions

5.58 Company pension contributions do not form part of aggregate remuneration described from paragraph 5.32 above. Instead, the Act requires separate disclosure of the aggregate value of company contributions paid, or treated as paid, to a money purchase pension scheme in respect of directors' qualifying services by a person other than the director. Contributions mean those according to which the rate or amount of any money purchase benefits that may become payable will be calculated. [SI 2008/409 3 Sch 1(1)(c); SI 2008/410 5 Sch 1(1)(d)].

5.59 In addition, a company must separately disclose the number of directors to whom retirement benefits are accruing under money purchase schemes and under defined benefit schemes in respect of qualifying services. [SI 2008/409 3 Sch 1(2); SI 2008/410 5 Sch 1(2)].

5.60 Although disclosure of contributions to money purchase schemes gives a reasonable indication of the benefit to a director, disclosure of contributions to defined benefit schemes may often not do so, as the level of funding will depend upon whether the scheme is in surplus or deficit. Schedule 8 to SI 2008/410 requires quoted companies (see para 5.6.3) to make detailed disclosures about directors' pension entitlements under defined benefit schemes (see section IV below). Because of the cost of obtaining information to satisfy the requirements of Schedule 8 to SI 2008/410, which would be considered unduly onerous for unquoted companies, disclosure of the number of directors to whom benefits are accruing must be disclosed to, at least, put members on notice that such schemes exist.

5.61 Pension schemes are defined as meaning the same as a retirement benefits scheme under section 611 of the Income and Corporation Taxes Act 1988 (ICTA). [SI 2008/409 3 Sch 10(1); SI 2008/410 5 Sch 13(1)]. Section 611 of ICTA defines a retirement benefits scheme as a scheme for the provision of benefits consisting of or including relevant benefits, but not including any national scheme providing such benefits. References to a scheme include references to a deed, agreement, series of agreements or other arrangements providing for relevant benefits notwithstanding that it relates or they relate only to:

- A small number of employees, or to a single employee (including company payments to personal pension plans – see example below).

- The payments of a pension starting immediately on the making of the arrangements.

> **Example – Payments to director's personal pension plan**
>
> A company makes a payment to a personal pension plan for one if its directors. The pension plan was arranged by the director some time before joining the company. Should these payments be disclosed under the Companies Act 2006 requirement to disclose company contributions to money purchase schemes?
>
> Yes, if the company makes the payments to the pension scheme, the payments should be disclosed in the aggregate of company contributions to money purchase schemes in respect of directors' qualifying services. [SI 2008/409 3 Sch 1(1)(c); SI 2008/410 5 Sch 1(1)(d)]. (If the company is quoted there should also be disclosure of the contributions in respect of each individual director – see further para 5.194.)

5.62 The definition of pension schemes above is generally interpreted as extending to unfunded pension arrangements. Accordingly, where a company makes provisions in respect of unfunded pensions of a money purchase type, it should disclose the amounts provided as contributions to money purchase schemes. Where it makes provisions in respect of unfunded pensions of a defined benefit type, it should take the related benefits provided to directors into account when determining the amounts to be disclosed in respect of directors' pension entitlements under defined benefit schemes.

5.63 Retirement benefits has the meaning given by section 612 of ICTA 1988. [SI 2008/409 3 Sch 10(1); SI 2008/410 5 Sch 13(1)]. That is, any pension, lump sum, gratuity or other like benefit given or to be given:

- on retirement; or

- on death; or

- in anticipation of retirement; or

- in connection with past service, after retirement or death; or

- to be given on or in anticipation of or in connection with any change in the nature of the service of the employee in question;

except that it does not include any benefit which is to be afforded solely by reason of the disablement by accident of a person occurring during his service or of his death by accident so occurring and for no other reason.

5.64 'Money purchase benefits' for the purpose of the requirement set out in paragraph 5.58 above means retirement benefits payable under a pension scheme the rate or amount of which is calculated by reference to payments made, or treated as made, by the director or by any other person in respect of the director and which are not average salary benefits. [SI 2008/409 3 Sch 10(3); SI 2008/410 5 Sch 13(4)].

5.65 'Company contributions' do not have to be paid by the company itself as the definition states that the term means any payments (including insurance premiums) made, or treated as made to the scheme in respect of the director by a person other than the director. [SI 2008/409 3 Sch 10(2); SI 2008/410 5 Sch 13(3)]. Thus, for instance, contributions paid by the company's parent undertaking would qualify for disclosure as company contributions.

5.66 A 'money purchase scheme' for the purpose of the requirement set out in paragraph 5.59 above means a pension scheme under which all of the benefits that may become payable to or in respect of the director are money purchase benefits. A 'defined benefit scheme' is a pension scheme that is not a money purchase scheme. [SI 2008/409 3 Sch 10(3); SI 2008/410 5 Sch 13(4)].

5.66.1 The disclosure for the purpose of directors' remuneration is based on the legal form of the pension scheme. This is particularly relevant where a company does not account for a pension scheme as defined benefit (where it is entitled to an exemption in the relevant accounting standard for pensions), as illustrated in the following example.

> **Example – Industry-wide pension scheme**
>
> Company F, a private company reporting under SI 2008/410, participates in an industry-wide defined benefit pension scheme. Company F is unable to identify its share of the scheme's underlying assets and liabilities and has taken the exemption available to it to account for the scheme as a defined contribution scheme, with the appropriate disclosure.
>
> In the disclosure of directors' remuneration required by the Companies Act 2006, should the scheme be treated as a defined contribution scheme so that the disclosures are consistent?
>
> The disclosure of the directors' remuneration required for a private company by Schedule 5 to SI 2008/410 is determined by the pension scheme's legal form and not by the accounting treatment. Company F should not make disclosure of the contributions paid to the industry-wide scheme as 'company contributions to money purchase schemes'.
>
> Disclosure should be made of the number of directors to whom benefits are accruing under the defined benefit scheme and, if the aggregate remuneration of the directors exceeds £200,000, the accrued benefit and accrued lump sum at the end of the year for the highest paid director. [SI 2008/410 5 Sch 1(2)(b), 2(2)].
>
> It may be useful to include some disclosure in the directors' remuneration note to the financial statements to explain the apparent inconsistency.

5.67 Where a pension scheme is a hybrid scheme and provides that any benefits that become payable will be the greater of money purchase benefits as determined under the scheme and defined benefits as determined, then the company may elect to treat the scheme as a money purchase scheme or as a defined benefit scheme, whichever seems more likely at the end of the financial year. [SI 2008/409 3Sch 10(4); SI 2008/410 5 Sch 13(6)].

5.68 The effect of the provision in the preceding paragraph is that where a pension scheme has both money purchase and defined benefit elements the company has an option as to how directors' remuneration disclosure is made. It can either take advantage of the provision and classify the scheme as money purchase or defined benefit in its entirety according to the type of benefits which appear to be higher in respect of the director at the end of the year. If the scheme is classified as a money purchase arrangement, the relevant disclosures as described in paragraph 5.58 above are made. If the scheme is classified as a defined benefit arrangement, the disclosure required by paragraph 5.59 is made.

5.69 Alternatively, the company can elect not to take advantage of the option and make separate disclosure of information relating to the money purchase element of the scheme following the requirement in paragraph 5.58 above. If this is done then the scheme is counted as a defined benefit scheme for the purpose of the requirement in paragraph 5.59.

5.70 The choice between the two alternatives may also be influenced by the requirement (discussed below from para 5.84) to disclose the pension entitlement of the highest paid director under any defined benefit scheme.

5.71 For the purpose of determining whether a pension scheme is a money purchase or defined benefit scheme any death in service benefits provided by the scheme are disregarded. [SI 2008/409 3 Sch 10(5); SI 2008/410 5 Sch 13(7)].

General — readily ascertainable from other information

5.72 Where the information discussed in the above sections is readily ascertainable from the other information that is shown, this satisfies the disclosure requirements. [SI 2008/409 3 Sch 4(2); SI 2008/410 5

Sch 6(2)]. For example, a quoted company that gives detailed information by individual director in its directors' remuneration report (as required by Schedule 8 to SI 2008/410) could satisfy the Schedule 5 to SI 2008/410 requirement for disclosure of the aggregate remuneration (described above) if the total is readily ascertainable, provided that there is a cross-reference from the notes to the financial statements (where the Schedule 5 to SI 2008/410 disclosure is required to be given) to the relevant part of the directors' remuneration report.

[The next paragraph is 5.74.]

Section II — Unquoted companies (including AIM companies)

5.74 In addition to the requirements described in section I, unquoted companies (other than small companies reporting under SI 2008/409 but including companies listed on AIM) must comply with the following requirements. Quoted companies (for definition see para 5.6.3) must comply instead with the requirements described in section IV.

Highest paid director's emoluments and other benefits

5.75 SI 2008/410 requires details of the highest paid director's emoluments and other benefits to be disclosed.

5.76 Quoted companies have to give details of individual directors' emoluments and other benefits (see section IV below) and so for them there is no requirement to give details of the highest paid director's emoluments separately, as such a requirement would be superfluous.

5.77 For unquoted (and AIM) companies the requirement to disclose additional information on the highest paid director enables the reader of the financial statements at least to determine the maximum amounts received or receivable by any director and thus to assess and evaluate this against company performance or whichever other criteria the reader chooses. Requirements recently introduced for AIM companies (see from para 5.120.1) include a breakdown of remuneration by individual director, but the three disclosure categories are slightly different from those required by the Act for highest paid director (see para 5.78), hence, a company meeting the AIM requirements is likely to need additional disclosure to meet the highest paid director disclosure requirements.

Ascertaining the highest paid director

5.78 There is a *de minimis* level below which the highest paid director's emoluments and other benefits need not be disclosed. If the total of the following items shown for all directors exceeds or is equal to £200,000, the information on the highest paid director must be given. These items are:

■ Aggregate emoluments paid to or receivable by directors in respect of qualifying services.

■ Aggregate amount of gains made by directors on exercise of share options (but see para 5.82).

■ Aggregate amount of (a) money paid to or receivable by directors under long-term incentive schemes in respect of qualifying services and (b) net value of assets (other than money and share options) received or receivable by directors under such schemes in respect of such services (but see para 5.82).

[SI 2008/410 5 Sch 2(1)].

5.79 The highest paid director is the director with the greatest part of the total calculated in paragraph 5.78 above. [SI 2008/410 5 Sch 10]. Note that only the elements listed above are included in the calculation. Other items, for example compensation for loss of office and company pension contributions, are not included in determining the highest paid director.

5.80 The total of the amounts listed in paragraph 5.78 is the figure to be taken into account in determining whether the £200,000 level is reached or exceeded.

5.81 The threshold figure of £200,000 is not increased or decreased when the financial year for which financial statements are prepared exceeds or is less than 12 months. This is because it is determined by reference to the actual figures disclosed (see para 5.78 above) which are those for the financial period, whether that period is 12 months or not.

5.82   For unquoted companies other than companies listed on AIM, the items described do not include the amounts of gains made on exercise of share options or the value of shares received under long-term incentive schemes, because these amounts do not have to be calculated or disclosed by such unquoted companies (see para 5.28 above).

Disclosure

5.83   If the limit of £200,000 is reached or exceeded, the following two amounts must be disclosed in respect of the highest paid director:

- The total of the aggregate amounts described in paragraph 5.78 above that is attributable to the director.

- The amount of any company contributions paid, or treated as paid to a money purchase pension scheme in respect of the director's qualifying services.

[SI 2008/410 5 Sch 2(1)].

5.84   If the highest paid director has also participated in a defined benefit pension scheme, in respect of his qualifying services during the year, then the following information must also be disclosed:

- The amount at the end of the year of his accrued pension.

- Where applicable, the amount at the end of the year of his accrued lump sum.

[SI 2008/410 5 Sch 2(2)].

5.85   Where a company is unquoted and not listed on AIM and, therefore, does not include details of gains on options exercised or the value of shares awarded under long-term incentive schemes, it must disclose:

- Whether the highest paid director exercised any share options.

- Whether any shares were received or receivable by that director in respect of qualifying services under a long-term incentive scheme.

[SI 2008/410 5 Sch 2(3)].

5.86   However, if the director has not been involved in any such transactions there is no need to state that fact. [SI 2008/410 5 Sch 2(4)].

5.86.1   Comparative figures are required for the director's emoluments information in the normal way – see paragraph 5.92 onwards below.

'Accrued pension' and 'accrued lump sum'

5.87   The terms 'accrued pension' and 'accrued lump sum' mean the amount of the annual pension and the amount of the lump sum that would be payable to the director when he reaches normal pension age if:

- He had left the company's service at the end of the financial year.

- There were no increase in the general level of prices during the period from the end of the year to the director's pension age.

- There was no question of there being any commutation of the pension or inverse commutation of the lump sum.

- Any amounts attributable to voluntary contributions (AVCs) paid by the director to the scheme, and any money purchase benefits payable under the scheme were disregarded.

[SI 2008/410 5 Sch 13(2)].

5.88   'Normal pension age' is the earliest date at which the director is entitled to receive a full pension on retirement of an amount determined without reduction to take account of its payment before a later age (but disregarding any entitlement to pension upon retirement in the event of illness, incapacity or redundancy). [SI 2008/410 5 Sch 13(5)]. This means that a pension is not a 'full pension' if the benefits are reduced to take account of early payment and that any entitlement in the event of illness, incapacity or redundancy is disregarded for these purposes.

5.89 The third bullet point in paragraph 5.87, which refers to commutation of the pension or inverse commutation of the lump sum, should be interpreted as follows. Disclosure of the amount of accrued lump sum should only be made where, under the pension scheme rules, the director will automatically receive a lump sum on retirement. No disclosure should be made of a lump sum when a lump sum may be payable by way of commutation (that is, reduction) of rights to an annual pension. In the same way, disclosure of the amount of accrued pension should not include any reverse commutation of a lump sum entitlement. In practice, schemes that have both lump sums and pensions are extremely rare outside the public sector.

5.90 If, for example, a director was entitled at the end of the year to an accrued pension of £30,000, but could commute that into a pension of £20,000 per annum and a lump sum of £100,000, the only disclosure to be made would be the accrued pension of £30,000. If he was entitled to a pension of £30,000 and a lump sum of £50,000 (without any reduction in the pension), both figures would be disclosed. If he was entitled to a pension of £30,000 and a lump sum of £50,000, but could commute the lump sum such that he could instead take a pension of £35,000 and no lump sum, then the figures to be disclosed would be £30,000 and £50,000, that is ignoring the right to the reverse commutation of the lump sum.

Example 1 – Accrued pension (no entitlement to lump sum)

The highest paid director is 50 at the beginning of the year. He joined the company when he was 40 and is entitled to retire at 60. His salary in the previous year was £120,000 per annum. In the current year his salary is also £120,000. His maximum pension is 20/30 of his final salary after 20 years, but he has no entitlement to a lump sum (although he may commute part of his pension and take a lump sum in place of the amount commuted).

The pension accrual would be calculated as follows:

Accrued pension at the end of the previous year	$10/30 \times £120,000 = £40,000$
Accrued pension at the end of the current year	$11/30 \times £120,000 = £44,000$
The disclosure would, therefore, be:	
Accrued pension of the highest paid director	£44,000 (previous year £40,000)

Example 2 – Accrued pension and lump sum

The highest paid director is 50 at the beginning of the year. He joined the company at 20 and is entitled to retire at 60. His salary in the previous year was £150,000 and is £160,000 in the current year. His maximum pension is 40/80 of his final salary after 40 years and he is also entitled to a maximum lump sum of 120/80 of his final salary after 40 years. (He may commute the lump sum by taking an increased pension instead of all or part of the lump sum.)

The pension accrued and accrual of the lump sum entitlement would be as follows:

Accrued pension at the end of the previous year	$30/80 \times £150,000 = £56,250$
Accrued pension at the end of the current year	$31/80 \times £160,000 = £62,000$
Accrued lump sum at the end of the previous year	90 (being $120 \times 30/40$ years)$/80 \times £150,000 = £168,750$
Accrued lump sum at the end of the current year	93 (being $120 \times 31/40$ years)$/80 \times £160,000 = £186,000$
The disclosure would, therefore, be:	
Accrued pension of highest paid director	£62,000 (previous year £56,250)
Accrued lump sum of highest paid director	£186,000 (previous year £168,750)

5.90.1 The examples below consider the implications for disclosure in respect of the highest paid director's pension entitlements when the director is appointed or retires in the year.

Example 1 – Director appointed in the year

A director was appointed during the year. He had previously been an employee of the (unquoted) company for many years. He is the highest paid director. In disclosing his accrued pension entitlement (in accordance with the requirements of Schedule 5 to SI 2008/410 for unquoted companies) should it be calculated on the basis of the period for which he has been a director or on the basis of the whole period for which he has been both an employee and a director?

The accrued pension entitlement disclosed under Schedule 5 to SI 2008/410 should be calculated and disclosed, based on the whole period of his service as an employee and a director. However, the company could add a note to explain how much of the entitlement was earned prior to his becoming a director.

This is further explained in the similar example for a quoted company – see further paragraph 5.203.

Example 2 – Director retires in the year

The highest paid director of an unquoted company retired during the year and started drawing his pension. What should be disclosed as the pension entitlement of the highest paid director at the year end under Schedule 5 to SI 2008/410?

For the purposes of the Schedule 5 to SI 2008/410 disclosure, the amount of the annual pension payable to the director should be disclosed, because up until his retirement he performed qualifying services by reference to which the final pension was calculated. A note could be given to explain that the figure disclosed was the pension entitlement at the date of retirement.

Examples of disclosure

5.90.2   The examples below illustrate disclosures in respect of the highest paid director.

Example 1 – Disclosure for highest-paid director (AIM company)

An example of disclosure in respect of the highest paid director that incorporates all of the above elements would be as follows for an AIM company:

Highest paid director	20X2	20X1
	£	£
Aggregate emoluments, gains on share options exercised and benefits under long-term incentive schemes	200,000	180,000
Company pension contributions to money purchase scheme	2,000	2,000
Defined benefit scheme:		
Accrued pension at end of year	30,000	25,000
Accrued lump sum at end of year	60,000	50,000

Example 2 – Disclosure for highest-paid director (unquoted company)

For an unquoted company that is not listed on AIM disclosure that incorporates all the above elements would be:

Highest paid director	20X2	20X1
	£	£
Aggregate emoluments and benefits (excluding gains on exercise of share options and value of shares received) under long-term incentive schemes	250,000	240,000
Company pension contributions to money purchase scheme	2,000	2,000
Defined benefit scheme:		
Accrued pension at end of year	60,000	53,000
Accrued lump sum at end of year	100,000	90,000

The highest paid director exercised share options during the year and received shares under the executive long-term incentive scheme.

General – readily ascertainable from other information

5.91   Where information on the highest paid director's emoluments is readily ascertainable from the other information that is shown, this satisfies the disclosure requirements. [SI 2008/410 5 Sch 6(2)].

Comparative figures

5.92   Comparative figures are required for the highest paid director's emoluments information in the normal way.

5.92.1   Where the highest paid director in the current year was not the highest paid in the previous year, we consider that the comparative figure disclosed should be the emoluments of the actual highest paid director last year. Therefore, the comparative figures may relate to a different person from the highest paid director this year. Where this is the case, the company may wish to indicate this in the disclosure.

5.92.2   Where a company reaches the £200,000 threshold (see para 5.78) in the current year and so is required to disclose the highest paid director's emoluments, the requirement to disclose comparatives applies even where the company did not reach the £200,000 threshold in the previous year and the information has not previously been disclosed.

5.92.3 Where a company is below the £200,000 threshold in the current year, it is not required to disclose the highest paid director's emoluments in the current year. However, if the company reached the £200,000 threshold in the prior year, our view is that it will not be exempt from disclosure for that year and so the comparative should be disclosed, together with an explanation that the company is exempt from disclosure in the current year. Furthermore, if the company is likely to reach the £200,000 threshold in the next year, it will be required to disclose information for that year with comparatives (see para 5.92.1). Therefore, the company should consider giving the disclosure for the current year, so that this is then available for the comparatives in next year's financial statements.

5.92.4 The above requirements for disclosure of comparatives in respect of the highest paid director's emoluments are summarised in the table below.

Current year	Prior year	Disclosure
£200,000 or more	£200,000 or more	Disclose highest paid director's emoluments for both years.
£200,000 or more	Less than £200,000	Disclose highest paid director's emoluments for both years (para 5.92.2).
Less than £200,000	£200,000 or more	No disclosure of highest paid director's emoluments for current year, but comparative disclosure required for prior year (para 5.92.3).
Less than £200,000	Less than £200,000	No disclosure of highest paid director's emoluments for both years.

Excess retirement benefits of directors and past directors

5.93 Except for small companies reporting under SI 2008/409, if retirement benefits paid to or receivable by directors or past directors are in excess of the retirement benefits to which they were entitled at the time when the benefits first became payable or 31 March 1997 (whichever is the later) the notes must disclose the aggregate amount of:

■ The amount of the excess benefits paid to or receivable by directors under pension schemes.

■ The amount of the excess benefits paid to or receivable by past directors, again under pension schemes.

[SI 2008/410 5 Sch 3(1)].

5.94 The excess amounts referred to above do not include amounts paid or receivable if:

■ The scheme's funding was such that the amounts were or could have been paid without recourse to additional contributions; and

■ The amounts were paid to or receivable by all pensioner members of the scheme on the same basis ('pensioner members' being persons entitled to the present payment of retirement benefits under the scheme).

[SI 2008/410 5 Sch 3(2), 3(3)].

5.95 The exception described above means that the excess retirement benefits disclosed do not include retirement benefits paid to all pensioners on the same basis out of an adequately funded pension scheme.

5.96 'Retirement benefits' for the purpose of the above includes benefits otherwise than in cash, and where benefits other than in cash are given the amount should be calculated as their estimated money value. The nature of any such benefit should also be disclosed. [SI 2008/410 5 Sch 3(4)].

Compensation for loss of office

5.97 Disclosure must be made of the aggregate amount of any compensation received or receivable by directors or past directors in respect of loss of office. [SI 2008/409 3 Sch 2(1); SI 2008/410 5 Sch 4(1)]. This disclosure should include amounts received or receivable in respect of the loss of office by the director of the reporting company. It should also include amounts received or receivable in respect of loss, while a director of the reporting company or in connection with ceasing to be a director of that company, of office as a director of any subsidiary undertaking or of any office that involved management of the affairs of the company or of any subsidiary undertaking. [SI 2008/409 3 Sch 2(2); SI 2008/410 5 Sch 4(2)]. 'Subsidiary undertaking' includes an undertaking at the time the services were rendered and a subsidiary undertaking immediately before the loss of office as a director. It also includes an undertaking where the director was a director, whilst being a director of the company, by virtue of the company's nomination (direct or indirect), whether or not it was in fact a subsidiary undertaking. [SI 2008/409 3 Sch 11; SI 2008/410 5 Sch 14].

5.98   Compensation for loss of office includes compensation for or in connection with a person's retirement from office. Where such retirement is caused by a breach of the person's contract with the company or with a subsidiary undertaking compensation includes payments made by way of damages for the breach or payments made in settlement or compromise of any claim in respect of the breach. [SI 2008/409 3 Sch 2(2); SI 2008/410 5 Sch 4(3)].

General – readily ascertainable from other information

5.99   Where information on compensation for loss of office is readily ascertainable from the other information that is shown this satisfies the disclosure requirements. [SI 2008/409 3 Sch 4(2); SI 2008/410 5 Sch 6(2)]. For example, if compensation had been paid to two people and each person's compensation is shown separately, but the aggregate can be readily ascertained this would satisfy the requirement to disclose the aggregate.

Pension scheme top ups

5.100   We consider that a payment made to top up a pension scheme for the benefit of a director on his retirement is disclosable as it is effectively a benefit in kind (see para 5.102 below). This would be so even if the top up were funded out of an existing scheme surplus [SI 2008/409 3 Sch 5(2); SI 2008/410 5 Sch 7(2)], because the reduction in the surplus would involve the company paying increased contributions to the scheme and the top up is, therefore, even in that case, indirectly a cost to the company.

Example – Enhanced pension on retirement

A director retired in the year and as part of his leaving package the company enhanced his pension by giving him extra years of pensionable service. The enhancement was funded out of a surplus in the company's pension scheme and the capital value of the added pension entitlement was £250,000. How should this be disclosed in the financial statements? Would the answer be different if the company had paid £250,000 into the pension scheme?

Since the pension enhancement was given in connection with the director's retirement, it should be included as part of the director's compensation for loss of office for disclosure under SI 2008/410. The amount to be disclosed would be £250,000, the capital value of the increase, because this is the value of the benefit to the retiring director. The disclosure would be the same, irrespective of whether the director's enhanced pension was funded out of a surplus in the scheme or by a special company contribution to the scheme.

5.101   An example of disclosure of a top up payment made by the company is given in Table 5.2.

Table 5.2 – Top up payment

XYZ Group Limited – Annual Report – 31 March 20X1

Directors' emoluments (extract)

During the year, Mr X, the previous chief executive, left the company. Mr X had a service contract with the company terminable by the company on one years' notice. The company has agreed to pay Mr X as compensation for loss of office an amount approximately equivalent to one year's salary and other benefits. This amount was £398,400, which is subject to deduction of tax, and includes a sum of £60,000 in respect of Mr X's pension arrangements.

(Note: This example is made up, but includes features from a real example of disclosure.)

Benefits in kind

5.102   In addition to any monetary payment, the term compensation for loss of office includes benefits received or receivable otherwise than in cash. The value of the benefit should be determined according to its estimated money value. [SI 2008/410 5 Sch 4(4)]. Except for small companies reporting under S1 2008/409 where compensation is given in kind, the company's financial statements should disclose its nature. [SI 2008/

410 5 Sch 4(4)]. For example, the compensation might be the gift to the director of a car that he had previously used, but that was owned by the company. In this situation, the money value of the car and the fact that the compensation is in the form of a car will have to be disclosed. Normally, the market value of the car at the time of transfer should be used for this purpose. If, however, compensation includes both cash and a car, only the nature and not the amount of the benefit relating to the car needs to be separately disclosed. The cash and the amount of the benefit may be shown as one figure.

Ex gratia payments

5.103   The statutory description of 'compensation to directors for loss of office' is widely drawn. In deciding whether compensation to a director or a former director is required to be disclosed, regard should be had to both the nature of the compensation and the circumstances in which it was made, rather than just to the description the company gives to it. For example, *'ex gratia'* payments made on either a director's retirement or his removal from office can be regarded not as gratuitous payments, but as payments in compensation for loss of office and they should be disclosed as such.

Payments made on retirement

5.104   In some cases, directors may have terms in their service contracts which entitle them to continue to receive remuneration for a period after they cease to be directors, perhaps in their capacity as employees. In other cases, they may have more than one service contract with different companies in a group. In such cases, the company may be obliged to make payments for periods after the directors cease to act as directors of the parent company. Where such arrangements exist or where they are terminated by payment of an additional lump sum on retirement as director we consider that the amounts should be disclosed as part of the compensation for loss of office disclosure.

5.105   Additionally, on retirement a director might enter into a consultancy agreement with a company whereby he is paid an annual retainer for one or more years. Again we consider that such arrangements should be disclosed. In some cases, where genuine services are to be provided, disclosure may be as a transaction in which a director is interested (caught by related party disclosures). In others where no genuine services will be provided or the services to be provided have a fair value that is less than the compensation payable by the company, we consider that the amounts payable under the arrangement are, in substance, compensation for loss of office. For quoted companies, see also paragraph 5.214.

5.106   A further benefit sometimes allowed to directors on retirement is that they may retain share options previously granted to them where such options would normally lapse on their leaving the company. Alternatively, they may be entitled to keep the options as a result of the terms in their service contract. Again, where there is a benefit to the retiring director to which he is not entitled under the scheme rules, the value of this benefit should be included in 'compensation' for loss of office and its nature disclosed in accordance with paragraph 5.102, disclosure should be made (see Table 5.3).

5.107   Further examples of disclosure of compensation which include the above features are set out in Tables 5.3 to 5.6 below.

Table 5.3 – Compensation for loss of office

XYZ plc (AIM company) – Annual Report and Accounts – 30 June 20X1

Remuneration of directors (extract)

Mr X resigned as a Director on 16th February 20X1 and his contracts of employment with the Company and a Group subsidiary undertaking in the USA were terminated with effect from 31st March 20X1. Under the terms of his contract with the Company, he has been paid £105,000 upon termination of that contract. Under the terms of his contract with the US subsidiary undertaking he is entitled, subject to certain conditions, to continue to receive his annual salary of US$635,000 and certain other incidental benefits for a period of up to three years from 31st March 20X1; these salary payments have been fully provided for in these accounts and are disclosed as payments for termination of executive office when paid. He will retain his participation in the cycle of the long-term performance-related incentive plan ending on 30th June 20X1, pro rata to the period during which he was an employee of the Group. Payments to him under this plan will be disclosed as payments to a former Director when paid. He retains his right to share options, numbering 93,217 at 31st March 20X1, which expire on dates up to 20th March 20X4.

(Note: This example is made up but includes features from a real example of disclosure.)

Table 5.4 – Compensation for loss of office

XYZ Limited – Report and Accounts – 31 December 20X1

7. EMOLUMENTS OF THE DIRECTORS OF THE HOLDING COMPANY (extract)

Mr. X, a former Director of the Company and of Subsidiary Y, resigned on 12 October 20X1. He will continue to receive cash and non-cash benefits under the terms of his contract of employment dated 19 March 199X for the two year period to 31 October 20X3. As compensation for his loss of office as Managing Director of Subsidiary Y, this contract was changed so that over the two year period he is free to undertake other employment, subject to certain non-compete conditions, and is to be available for consultation by the Company. The estimated money value of the benefit to Mr. X, being the estimated total cash and non-cash benefits, is £670,000.

(Note: This example is made up but contains features from a real example of disclosure.)

Table 5.5 – Compensation for loss of office

XYZ Limited – Annual Report and Accounts – 31 December 20X1

Directors and employees (extract)

Following Mr X's resignation as director on 6 July 20X1, Mr X and Associates, of which Mr X is a partner, entered into a consultancy agreement with the company. The agreement has a term of two years from 1 August 20X1. Under the provisions of the agreement, Mr X and Associates will provide consultancy services as required by the company and receive remuneration comprising a day rate and payments at specified intervals. The agreement also provides for the partnership to receive a start-up loan of £50,000 free of interest but repayable by three instalments at specified dates in 20X2 and 20X3. The amount paid to the partnership for the services rendered in 20X1 was £95,750. The amount payable in 20X2 and 20X3, provided the agreement is not terminated, will depend on the work undertaken but will include specified payments which may total a maximum of £145,000.

(Note: This example is made up but contains features from a real example of disclosure.)

Table 5.6 – Disclosure of compensation for loss of office

X plc (AIM company) – Annual Report and Accounts – 2 April 20X3

SUPPLEMENTARY PROFIT AND LOSS INFORMATION (extract)

The value of the compensation received by a former director for loss of office amounted to £100,000 (20X2 — £1,162,536 relating to five directors). He also retained and has exercised options over 113,732 shares (granted under the executive share option scheme in May 20X1), and 144,975 shares (granted in May 20X2).

(Note: This example is made up but contains features from a real example of disclosure.)

Requirement for member approval

5.108   The Companies Act 2006 requires companies to obtain member approval for payments made to a director (or former director) or to persons connected with them relating to loss of office. This includes payments by way of compensation for loss of office and those in connection with the directors' retirement and includes payments relating to the loss of office from a subsidiary undertaking or any other office in connection with the company's management. The provisions are set out in sections 215 to 222 of the Companies Act 2006, including some exceptions, for wholly-owned subsidiaries and non-UK incorporated entities, and are effective for retirements occurring on or after 1 October 2007.

5.109   In addition to the exemptions for wholly-owned subsidiaries and non-UK incorporated entities, certain further exceptions to the requirement for shareholder approval are set out in the Act. A company will not be required to seek shareholder approval where the payment is made in good faith:

■   in discharge of an existing legal obligation (namely an obligation that was not entered into in connection with, or in consequence of, the event giving rise to the payment for loss of office);

■   by way of damages for breach of an existing legal obligation;

■   by way of settlement or compromise of any claim arising in connection with the termination of a director's office or employment; or

■   by way of pension in respect of past services.

[CA06 Sec 220].

5.109.1 There is also a *de minimis* exception, such that shareholder approval is not required if the total value of the payment does not exceed £200. [CA06 Sec 221].

> **Example – Compensation for loss of office to be approved at the next AGM**
>
> An ultimate parent company with a 31 December 20X8 year end is proposing to make a payment to a director for loss of office. The payment is to be approved by the members at the AGM on 15 March 20X9.
>
> No expense should be charged in the 2008 financial statements for this proposal. Compensation for loss of office proposed to be paid by the directors is not a liability of the company until approved by the members. The payment for compensation for loss of office should be accrued for in the 31 December 20X9 financial statements. This is similar to the situation for the accounting for final dividends (see chapters 22 of the Manual of Accounting – IFRS for the UK and the Manual of Accounting – UK GAAP).
>
> Consideration should also be given to providing disclosure in the directors' remuneration note to the accounts or the remuneration report under Schedules 5 and 8 to SI 2008/410 respectively.

Disclosure in the financial statements

5.110 Amounts to be disclosed include all relevant sums paid by or receivable from the company, the company's subsidiary undertakings and any other person, unless the director has to account for the sums to the company, its subsidiaries or to members. [SI 2008/409 3 Sch 5(2); SI 2008/410 5 Sch 7(2)].

5.111 For this purpose, a subsidiary undertaking includes a company that was a subsidiary undertaking immediately before the date on which the director lost office. It also includes an undertaking of which the director, while a director of the company, was a director by virtue of the company's nomination (direct or indirect), whether or not it is or was in fact a subsidiary undertaking of the company. [SI 2008/409 3 Sch 11(1); SI 2008/410 5 Sch 14(1)].

5.112 Compensation paid to a director for loss of office should not be included in the disclosure of that person's aggregate remuneration as described from paragraph 5.32; it is a separate disclosure requirement for unquoted companies. However, it is worth noting that quoted companies are required to present a table in the directors' remuneration report disclosing various elements of the pay of each of the directors and stating the total of those amounts for each director. Compensation for loss of office is one of the elements that must be separately disclosed; that is, for quoted companies, compensation for loss of office is included in total pay rather than being an entirely separate disclosure. See further from paragraph 5.163.

Sums paid to third parties in respect of directors' services

5.113 Paragraph 3 of Schedule 3 to SI 2008/409 and paragraph 5 of Schedule 5 to SI 2008/410 require companies to disclose in their financial statements any consideration paid to or receivable by third parties for making available the services of any person:

■ As a director of the company.

■ While a director of the company, as director of any of its subsidiary undertakings, or otherwise in connection with the management of the affairs of the company or any of its subsidiary undertakings.

[SI 2008/409 3 Sch 3(1); SI 2008/410 5 Sch 5(1)].

5.114 In this context, third parties do not include:

■ The director himself or a person connected with him or a body corporate controlled by him.

■ The company or any of its subsidiary undertakings.

[SI 2008/409 3 Sch 3(3); SI 2008/410 5 Sch 5(3)].

5.115 For the purpose of this disclosure 'subsidiary undertaking' includes an undertaking which is a subsidiary undertaking at the time the services were rendered and an undertaking where the director, while a director of the company, was a director by virtue of the company's nomination (direct or indirect), whether or not it is or was in fact a subsidiary undertaking. [SI 2008/409 3 Sch 11; SI 2008/410 5 Sch 14(1)]. See further paragraph 5.15.

5.116 For the purposes of this disclosure, the definition of consideration includes non-cash benefits. Where a benefit is given, its amount should be determined by reference to its estimated money value. The nature of the non-cash benefit must also be disclosed. [SI 2008/409 3 Sch 3(2); SI 2008/410 5 Sch 5(2)].

5.117 The requirement to disclose amounts paid to third parties for making available the services of a director is illustrated in the following example.

> **Example – Amounts paid to third party**
>
> Company A borrows money from a venture capital company. As part of the financing arrangement, a director of the venture capital company has been appointed to the board of directors of company A. Company A pays £10,000 per year to the venture capital company in respect of the director's services. The director is remunerated by the venture capital company and does not receive the money paid in respect of his services by company A personally. In this situation, the amount of £10,000 would be disclosed in company A's financial statements as sums paid to third parties in respect of directors' services in accordance with paragraph 3 of Schedule 3 and paragraph 5 of Schedule 5 to SI 2008/410.

5.117.1 A further example is given in Table 5.7.

Table 5.7 – Sums paid to third parties in respect of directors' services

XYZ Limited – Report and Accounts – 2 May 20X2

EMOLUMENTS OF DIRECTORS (extract)

ABC Bank plc, of which Mr X was a director, were paid fees of £23,000 during the period for the release of Mr X's services during the illness of the then Chairman.

(Note: This example is made up but contains features from a real disclosure example.)

5.117.2 The disclosure applies where third parties make available the services of a director. It does not apply to other services, as illustrated in the following example.

> **Example – Payments to a head hunter**
>
> Company B is looking to recruit a new director and agrees to use the services of a head hunter. Once the director has been employed, should the payments made to the head hunter be included with the emoluments disclosures?
>
> Paragraph 3 of Schedule 3 to SI 2008/409 and paragraph 5 of Schedule 5 to SI 2008/410 (for small and medium and large unquoted companies respectively) require disclosure of the aggregate amount of any consideration paid to or receivable by third parties for making available the services of any person as a director of the company. (Note that paragraph 16 of Schedule 8 to SI 2008/410 (for quoted companies) requires the information to be disclosed by individual director.)
>
> Where the fees paid by company B to a head hunter relate solely to services to the company for finding and introducing the person, we consider that a head hunter is not making available the services of a person as director in the sense envisaged in SI 2008/410. The head hunter receives a fee for finding the person who the company appoints to perform the services, but is not being paid in respect of the services. Our interpretation is that SI 2008/410 only applies to third parties who make the services of the director available (for instance, where another company lends a director part-time).

Disclosure examples

5.117.3 An example of directors' remuneration disclosure under the 2006 Act by an unquoted company not listed on AIM is given below.

Example – Disclosure of directors' remuneration (unquoted company)

	20X2	20X1
	£	£
Aggregate emoluments	350,000	320,000
Amounts (excluding shares) receivable under long-term incentive schemes	50,000	40,000
Company pension contributions to money purchase schemes	5,000	5,000
Compensation for loss of office	100,000	—
Sums paid to third parties for directors' services	—	20,000
Excess retirement benefits – current directors	5,000	5,000
– past directors	10,000	10,000

Two directors exercised share options in the year (20X1: two) and one director became entitled to receive shares under the long-term incentive scheme (20X1: three). Retirement benefits are accruing to two directors under the company's money purchase pension scheme (20X1: two) and to one director under a defined benefit scheme (20X1: one).

(Note: details of the highest paid director's emoluments must also be disclosed. An example of disclosure is given in para 5.90.2.)

An example of disclosure under the Act by an AIM company is given in the next section in paragraph 5.120.

Section III — AIM companies

5.118   AIM companies are effectively treated as unquoted companies by the Companies Act 2006. Therefore, unlike quoted companies (see para 5.6.3) they are not required to produce a directors' remuneration report in the form set out in Schedule 8 to SI 2008/410.

5.119   However, AIM companies do have to give certain information that other unquoted companies not listed on AIM do not have to give. The additional requirements are set out in the Companies Act 2006 and the AIM Rules as follows.

Companies Act 2006 disclosure requirements

5.119.1   Schedule 5 to SI 2008/410 requires AIM companies to provide disclosures of aggregate gains made by directors on the exercise of share options and the aggregate net value of shares received or receivable under long-term incentive schemes. [SI 2008/410 5 Sch 1(b), (c)].

5.119.2   In addition, in their disclosure of highest paid director's emoluments, AIM companies also have to include amounts in respect of gains on the exercise of share options and the net value of shares received or receivable under long-term incentive schemes. [SI 2008/410 5 Sch 2(1)(a)].

5.120   These points are dealt with in section I and section II above, which distinguish, where applicable, the provisions relating to AIM companies from those relating to unquoted companies not listed on AIM. In general, however, the requirements for AIM companies are, with the above exceptions, the same as those for other unquoted companies. An example of disclosure under the 2006 Act by an AIM company is given below.

Example – Disclosure of directors' remuneration (AIM company)

	20X2	20X1
	£	£
Aggregate emoluments	650,000	580,000
Gains made on exercise of share options	50,000	—
Amounts receivable under long-term incentive schemes	400,000	350,000
Company pension contributions to money purchase schemes	50,000	50,000
Compensation for loss of office	—	100,000
Sums paid to third parties for directors' services	20,000	20,000
Excess retirement benefits – current directors	5,000	5,000
– past directors	10,000	10,000

Retirement benefits are accruing to two directors under the company's money purchase pension scheme and to one director under a defined benefit scheme.

(Note: details of highest paid director's emoluments must also be disclosed. An example of the disclosure is given in para 5.90.2. In addition, disclosure of three categories of remuneration by individual director must be disclosed under the AIM Rules, as explained from para 5.120.2.)

[The next paragraph is 5.120.2.]

AIM Rules disclosure requirements

5.120.2   AIM Rule 19 requires the following to be disclosed for each director:

- Emoluments and compensation (this will include both cash and non-cash benefits).

- Details of share options and other long-term incentive schemes (this will include information on all outstanding options and awards).

- The value of any company contribution made to a pension scheme.

5.120.3   There is limited detailed guidance on the new requirements, for example, there is little clarity on the extent of the detail to be provided in relation to share options and long-term incentive schemes. AIM-listed entities may, therefore, wish to look to the current requirements in Schedule 5 (requirements for all entities) and Schedule 8 (requirements for quoted entities) to SI 2008/410 for further guidance. Detailed guidance on these schedules is set out from paragraphs 5.27 (Schedule 5) and 5.163 (Schedule 8).

5.120.4   AIM Rule 19 refers to the requirement to disclose remuneration earned *"by each director of the AIM company acting in such capacity during the financial year"*. The definition in Schedule 5 to SI 2008/410 is more specific, requiring all companies to disclose aggregate remuneration paid to or receivable by directors in respect of qualifying services. Qualifying services are defined in paragraph 5.33. We believe that, consistent with SI 2008/410's definition, disclosures should be in respect of remuneration of directors for their work for the whole group, not just work for the parent company.

Position of the auditor

5.120.5   While the notice issued by the London Stock Exchange states that the AIM Rules do not require the new directors' remuneration disclosures to be audited, the location of the disclosure could mean that the additional information on individual directors' remuneration is subject to audit. In addition, given the nature of the disclosures, and the following analysis, it is likely in practice that such balances would be audited.

- The introductory sentence to AIM Rule 19 states: *"an AIM company must publish annual audited accounts. . ."*. Therefore, the later reference in Rule 19 stating that *"the accounts produced in accordance with this rule must provide disclosure of. . .directors' remuneration. . ."* could be read as implying that these disclosures are subject to audit, despite the contradiction to the explicit statement in the London Stock Exchange's notice that the disclosures are not required to be audited.

- If the directors' remuneration disclosures required by AIM Rule 19 are included within the notes to the financial statements, these would need to be audited, consistent with other notes (unless headed up as 'unaudited', which would be unusual).

■ AIM-listed entities are not required to prepare a remuneration report in accordance with Schedule 8 to SI 2008/410 because they do not meet the definition of a quoted company under section 385(2) of the Companies Act 2006. However, if a voluntary remuneration report were produced or the disclosures were included within the directors' report, then section 496 of the Act and ISA (UK&I) 720A (revised), 'The auditor's responsibilities relating to other information in the documents containing audited financial statements (2009)', would apply. Section 496 of the Act requires the auditor to opine on *"whether the information given for the financial year of which the accounts are prepared is consistent with those accounts"*, including seeking to resolve any identified inconsistencies and providing details in the audit report if any material inconsistency is not resolved.

■ As mentioned above, AIM Rule 19 states that the disclosures are required to be made in the 'accounts' and this could be interpreted as meaning the financial statements. In any event, given the nature of the disclosures it is likely in practice that such balances would be audited even if included in the front end of the financial statements.

Section IV — Quoted companies (excluding companies listed on AIM)

Remuneration report

5.121 SI 2008/410 contains requirements for quoted companies (for definition see para 5.6.3) which substantially duplicates the requirements contained in the FSA Listing Rules. The requirements of SI 2008/410 also contain additional disclosures over and above those contained in the Listing Rules. As explained in paragraph 5.6.5, there are some differences between the requirements of the Listing Rules and those of SI 2008/410 and so the disclosures could be complicated. An illustrative example is given in the directors' remuneration report for IFRS GAAP plc (see separate publication containing illustrative financial statements). The requirements of the Listing Rules are covered in this section in addition to those in SI 2008/410.

5.122 Quoted companies must comply with the disclosure requirements that are applicable to all companies, and these are described above in section I of this chapter. Sections 420 to 422 of the Companies Act 2006 require that the directors of a quoted company prepare a directors' remuneration report that contains the information specified in Schedule 8 and complies with any requirement of that Schedule as to how the information is to be set out in the report. Section 421 of the Companies Act 2006 gives the Secretary of State power to make provision by regulations as to the information that must be contained in a directors' remuneration report and how it should be set out. These matters are set out in Schedule 8 to SI 2008/410.

5.123 The directors' remuneration report must be approved by the board and signed on its behalf by a director or the secretary of the company. [CA06 Sec 422(1)].

5.124 Schedule 8 to SI 2008/410 contains four parts:

■ Introductory.

■ Information not subject to audit — information about remuneration committees, performance related remuneration and liabilities in respect of directors' contracts.

■ Information subject to audit — detailed information about directors' remuneration.

■ Interpretation and supplementary.

5.125 This section of the chapter considers the provisions of Schedule 8 to SI 2008/410 in two parts: first, the information that is not subject to audit and second, the information that is subject to audit, which was mainly derived from the requirements of the Listing Rules, but with some changes – notably on pensions disclosure.

5.126 The introductory part of Schedule 8 to SI 2008/410 merely states that the directors' remuneration report shall show the information specified in the Schedule and that information required to be shown in the report for, or in respect of, a particular person shall be shown in the report in a manner that links the information to that person identified by name. [SI 2008/410 8 Sch 1].

5.127 The information not subject to audit covers:

■ Consideration by the directors of matters relating to directors' remuneration.

■ A statement of policy on directors' remuneration.

- Statement of consideration of conditions elsewhere in the company and group.

- Performance graph.

- Service contracts.

- Compensation for past directors (explanation for awards).

There is also some discussion on the interaction between the UK Corporate Governance Code and the remuneration report at the end of this section.

5.128 The information that is subject to audit covers:

- Individual directors' emoluments and compensation.

- Share options.

- Long-term incentive schemes.

- Pensions.

- Excess retirement benefits of directors and past directors.

- Compensation for past directors (details of awards).

- Sums paid to third parties in respect of directors' services.

5.129 Each of these above requirements is considered below and finally the approval and audit requirements are described.

Information not subject to audit

Consideration by the directors of matters relating to directors' remuneration

5.130 SI 2008/410 requires that if a committee of a company's directors has considered matters relating to directors' remuneration for the year, the names of each of the directors on the committee must be given in the remuneration report. [SI 2008/410 8 Sch 2(1)(a)].

5.131 The name must be given of anyone (which may include a director who was not a member of the committee) who provided advice or services that materially assisted the committee in considering any matter relating to directors' remuneration. For anyone so named, who is not a director of the company, further information must be given as follows:

- The nature of any other services that the person provided to the company during the year.

- Whether the person was appointed by the committee.

[SI 2008/410 8 Sch 2(1)(b)(c)].

5.132 This requirement is illustrated in the following examples.

> **Example 1 – Report benchmarking remuneration**
>
> The remuneration committee of a quoted company engaged an HR consultant to prepare a report benchmarking the remuneration of the company's directors against the remuneration of directors of comparable companies. Does this constitute material assistance for the purpose of disclosure under Schedule 8 of SI 2008/410?
>
> This would be material assistance. The HR consultant prepared a report with the purpose of assisting the remuneration committee in their consideration of directors' remuneration by benchmarking against similar companies.

Example 2 – Independent benchmarking survey

A different HR consultant has prepared and published widely an independent benchmarking survey that the remuneration committee has used when considering whether the relative importance of performance-related and non-performance-related remuneration is appropriate. Would this constitute material assistance?

This would not be material assistance. The HR consultant prepared a report for the purposes of general publication, which the remuneration committee used to assist itself in its consideration of directors' remuneration. No assistance was given by the HR consultant to this remuneration committee.

Example 3 – Preparation of performance graph

A third HR consultant was engaged by the same remuneration committee to prepare the total shareholder return graph for inclusion in the directors' remuneration report. Would this constitute material assistance?

This would not be material assistance. The HR consultant is putting together a graph of factual information, all of which is publicly available, for the purposes of disclosure and not to assist the remuneration committee in its consideration of directors' remuneration.

Example 4 – Auditors' review of remuneration report

During the course of an audit, the auditors reviewed the directors' remuneration report and made some comments to the directors on the presentation and content of the remuneration report. Would this constitute material assistance?

This would not be material assistance. The review of the directors' remuneration report is undertaken by the auditor as part of the audit and does not assist the remuneration committee in its consideration of directors' remuneration.

5.133 An example of disclosure that complies with the requirement to provide details of anyone who provided advice or services to the remuneration committee is given in Table 5.8.

Table 5.8 – Remuneration committee membership and advisors

Anglo American plc – Annual Report 2011 – 31 December 2011

1. REMUNERATION COMMITTEE (extract)

1.2 Membership of the Committee

The Committee comprised the following non-executive directors during the year ended 31 December 2011:

- Sir Philip Hampton (Chairman)
- David Challen
- Sir CK Chow
- Jack Thompson
- Peter Woicke

The Company's chief executive attends the Committee meetings by invitation and assists the Committee in its deliberations, except when issues relating to her own compensation are discussed. No directors are involved in deciding their own remuneration. In 2011, the Committee was advised by the Company's Human Resources and Finance functions and, specifically, by Mervyn Walker and Chris Corrin. It also took external advice as shown in Figure 1. Certain overseas operations within the Group are also provided with audit related services from Deloitte's and PwC's worldwide member firms and non-audit related services from Mercer's worldwide member firms.

A summary of the letter from Mercer Limited containing the conclusions of their review of the Committee's executive remuneration processes for 2011 can be found on page 116.

Figure 1: External advice provided to the Committee

Advisers		Other services provided to the Company
PricewaterhouseCoopers LLP (PwC)	Appointed by the Company, with the agreement of the Committee, to provide specialist valuation services and market remuneration data	Investment advisers, actuaries and auditors for various pension schemes; advisers on internal audit projects; taxation, payroll and executive compensation advice
Linklaters LLP (Linklaters)	Appointed by the Company, with the agreement of the Committee, to provide legal advice on long-term incentives and directors' service contracts	Legal advice on certain corporate matters

Mercer Limited (Mercer)	Engaged by the Committee to review the Committee's processes on an annual basis, in order to provide shareholders with assurance that the remuneration processes the Committee has followed are in line with stated policy and that the Committee has operated within its Terms of Reference	Investment advisers and actuaries for various pension schemes
Deloitte LLP (Deloitte)		In their capacity as Group auditors, Deloitte undertake an audit of sections 10 and 11 of the remuneration report annually. However, they provide no advice to the Committee

Statement of policy on directors' remuneration

5.134 The directors' remuneration report should contain a statement of the company's policy on directors' remuneration for the following year and for subsequent financial years. [SI 2008/410 8 Sch 3(1)]. For companies listed in the UK, the Listing Rules also require a statement of the company's policy on executive directors' remuneration. [LR 9.8.8R (1)]. The policy statement required under the Act should include:

- For each director, a detailed summary of any performance conditions to which the director's entitlement to share options or long-term incentive awards is subject, together with an explanation as to why those performance conditions were chosen.

- A summary of the methods to be used to assess whether the performance conditions are met and an explanation of why those methods have been chosen.

- If any of the performance conditions involves comparison with factors external to the company, a summary of the factors to be used in the comparison. If any of the factors relates to the performance of another company, or of two or more companies, or of an index on which a company or companies are listed, the identity of the company or companies or of the index must be given.

- A description of, and explanation for, any significant amendment that is proposed to the terms and conditions of any entitlement of a director to share options or under a long-term incentive scheme.

- If there are no performance conditions attached to the entitlement of a director to share options or under a long-term incentive scheme, an explanation as to why that is the case.

[SI 2008/410 8 Sch 3(2)].

5.135 The policy statement must, in respect of each director's terms and conditions relating to remuneration, explain the relative importance of the elements that are related to performance and those that are not. [SI 2008/410 8 Sch 3(3)].

5.136 The Listing Rules also require an explanation and justification of any element of remuneration, other than basic salary, which is pensionable. [LR 9.8.8R (7)].

5.136.1 In addition to the above disclosure required by the Act in respect of performance conditions and of any significant amendments to the terms of share options or long-term incentive schemes, the Listing Rules also require a statement of the company's policy on the granting of options or awards under its employees' share schemes and other long-term incentive schemes, explaining and justifying any departure from that policy in the period under review and any change in the policy from the preceding year. [LR 9.8.8R (10)].

5.137 As detailed in paragraph 5.134, SI 2008/410 requires certain disclosures in respect of performance conditions to which the director's entitlement to share options or long-term incentive awards is subject. SI 2008/410 does not distinguish between performance conditions and additional service conditions that have to be met before an award vests. This is considered in the example below.

Example – Service conditions outstanding

A quoted company is preparing a directors' remuneration report. A director has been awarded share options that vest if the company meets certain targets for the first three years of the scheme and he remains employed by the company for a further two years. Is the requirement for him to stay for the further two years a performance condition?

SI 2008/410 does not distinguish between performance conditions and service conditions that must be met before an award under a share option scheme is exercisable or under an LTIP is receivable. Although it is possible to interpret the Act to have a narrow definition of 'performance conditions', we believe that the intention of the Act is that service conditions should be included within the umbrella of 'performance conditions'. This is consistent with both the company's perspective that during the period in which the director is fulfilling his service conditions, the company is receiving qualifying services. It is also consistent with IFRS 2 (FRS 20) which recognises the charge to the income statement (UK – profit and loss account) for employee services received over the vesting period which includes the performance and service periods.

Hence, given that the director is not entitled to exercise his share options unless he remains employed by the company for a period of five years, it would be appropriate to explain this fact in the remuneration report. We believe that it is good practice to disclose the service condition as a performance condition under paragraph 3 of Schedule 8 to SI 2008/410.

5.137.1   The directors who are covered by the detailed requirements in paragraphs 5.134 to 5.135 above are those who are serving as directors at any time in the period from the end of the financial year to the date on which the directors' remuneration report is laid before the company in general meeting. [SI 2008/410 8 Sch 3(5)].

5.137.2   Further disclosure requirements in respect of share options are given from paragraph 5.170 onwards and in respect of long-term incentive schemes are given from paragraph 5.180.

5.138   The remuneration policy statement must also summarise and explain the company's policy on:

- The duration of contracts with directors.

- Notice periods and termination payments under such contracts.

[SI 2008/410 8 Sch 3(4)].

5.139   We believe that this requirement relates to the company's general policy on contracts and notice periods and, therefore, would apply to anyone who is a director during the year or in the period up to the date that the remuneration report is signed.

5.140   Examples of notes that deal with policy for service contracts and termination payments are given in Table 5.9. Further disclosure requirements in respect of service contracts are given from paragraph 5.149.

Table 5.9 – Policy on service contracts and termination payments

GlaxoSmithKline plc – Annual report and accounts – 31 December 2011

Remuneration report (extract 1)

Executive Director terms and conditions

Executive Director contracts

The policy set out below provides the framework for contracts for Executive Directors.

	Policy
Notice period on termination by employing company or Executive	12 calendar months
Termination payment	1 x annual salary payable on termination by the company
Vesting of LTIs	Rules of relevant incentive plan, as approved by shareholders
Pensions	Based on existing arrangements and terms of relevant pension plan
Non-compete clause	12 months from termination notice date*

* The ability to impose a 12-month non-compete period (and a non-solicitation restriction) on an Executive is considered important by the company to have the ability to protect the Group's intellectual property and staff. In light of this, the Committee believes that it would not be appropriate to provide for mitigation in the contracts.

The contracts for new Executives will not normally include a bonus element in any termination payment.

Disclosure of directors' remuneration

The terms of the contracts seek to balance commercial imperatives and best practice. Where the company considers it important that an individual does not work elsewhere during his or her notice period, it may make a compensatory payment in respect of bonus for the period of restraint.

Julian Heslop retired early from the company on 31 March 2011. Under the terms of his contract entered into in 2005, prior to the above framework being introduced, he was entitled to receive one year's notice on termination and his payment included one year's annual salary and a 12 months' on-target bonus.

Simon Dingemans joined the Board on 4 January 2011 and was appointed CFO on 1 April 2011 following Julian Heslop's early retirement. In line with the company's policy, Simon Dingemans' contract provides for a termination payment based on one year's base salary only.

The following table sets out the details of the Executive Directors' service contracts:

Current Directors	Date of contract	Effective date	Expiry date
Sir Andrew Witty*	18 June 2008	22 May 2008	31 August 2024
Simon Dingemans	8 September 2010	4 January 2011	30 April 2028
Dr Moncef Slaoui**	21 December 2010	21 December 2010	1 August 2019

* Sir Andrew Witty's contract was renewed in June 2008 following his appointment as CEO, and was amended on 4 February 2010 to remove the entitlement to bonus as part of his severance terms.

** Dr Moncef Slaoui's previous contract dated 16 May 2008 was replaced with a new contract on 21 December 2010 to reflect the changes to his severance terms outlined above.

No termination payments will be made in respect of any part of a notice period extending beyond the contract expiry date.

Other entitlements

In addition to the contractual provisions outlined above, in the event that Dr Moncef Slaoui's service agreement is terminated by his employing company, the following will apply:

- in the case of outstanding awards due under the GlaxoSmithKline Annual Investment Plan (which was closed to new deferrals with effect from the first quarter of 2006), provided that his agreement is terminated other than for cause, Dr Moncef Slaoui must exercise any Bonus Investment Rights within six months of termination to receive any deferred amounts, and any income and gains; and

- in line with the policy applicable to US senior executives, Dr Moncef Slaoui may become eligible, at a future date, to receive continuing medical and dental insurance after retirement.

Remuneration report (extract 2)

Chairman and other Non-Executive Directors

How Non-Executive Director fees are set

The company aims to provide the Chairman and other Non-Executive Directors with fees that are competitive with those paid by other companies of equivalent size and complexity, subject to the limits contained in GSK's Articles of Association.

The Chairman and the CEO are responsible for evaluating and making recommendations to the Board on the fees payable to the Non-Executive Directors.

Fees

The Chairman's fees are currently £540,000 per annum plus an allocation of shares to the value of £135,000 per annum.

The other Non-Executive Directors' fees applying at 31 December 2011 are as follows:

	Per annum
Standard annual cash retainer fee	£75,000
Supplemental fees	
Chairman of the Audit & Risk Committee*	£80,000
Senior Independent Director and Scientific/Medical Experts	£30,000
Chairmen of the Remuneration and Corporate Responsibility Committees	£20,000
Non-Executive Director undertaking intercontinental travel to meetings	£7,500
	per meeting

* The fee for the Chairman of the Audit & Risk Committee reflects the increased focus within the Group on compliance and risk, and the time commitment required from the Committee Chairman of approximately 80 days per annum. Full details of the operation of the Audit & Risk Committee are given on pages 97 to 101.

†Sir Christopher Gent is the Chairman of the Corporate Responsibility Committee, but does not receive the additional fee listed above.

In recent years, there has been an increase in the time commitment, demands and responsibility placed on the role of a non-executive director, and this has generally led to an increase in their fees. As a result of these developments in the market, Non-Executive Director fees at GSK were independently reviewed during 2011. The review highlighted that there was scope to increase Non-Executive Director fees. However, in the light of the current environment, it was decided not to increase the fees at this time. They will continue to be kept under review.

Non-Executive Directors' share allocation plan

To enhance the link between Directors and shareholders, GSK requires Non-Executive Directors to receive a significant part of their fees in the form of shares. At least 25% of the Non-Executive Directors' total fees, excluding those of the Chairman, are paid in the form of shares or ADS and allocated to a share account. The Non-Executive Directors may also take the opportunity to invest part or all of the balance of their fees into the same share or ADS account.

The shares or ADS which are notionally awarded to the Non-Executive Directors and allocated to their interest accounts are set out in the table on page 125 and are included within the Directors' interests table on page 126. The accumulated balance of these shares or ADS, together with notional dividends subsequently reinvested, are not paid out to the Non-Executive Directors until retirement from the Board. Upon retirement, the Non-Executive Directors will receive either the shares or ADS, or a cash amount equal to the value of the shares or ADS at the date of retirement, or date of payment if later.

Letters of appointment

The terms of engagement of the Non-Executive Directors are set out in letters of appointment which are available for inspection at the company's registered office and at the AGM. For each Non-Executive Director, his or her initial appointment and any subsequent reappointment are subject to election and, thereafter, periodic re-election by shareholders.

The Non-Executive Directors' letters of appointment do not contain provision for notice periods or for compensation if their appointments are terminated.

The following table shows the date of the initial letter of appointment of each Non-Executive Director:

Non-Executive Director	Date of letter of appointment
Sir Christopher Gent	26 May 2004
Professor Sir Roy Anderson	28 September 2007
Dr Stephanie Burns	12 February 2007
Stacey Cartwright	3 March 2011
Larry Culp	9 June 2003
Sir Crispin Davis	9 June 2003
Judy Lewent	3 March 2011
Sir Deryck Maughan	26 May 2004
James Murdoch	26 February 2009
Dr Daniel Podolsky	3 July 2008
Tom de Swaan	21 December 2005
Sir Robert Wilson	9 June 2003

In Sir Christopher Gent's letter of appointment, it was agreed that he would serve the company as Deputy Chairman until 31 December 2004 and from 1 January 2005 as Chairman until the conclusion of the AGM following the third anniversary of his appointment. This was extended for a term of three years by mutual agreement, with effect from his re-election as a Director at the AGM held on 21 May 2008. This has been further extended for a period of five years with effect from 1 January 2011, subject to annual re-election at AGMs.

5.141 The principles of the UK Corporate Governance Code that relate to directors' remuneration are described in Annex 1 to this chapter. Whilst the legal requirements above set out what must be disclosed, the UK Corporate Governance Code also contains best practice provisions for a range of issues including setting remuneration levels, awarding options, long-term incentive schemes and the terms of service contracts.

5.141.1 A number of other organisations, including industry commentators such as the NAPF, ABI and RiskMetrics Group have also published good practice guidance on remuneration. This guidance is discussed from paragraph 5.223.1 below.

Statement of consideration of conditions elsewhere in the company and group

5.142 Under the Companies Act 2006, there is a requirement for quoted companies to report in their directors' remuneration report on how they have taken pay and employment conditions elsewhere in the group into account when determining directors' remuneration for the relevant financial year. [SI 2008/410 8 Sch 4]. An example of disclosure of consideration of conditions elsewhere in the group is given in Table 5.10. A further example which refers to the Government's ongoing review of executive remuneration is given in Table 5.11.

Table 5.10 – Consideration of pay and employment conditions throughout the group

Tesco PLC – Annual report – 25 February 2012

Directors' remuneration report (extract)

Remuneration arrangements throughout the Group

Remuneration arrangements at Executive Director level and throughout the Group are designed around a set of common Tesco pay values. Ensuring that employees are focused on delivering the same core objectives is an important part of Tesco's reward philosophy:

- **Annual bonus** – Annual bonuses throughout the Group are linked to local business performance but are consistent in structure to that of the Executives with a focus on underlying profit growth and performance against key strategic objectives.

- **Share incentives** – Over 5,000 of our senior employees across the globe participate in the Performance Share Plan based on the same performance conditions as Executive Directors. This senior population also receives some of their bonus in Tesco shares deferred for a period.

- **Employees as shareholders** – It is an important part of the Tesco values that all of our employees, not just senior management, have the opportunity to become Tesco shareholders. Over 210,000 of our people participate in our all-employee schemes and we delivered over 26 million shares in 2011 under our Shares In Success Plan, a plan which awards free shares to all UK employees based on Company performance.

When determining Executive remuneration arrangements the Committee takes into account pay conditions throughout the Group to ensure that the structure and quantum of executive pay remains appropriate in this context. When considering salary increases the Committee considers the general Group wage increase. In the last few years executive salary increases have been at a similar level to the general employee increase.

Table 5.11 – Consideration of pay and employment conditions throughout the group

Booker Group Plc – Annual report – 30 March 2012

Remuneration report (extract)

Unaudited Information

The Committee aims to ensure that the remuneration policies of the Company are in line with the proposals set out by the Secretary of State for Business and Enterprise as part of the recent review of executive remuneration conducted by the Department for Business Innovation & Skills ("BIS"). Among the more prominent objectives set out in that consultation exercise were that: 1) Directors should not be rewarded for failure; 2) incentives for senior management should be more closely linked to performance, thus aligning better the interests of executives and shareholders; and 3) Director rewards should be correlated with those received by other employees of the business. The Committee believes that the Company's remuneration system conforms with these objectives whilst retaining and attracting individuals capable of promoting the success of the business. As the BIS consultation process is ongoing the Committee is monitoring developments in this area and will continue to adopt best practice wherever possible.

The Committee believes that it has met these objectives for the period to 30 March 2012 in the following ways:-

- Base pay: All employees are eligible for an annual pay award. The average salary increase during the year under review for all employees of the Group was 2.9%, and the average base salary increase for Executive Directors was 1.7%.

- Bonus: Of the Group's 9,375 employees, 6,500 employees are eligible for a bonus payment based on "customer satisfaction". Customer satisfaction is measured independently by calling 35 customers selected at random for each of our 172 branches on a quarterly basis to ask them to rate key areas of service. In the past year 5,226 employees received a bonus payment. Of the remaining employees, 1,174 are eligible for a quarterly bonus payment based on achieving productivity and efficiency targets at the site at which they are employed. 1,200 employees (excluding the CEO) are eligible for a bonus based on increasing Group EBITDA year on year.

- Long term incentives: 2,517 employees are in the 2011 SAYE scheme and 900 have PSP options. Both schemes provide rewards which are based on increasing equity value. The high number of employees participating in these schemes is a testament to the Group's policy of ensuring that the remuneration of senior management is aligned with that of the overall workforce and with the interests of shareholders. Since 2007 when we completed the reverse takeover of Blueheath and became admitted to trading on AIM, the equity value has increased from approximately £300m to over £1,100m. The value of the PSP options awarded has been equivalent to 2% of the value generated.

Alignment between the senior management and shareholders is also significantly increased by personal shareholdings. Directors, senior managers and colleagues own in aggregate approximately 10% of the issued share capital of the Company.

The Committee is of the view that, when the above schemes are looked at in combination, we have a structure of reasonable base pay, bonuses which are paid for increasing cash profit and customer satisfaction and long term incentives which are aligned to the creation of shareholder value. Director pay inflation is running in line with employees, the best paid Director basic salary is circa's 36 times the basic salary of the median employee and the average basic salary of the Executive Directors is circa 23 times the basic salary of the median employee.

The Committee believes that this remuneration system is simple to understand, has a proven track record of encouraging strong performance, does not "reward failure" and reflects the Company's goals of continuing to improve services to customers and to create value for shareholders.

Performance graph

5.143 The directors' remuneration report is required to include a performance graph showing the total shareholder return for the company against an index.

5.144 The detailed requirement is for a line graph to be presented that shows the total shareholder return for each of:

- A holding of shares of the company's equity share capital whose listing or admission to dealing has led to the company being defined as a quoted company (for definition see para 5.6.3 above).

- A hypothetical holding of shares made up of shares of the same kind and number as those by reference to which a broad based equity market index is calculated.

[SI 2008/410 8 Sch 5(1)(a)].

5.145 The name of the index selected for the purpose of the graph and the reason for selecting that index should be disclosed. [SI 2008/410 8 Sch 5(1)(b)].

5.146 The line graph should cover five financial years of which the last is the current financial year (that is, the year for which financial statements are being presented). However, if the company has been in existence for less than five years, a shorter period may be given comprising only the number of financial years completed since the company came into existence. For example, if the current financial year is the company's third, the graph would cover three financial years. [SI 2008/410 8 Sch 5(2)(3)]. The situation where the company has been listed for less than five years, despite existing for longer is dealt with in paragraph 5.148.2 below. The situation where the index itself has existed for less than five years is considered in paragraph 5.148.4 below.

5.147 Total shareholder return is calculated using a fair method that:

- Starts with the percentage change in the market price of the holding over the period.

- Makes the following assumptions as to reinvestment of income:

  (a) That any benefit in the form of shares of the same kind as those in the holding is added to the holding when that benefit becomes receivable.

  (b) That any benefit in cash, and the value of any benefit not in cash and not falling into (a) above, is used when the benefit becomes receivable to purchase shares of the same kind as the existing holding at market price and that the notional shares so purchased are added to the existing holding at that time.

  (c) 'Benefit' in paragraphs (a) and (b) means any benefit (including dividends) receivable in respect of the holding from the company of whose share capital the holding forms part.

- Makes the following assumptions as to the funding of liabilities:

  (a) Where the holder has a liability to the company of whose share capital the holding forms part, shares are sold from the holding:

    (i) immediately before the time by which the liability is due to be settled; and

    (ii) they are sold in such numbers that, at the time of sale, the market price of the shares sold equals the amount of the liability in respect of the shares in the holding that are not sold.

  (b) in paragraph (a) 'liability' means a liability in respect of any shares in the holding or from the exercise of a right attached to any of those shares.

  [SI 2008/410 8 Sch 5(4)-(8)].

- Makes provision for any replacement of shares in the holding by shares of a different description.

The same method must be used for each of the holdings mentioned in paragraph 5.144.

[SI 2008/410 8 Sch 5(4)-(8)].

5.148 In general there are a number of indices that are widely available and which show total returns. For example the UK Series of the FTSE Actuaries Share indices include Total Return indices. As noted in paragraph 5.145, SI 2008/410 requires disclosure of the name of the index, therefore, it is not acceptable to use an index created by the company alone, although it may be possible to give some disclosure as additional information. This is considered in the example below.

> **Example – Selection of index for total shareholder return graph**
>
> A quoted company is preparing its directors' remuneration report and is selecting the index to use in the total shareholder return graph. Can the company 'create' an index of companies of a similar size and nature? If not, which index should it use?
>
> Given the Companies Act's requirement for disclosure of the name of the index (see para 5.145 above), using an index created by the company alone is not acceptable.
>
> There are a number of published indices for total shareholder return that are publicly available. These include indices that are industry-based, such as the TechMark index, as well as indices that are size-based, such as the FTSE 100.
>
> We consider that when selecting an index, the directors should generally use an index of which the company is a constituent and that they use internally to measure the company's performance against its peers. The remuneration committee should consider a range of appropriate indices and, based on the relative merits of each, select the index that is, in their opinion, most appropriate.
>
> However, we also consider that, if a company has also devised a more specific index for a peer group of companies, that it actually uses for the purpose of setting performance targets, a total return graph, plotting the company's performance against the performance of the peer group, could be given as additional information. The composition of the peer group, the basis of preparation of the graph and reasons for producing it, should be given.

5.148.1 A straightforward example of disclosure is given in Table 5.12 below. See also the example in Table 5.13, which gives the information required by the legislation in the first graph and additional information in subsequent graphs. The example compares the company's performance with three indices, each of which is relevant because each gives a different perspective on the group's performance.

Table 5.12 – Performance graph

Rolls-Royce Holdings plc – Annual Report – 31 December 2011

TSR over five years

The Company's TSR performance over the previous five years compared to a broad equity market index is shown in the graph below. The FTSE 100 has been chosen as the comparator index because it contains a broad range of other leading UK listed companies.

The graph shows the plc growth in value of a hypothetical £100 holding in Rolls-Royce Holdings plc (previously Rolls-Royce Group plc) ordinary shares over five years, relative to the FTSE 100 index. The values of the hypothetical £100 holdings at the end of the five year period were £194.00 and £107.90 respectively.

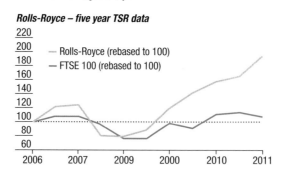

Table 5.13 – Performance graph

Pearson Plc – Annual Report – 31 December 2011

Total shareholder return performance

Below we set out Pearson's total shareholder return on three bases. Pearson is a constituent of all the indices shown. First, we set out Pearson's total shareholder return performance relative to the FTSE All-Share index on an annual basis over the five-year period 2006 to 2011. We have chosen this index, and used it consistently in each report on directors' remuneration since 2002, on the basis that it is a recognisable reference point and an appropriate comparator for the majority of our investors.

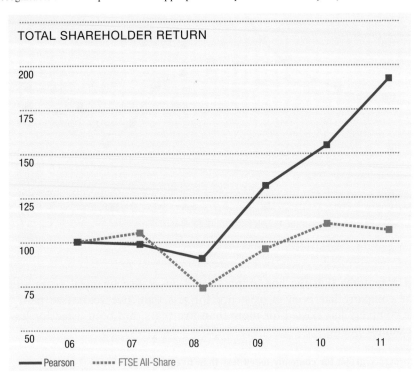

Secondly, to illustrate performance against our sector, we show Pearson's total shareholder return relative to the FTSE Media index over the same five-year period.

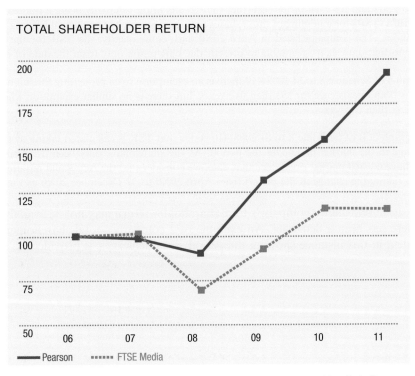

And thirdly, we show Pearson's total shareholder return relative to the FTSE All-Share and Media indices on a monthly basis over 2011, the period to which this report relates.

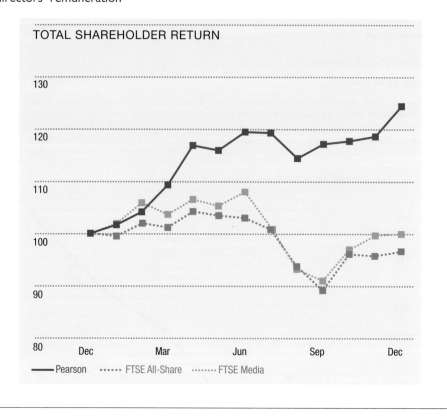

5.148.2 SI 2008/410 requires that the line graph should cover five financial years and it deals with the situation where the company has been in existence for less than five years (see para 5.146 above). The situation where the company has existed for more than five years, but been listed for less than five years in considered in the example below.

> **Example – Performance graph for company listed less than five years**
>
> A quoted company is preparing its directors' remuneration report for the year ended 31 December 20X2. Paragraph 5 of Schedule 8 to SI 2008/410 requires the company to present, in the remuneration report, a line graph showing, for the previous five years and for each of the securities that results in the company being a quoted company, the Total Shareholder Return (TSR) for a holding of those shares and the TSR for a hypothetical holding of shares on a broad equity market index. The company listed in April 20X0 and, consequently, the TSR for the company cannot be calculated prior to that date. Is it acceptable to present the TSR graph only from the date of listing?
>
> Within paragraph 5 of Schedule 8 to SI 2008/410 there is an exemption from presenting the full five year history when the company has been in existence for less than five years, but there is no similar exemption where the company has been listed for less than five years.
>
> However, paragraph 5(4) of Schedule 8 to SI 2008/410 states that TSR is calculated taking as the starting point the percentage change in the market price over the period. As the shares have only been listed since April 20X0 and, therefore, only have a listed market price since that date, we consider that the Act would require the company's TSR to be calculated taking the change in the period from April 20X0 to 31 December 20X0 as the starting point.

5.148.3 Another situation where a company's total shareholder return may not be available for the five year period is where there has been a demerger. An example of a company's total shareholder return compared with a relevant index, in this instance showing the period since demerger, is provided in Table 5.14.

Table 5.14 – Performance graph

Home Retail Group plc – Annual report – 28 February 2009

Directors' remuneration report

Performance graph

The graph below compares the TSR for Home Retail Group against the FTSE 350 index of general retailers for the period from demerger to the end of the period under review. The directors feel that the FTSE 350 index of general retailers is the most appropriate choice of index as it is a relevant comparator group for a retail business. The graph has been prepared in accordance with the assumptions contained in the relevant legislation.

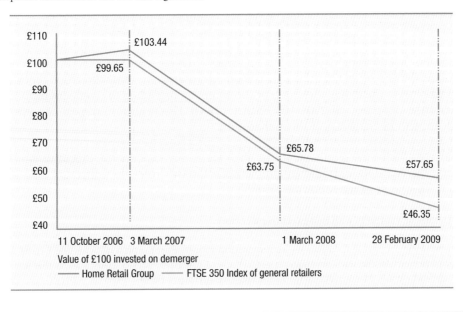

5.148.4 The situation can also arise where the index being used has existed for less than five years. This is considered in the following example.

Example – New index used for total shareholder return graph

A quoted company is preparing its directors' remuneration report for the year ended 31 December 20X2 and is selecting the index to use in the total shareholder return graph. The remuneration committee consider that the most appropriate index to use would be a new index, but this has only existed since 20X1. The remuneration committee consider that the second most appropriate index would be the FTSE All Share index. The remuneration committee do not want to have to use the FTSE All Share index until 20X6 and then change to the new index and explain the change. What should they do?

As the information for the new index is not available for the full five year period, then to select this index would not comply with the Act's requirements.

SI 2008/410 does not prohibit the presentation of two performance graphs: one showing a five year comparison against the FTSE All Share index and one showing a two year comparison with the new index. The remuneration committee can disclose both graphs and explain the reasoning, then in 20X6 when a five-year history for the new index is available, they can drop the disclosure of the FTSE All Share index.

5.148.5 In other examples, not reproduced here, several companies have given explanations of how their long-term incentive scheme criteria differ from the measure of performance provided by comparison with stock exchange indices and this provides useful additional information. Others, as in Table 5.19 above, have given explanations of how significant changes in the composition of the group, such as mergers or demergers, have been dealt with. Where companies have been listed for only part of the five year period required, and thus a market price has not been available, the shorter period since listing has generally been used as explained in paragraph 5.148.2 above.

Service contracts

5.149 The remuneration report is required to contain details of the service contract or contract for services of each person who has served as a director at any time during the financial year. The details required to be disclosed are:

- The date of the contract, the unexpired term and details of any notice periods.

- Any provision for compensation payable on early termination of the contract.

- Such details of other provisions in the contract as are necessary to enable shareholders to estimate the liability of the company in the event of early termination of the contract.

[SI 2008/410 8 Sch 6(1)].

5.149.1 The requirement to disclose any provision for compensation payable on early termination of the contract refers to the contract's terms and includes 'golden parachute' provisions in service contracts, that is, where the directors receive a payment if they leave, for example, following a hostile take-over bid (see also para 5.149.2 below).

5.149.2 In addition, a UK company that has securities carrying voting rights admitted to trading on a regulated market at the end of its financial year is required to disclose, in its directors' report, details of any agreement with employees (including directors) of the company providing for compensation for loss of office on the takeover of the company. [SI 2008/410 7 Sch 13(2)(k)]. Disclosures in respect of contracts relating to takeovers are dealt with in chapter 3 of this publication.

5.149.3 The above disclosure requirements in the Act apply equally to executive and non-executive directors, because the Act does not differentiate between the two roles that directors take within a quoted company. This is illustrated in the following example.

> **Example – Details of contracts with non-executive directors**
>
> A quoted company is preparing its directors' remuneration report. Paragraph 6 of Schedule 8 to SI 2008/410 requires the company to present, in the remuneration report, details of directors' service contracts. Is this just for the executive directors or should details of contracts with non-executive directors be disclosed as well?
>
> As noted above, the disclosure requirements contained in Schedule 8 to SI 2008/410 apply equally to executive and non-executive directors, because the Act does not differentiate between the two roles that directors take within a quoted company.
>
> The requirement in paragraph 6 of Schedule 8 to SI 2008/410 surrounds the disclosure of certain, specified, details of each "... *contract of service or contract for services of each person who has served as a director of the company at any time during the relevant financial year ...*". [SI 2008/410 8 Sch 6(1)]. We consider that the term 'contract for services' encompasses all written agreements between a director and the company under which the director agrees to perform services for the company, regardless of the legal form that those agreements may take.

5.150 In addition, for companies listed in the UK, the Listing Rules require disclosure of:

- Details of any directors' service contract with a notice period in excess of one year or with provisions for pre-determined compensation on termination which exceeds one year's salary and benefits in kind, giving the reasons for such notice period.

- The unexpired term of any directors' service contract of a director proposed for election or re-election at the forthcoming annual general meeting and, if any director proposed for election or re-election does not have a directors' service contract, a statement to that effect.

[LR 9.8.8R (8), (9)].

5.151 An example of disclosure in respect of all the matters in the bullet points in paragraph 5.149 is given in Table 5.15 below.

Table 5.15 – Details of service contracts

BG Group plc – Annual Report – 31 December 2010

Remuneration report (extracts)

Service contracts

The Executive Directors' service contracts, including arrangements for early termination, are carefully considered by the Committee and are designed to recruit, retain and motivate directors of the quality required to manage the Company. The Committee considers that a rolling contract with a notice period of one year is appropriate.

In line with the Company's policy, the Executive Directors' service contracts contain change of control provisions. Should the Directors' employment be terminated within 12 months of a change of control, they are entitled to liquidated damages. The amount

---

of liquidated damages is equal to one year's gross salary and a credit of one year's pensionable service (less any deductions the employer is required to make), which the Committee considers to be a genuine pre-estimate of loss. The Committee considers that these provisions assist with recruitment and retention and that their inclusion is therefore in the best interests of shareholders.

Other than change of control, the Executive Directors' service contracts do not contain provisions for compensation in the event of early termination. When calculating termination payments, the Committee takes into account a variety of factors, including individual and Company performance, the obligation for the Director to mitigate his or her own loss (for example, by gaining new employment) and the Director's length of service. Further details of the Executive Directors' service contracts can be found on page 70.

Executive Directors' service contracts

Details of the service contracts of the Executive Directors who served during the year are set out below:

Executive Directors	Contract date	Unexpired term	Notice period	Compensation payable upon early termination[a]
Ashley Almanza	01 Aug 02	rolling 1yr	1yr	n/a
Frank Chapman	14 Sep 00	rolling 1yr	1yr	n/a
Martin Houston	03 Feb 09	rolling 1yr	1yr	n/a

(a) Other than the change of control provisions, the Executive Directors' service contracts do not contain provisions for compensation payable upon early termination.

Change of control (extract from page 70)

As described on page 65, the Executive Directors' service contracts contain change of control provisions.

For the purposes of these provisions, a change of control is deemed to occur if the Company becomes a subsidiary of another company; or if 50% or more of the voting rights of the Company or the right to appoint or remove the majority of the Board of the Company become vested in any individual or body or group of individuals or bodies acting in concert; or if all or substantially all of the business, assets and undertakings of the Company become owned by any person, firm or company (other than a subsidiary or associated company). A change of control is also deemed to occur if the whole of the issued capital of BG Energy Holdings Limited or a substantial part of the undertaking of that Company (including its subsidiaries) is transferred to another company, unless that transferee company is a subsidiary of the Company, or a company ultimately owned by substantially the same shareholders as are the ultimate owners of the Company.

However, a change of control does not occur if (and only if) through a process of reconstruction the Company becomes a subsidiary of another company owned by substantially the same shareholders as are the shareholders of the Company. The Executive Directors' service contracts provide that any payments made pursuant to these provisions will be made, less any deductions the employer is required to make. Any such payments shall be in full and final settlement of any claims the Executive Director may have against the employer or any associated company arising out of the termination of employment, except for any personal injury claim, any claim in respect of accrued pension rights, or statutory employment protection claims.

Non-Executive Directors (extract)

The Board aims to recruit Non-Executive Directors of a high calibre, with broad commercial, international or other relevant experience. Non-Executive Directors are appointed by the Board on the recommendation of the Nominations Committee. Their appointment is for an initial term of three years, subject to election by shareholders at the first annual general meeting following their appointment and annual re-election thereafter. The terms of engagement of the Non-Executive Directors are set out in a letter of appointment.

The basic annual fee paid to Non-Executive Directors increased from £75 000 to £77 500 on 1 July 2010. Additional fees are also payable, for example, for membership of, or chairing, a Committee of the Board and acting as Senior Independent Director. The current remuneration policy for NonExecutive Directors requires that fees are reviewed every two years, taking into account time commitment, competition for high-quality non-executive directors and market movements.

Non-Executive Directors are not eligible to participate in any of the Company's share schemes, incentive schemes or pension schemes.

To facilitate the alignment of the interests of the Non-Executive Directors with those of shareholders, the Group has put in place a Non-Executive Directors' share purchase programme through which Non-Executive Directors may elect to invest a proportion of their fees, net of tax and on a regular basis, to acquire BG Group shares on the open market. The first deductions were made under this programme in January 2010.

Chairman

Sir Robert Wilson was initially appointed as Chairman with effect from 1 January 2004. He was first re-appointed for a three-year term with effect from 1 January 2007 and following due consideration was re-appointed with effect from 1 January 2010, at which point his fee was increased to £700 000 per annum. In line with the Non-Executive Directors, Sir Robert Wilson's re-appointment is for a three-year term, subject to annual re-election by shareholders at the annual general meeting, and there is no notice period and no provision for payment in the event of early termination. Sir Robert Wilson's fee was raised with effect from 1 January 2011 to £725 000 and is next subject to review on 1 January 2012.

Chairman and Non-Executive Directors' letters of appointment

	Date of appointment or re-appointment	Expiry date
Sir Robert Wilson	1 Jan 10	Jan 13
Peter Backhouse	12 May 10	May 14
Baroness Hogg	14 May 08	May 14
Dr John Hood	14 May 08	May 14
Caio Koch–Weser	1 Nov 10	Nov 13
Sir David Manning	1 July 08	May 14
Mark Seligman	3 Dec 09	Dec 12
Lord Sharman	12 May 10	May 11
Patrick Thomas	15 Dec 10	Dec 13
Philippe Varin	12 May 10	May 12

The Non-Executive Directors' letters of appointment do not contain any notice period or provision for compensation in the event of early termination of their appointment.

Compensation for past directors

5.152 The remuneration report must contain an explanation for any significant award made in the circumstances described in paragraph 15 of Schedule 8 to SI 2008/410 to a past director, including, in particular, compensation for loss of office and pensions but excluding any sums shown separately in the table of individual directors' emoluments or as compensation in accordance with the requirement of paragraph 7(1)(d) of Schedule 8 to SI 2008/410. [SI 2008/410 8 Sch 6(2)].

5.153 Paragraph 15 of Schedule 8 to SI 2008/410 contains a 'sweep-up' requirement to disclose any significant award to a past director that has not already been disclosed in the table of individual directors' emoluments and compensation (see below from para 5.209). This is disclosed in the 'auditable part' of the remuneration report. The requirement of paragraph 6(2) of Schedule 8 to SI 2008/410, which is outside the auditable part, is to give an explanation for any such payment.

Interaction between the UK Corporate Governance Code and the remuneration report

5.154 The Listing Rules require a listed company to comply with the provisions of the UK Corporate Governance Code or to explain any departures (see chapter 4). The UK Corporate Governance Code recommends that where a company releases an executive director to serve as a non-executive director elsewhere, the remuneration report should include a statement as to whether or not the director will retain such earnings and, if so, what the remuneration is. [CC B.1.4; UK CGC D.1.2]. An example disclosure is provided in Table 5.16. Further details on the principles and provisions of the UK Corporate Governance Code that relate to directors' remuneration are set out in Annex 1.

Table 5.16 – Executive directors retain fees for services provided as non-executive directors elsewhere

Pearson plc – Annual report and accounts – 31 December 2010

Report on directors' remuneration (extract)

Executive directors' non-executive directorships

The committee's policy is that executive directors may, by agreement with the board, serve as non-executives of other companies and retain any fees payable for their services.

The following executive directors served as non-executive directors elsewhere and received fees or other benefits for the period covered by this report as follows:

	Company	Fees/benefits
Marjorie Scardino	Nokia Corporation	€150,000
	MacArthur Foundation	$27,000
Rona Fairhead	HSBC Holdings plc	£151,844
	Spencer Stuart Advisory Board	£15,000

Other executive directors served as non-executive directors elsewhere but did not receive fees.

[The next paragraph is 5.163.]

Information subject to audit

Individual directors' emoluments and compensation

5.163   Schedule 8 to SI 2008/410 requirements for disclosure of individual directors' emoluments and compensation are similar to those contained in the Listing Rules. This section of the chapter deals mainly with the legal requirements for quoted companies, but also refers to the requirements of the Listing Rules where appropriate.

5.164   For quoted companies, the remuneration report is required to show, in tabular form, for each director of the company who served as such at any time in the financial year, each of the following:

- The total amount of salary and fees paid to or receivable by the director in respect of qualifying services (see para 5.33).

- The total amount of bonuses paid or receivable, the amount of which is determined by reference to service or performance within a single year (see para 5.181).

- The total amounts paid by way of expenses allowance that are:

    (a)   chargeable to UK income tax, or would be if the person was an individual; and

    (b)   paid to or receivable by the director in respect of qualifying services.

- The total amount of:

    (a)   any compensation for loss of office paid to or receivable by the director (see para 5.168 below); and

    (b)   any other payments paid to or receivable by the director in connection with the termination of qualifying services.

- The total estimated value of any benefits received by the director otherwise than in cash (see para 5.166 below) that:

    (a)   do not fall within any of the bullet points above or which are not included in the other information required to be disclosed in the auditable part of the remuneration report in respect of share options and long-term incentive schemes;

    (b)   are emoluments of the director; and

    (c)   are received by the director in respect of qualifying services.

- The total of the sums mentioned in the bullet points above.

[SI 2008/410 8 Sch 7(1), 7(4)].

5.164.1   In respect of comparative amounts, the Act states that *"the directors' remuneration report shall show, for each person who has served as a director of the company at any time during the relevant financial year, the amount that for the financial year preceding the relevant financial year is the total of the sums mentioned in paragraphs (a) to (e) of sub-paragraph (1)"*. Therefore, comparative amounts for the total referred to in the last bullet point above must be given for each director. [SI 2008/410 8 Sch 7(2)]. Comparatives for each component of the total are not required.

5.164.2   Comparatives are required in respect of each person who has served as a director of the company at any time during the *relevant financial year*. The relevant financial year means the financial year in respect of which the report is prepared. [SI 2008/410 8 Sch 1(1)]. Therefore, strictly, SI 2008/410 does not require disclosure of the comparatives in respect of individual directors who retired last year. However, it is common practice for such disclosure to be made. It provides useful additional information for readers and it means that the figures in the directors' remuneration report can be reconciled to the aggregate figures disclosed in the notes to the financial statements under Schedule 5 to SI 2008/410.

5.165   For companies listed in the UK, the Listing Rules require disclosure of:

- The amount of each element in the remuneration package for the period under review of each director by name, including, but not restricted to, basic salary and fees, the estimated money value of benefits in kind, annual bonuses, deferred bonuses, compensation for loss of office and payments for breach of contract or other termination payments.

- The total remuneration for each director for the period under review and for the corresponding prior period.

- Any significant payments made to former directors during the period under review.

[LR 9.8.8R (2)(a)-(c)].

5.165.1 In addition, the Listing Rules require listed companies to disclose particulars of any arrangement under which a director has either waived or agreed to waive any future or current emoluments and details of such waivers. This applies in respect of emoluments from either the company or any of its subsidiaries. [LR 9.8.4R (5)].

5.166 For quoted companies, separate disclosure of benefits by individual director is required. The nature of any element of each director's remuneration package that is not cash must also be stated. [SI 2008/410 8 Sch 7(3)]. However, the amount attributed to each non-cash element of a director's remuneration does not need to be disclosed. Further guidance on benefits is kind (applicable to all companies) is given from paragraph 5.42 onwards and in the example below.

> **Example – Flexible benefits scheme**
>
> A quoted company has a flexible benefits scheme, whereby a director may apply part of his/her salary in purchasing additional benefits, such as increased holiday or health cover. Assuming the director takes advantage of this and purchases, say, two weeks additional holiday, should the value of this be disclosed in the individual directors' remuneration table required by Schedule 8 to SI 2008/410 as salary/fees or as benefits in kind?
>
> We consider that in a case such as this the basic salary figures should not be adjusted (reduced). This is because the director is entitled to the basic salary and it is his/her option to apply it in purchasing whatever he/she wants. The fact that holiday/other benefits are purchased from the company rather than from some third party is not relevant. If, however, the additional benefits and reduction in base salary were imposed on the director (that is, it was not at his/her option) the amounts would be adjusted and the benefit included in the total of his/her benefits disclosed in the individual directors' remuneration table with the nature of the benefit also being disclosed. [SI 2008/410 8 Sch 7(1), (3)].

5.167 Where a director is appointed during the year, only the remuneration while he is a director of the company is disclosable as director's remuneration, as explained in the following example.

> **Example – Employee appointed as director during year**
>
> As noted above, quoted companies are required to disclose details of each element of the remuneration of each director by name and the total for each director. If a person has been an employee for part of the year and is then appointed a director during the year, should the figures disclosed for him include remuneration paid to him whilst he was an employee or should it just include remuneration paid to or receivable by him whilst a director?
>
> Schedule 8 to SI 2008/410 requires only the amounts paid to or receivable by the person in respect of 'qualifying services' to be disclosed. Qualifying services means services as a director of the company or whilst a director of the company, as a director of a subsidiary undertaking or as director of any other company of which he is a director as a result of the company's nomination (direct or indirect) or otherwise in connection with the management of the affairs of the company or any such subsidiary or other undertaking. Therefore, only the remuneration while he is a director of the company is disclosable as director's remuneration.
>
> Note that for companies reporting under IFRS, additional disclosure for the whole period may be necessary. IAS 24 requires disclosure of remuneration (in total and split into five categories) for key management personnel in respect of services provided to the entity. In this context we consider that the services provided to the entity means services while the person is a member of key management personnel. Where a director fell into the key management classification prior to appointment as a director, remuneration for the whole period under review should be given in the aggregate IAS 24 disclosure.

5.167.1 In some situations, directors are remunerated in a currency that differs from the company's presentation currency. This is considered in the following example.

> **Example – Director paid in foreign currency**
>
> A quoted company is preparing its remuneration report. Although most of the directors are UK resident and are paid by the company in pounds sterling (which is both the company's functional and presentation currency), one of its directors is resident in the United States and is paid by the UK company in US dollars. Should his emoluments be disclosed in US dollars or pounds?

Paragraph 7 of Schedule 8 to SI 2008/410 requires disclosure of a table disclosing the emoluments paid to or receivable by each director in respect of qualifying services. The legislation is silent as to the currency in which the directors' remuneration should be denominated.

We consider, however, that it would be misleading and confusing to users of the remuneration report to denominate different directors' emoluments in different currencies, as it hinders the comparability of the information. In addition, the amounts disclosed for the individual directors should be consistent with those amounts included in the 'aggregate emoluments' disclosure requirement that applies to all companies. We consider, therefore, that the individual directors' remuneration should all be disclosed in the company's presentation currency and that, where this requires the translation of directors' remuneration, the exchange rate used for that translation should be disclosed. Each director's emoluments could also be disclosed in the currency in which the director is paid.

This enables users of the remuneration report to make meaningful comparisons of the directors' remuneration packages whilst fully understanding their nature.

5.168 As noted in paragraph 5.164 above, quoted companies are required to disclose for each director the total amount of compensation for loss of office paid to or receivable by the director and any other amounts paid or receivable in connection with the termination of qualifying services. This disclosure is required to be given in the table of directors' emoluments. The amount that should be disclosed when the compensation is conditional on uncertain future events is considered in the example below. Further guidance on compensation for loss of office (applicable to all companies) is given in paragraph 5.97 onwards. There is a further 'sweep-up' requirement for quoted companies, which is discussed in paragraph 5.209 onwards.

Example – Compensation contingent on uncertain future events

A director of a quoted company resigned during the year. Contractually, he is entitled to receive compensation for loss of office of one year's annual salary in twelve equal monthly instalments during the year post-resignation. If at any point during the twelve months immediately following his resignation he secures alternative employment on the same (or higher) salary, payments to the director will cease, but there are no provisions for the company to claw-back any payments already made to him pursuant to this arrangement.

The company's year end is 31 December, the director resigned on 31 August and the directors' remuneration report is signed on 28 February. The monthly instalment is £10,000. The company has recognised the full £120,000 as an expense in the income statement (UK – profit and loss account) for the period, as it considers it probable that the full amount will become payable.

What should be included as the director's compensation for loss of office in the annual report in the year in which he resigns?

Paragraph 7 of Schedule 8 to SI 2008/410 requires disclosure of compensation for loss of office, which is defined in terms of amount paid to or receivable by a director in connection with loss of office.

Of the full £120,000 that the director may be entitled to, £40,000 has been paid at the year end. Consequently, £40,000 meets the definition of compensation for loss of office and must be disclosed as compensation for loss of office.

Although the remaining £80,000 is not technically receivable by the director at the year end, our view is that it is to be paid to him in the future as part of his compensation for leaving office and should also be included in the remuneration table as compensation for loss of office, taking the total to £120,000. This is consistent with the accounting treatment. Disclosure should be made in a footnote to the table (that the amount in the table should be cross-referred to) of full details of the contingency, to draw readers' attention to the fact that an element of the amount disclosed may not become payable. The 'full details' in the footnote should include the nature of the contingency, the amount that was paid during the year (£40,000) and the amount that was paid between the year end and the date of signing of the remuneration report (£20,000).

An alternative view, which is also acceptable and compliant with the SI 2008/410, is to include only the £40,000 that technically meets the definition of compensation for loss of office in the emoluments table prepared in accordance with paragraph 7 of Schedule 8 to SI 2008/410. Full disclosure must be made in a footnote to the table (that the amount in the table should be cross-referred to) of full details of the arrangements to draw readers' attention to the fact that the total compensation payable may be higher. The 'full details' in the footnote should note that the amount included in the table is only that which was paid during the year, disclose the maximum that could become payable (an additional £80,000) and the amount that was paid between the end of the year and the date of signing of the remuneration report (£20,000). In the following year, the director may be omitted from the tabular disclosures required by paragraph 7 (see para 5.164.2), but all amounts paid to or receivable by him will meet the definition of an 'award to a former director' and will be required to be disclosed in the remuneration report (albeit outside the table) by paragraph 15 of Schedule 8 to SI 2008/410.

Under either option, there will be a 'payment to a former director' in the subsequent year, which must be disclosed in accordance with the Listing Rules (see para 5.165). [LR 9.8.8 R (2)(c)].

5.169 An example is given below of the sort of presentation that may be given to comply with the legislation. In Table 5.17 details are given by individual director of salaries/fees, bonuses, compensation for loss of office (referred to as termination payments), expense allowances, benefits and totals.

Table 5.17 – Directors' emoluments

BT Group plc – Annual Report – 31 March 2011

Directors' emoluments

Directors' emoluments for the 2009/10 financial year were as follows:

	Basic salary and fees	Pension allowance net of pension contributions	Total salary and fees	Annual bonus	Expense allowance	Other benefits excluding pension	Total 2011	Total 2010	Deferred bonus plan 2011	2010
	£000	£000	£000	£000	£000	£000	£000	£000	£000	£000
Sir Michael Rake[c]	613	–	613	–	–	25	638	670	–	–
I Livingston[c]	892	32	924	1,415	–	20	2,359	2,105	1,415	1,206
T Chanmugam[c,d,e]	504	151	655	604	19	12	1,290	1,109	453	346
G Patterson[c,d]	521	104	625	645	19	11	1,300	1,133	484	365
T Ball	73	–	73	–	–	–	73	53	–	–
C Brendish	82	–	82	–	–	–	82	80	–	–
J E Daniels	76	–	76	–	–	–	76	75	–	–
P Hewitt	152	–	152	–	–	–	152	128	–	–
P Hodkinson	102	–	102	–	–	–	102	100	–	–
N Rose[f]	16	–	16	–	–	–	16	–	–	–
C G Symon[g]	152	–	152	–	–	16	168	174	–	–
J Whitbread[h]	14	–	14	–	–	–	14	–	–	–
	3,197	287	3,484	2,664	38	84	6,270	5,627	2,352	1,917

Termination payments

							Total 2011	Total 2010		
H Lalani[i]							612	131		
							6,882	5,758		

a Pension allowance paid in cash for 2011 – see 'Pensions' on page 78.

b Deferred annual bonuses payable in shares in three years' time, subject to continued employment.

c Other benefits include some or all of the following: company car, fuel or driver, personal telecommunications facilities and home security, medical and dental cover for the directors and immediate family, special life cover, professional subscriptions, personal tax advice, and financial counselling.

d Expense allowance in the above table includes a monthly cash allowance in lieu of a company car or part of such allowance which has not been used for a company car.

e Tony Chanmugam was granted a retention cash award in early 2008 prior to his appointment as a director. He received a payment of £315,000 in May 2010.

f Nick Rose was appointed as a director on 1 January 2011.

g Includes an additional fee for regular travel to Board and Board committee meetings.

h Jasmine Whitbread was appointed as a director on 19 January 2011.

i Hanif Lalani's contract was terminated on 11 January 2010. In accordance with his contract, his salary of £585,000 per annum and the value of his benefits to which he was entitled amounting to £195,000 per annum, continued to be provided until 10 January 2011.

Share options

5.170 The remuneration report must contain details, by individual director, of share options granted in respect of qualifying services. The information in (a) to (d) of paragraph 5.170.1 below should be in tabular form, but may be aggregated to avoid excessively lengthy reports (see para 5.174). [SI 2008/410 8 Sch 8(1)-(3)]. The Listing Rules require disclosure of information on share options, including SAYE options, for each director by name in accordance with the requirements of Schedule 8 to SI 2008/410. [LR 9.8.8R (2)(d)].

5.170.1 The information to be given (in tabular form for (a) to (d) below) for each director who served as such at any time in the financial year is:

(a) Number of shares subject to a share option at the beginning of the financial year or, if later, at the date of appointment as a director (differentiating between options having different terms and conditions).

(b) Number of shares at the end of the financial year or, if earlier, at the date of ceasing to be a director (differentiating between options having different terms and conditions).

(c) Details of options awarded, options exercised, options expiring unexercised and options whose terms and conditions have been varied in the financial year.

(d) For each share option that is unexpired at any time in the financial year:

  (i) The price paid, if any, for its award.

  (ii) The exercise price.

  (iii) The date from which the option may be exercised.

  (iv) The date on which the option expires.

(e) A description of any variation made in the year to the terms and conditions of a share option.

(f) A summary of any performance criteria on which the award or exercise of an option is conditional and a description of any variation in such performance criteria made in the year.

(g) For each option that has been exercised in the financial year, the market price of the shares in relation to which the option was exercised, at the date of exercise (see also para 5.48 above).

(h) For each option that is unexpired at the end of the financial year:

  (i) The market price of the related shares at the end of that year.

  (ii) The highest and lowest market prices of the related shares in that year.

[SI 2008/410 8 Sch 8, 9].

5.171 The following extracts illustrate some of the disclosure requirements above. In Table 5.18, performance conditions are explained and options are disclosed at the beginning and end of the year together with options granted and exercised.

Table 5.18 – Share options

AVEVA Group plc – Annual Report & Accounts – 31 March 2012

Remuneration Committee report (extract)

Share awards (extract)

Long-Term Incentive Plan (LTIP)
Under the LTIP, options are granted to selected individuals to acquire ordinary shares at an exercise price equal to the nominal value of the shares (3.33 pence); these options will be exercisable only if stretching performance criteria are met. For 2011/12 and 2012/13 the market value of awards under the LTIP awarded to Richard Longdon and James Kidd amounted to 120% and 100% of basic salary respectively (2010/11 – 100%). The increase in the level of LTIP awards compared to 2010/11 was the result of a review conducted at that time into the remuneration arrangements for Executive Directors and comparison with remuneration packages for Directors of other similar sized companies.

Currently, there are no rules under the LTIP scheme which govern the maximum awards that can be made to participants. However, as set out above, following feedback received from ISS last year, the Committee has decided to introduce a maximum limit on the LTIP. Going forward the maximum award under the LTIP will be 250% of salary, which will only be awarded in exceptional circumstances, e.g. on recruitment.

The Committee continues to believe that earnings per share growth is an appropriate performance measure for awards under the LTIP, as growing earnings is strongly aligned with our long-term business strategy and the creation of shareholder value.

In determining each of the awards under the LTIP, the Remuneration Committee considered and concluded that the performance conditions set were challenging in the context of internal and external expectations at the time of the awards.

Details of the outstanding awards under the LTIP are as follows:
2008/9 awards
In 2008/09, a total of 17,929 nominal value share options were conditionally awarded to the Executive Directors under the LTIP. The performance conditions were based on average growth in EPS over the years from 2009/10 to 2010/11. If average EPS growth is greater than 14% per annum then all of the shares shall vest. If average EPS is less than 10% per annum then none of the shares shall vest. If average EPS growth is between 10% and 14% per annum then the number of shares that shall vest shall be determined by linear interpolation. The performance conditions attached to this award were not met and therefore these awards all lapsed.

2009/10 awards
In 2009/10, a total of 36,628 nominal value share options were conditionally awarded to the Executive Directors under the LTIP. In view of the general economic background, the Remuneration Committee gave especially careful consideration to what performance conditions would be appropriate and finally agreed that they should be based on average diluted EPS over the three years from 2009/10 to 2011/12. All shares under this option shall vest if average diluted EPS for the three years ending 31 March 2012 is equal to or above 52.14 pence. Should average diluted EPS for the period be below 52.14 pence, then no shares will vest and the option will lapse. Although the vesting date has not yet been reached, it is anticipated that the performance conditions attached to this award will be met following finalisation of the 2011/12 financial results and 100% of the award will vest. However this is subject to the approval of the Remuneration Committee at the time of announcement of the results.

Disclosure of directors' remuneration

2010/11 awards

In 2010/11, a total of 37,961 nominal value share options were awarded to Executive Directors under the LTIP. The performance conditions are based on average EPS growth over the three years from 2010/11 to 2012/13. If average diluted EPS growth is more than 12% above RPI for the same period then all of the shares under this option will vest. If average diluted EPS growth is less than 4% above RPI then none of the shares will vest. If average EPS growth is between 4% and 12% per annum then the number of shares that shall vest shall be determined by linear interpolation.

2011/12 awards

In 2011/12 a total of 35,155 share options were awarded to the Executive Directors under the LTIP. The performance conditions attached to this award are based on EPS growth over the three years from 2011/12 to 2013/14. If average diluted EPS growth is more than 12% above RPI for the same period then all the shares under this option will vest. If average diluted EPS growth is less than 5% above RPI then none of the shares will vest. If average EPS growth is between 5% and 12% per annum above RPI then the number of shares that shall vest shall be determined by linear interpolation.

2012/13 awards

It is intended that share options be awarded to Executive directors at at 120% of salary for Richard Longdon and 100% for James Kidd and that performance conditions should be based on EPS growth over a three year period from 2012/13 to 2014/15. As set out above, given the international nature and scope of our business, the Committee has decided to de-link the LTIP performance condition from RPI for awards made in 2012 onwards. EPS targets have been re-calibrated to ensure a similar level of stretch to the EPS targets for 2011 awards. It is proposed that if average annual diluted adjusted EPS growth is more than 15% then all shares under this option will vest. If average annual diluted adjusted EPS growth is less than 8% then no shares will vest. At 8% average annual adjusted diluted EPS growth, 25% of shares will vest and between 8% and 15%, the number of shares that vest will be determined by linear interpolation between 25% and 100%.

Summary of LTIP targets

Award	Performance targets
2008/09 – 2010/11	EPS growth 10% p.a. to 14% p.a
	These targets were not met and therefore these awards lapsed in full
2009/10 – 2011/12	Average diluted EPS of 52.14 pence
	This target was met and the award will vest in full
2010/11 – 2012/13	EPS growth of RPI plus 4% p.a. – RPI plus 12% p.a.
2011/12 – 2013/14	EPS growth of RPI plus 5% p.a. – RPI plus 12% p.a.
2012/13 – 2014/15	EPS growth of 8% p.a. – 15% p.a.

Deferred annual bonus share plan

As described above, part of the annual bonus earned by Executive Directors in the year is used to determine eligibility for an award of of deferred shares under the Deferred Share Scheme. In order to deliver shares under the Deferred Share Scheme, an Employee Benefit Trust (EBT) was established following shareholder approval at the 2008 Annual General Meeting. Awards of deferred shares are made by the trustee of the EBT using shares purchased in the market.

On 4 July 2011 the EBT awarded 8,536 and 1,464 deferred shares to Richard Longdon and James Kidd respectively in respect of the bonus arrangements for the year ended 31 March 2011.

Following the achievement of the objectives for 2011/12, it is anticipated that 4,190 and 2,010 deferred shares will be awarded to Richard Longdon and James Kidd respectively in respect of the bonus arrangements for the year ended 31 March 2012.

Share options

The interests of Directors in options to acquire ordinary shares were as follows:

	Scheme	As at 1 April 2011 Number	Granted Number	Exercised Number	Forfeited Number	As at 31 March 2012 Number	Gain on exercise £	Exercise price Pence	Earliest date of exercise	Date of expiry
Richard Longdon										
	LTIP	10,891	—	—	(10,891)	—	—	3.33	07.07.11	07.07.15
	LTIP	22,264	—	—	—	**22,264**	—	3.33	07.07.12	07.07.16
	LTIP	25,038	—	—	—	**25,038**	—	3.33	26.07.13	26.07.17
	LTIP	—	25,115	—	—	**25,115**	—	3.33	06.07.14	06.07.18
	Deferred Share Scheme (2008)	4,094	—	4,094	—	—	68,247	0.00	26.05.09	Note 1
	Deferred Share Scheme (2009)	14,991	—	7,496	—	**7,495**	124,958	0.00	26.05.10	Note 1
	Deferred Share Scheme (2010)	12,471	—	4,157	—	**8,314**	69,297	0.00	26.05.11	Note 1
	Deferred Share Scheme (2011)	—	8,536	—	—	**8,536**	—	0.00	26.05.12	Note 1

James Kidd

LTIP	2,101	—	—	(2,101)	—	—	3.33	07.07.11	07.07.15
LTIP	4,289	—	—	—	**4,289**	—	3.33	07.07.12	07.07.16
LTIP	2,435	—	—	—	**2,435**	—	3.33	26.07.13	26.07.17
LTIP	—	10,040	—	—	**10,040**	—	3.33	06.07.14	06.06.18
Deferred Share Scheme (2009)	886	—	443	—	**443**	7,385	0.00	26.05.10	Note 1
Deferred Share Scheme (2010)	737	—	245	—	**492**	4,084	0.00	26.05.11	Note 1
Deferred Share Scheme (2011)	—	1,464	—	—	**1,464**	—	0.00	26.05.12	Note 1

The last date of the exercise is the end of the 42-day period following the announcement of the final results of the Group in the third calendar year following that in which the option was granted or (if applicable) such later date as the remuneration Committee may specify.

The market price as at 31 March 2012 was £16.57 (31 March 2011 — £16.15) with a high-low spread for the year of £12.98 to £17.99.

During the year Richard Longdon and James Kidd exercised options over 15,747 and 688 ordinary shares under the Deferred Share Scheme respectively at an exercise price of nil. The market price on the date of exercise was £16.67 which resulted in an aggregate gain on exercise of £262,502 for Richard Longdon and £11,469 for James Kidd. Richard Longdon retained 7,541 and James Kidd 329 of the shares over which options were exercised.

At 31 March 2012, Richard Longdon owned 385,565 ordinary shares (2011 – 378,024 ordinary shares) and options over 96,762 ordinary shares (2011 – 89,749 options). James Kidd owned 3,555 ordinary shares (2011 – 3,226 ordinary shares) and options over 19,163 ordinary shares (2011 – 10,448 options).

Options under the LTIP are normally exercisable in full or in part between the third and tenth anniversaries of the date of grant.

5.172 In Table 5.19 details are given of rebasing of share options as to volume and price terms.

Table 5.19 – Rebasing of share options

National Grid plc – Annual Report – 31 March 2011

Directors' remuneration report (extract)

3. Directors' interests in share options

Executive Share Option Plan (ESOP)

No further awards will be made under this plan but there are outstanding options granted in previous years. Such options will normally be exercisable between the third and tenth anniversary of the date of grant, subject to a performance condition.

Options worth up to 100% of an optionholder's base salary will become exercisable in full if TSR, measured over the period of three years beginning with the financial year in which the option is granted, is at least median compared with a comparator group of energy distribution companies; and UK and international utilities.

Grants in excess of 100% of salary vest on a sliding scale and become fully exercisable if the Company's TSR is in the top quartile.

The outstanding options have reached the required performance criteria and remain subject to exercise only.

The table below provides details of the Executive Directors' holdings of share options awarded under the ESOP, the Share Matching Plan (Share Match) and Sharesave schemes.

Table 3 **Steve Holliday**	Adjusted no. of options held at 1 April 2010 or, if later, on appointment* (i)	Adjusted no. options exercised or lapsed during the year (i)	Market price at exercise (pence)	Options granted during the year	Adjusted no. of options held at 31 March 2011 or, if earlier, on retirement † (i)	Adjusted exercise price per share (pence) (ii)	Normal exercise period
ESOP	77,129	–	–	–	77,129	421.36	Jun 2005 to Jun 2012
Share Match	11,827	–	–	–	11,827	100 in total	Jun 2005 to Jun 2012
	16,092	–	–	–	16,092	100 in total	Jun 2006 to Jun 2013
	21,383	–	–	–	21,383	nil	May 2007 to May 2014
Sharesave	3,921	–	–	–	3,921	427.05	Apr 2014 to Sep 2014
Total	**130,352**	**–**		**–**	**130,352**		

Disclosure of directors' remuneration

Andrew Bonfield							
Sharesave	_*	–	–	3,421	3,421	445	Apr 2016 to Sep 2016
Total	**_***	**–**		**3,421**	**3,421**		
Steve Lucas (iii)							
ESOP	62,167 (iv)	–	–	–	62,167 †	380.02	Jan 2011 to Dec 2011
Sharesave	3,416 (iv)	–	–	–	3,416 †	455.06	Jan 2011 to Jun 2011
Total	**65,583**	**–**		**–**	**65,583 †**		
Mark Fairbarn (iii)							
Sharesave	2,011 (v)	–	–	–	2,011	488.31	Apr 2011 to Sep 2011
	585 (v)	–	–	–	585	573.19	Apr 2011 to Sep 2011
Total	**2,596**	**–**		**–**	**2,596**		

(i) The option numbers shown, for awards granted prior to the rights issue which completed on 14 June 2010, were adjusted using an adjustment factor of 1.14271765.

(ii) The exercise prices shown above, for awards granted prior to the rights issue which completed on 14 June 2010, were adjusted using an adjustment factor of 0.87510681.

(iii) On 1 April 2010, the first day of the financial year, Steve Lucas and Mark Fairbairn exercised Sharesave options over 1,693 and 862 shares respectively as reported in footnote (i) of Table 3 of the 2009/10 Directors' Remuneration Report. As a result, these options were not adjusted for the rights issue which completed on 14 June 2010 and are not included in this table.

(iv) On leaving, Steve Lucas was permitted 12 months from his termination date in which to exercise his ESOP options and six months to exercise his Sharesave options.

(v) On leaving, Mark Fairbairn was permitted six months from his termination date in which to exercise his Sharesave options.

5.173 If disclosure of the details set out in paragraph 5.170.1 above would result in disclosure of excessive length, the disclosure may be summarised as follows:

- Information disclosed in relation to an individual director need not differentiate between options having different terms and conditions (para 5.170.1 (a) and (b) above).

- In respect of the disclosure of the price paid for the award and the exercise price of options that are unexpired at any time in the year (para 5.170.1 (d)(i) and (ii) above) and in respect of disclosure of the market price at the end of the year and the highest and lowest prices in the year for shares related to options unexpired at the end of the year (para 5.170.1 (h) above), share options may be aggregated and, instead of disclosing prices for each option, disclosure may be made of weighted average prices of aggregated share options.

- In respect of disclosure of dates from which options may be exercised or of dates of expiry of options that are unexpired at any time in the year (para 5.170.1 (d)(iii) and (iv) above) options may be aggregated and, instead of disclosing dates for each option, disclosure may be made of ranges of dates for aggregations of share options.

[SI 2008/410 8 Sch 10(1)].

5.174 The relaxations in the last two bullet points above are, however, subject to the condition that options in relation to shares whose market price at the end of the year is below the option exercise price (out of the money options) may not be aggregated with options relating to shares whose market price at the end of the year is equal to or above the option exercise price (in the money options). [SI 2008/410 8 Sch 10(2)].

5.175 The relaxations in the bullet points above do not apply in respect of options that have been awarded or exercised or had their terms and conditions varied in the year. [SI 2008/410 8 Sch 10(3)].

5.176 The following examples illustrate aggregated disclosures as permitted by these provisions. In Table 5.20 aggregated disclosures are given for options, but the table shows separately options that are out of the money from those that are in the money.

Table 5.20 – Separate disclosure for out of the money options

AstraZeneca PLC – Annual Report and Accounts – 31 December 2011

Directors' Remuneration Report (extract)

Share options

The interests of Directors who served during 2011, in options to subscribe for Ordinary Shares, granted under the SOP are included in the following table. None of the Directors in the table below holds options under the AstraZeneca Savings-Related Share Option Plan. There were no grants of options made to Directors under any of the plans in 2011.

		Number of Ordinary Shares under option[1]	Exercise price per Ordinary Share[2]	Market price on date of exercise	First day exercisable[3,4]	Last day exercisable[3,4]
David Brennan	At 1 January 2011– options over Ordinary Shares	592,975	2375p		24.03.09	26.03.19
	- market price above option price (Ordinary Shares)	505,244	2271p		19.05.09	26.03.19
	- market price at or below option price (Ordinary Shares)	87,731	2975p		24.03.09	23.03.16
	At 31 December 2011 – options over Ordinary Shares	592,975	2375p		24.03.09	26.03.19
	- market price above option price (Ordinary Shares)	505,244	2271p		19.05.09	26.03.19
	- market price at or below option price (Ordinary Shares)	87,731	2975p		24.03.09	23.03.16
	At 1 January 2011 – options over ADSs	322,519	$45.35		29.03.04	23.03.15
	- market price above option price (ADSs)	110,987	$40.35		24.03.08	23.03.15
	- market price at or below option price (ADSs)	211,532	$47.97		29.03.04	25.03.14
	Exercised 18 February 2011	(29,354)	$47.14	$49.10	29.03.04	28.03.11
	Exercised 18 February 2011	(39,942)	$47.73	$49.10	29.06.04	28.06.11
	At 31 December 2011 – options over ADSs	253,223	$44.76		28.03.05	23.03.15
	- market price above option price (ADSs)	110,987	$40.35		24.03.08	23.03.15
	- market price at or below option price (ADSs)	142,236	$48.21		28.03.05	25.03.14
Simon Lowth	At 1 January 2011	135,269	2074p		28.03.11	26.03.19
	- market price above option price	135,269	2074p		28.03.11	26.03.19
	- market price at or below option price	-	n/a		n/a	n/a
	Exercised 9 August 2011	(70,138)	1882p	2568p	28.03.11	27.03.18
	At 31 December 2011	65,131	2280p		27.03.12	26.03.19
	- market price above option price	65,131	2280p		27.03.12	26.03.19
	- market price at or below option price	-	n/a		n/a	n/a

1 Vesting is subject to satisfying the relevant performance conditions set out in each of the relevant share option plans. Further information on the performance conditions applicable to the SOP is set out in the AstraZeneca Share Option Plan section on page 122.
2 Exercise prices are weighted averages.
3 First and last exercise dates of groups of options, within which period there may be shorter exercise periods.
4 UK date convention applies.

Gains by Directors on exercise of share options

The aggregate gains made by Directors on the exercise of share options during the year and the two previous years is set out below.

Year	Gains made by Directors on the exercise of share options $	Gains made by the highest paid Director $
2011	882,089	112,254
2010	260,182	11,454
2009	-	-

During 2011, the market price of Ordinary Shares or ADSs was as follows:

Stock Exchange	Ordinary Share/ADS market price at 31 December 2011	Range of the Ordinary Share/ADS market price during 2011
London	2975p	2543.5p to 3194p
Stockholm	316.0 SEK	269.3 SEK to 328.5 SEK
New York	$46.29	$40.95 to $52.40

5.177 It should be noted that there is a difference between the definition of share options required to be disclosed by quoted companies in the directors' remuneration report under Schedule 8 to SI 2008/410 and the definition of share options for the purposes of the requirement in Schedule 5 to SI 2008/410 for the disclosure of aggregate gains made on the exercise of share options. In Schedule 8 to SI 2008/410, share options are defined as options granted in respect of qualifying services of the person. [SI 2008/410 8 Sch 8(4)]. However, share options in Schedule 5 to SI 2008/410 are defined merely as rights to acquire shares (that is, it includes share options that are not in respect of qualifying services). [SI 2008/410 5 Sch 12(b)]. This is illustrated in the following example:

Example – Definition of share options

Three years ago, company A acquired 100 per cent of the share capital of company B from Mr C, a director of both companies. As part of the consideration, Mr C was granted options to subscribe for shares in company A at 25p per share. These options have recently been exercised at a time when the market price of company A's shares was 75p. Will the gain on exercising these options be disclosable as part of directors' emoluments in company A's financial statements?

Under paragraph 1(1)(b) of Schedule 5 to SI 2008/410 disclosure is required of the aggregate amount of gains – being the difference between the market price of the shares on the day on which the options were exercised and the price actually paid – on the exercise of any right to acquire shares. However, in the case of a company that is not quoted (as defined in section 385(2) of the 2006 Act) or listed on AIM, only the number of directors who exercised options should be shown.

If company A is quoted, it seems that disclosure of the gains made by Mr C would be required. Under the provisions of Schedule 5 to SI 2008/410, only aggregate disclosure would be required, so Mr C's gains could be combined with those of the other directors and a single figure disclosed. It is arguable that such disclosure does not belong in a note concerning directors' emoluments, as Mr C was granted the options only as consideration for the acquisition of company B. Indeed, each of the other requirements of paragraph 1 of Schedule 5 to SI 2008/410 (that is, other than the gains on the exercise of share options) refers specifically to 'qualifying services' and these options were not a reward for qualifying services. However, the fact that reference to qualifying services is not included in the requirement must be relevant. Hence, we consider that disclosure of Mr C's gains in the aggregate figure required by Schedule 5 to SI 2008/410 would be appropriate.

There is a further disclosure requirement in Schedule 8 to SI 2008/410 for quoted companies to disclose, in tabular form, by individual director, details of share options. In this case, however, paragraph 8(4) of Schedule 8 to SI 2008/410 specifically states that 'share option' (for the purpose of the Schedule 8 to SI 2008/410 disclosures) means a share option granted in respect of qualifying services of a person. Therefore, as the options were not granted in respect of Mr C's services to company A, the options are not disclosed in the table of individual directors' share options.

5.178 The examples below consider the disclosure requirements when share options are exercised by a director after retirement.

Example 1 – Options exercised immediately after retirement

A director of a quoted company (for definition see para 5.6.3) resigned during the year. He was allowed to retain and exercise his share options early and did so one day after resignation (but still during the year). He is the only director who has exercised options. At present the company has not included the director in the disclosure table of directors' individual interests in options required by Schedule 8 to SI 2008/410, but has included a footnote with some but not all the information. For example, it has not disclosed the gain on exercise of the options. Should this be disclosed?

If the director had exercised his option whilst still a director then disclosure of the gain would be required by SI 2008/410 requirements for disclosure of aggregate gains made by directors on exercise of options. However, as he exercised them a day after resigning it is not caught by this requirement.

If the options were retained not as an entitlement of employment, but as part of compensation for leaving, they form part of the director's compensation for loss of office. The question arises generally as to whether if a director retains options on leaving the company, but exercises them in the following year, the gain needs to be disclosed. In that situation our view is that no disclosure is required, but there should have been full disclosure at the time of leaving (see example 2 below).

In this case, however, the early exercise of options is connected with the resignation and took place immediately afterwards. Therefore, we consider there should be disclosure of the exercise of the options in the compensation for loss of office note. This can be done by including the director in the individual directors' share options table which should cover directors during the year and not just those at the year end. Schedule 8 to SI 2008/410 requires disclosure (in tabular form) in the directors' remuneration report of interests in options of each person who has served as a director at any time in the financial year. It requires, therefore, that the director is included in the table and the director's interest should be disclosed as at the date of his resignation. [SI 2008/410 8 Sch 8, 9]. A note should then be added to say that the director was permitted to retain the options on resigning and that they have subsequently been exercised. In addition, we consider that the gain on exercise should be disclosed by way of a note. Schedule 8 to SI 2008/410 requires disclosure of compensation for loss of office not otherwise disclosed in the table of individual directors' emoluments. [SI 2008/410 8 Sch 15].

Example 2 – Options exercised by former directors

Two directors of a quoted company (for definition see para 5.6.3) retired in the previous financial year and, at the end of that year, the financial statements disclosed that they had retired and had been permitted to retain their share options, giving details as part of the disclosure on compensation for loss of office. In the course of this year, those former directors exercised their options. Does any disclosure have to be given under the Companies Act relating to directors' remuneration?

There is no Companies Act requirement to disclose the gains as the directors left before the end of the previous year. Schedule 8 to SI 2008/410 requires significant awards of compensation to former directors to be disclosed, but the exercise of share options after retirement is not the same as a payment or award made to the former director by the company. [SI 2008/410 8 Sch 15]. Therefore, there does not appear to be any requirement in the Act to disclose anything this year (given full disclosure of the retained options in last year's financial statements), but the company could disclose, if it wished, in the spirit of 'full disclosure'.

Long-term incentive schemes

5.179   A long-term incentive scheme is defined under SI 2008/410 as '...*any agreement or arrangement under which money or other assets may become receivable by a person and which includes one or more qualifying conditions with respect to service or performance that cannot be fulfilled within a single financial year*'. [SI 2008/410 8 Sch 11(5)].

5.180   A long-term incentive scheme does not include bonuses the amount of which fall to be determined by reference to service or performance within a single financial year. [SI 2008/410 8 Sch 11(5)]. A feature of many bonus arrangements is that a bonus is payable after the end of the financial year and only if the director is in office at the payment date. In such circumstances we consider that under SI 2008/410 the bonus may fall within the definition of a long-term incentive scheme.

Example – Bonuses paid after the end of the period

A company calculates its directors' bonuses by reference to the company's results for the year ended 31 December 20X5. However, under the terms of the bonus scheme, the bonuses are paid on 28 February 20X6. If the director is not in office at 28 February 20X6, entitlement to the bonus is forfeited.

We consider that the amount of the bonus is not calculated by reference to service or performance conditions that can be fulfilled within a single financial year. Instead it is calculated by reference to the company's performance for the financial year ended 31 December 20X5 and the directors' service for the fourteen month period to 28 February 20X6. Thus, we consider that the most appropriate disclosure of these bonuses is as long-term incentive schemes.

However, the definitions under the Listing Rules differ from those in the Act, which can impact on disclosure – see further the example in paragraph 5.188.1.

5.181   A long-term incentive scheme does not include compensation for loss of office, payments for breach of contract and other termination payments. Nor does it include retirement benefits. [SI 2008/410 8 Sch 11(5)].

5.182   Bonuses and deferred bonuses and compensation for loss of office would instead be disclosed in the table of each director's emoluments and compensation (see para 5.164 above). Pensions and other retirement benefits would be separately disclosed (see para 5.193 onwards below).

5.183 The difference between a long-term incentive scheme and a deferred bonus may sometimes be difficult to determine. For example, if a three-year performance scheme is introduced whereby a director is entitled to an award if the performance of the company over the three years satisfies certain conditions, this is a long-term incentive scheme. This is because the award relates to a three-year period and the conditions cannot be fulfilled within a single financial year.

5.183.1 The example below considers the disclosure requirements for a long-term incentive scheme where the performance conditions have been met, but the final award of shares is still subject to approval.

> **Example – Share awards subject to approval**
>
> A quoted company (for definition see para 5.6.3) operates a long-term incentive plan (LTIP) for directors based on performance conditions over a three-year period. At the end of the current reporting period, the performance conditions have been met, but the final award of shares will not be approved until after the date of approval of the financial statements. What should be disclosed for directors' remuneration?
>
> Paragraph 1(1)(c) of Schedule 5 to SI 2008/410 requires separate disclosure of the aggregate of (i) the amount of money paid to or receivable by directors under long-term incentive schemes in respect of qualifying services and (ii) the net value of assets (other than money and share options) received or receivable by directors under such schemes in respect of such services.
>
> Therefore, the Schedule 5 to SI 2008/410 disclosure will depend upon when the amounts were receivable (and can be quantified). The relevant amount would be measured as at the date the shares were receivable by the directors, that is, no longer contingent. If the award is subject to approval after the date of approval of the financial statements, the amounts would be contingent at that date and would, therefore, not be disclosed as finally awarded until the following year.
>
> The LTIP awards are not included in the table showing directors' individual emoluments, as Schedule 8 to SI 2008/410 requires separate disclosure (in tabular form) of details of any long-term incentive schemes (see para 5.189 below for the information to be disclosed).
>
> This disclosure, required by Schedule 8 to SI 2008/410, is similar to that in Listing Rule 9.8.8R (3) (see para 5.189.2 below) and so compliance with SI 2008/410 will also cover the requirements of the Listing Rules. If the awards were not receivable at the year end (because they are still awaiting formal approval), then the shares will be included in the scheme interests at the end of the year. A note should, however, be included to indicate that the performance conditions have been met, but that the award is still subject to formal approval after the date of approval of the financial statements and, therefore, further details of the final determination of the award will be included in the following year.

5.184 If, however, there is a scheme that lasts three years, but a director receives an award in each of those three years dependent on the performance of that year, this is a bonus. If the three years of bonus is only payable after the end of the three years it is a deferred bonus, but not a long-term incentive, because the conditions were satisfied by reference to performance in each of the three years, considered separately. However, if the three years of bonus, although earned by reference to each of the individual years is only payable if the director stays for the three years, this may fall within the definition of a long-term incentive scheme as there is then an additional service condition that cannot be satisfied within one year (see also para 5.188.1 below).

5.185 Sometimes a scheme may provide for a bonus payable in respect of the year, but where part of the bonus may be taken in shares, which if held for a further three years are then supplemented by a further award of shares, dependent on cumulative performance over the three years. In this case, the whole of the initial bonus, whether reinvested in shares or not, is emoluments in year one because it is receivable in respect of that year, but the additional potential award may be treated as a long-term incentive.

5.186 The remuneration report is required to disclose details of long-term incentives by individual director in tabular form (see para 5.189). [SI 2008/410 8 Sch 11(1), (3)].

5.187 Details of share options are not required to be included. This is because they are separately disclosed (see from para 5.170 above). [SI 2008/410 8 Sch 11(2)]. Awards of long-term incentives are sometimes received in the form of options with a nil exercise price, which also require this separate disclosure. Thus, there may sometimes be a cross over between the disclosure of long-term incentives and the disclosure of share options as illustrated in the example below. In such cases, full details of the options, often referred to as 'nil cost options', and a clear cross-reference between information contained in each of the tables should be given.

Example – Gain on exercise of nil cost options awarded under LTIP

A quoted company (for definition see para 5.6.3) has had a long-term incentive scheme in operation for three years, whereby three years ago directors were awarded the right to receive a number of shares that would vary depending on the company's performance over three years. The scheme has always, to date, been disclosed and described as a long-term incentive scheme. This year the final awards were made and the shares vested with the directors. Normally the disclosures required would be the value of the shares awarded on the date they vested. However, it transpires that the form of the award is the grant of nil cost options exercisable from that date. As these are options, is the requirement of the Act to give the total gain on the exercise of options, calculated as at the date of exercise and not, as with long-term incentive schemes, as at the date of vesting?

In this case we consider that the substance of the scheme is a long-term incentive scheme and that there is no difference in reality between vesting the shares in the directors at a particular date and awarding them nil cost options exercisable from that date. For this reason we consider that the disclosures should be made as if the scheme were a long-term incentive scheme and not an option scheme. Thus the disclosures should be made, by individual director, of the value of the shares received on the vesting date. This is because the options are exercisable immediately so that it is the same as if an outright award of shares had been made on the same day. Details of the awards should be given in the table of individuals' interests in long-term incentive schemes required by paragraphs 11 and 12 of Schedule 8 to SI 2008/410 and the resulting options should then also be disclosed in the table of share options required by paragraphs 8 and 9 of Schedule 8 to SI 2008/410. There will need to be a note and cross-reference to describe the situation so that it is clear to a reader of the remuneration report.

5.187.1   A further complication can arise as a result of different definitions in SI 2008/410 and in the Listing Rules. This is explained in the example below.

Example – Deferred bonuses

The directors of a quoted company (for definition see para 5.6.3) have met performance targets for this financial year and have been allocated shares as a bonus. The shares will vest with the directors unconditionally in three years' time if the directors are still with the company. How should such bonuses be disclosed in the annual report?

Under SI 2008/410 an arrangement conditional on fulfilment of one or more qualifying conditions with respect to service or performance that cannot be fulfilled in a single financial year is classed as a 'long-term incentive scheme'. Bonuses whose amount can be determined by reference to service or performance within a single financial year are disregarded for this purpose. [SI 2008/410 8 Sch 11(5)].

Although the amount is initially determined by reference to performance within a single year, this amount is only provisional. The final amount receivable (all or nothing in this case) depends on a further service condition. Therefore, the final amount of the bonus cannot be determined by performance or service within one year and so qualifies as a long-term incentive scheme under SI 2008/410. Therefore, the award should be treated as a long-term incentive and disclosed by individual director in tabular form in the directors' remuneration report required by SI 2008/410.

If, in practice, the service conditions were not observed such that a director would receive the shares whether or not he stayed with the company for three years, this would not be a long-term incentive scheme. If the service condition either does not exist or is not observed, the bonus would be treated as an amount to be disclosed in the table of individual directors' emoluments as a bonus under paragraph 7(1)(b) of Schedule 8 to SI 2008/410.

Under the Listing Rules deferred bonuses are defined as *"any arrangement pursuant to the terms of which an employee or director may receive a bonus (including cash or any security) in respect of service and/or performance in a period not exceeding the length of the relevant financial year notwithstanding that the bonus may, subject only to the person remaining a director or employee of the group, be receivable by the person after the end of the period to which the award relates"*. This definition effectively requires the service period to be ignored and thus the bonus would be disclosed in the year as remuneration for the purpose of the Listing Rules.

There is, therefore, a difference between the disclosure under the legal requirements (as a long-term incentive) and the disclosure under the Listing Rules (as directors' emoluments for the year). We suggest that this is dealt with by excluding the amount from the detailed directors' remuneration table given under the Listing Rules, but including a note to that table to say that the amount is included in the long-term incentive scheme table given in accordance with SI 2008/410. The note to the detailed directors' remuneration table should also give the amount of the bonus by individual director and the total emoluments that would be disclosed under the Listing Rules, if the bonus were to be included in the table of emoluments required by the Listing Rules. The bonus should then be included in accordance with SI 2008/410 in the disclosure of directors' long-term incentive scheme interests.

In addition, for companies reporting under IFRS, there could be a further difference. Under IAS 24, long-term benefits include long-service, profit-sharing, bonuses and deferred compensation not payable wholly within 12 months of the end of the period. SI 2008/410 does not rigidly divide bonuses between amounts *payable* within a year of the period end and amounts payable thereafter as the IAS 24 definitions do, but rather divides them by reference to the *period of service to which they relate*. That is, SI 2008/410 divides them between the amounts payable in respect of the year and amounts not payable specifically in respect of the year.

5.188   For quoted companies, the information to be disclosed by individual director in tabular form is as follows:

- Details of the scheme interests of each director at the beginning of the financial year or date of appointment as director, if later. For this purpose and for the purpose of the remaining disclosure requirements 'scheme interest' means an interest under a long-term incentive scheme whereby assets may become receivable in respect of the director's qualifying services. [SI 2008/410 8 Sch 11(4)(a), 12(1)(a)].

- Details of scheme interests awarded to each director during the financial year, including (if shares may become receivable) the number of shares, the market price of those shares at the date of award and details of performance conditions. [SI 2008/410 8 Sch 12(2), 12(1)(b)].

- Details of scheme interests of each director at the end of the financial year or on ceasing to be a director, if earlier. [SI 2008/410 8 Sch 12(1)(c)].

- For each scheme interest referred to above:

  (i)   The end of the period over which the qualifying conditions for that interest have to be met (or the end of the last such period where there are different periods for different conditions).

  (ii)   A description of any variation in the terms and conditions of the scheme interests in the year.

  [SI 2008/410 8 Sch 12(1)(d)].

- For each scheme interest that has vested in the year:

  (i)   the relevant details of any shares, that is the number of shares, the date on which the scheme interest was awarded, the market price of each of those shares when the scheme interest was awarded, the market price when the scheme interest vested and details of performance conditions;

  (ii)   the amount of any money; and

  (iii)   the value of any other assets;

  that have become receivable in respect of the interest. [SI 2008/410 8 Sch 12(1)(e), 12(3)].

- For the purpose of the disclosure in the last bullet point above a scheme interest vests at the earliest date when:

  (i)   It has been ascertained that the qualifying conditions have been met.

  (ii)   The nature and quantity of the assets receivable under the scheme in respect of the interest have been ascertained.

  [SI 2008/410 8 Sch 11(4)(b)].

5.188.1   It should be noted that there is a distinction between the disclosures required to be made by quoted companies and those by unquoted companies. Quoted companies have to disclose the amounts that *may* become receivable (the 'scheme interests') and also give information regarding performance conditions, so that the reader of the remuneration report can understand what will have to occur for the director to earn that amount. If the director earns the right to the award in the period (that is, it vests), this must also be disclosed. Unquoted companies only have to disclose the amount that is received or receivable by the director in the period (see para 5.27) — that is, the amount that the director has earned the right to (in other words, the amount that has vested).

5.188.2   For companies listed in the UK, the Listing Rules require disclosure of details of any long-term incentive schemes, other than share options (details of which are disclosed separately), including:

- The interests of each director by name in the long-term incentive schemes at the start of the period under review.

- Entitlements or awards granted and commitments made to each director under such schemes during the period, showing which crystallise either in the same year or subsequent years.

■ The money value and number of shares, cash payments or other benefits received by each director under such schemes during the period.

■ The interests of each director in the long-term incentive schemes at the end of the period.

[LR 9.8.8R (3) to (6)].

5.189 The example below considers the disclosure implications for long-term incentives where the incentive was awarded before appointment as a director.

Example – LTIP awarded before appointment as a director

A director of a quoted company (for definition see para 5.6.3) is appointed during the year. Immediately prior to being appointed a director, he had been awarded benefits under a long-term incentive plan (LTIP) and at the date of appointment and the year end date, the performance conditions remain unfulfilled.

(a) Does the director's interest in the LTIP need to be disclosed in the directors' remuneration report?

(b) If the award had been made a number of years ago and he had completed his performance criteria, but is required to remain in the company's employment for a further period, does this make any difference?

Paragraphs 11 and 12 of Schedule 8 to SI 2008/410 require disclosure of each director's interests in LTIPs that are receivable *"in respect of qualifying services"*.

(a) Where a director is appointed during the period and has outstanding performance conditions in respect of an award made under an LTIP prior to his appointment, we consider that the award is receivable in respect of qualifying services, because he must perform those qualifying services in order to be entitled to receive that award. Consequently, disclosure of the interest in the LTIP is required in the directors' remuneration report.

(b) SI 2008/410 does not distinguish between performance conditions and service conditions (see para 5.137). Where a director is required to remain in the company's employment in order for an entitlement under an LTIP to vest, the company is receiving performance from that director over that extended period, so it would be included as a performance condition under SI 2008/410. Consequently, if the director is required to remain in employment after his date of appointment in order to become entitled to receive the award, then we would consider that the award is in respect of qualifying services and disclosure of the interest in the LTIP is required in the directors' remuneration report. However, an explanation could be given in a note of the circumstances, that is, that the performance conditions were satisfied before becoming a director and only the service condition remains to be satisfied.

5.189.1 The example below summarises the disclosures required under SI 2008/410 in respect of performance conditions relating to awards that have not vested at the year end.

Example – Performance conditions

A quoted company is preparing a directors' remuneration report. Several of the directors have awards that have been granted to them under the company's share option scheme and Long-Term Incentive Plan (LTIP), but which are yet to vest. Do the performance criteria upon which vesting depends need to be disclosed in the remuneration report?

Paragraph 3 of Schedule 8 to SI 2008/410 requires disclosure of a policy statement that explains the company's policy on directors' remuneration for the following financial year and for financial years subsequent to that. The policy statement should include a summary of performance criteria to which any entitlement under a share option scheme or LTIP is subject and an explanation as to why those performance criteria were chosen (see para 5.134).

Paragraph 9(e) of Schedule 8 to SI 2008/410 also requires a summary of performance criteria on which the award or exercise of a share option is conditional, including a description of any variation in the year, to be given (see para 5.170.1).

Paragraphs 12(2) and 12(3) of Schedule 8 to SI 2008/410 require disclosure of performance conditions in respect of scheme interests awarded in the year and scheme interests that been received or become receivable in the year respectively (see para 5.189).

An award under a share option scheme or an LTIP forms part of the director's remuneration in the year in which the share options are exercised or when the awards under the LTIP are received or receivable.

Consequently, if an award under either a share option scheme or an LTIP is outstanding at the year end, it will form part of the director's remuneration in the following or subsequent periods and the performance criteria on which vesting depends should be disclosed, together with an explanation as to why those performance criteria were chosen.

5.190   Table 5.21 is an example of disclosure of performance conditions attaching to a scheme. In this case the performance condition is related to total shareholder return and adjusted earnings per share.

Table 5.21 – Performance conditions

SSE plc – Annual Report – 31 March 2012

Remuneration Report (extract)

Executive Directors' salary and incentive plans 2011/12 (extract)

Performance Measure	Purpose – link to strategy	Policy and decisions
Performance Share Plan 2009-2012 For awards granted in 2009 performance is measured against the following two elements over a three-year period.	The two elements of TSR and EPS reflect relative and absolute measures of performance.	**0% awarded** Maximum award of 150% of base salary each year. Awards are released to the extent performance conditions are met.
Total Shareholder Return (TSR) • 100% vests at or above 75th percentile • 25% vests at median • straight-line basis between median and 75th percentile • no vesting of award if median performance not achieved	The relative TSR measure is dependent on SSE's relative long-term share price performance and dividend return. It is therefore directly linked to the strategic objective of sustained real dividend growth.	**TSR (max 50%)** Out-turn below median of FTSE 100 and 0% of TSR element awarded; the graph on page 81 reflects performance over a five-year period.
Adjusted Earnings per Share* (EPS) • 100% vests where EPS is 9% RPI • 25% vests where EPS is 3% above RPI • straight-line basis between 3% and 9% above RPI • no vesting if EPS minimum growth of RPI +3% is not achieved	Adjusted EPS* is used to monitor SSE's performance over the medium term because it is straightforward: it defines the amount of profit after tax that has been earned for each Ordinary Share. Profit is required to support the payment of, and increases in, the dividend.	**EPS (max 50%)** Out-turn growth below the EPS minimum growth target RPI + 3% and 0% of EPS element awarded.

Long-term incentive scheme for an individual

5.191   Where the only participant of a long-term incentive scheme is a director (or a prospective director) and the arrangement is established specifically to facilitate, in unusual circumstances, the recruitment or retention of the relevant individual, disclosure of the following details are required to be given in the first annual report and accounts published by the company following the date on which the individual becomes eligible to participate in the arrangement:

■   The full text of the scheme or a description of its principal terms.

■   Details of trusteeship in the scheme or interest in the trustees, if any, of directors of the company.

■   A statement that the principal provisions of the scheme (set out in detail in rule 13.8.11R (3) of the Listing Rules) cannot be altered to the advantage of the participant without shareholders' approval.

■   A statement as to whether benefits under the scheme will be pensionable and if so the reasons for this.

■   The name of the sole participant.

■   The date on which he or she first became eligible to participate in the arrangement.

■   An explanation as to why the circumstances in which the arrangement was established were unusual.

■   The conditions to be satisfied under the arrangement's terms.

■   The maximum award(s) under the arrangement's terms, or, if there is no maximum, the basis on which the awards will be determined.

[LR 9.4.3R, 13.8.11R].

An example of disclosure is given in Table 5.22 below.

Table 5.22 – Aviva plc – Annual report and accounts – 31 December 2010

Directors' remuneration report (extract)

Policy	How delivered
Other benefits Other benefits are provided on a market competitive basis.	■ Cash car allowance ■ PMI
CFO Recruitment Share Awards Plan The CFO Recruitment Share Awards Plan was approved by the committee in 2010 for the granting of one-off share awards to Patrick Regan as part of the recruitment offer made to him. The following awards were granted to Mr Regan under the rules of this plan and are subject to clawback provisions: ■ Replacement Restricted Share Award (RRSA) with a grant value of £1.65 million to compensate for the loss of unvested Willis Group Holdings Limited restricted shares and share options. ■ Bonus Replacement Deferred Share Award (BRDSA) with a grant value of £283,333, two-thirds of the compensation for the loss of bonus which would have been paid to Mr Regan by Willis Group Holdings Limited for the 2009 financial year. ■ One Aviva, Twice the Value Award (OATTV) with a grant value of 75% of the BRDSA	■ RRSA will vest in three equal tranches on the first, second and third anniversaries of Mr Regan's employment start date, subject to Mr Regan's performance being considered to be at lease 'Mid Range', as assessed by the chairman of the Company and the group chief executive, and no dealing restrictions being in place on the vesting date. Otherwise the principal terms of the RRSA are generally the same as those of the ABP, except that on cessation of employment, Mr Regan's unvested awards will generally lapse unless he leaves by reason of death, ill-health, injury, disability, redundancy or a sale of an employing subsidiary or business. ■ BRDSA will vest under the same terms as outlined above for the ABP and is therefore not subject to performance conditions. ■ OATTV will vest under the same terms as outlined above for the OATTV Plan. ■ Awards granted under the CFO Recruitment Share Awards Plan are not pensionable. Any amendments to the plan which are to the advantage of the participant (other than certain minor amendments) are subject to shareholder approval.

Patrick Regan, chief financial officer*

Element	Amount	Commentary**
Basic Salary	£511,539 during the year.	Mr Regan commenced employment on 22 February 2010 with an annual basic salary of £600,000.
ABP	£668,850 (111.5% of basic salary) (£222,950 delivered in cash and £445,900 deferred into shares for three years)	Bonus is a function of the degree of achievement of 2010 targets as follows: Financial 40.8% (maximum 50%) Employee 0.9% (maximum 10%) Customer 5.9% (maximum 10%) Personal 26.7% (maximum 30%)
LTIP – Face Value of grant	£900,000	The face value of the grant represented 150% of Mr Regan's basic salary on 28 February 2010.
CFO Recruitment Share Awards Plan ■ RRSA	£1,650,000	RRSA was granted over Restricted Shares and will vest in three equal tranches per year over a three-year period. The grant is compensation for the loss of share awards and share options from previous employer (see section 10 for more details).
■ BRDSA	£283,333	BRDSA was granted over Restricted Shares and will vest on third anniversary of the date of grant (see section 10 for more details).
■ OATTV	£212,500	The face value of 75% of the BRDSA. Vests subject to performance condition outcome of 2010 OATTV award (see section 10 for more details).
Defined Contribution Pension		See section 23 for details.
Other Benefits	£13,811 cash car allowance during the year PMI £141,667 compensation for loss of bonus from previous employer	Annual car allowance of £16,200. Mr Regan received £425,000 compensation for loss of bonus from previous employer. This payment was paid one-third in cash (£141,667) with the remaining £283,333 deferred into restricted shares for three years (BRDSA as detailed above).

* Patrick Regan joined the Company and Board on 22 February 2010.
** Percentages do not necessarily add up due to rounding.

Pensions

5.192   The definitions of pension scheme, money purchase scheme, money purchase benefits and retirement benefits are the same under Schedule 8 to SI 2008/410 as they are for the purpose of the requirement to disclose total emoluments under Schedule 5 to SI 2008/410. The definitions are described from paragraph 5.61 above.

5.193   The disclosure requirements for money purchase schemes are to show, by individual director, the details of company contributions paid or payable in respect of the director for the year or paid by the company in the year in respect of another financial year. [SI 2008/410 8 Sch 13(3)]. This is similar to the requirement in the Listing Rules for disclosure of details of the contribution or allowance payable or made by the company in respect of each director during the period under review. [LR 9.8.8R (11)].

5.194 'Company contributions' means any payments (including insurance premiums) made, or treated as made, to the scheme in respect of the director by anyone other than the director, that is the term would include payments by parties other than the company in respect of the director. [SI 2008/410 8 Sch 17]. This definition is consistent with that given for the purpose of disclosure of aggregate contributions by all companies (see para 5.65 above). See further paragraph 5.202 for practical application of the rules.

5.194.1 An example of disclosure of company contributions to money purchase schemes is given in Table 5.23.

Table 5.23 – Money purchase pension schemes

Aggreko PLC – Annual Report – 31 December 2010

Pension entitlements

Executive Directors participate in defined contribution plans that are designed to be in line with the median practice in the relevant country but Executive Directors who reside in the United Kingdom and who joined the Board before 1 April 2002 participate in a defined benefits plan.

Rupert Soames, Kash Pandya and Bill Caplan are members of the Aggreko plc Group Personal Pension Plan. Rupert Soames is entitled to a pension contribution from the Company of 25% of his basic salary and Kash Pandya and Bill Caplan are entitled to a Company contribution of 20%. Kash Pandya has chosen not to take his entire Company contribution into the Group Personal Pension Plan and takes a proportion as a cash payment, shown as Other Pay in the Emoluments table on page 72.

George Walker is entitled to participate in the Employees' Savings Investment Retirement plan and the Supplemental Executive Retirement plan of Aggreko LLC, which are governed by the laws of the United States. These plans allow contributions by the employee and the Group to be deferred for tax.

Contributions paid by the Company under the defined contribution plans during the year are as follows:

	Notes	Company contributions during 2010 £	Company contributions during 2009 £
Rupert Soames		137,500	125,000
George Walker	1	99,539	111,271
Kash Pandya		15,840	15,840
Bill Caplan		55,000	40,500

5.195 The Schedule 8 to SI 2008/410 disclosure requirements in respect of directors' rights under defined benefit schemes are to show, for each director of the company who has served as such at any time during the financial year, the following information:

- Changes in the director's accrued benefits during the year.

- Details of the director's accrued benefits at the end of the year.

- Transfer value of the director's accrued benefits at the end of the year, calculated in accordance with 'Retirement Benefit Schemes – Transfer Values (GN11)' published by the Institute of Actuaries and the Faculty of Actuaries and dated 6 April 2001.

- Transfer value of the director's accrued benefits, either at the end of the previous year as shown in the previous period's remuneration report or, if none was produced, as at the beginning of the financial year.

- The amount of the difference between the two transfer values disclosed in the previous two bullet points, less the amount of any contributions made to the scheme by the director during the year.

[SI 2008/410 8 Sch 13(1), (2)].

5.195.1 An example of disclosures required under Schedule 8 to SI 2008/410 might be as follows:

Director	Increase in accrued benefits	Accrued benefits at 31 December 2002	Transfer value 31 December 2002	Transfer value 31 December 2001	Increase in transfer value less director's contributions
	£	£	£	£	£
A Smith	2,000	30,000	216,000	190,000	21,000
B Jones	10,000	150,000	1,500,000	1,360,000	137,000

See further paragraph 5.203 for practical application of the rules.

5.196 For companies listed in the UK, the Listing Rules disclosure requirements in respect of directors' rights under defined benefit schemes are to show the following information:

■ details of the amount of the increase during the period under review (excluding inflation) and of the accumulated total amount at the end of the period in respect of the accrued benefit to which each director would be entitled on leaving service or is entitled having left service during the period under review;

■ and either:

■ the transfer value (less director's contributions) of the relevant increase in accrued benefit (to be calculated in accordance with Actuarial Guidance Note GN11, but making no deduction for any underfunding) as at the end of the period; or

■ so much of the following information as is necessary to make a reasonable assessment of the transfer value in respect of each director:

■ current age;

■ normal retirement age;

■ the amount of any contributions paid or payable by the director under the scheme's terms during the period under review;

■ details of spouse's and dependants' benefits;

■ early retirement rights and options, expectations of pension increases after retirement (whether guaranteed or discretionary); and

■ discretionary benefits for which allowance is made in transfer values on leaving and any other relevant information which will significantly affect the value of the benefits.

Voluntary contributions and benefits should not be disclosed.

[LR 9.8.8R (12)].

5.197 There is some overlap between the disclosure requirements in respect of defined benefit pensions in the Listing Rules and the legal requirements in SI 2008/410, but there are differences. The legal disclosure requirements go much further than the requirements of the Listing Rules. This is principally because SI 2008/ 410 specifically requires the transfer value of a director's accrued pension at the beginning and end of the year to be given, which is not a requirement of the Listing Rules. The difference between these two values less the director's contributions also has to be disclosed. Under the Listing Rules either the transfer value of the increase in accrued pension or sufficient information to enable it to be ascertained only has to be given. The main disclosures, which are considered further below, are as follows:

■ The SI 2008/410 requires disclosure of any changes during the year in a director's accrued benefits under a pension scheme, which includes inflation, whereas the Listing Rules requirement excludes inflation (see para 5.199 below).

■ The SI 2008/410 requires disclosure of the change in the transfer value of accrued benefits (based on the opening and closing values of the transfer value), whilst the Listing Rules require the transfer value of the increase in the accrued benefit to be disclosed (or sufficient information about the Director's pension entitlements from which that value can be derived) (see para 5.200 below).

5.198 The Listing Rules require disclosure of the increase excluding inflation of the director's accrued benefit during the period under review, whereas SI 2008/410 requires disclosure of any changes during the relevant financial year in the person's accrued benefits under the scheme, which would include inflation. [LR 9.8.8 R (12)(a); SI 2008/410 8 Sch 13(2)(a)(i)]. Although the only difference between the disclosures is the inflationary element, they are aimed at telling different stories: the SI 2008/410 disclosure is aimed at telling the reader the difference between the annual pension that each director would have received if they had retired at the end of the year and the annual pension that they would have received if they had retired at the end of the previous year. However, the Listing Rules disclosure is designed to disclose the element of the director's increase in their accrued benefit that is earned during the year. If the director's annual pension entitlement increased only because of inflation, they would have earned no additional pension benefit by reason of employment, as their pension would have been increased by an inflationary element even if they had left. An example of an adjustment for inflation is given below.

Example – Adjustment for inflation

This example shows how the entitlement should be calculated for a director given the relevant facts as follows:

A director has ten years' service at the beginning of the year and earns £120,000 per annum. He is entitled to a pension of one-sixtieth of final pensionable salary for each year of pensionable service. At the end of the year his salary was £130,000. The increase for the year and the accumulated total at the year end are calculated as follows:

Accumulated totals

At the beginning of the year: $10/60 \times £120,000 = £20,000$

At the end of the year: $11/60 \times £130,000 = £23,833$

Calculation of increase in the year (excluding inflation)

Increase: $£23,833$ less $£20,000 = £3,833$

Inflation is assumed to be 5%.

The increase due to inflation is: $£20,000 \times 5\% = £1,000$

The increase excluding inflation is, therefore, £2,833.

Note: The inflation rate used should be that published by the Secretary of State for Social Security each year (Schedule 3 of the Pension Schemes Act 1993).

5.199 A further difference between the Listing Rules and the legal requirements is that the Listing Rules require disclosure of the transfer value (less director's contributions) of the relevant increase in accrued benefit as at the end of the period or sufficient information about the director's pension entitlements from which that value can be derived. [LR 9.8.8R (12)(b)]. SI 2008/410, however, requires disclosure of the amount obtained by subtracting the transfer value of the person's accrued benefits at the end of the previous period from the transfer value of his accrued benefits at the end of the current period, then subtracting the director's personal contributions from that total. [SI 2008/410 8 Sch 13(2)(d)]. The transfer value of the increase in accrued benefits, required by the Listing Rules, discloses the current value of the increase in accrued benefits that the director has earned in the period, whereas the change in the transfer value, required by SI 2008/410 discloses the absolute increase or decrease in the director's transfer value and includes the change in value of the accrued benefits that results from applying a different actuarial factor to the accrued benefits at the beginning of the period, as well as the additional value earned in the year.

5.200 The above differences between SI 2008/410 requirements and those of the Listing Rules are illustrated in the following example.

Example – Transfer values under SI 2008/410 and the Listing Rules

A UK listed company is preparing its directors' remuneration report in compliance with the disclosure requirements in the Listing Rules and Schedule 8 to SI 2008/410. The company's executive directors are members of the company's defined benefit pension scheme. The Listing Rules require disclosure of the transfer value of the increase in each director's accrued benefits under the scheme, excluding inflation, while SI 2008/410 requires disclosure of the increase in the transfer value of their accrued benefits less the director's personal pension contributions.

What is the difference between these disclosures and does the company need to disclose both figures?

A transfer value is an actuarially calculated value that measures the fair value of a pension scheme's liability in respect of a director's accrued benefit. The Listing Rules require disclosure of the transfer value of the increase in the director's accrued benefit excluding inflation. So, using an example, if a director's accrued benefit at the end of 20X2 was £100,000 and his accrued benefit at the end of 20X3 was £110,000, inflation was steady at 3% and the actuarially calculated 'factor' for this director to be applied is 9.27, the transfer value of the increase in accrued benefit excluding inflation is £64,890, being $9.27 \times (£110,000 - (103\% \times £100,000))$.

SI 2008/410 requires disclosure of the difference between the transfer value at the year end and the transfer value at the beginning of the year, less any personal contributions paid by the director. Using the same facts as in the example above and assuming that the 'factor' at the end of 20X2 was 8.5 and the director contributed £500 per month (gross), the figure disclosed will be £163,700 (the difference between the transfer value at the end of 20X3 (£110,000 × 9.27 = £1,019,700) and the transfer value at the end of 20X2 (£100,000 × 8.5 = £850,000), less the director's personal contributions of £6,000).

So, although the requirements of the Listing Rules and SI 2008/410 may appear similar, the resulting disclosures can be significantly different. The company will need to comply with both requirements.

5.200.1 An example of disclosure that gives the information required by both SI 2008/410 and the Listing Rules is Table 5.24.

Table 5.24 – Disclosure of directors' pension benefits

Vodafone Group plc – Annual Report – 31 March 2012

Directors' remuneration (extract)

Pensions (extract)

Pension benefits earned by the director in the year ended 31 March 2012 were:

	Total accrued benefit at 31 March 2012[1] £'000	Change in accrued benefit over the year[1] £'000	Transfer value at 31 March 2011[2] £'000	Transfer value at 31 March 2012[2] £'000	Change in transfer value over year less member contributions £'000	Change in accrued benefit in excess of inflation[3] £'000	Transfer value of change in accrued benefit net of member contributions £'000	Employer allocation/ contribution to defined contribution plans £'000
Andy Halford	18.7	0.9	701.2	846.9	145.7	(0.1)	(4.8)	–

Notes:

[1] Andy Halford took the opportunity to take early retirement from the pension scheme due to the closure of the scheme on 31 March 2010 (aged 51 years). In accordance with the scheme rules, his accrued pension at this date was reduced with an early retirement factor for four years to reflect the fact that his pension is being paid before age 55 and is therefore expected to be paid out for a longer period of time. In addition, Andy Halford exchanged part of his early retirement pension at 31 March 2010 for a tax-free cash lump sum of £118,660. The pension in payment at 31 March 2010 was £17,800 per year, and this increased on 1 April 2011 by 5%, in line with the scheme rules, to £18,700 per year and remained so at 31 March 2012, as shown above. No member contributions are payable as Andy Halford is in receipt of his pension.

[2] The transfer value at 31 March 2012 has been calculated on the basis and methodology set by the trustees after taking actuarial advice, as set out in the papers entitled "Calculation of cash equivalent transfer values" dated January 2011 and "Sex-specific actuarial factor" dated March 2011. No director elected to pay additional voluntary contributions. The transfer value disclosed above does not represent a sum paid or payable to the individual director. Instead it represents a potential liability of the pension scheme.

[3] Inflation has been taken as the increase in the retail price index over the year to 30 September 2011.

Practical application of pensions disclosures

5.201 As noted in paragraph 5.194, quoted companies are required to show, by individual director, the details of company contributions paid or payable in respect of the director to money purchase pension schemes. This requirement applies both to company pension schemes and to company payments to personal pension schemes (see further para 5.61 above).

5.201.1 However, contributions that directors themselves pay by way of a compulsory deduction from salary are disclosed as part of directors' emoluments, rather than pension contributions (see para 5.37 above). Similarly, payments made directly to a director, which the director then elects to pay into a pension scheme should be disclosed as emoluments, rather than pension contributions, as illustrated in the examples below.

Example 1 – Cash in lieu of pension contributions

A quoted company is preparing its directors' remuneration report in accordance with Schedule 8 to SI 2008/410. Some of the directors have contributions paid by the company into its defined contribution scheme. Other directors elected instead to receive a direct payment through payroll, in lieu of the contributions that would have been made by the company to the defined contribution scheme. Although it is expected that they will use the cash in a personal pension scheme, they are under no obligation to do so. How should the payments be presented in the remuneration report?

Because the cash in lieu of pension contributions is paid directly to the directors through the payroll system it cannot be classified as a company contribution to a pension scheme.

The cash received in lieu of pension contributions is remuneration and should be included appropriately in the tabular disclosure given under Schedule 8 to SI 2008/410. Although it is not a company pension contribution, in our view it is equally not salary, bonus, expense allowance or benefit in kind (which are required to be disclosed separately – see para 5.164). In the interests of transparency we believe that the company should disclose the amounts in the emoluments table in a separate column, explaining the nature of the payment.

Example 2 – Waiver of bonus in favour of pension contributions

A director of a quoted company is entitled to an annual salary and other benefits, including an annual bonus. After the end of the year, the value of his bonus is determined and he is given three options:

(a)   He receives the bonus in cash.

(b)   He waives the bonus and the company pays the same amount into his defined contribution pension arrangement.

(c)   He waives the bonus and the company pays the same amount into his final salary-based pension to buy additional years' service in the scheme.

What would be disclosed in the remuneration report under each of these options?

Would the answer be any different if he waived part of his salary, rather than his bonus?

Paragraph 7 of Schedule 8 to SI 2008/410 requires disclosure, in a table, of the emoluments (including bonus) paid to or receivable by each director in respect of qualifying services for the financial year.

The bonus was receivable by the director in respect of qualifying services and it would be his choice to convert the bonus into a pension contribution, so if this happens the amount should continue to be disclosed as emoluments.

If emoluments are waived, then they are excluded from the emoluments table, but disclosed in the remuneration report, as required by the Listing Rules. [LR 9.8.4R (5)]. However, the bonus has not, in substance, been waived as the director has received consideration (additional pension contributions) for the waiver, therefore, the amount should continue to be disclosed as emoluments.

5.202   The examples below consider the implications for disclosure in respect of pension entitlements in various situations, including when the director is appointed or retires in the year. The examples cover the following situations:

- A director (who was previously an employee) is appointed during the year (example 1). (For unquoted companies see para 5.90.1.)

- Serving director receives pension (example 2).

- Retired director becomes non-executive director (example 3).

- Director retires during year, but remains an employee (example 4).

- Director retires and commutes pension (example 5).

Example 1 – Director (previously an employee) appointed during the year

A quoted company is preparing its directors' remuneration report. One of the directors has been an employee of the company and a member of its defined benefits pension scheme, for a number of years, but was appointed as a director of the company during this year.

(a) Under Schedule 8 to SI 2008/410, should the disclosures in respect of the benefits accruing to that director under the defined benefits scheme include all benefits accruing or just those that have accrued to him in respect of qualifying services?

Paragraph 13 of Schedule 8 to SI 2008/410 requires disclosure of specified information (see para 5.196) in respect of a director, where *"...the person has rights under a ... defined benefit scheme ... and any of those rights are rights to which he has become entitled in respect of qualifying services..."*. This means that the disclosures apply where any of the rights are earned in respect of qualifying services. As the director was appointed in the year and some of the benefits accrued at the year-end are in respect of the qualifying services performed since the appointment date, this means that the disclosures apply. These disclosure requirements do not state that they should be made only in respect of the period since appointment and they should, therefore, be calculated based on the director's total accrued benefit under the scheme and not just on the portion that has been earned in respect of qualifying services.

(b) Should the change in the director's accrued benefit disclosed under Schedule 8 to SI 2008/410 be the difference between his accrued benefit at the end of the year and at the beginning of the year or the date of appointment?

Paragraph 13 of Schedule 8 to SI 2008/410 requires disclosure of the change in the director's accrued benefit during the year and does not contain a *proviso* that where the director was appointed during the year the change should be given only since the date of appointment. Therefore, the change in the director's accrued benefit disclosed should be the total difference between the director's accrued benefit at the end of the year and at the beginning of the year. However, whilst disclosing the full year's increase an explanation could be added to the effect that the increase for the year of £x arose after the director became a director.

Example 2 – Serving director receives pension

The chairman of a quoted company is past retirement age and has been receiving a pension from the company for the whole of the current year, in addition to his emoluments (which are not pensionable). Does the table of accrued pension benefits, required by paragraph 13 of Schedule 8 to SI 2008/410 have to include, in respect of the chairman, details of the change (if any) in his accrued benefit, the accrued benefits at the end of the year and the transfer values?

The disclosure requirements for the chairman's defined benefit pension entitlement are the same as the requirements in respect of each of the other directors and are as set out in paragraph 13(2) of Schedule 8 to SI 2008/410. The Act requires disclosure of the information specified in paragraph 13 of Schedule 8 to SI 2008/410 in respect of each person's defined benefit pension entitlements where that person has performed qualifying services at any point during the year (which the chairman has) and has benefits accruing to him/her under a defined benefits scheme (which the chairman has), any of which were accrued in respect of qualifying services. So even though the chairman received no pensionable emoluments during the year (so no further benefits accrued to him during the year), full disclosure is required.

The requirement in Schedule 8 to SI 2008/410 differs from the requirement in Schedule 5 to SI 2008/410 (for unquoted companies) and from the Listing Rules (for UK listed companies).

Schedule 5 to SI 2008/410 requires disclosure (by unquoted companies) of the highest paid director's accrued benefits (and accrued lump sum where applicable) only if the director has performed qualifying services in the year that earn pension entitlements, which a director who is drawing his pension will normally not do. This requirement applies only to the highest paid director.

The Listing Rules require disclosure (by UK listed companies) of the increase in the accrued benefit (excluding inflation) and the transfer value of that increase (which can be substituted by specified details as outlined in the Listing Rules) for each director (or person who resigned as a director during the year). As the chairman is receiving a pension, there will be no increase in the accrued benefit and, consequently, no disclosure is required by the Listing Rules.

However, Schedule 8 to SI 2008/410 requires disclosure (by quoted companies) of pension entitlements where a director has rights under a scheme and any of those rights are rights to which he has become entitled in respect of qualifying services. However, it does not make disclosure conditional on his having performed qualifying services in the year that accrue pension entitlements.

Therefore, the Schedule 8 to SI 2008/410 requirements differ from those of the Listing Rules and under Schedule 8 to SI 2008/410, even if a person has retired and is performing non-qualifying services as a director of the company, perhaps in a non-executive capacity, such that the accrued benefit does not increase, all the pensions entitlement disclosures of Schedule 8 to SI 2008/410 are still required to be given in the directors' remuneration report, as he has rights under the pension scheme that were earned in respect of qualifying services in the past (before he retired).

Example 3 – Retired director becomes non-executive director

A director of a quoted company is a member of the company's defined benefit pension scheme. During the prior year, he reached retirement age, stood down as an executive director and was appointed a non-executive director. He is receiving his pension from the pension scheme in addition to fees in respect of his services as a non-executive director.

(a) Does the director's annual pension received need to be included in his emoluments?

Paragraph 7 of Schedule 8 to SI 2008/410 requires disclosure, in a table, of the emoluments paid to or receivable by each director in respect of qualifying services for the financial year. The pension payment is receivable by the director, but it was accrued in respect of qualifying services in years prior to his retirement, so is not receivable in respect of qualifying services for the period and should be excluded from the disclosure of his emoluments.

(b) Should the director be included in the defined benefit pension disclosures?

Paragraph 13 of Schedule 8 to SI 2008/410 requires disclosure of specified information (see para 5.196) in respect of a director, where *"...the person has rights under a ... defined benefit scheme ... and any of those rights are rights to which he has become entitled in respect of qualifying services..."*. This means that the disclosures apply where the director (the Act does not differentiate between executive and non-executive directors) has any entitlement under a defined benefit scheme and any of those rights are earned in respect of qualifying services.

As the director served as a director during the year and has an entitlement under a defined benefit scheme, some of which was accrued in respect of qualifying services (albeit in years prior to his retirement), the above disclosures are required in respect of him, even though pension entitlements were not accruing in respect of services during the period.

Example 4 – Director retires during year, but remains an employee

A quoted company is preparing its directors' remuneration report. One of the directors, who is a member of its defined benefits pension scheme, resigned as a director of the company during this year, but will remain an employee of the company, accruing further pensionable service.

(a) Should the disclosures in respect of the benefits accruing to that director under the defined benefits scheme include all benefits accruing or just those that have accrued to him in respect of qualifying services?

Schedule 8 to SI 2008/410 requires disclosure of specified information (see para 5.196) in respect of any person who has served as a director at any time during the year and has defined benefit pension entitlements, any of which were accrued in respect of qualifying services. This means that the disclosures apply where any of the rights are earned in respect of qualifying services. As the director resigned in the year and some of the benefits accrued at the year end are in respect of qualifying services, this means that the disclosures are required in respect of all benefits accrued (that is, determined as at the year end, rather than at the date of retirement).

(b) Should the change in the director's accrued benefit disclosed be the difference between his accrued benefit at the beginning of the year and at the end of the year or at the date of resignation?

Paragraph 13 of Schedule 8 to SI 2008/410 requires disclosure of the change in the director's accrued benefit during the year and does not contain a *proviso* that where the director resigned during the year the change should be given only until the date of resignation. Therefore, the change in the director's accrued benefit disclosed should be the total difference between the director's accrued benefit at the end of the year and at the beginning of the year.

Example 5 – Director retires and commutes pension

A quoted company is preparing its directors' remuneration report for the year ended 31 December 20X4. One of its directors retired during the year and, as permitted by the rules of the defined benefit pension scheme, commuted part of her pension entitlement into a tax-free lump sum. In the 20X3 remuneration report, her disclosed accrued benefit was £100,000 and the transfer value of her accrued benefit at that date was £950,000. When she retired, she elected to forfeit £25,000 of her annual pension entitlement in consideration for a cash receipt of £235,000. At 31 December 20X4, her accrued pension is £76,000 (the £1,000 increase being inflationary) and the transfer value is £724,000. She made no personal contributions during the year.

What should be disclosed in this year's remuneration report under the Companies Act?

Schedule 8 to SI 2008/410 requires disclosure of specified information (see para 5.196) in respect of any person who has served as a director at any time during the year and has defined benefit pension entitlements, any of which were accrued in respect of qualifying services. So full disclosure in accordance with paragraph 13 of Schedule 8 to SI 2008/ 410 is required of information about the director's pension entitlement.

A literal reading of SI 2008/410 requirements would lead to disclosure of her accrued benefits of £76,000, the reduction in accrued benefit of £24,000, the transfer values at 1 January 20X4 and 31 December 20X4 of £950,000 and £724,000 respectively and the reduction in transfer value (excluding personal contributions) of £226,000. However, disclosure of this information without disclosure of the cash lump sum of £235,000 would be misleading to the user of the remuneration report so disclosure of this must be given.

An alternative view is that a more representative disclosure would be based on her entitlement had she not commuted her benefit into cash. That is, disclosure of her accrued benefit of £101,000 and a transfer value at the end of the year calculated by reference to that amount. However, as this is not the benefit that she will actually receive, in order that the readers of the remuneration report are not misled, a footnote must be given, explaining that she has commuted 25% of her benefit and received a cash lump sum.

In our view, either disclosure is acceptable, but either disclosure must be clear to the users of the remuneration report.

Excess retirement benefits of directors and past directors

5.203 The remuneration report must disclose, for each director who served during the year and for each past director, the amount of excess retirement benefits paid to or receivable by that director or past director under pension schemes. [SI 2008/410 8 Sch 14].

5.204 The requirement for disclosure by individual director or past director in the remuneration report prepared by quoted companies is subject to similar criteria and definitions as the aggregate disclosure requirement that applies only to unquoted companies (see para 5.93). Thus, for example, the excess amounts referred to above do not include amounts paid or receivable if:

■ the scheme's funding was such that the amounts were or could have been paid without recourse to additional contributions; and

■ the amounts were paid to or receivable by all pensioner members of the scheme on the same basis ('pensioner members' being persons entitled to the present payment of retirement benefits under the scheme).

[SI 2008/410 8 Sch 14(3)].

5.205 Retirement benefits, for the purpose of the above, includes benefits otherwise than in cash and where benefits otherwise than in cash are given, the amount is their estimated money value. The nature of any such benefit should also be disclosed. [SI 2008/410 8 Sch 14(4)].

5.206 Retirement benefits means retirement benefits to which the director or past director became entitled in respect of his qualifying services. [SI 2008/410 8 Sch 14(2)].

Compensation for past directors

5.207 The general rules for disclosure of compensation for loss of office, applicable for all companies, are dealt with in paragraph 5.97 onwards. In addition, for quoted companies, the remuneration report is required to disclose details of compensation for loss of office for individual directors (see para 5.163). However, there may be other payments or benefits given to past directors that may not legally qualify as compensation for loss of office and so SI 2008/410 contains a 'sweep-up' requirement for such awards to be disclosed.

5.208 The requirement is to disclose details of any significant award made in the financial year to any director who was not a director at the time when the award was made, but was previously a director. This requirement covers, in particular, compensation for loss of office and pensions, but excludes any sums already disclosed in the table of individual directors' emoluments and compensation for loss of office. [SI 2008/410 8 Sch 15].

Example – Awards to former directors

(i) Paragraph 15 of Schedule 8 to SI 2008/410 requires disclosure of the details of any significant award made in the financial year to any director who was not a director at the time when the award was made, but was previously a director. How should this be interpreted for awards in the current period to:

(a) A director who retires in the period?

Paragraph 7(1) of Schedule 8 to SI 2008/410 requires disclosure in respect of each person who has served as a director of the company at any time during the year. Therefore, if a director retires in the period then his emoluments (for qualifying services) should be included in the analysis by individual director as normal. This analysis would also include any compensation for loss of office. Any further awards made after the person ceased to be a director that are not included in compensation would fall to be disclosed separately under paragraph 15 of Schedule 8 to SI 2008/410.

(b) A director who retired in the previous period?

We interpret significant awards to former directors during the year to include awards (cash or non-cash) to former directors who had ceased to be directors by the beginning of the current accounting period. These awards would be picked up by the paragraph 15 of Schedule 8 to SI 2008/410 requirement detailed above.

(ii) Do significant awards to former directors have to be disclosed by individual director, naming them, or can they just be disclosed in aggregate, without names?

If the awards are not already disclosed in the table by individual director as compensation under paragraph 7 of Schedule 8 to SI 2008/410, they would be separately disclosed by director under paragraph 15 of Schedule 8 to SI 2008/410. Disclosure by individual director is clearly required by the wording of paragraph 15 of Schedule 8 to SI 2008/410.

5.209 Of particular note is that the requirement also relates to pensions and so will lead to disclosure of any pension top-ups (see para 5.100 onwards) or benefits in respect of early retirement not disclosed elsewhere.

5.209.1 In addition, for companies listed in the UK, the Listing Rules require disclosure of any significant payments made to former directors during the period under review. [LR 9.8.8R (2)(c)].

5.210 Examples of items that may fall to be disclosed under these requirements are contained in Table 5.35 (see para 5.208 above). This example has been used above to illustrate disclosure of excess retirement benefits required to be disclosed separately (see from para 5.204), but also includes disclosure that may fall under this section of other significant awards to former directors that are not compensation for loss of office or excess retirement benefits.

5.211 Another example might be one such as that shown in Table 5.21 in paragraph 5.154 of a payment made in respect of a dispute with a former director, which is resolved several years after the director ceased to act as such.

5.212 Another example might be a consultancy contract entered into with a former director. This is considered in the example below.

Example – Consultancy contract with former director

A quoted company is preparing its directors' remuneration report. During the year it entered into a contract for services with a person who was previously a director of the company, but who had resigned as a director three years previously. The rate being paid to the former director is in excess of the market rate for the services he is contracted to provide.

(a) Is there any disclosure requirement in the directors' remuneration report?

(b) Would it make any difference if the payment for services was an arm's length rate?

As noted in paragraph 5.210 above, paragraph 15 of Schedule 8 to SI 2008/410 requires disclosure in the directors' remuneration report of *"…any significant award made in the relevant financial year to any person who was not a director of the company at the time the award was made but had previously been a director of the company…"*.

Paragraph 6(2) of Schedule 8 to SI 2008/410 requires disclosure of an explanation for any significant award made in the circumstances described in paragraph 15 of Schedule 8 to SI 2008/410.

(a) Where the director receives reward for the services he provides to the company at a value in excess of arm's length, this would be an award under the terms of paragraph 15 of Schedule 8 to SI 2008/410 and disclosure would be required of amounts received by him, together with an explanation.

(b) Where the director receives payment at a value that is arm's length, the award of the contract to the former director would require disclosure under paragraph 15 of Schedule 8 to SI 2008/410, together with an explanation, in the year in which it is awarded. In subsequent accounting periods, there will be no SI 2008/410 disclosure requirements in respect of the ongoing arm's length contract because there will be no award in those years.

In either case, the Listing Rules require disclosure of significant payments to former directors and would require disclosure of this payment in the directors' remuneration report (see para 5.165). [LR 9.8.8R 2(c)].

[The next paragraph is 5.216.]

Sums paid to third parties in respect of directors' services

5.216 SI 2008/410 contains a requirement for quoted companies to disclose, by individual director, the aggregate amount of any consideration paid to or receivable by third parties for making available the services of the director.

■ As a director of the company.

■ While a director of the company:

(i) as director of any of its subsidiary undertakings;

(ii) as director of any other undertaking of which he was a director by virtue of the company's nomination (direct or indirect); or

(iii) otherwise in connection with the management of the affairs of the company or any such other undertaking.

[SI 2008/410 8 Sch 16(1)].

5.217 In this context, third parties do not include:

■ The director himself or a person connected with him or a body corporate controlled by him.

■ The company or any other undertaking of which he is a director (while director of the company) by virtue of the company's nomination (direct or indirect).

[SI 2008/410 8 sch 16(3)].

5.218 This part of SI 2008/410 does not specifically exclude from the definition of third party the company's subsidiary undertakings, whilst the rule relating to disclosure of aggregate amounts by unquoted companies in paragraph 5(3) of Schedule 5 to SI 2008/410 does do so (see para 5.114 above). This may be an oversight and common sense would suggest that subsidiary undertakings should also be excluded.

5.219 The reference to consideration includes benefits otherwise than in cash and where such benefits are given the amount to be disclosed is the estimated money value of the benefit. [SI 2008/410 8 Sch 16(2)]. An example of disclosure of sums paid to third parties is given in Table 5.11 in paragraph 5.117.1 above.

5.220 The disclosure applies where third parties make available the services of a director. It does not apply to other services, for example, payments to a head hunter that relate solely to services to the company for finding and introducing a director. This is illustrated in the example in paragraph 5.117.2 above.

[The next paragraph is 5.222.]

Approval of remuneration report

5.222 Section 447 of the 2006 Act requires that the remuneration report (quoted companies only – see para 5.6.3 for definition) has to be approved by the board of directors and signed on behalf of the board by a director or the secretary of the company. [CA06 Sec 447(3)].

5.223 Quoted companies are required by section 439 of the 2006 Act to give notice to members, prior to the general meeting at which accounts are laid, of an ordinary resolution to approve the directors' remuneration report for the year. However, no entitlement of a director to remuneration is made conditional on the resolution being passed by reason only of the requirements in section 439 of the 2006 Act. [CA06 Sec 439(2)]. In other words, the success or failure of the resolution does not affect the entitlement of the directors to the remuneration disclosed in the report. This is because remuneration will already be the subject of contracts that cannot be overturned. However, any 'no vote' or significant opposition is likely to spell trouble for the company in terms of investor relations.

Good practice guidance

5.223.1 Executive remuneration is one of the most sensitive and heavily scrutinised areas of corporate reporting. However, many remuneration reports are framed to disclose no more than the law requires. Good reporting should explain how the remuneration committee has spent its time in the year, how it has arrived at its decisions, and how it is continuing to refine the alignment of executives' interests with those of shareholders. It should also explain how the remuneration of executives is linked to the strategy and performance of the business. The Government has expressed concern that there is a disconnect between executive pay and performance, with pay levels in recent years increasing at rates that are out of line with the rates of improvement in company performance. To improve shareholder engagement with companies, the Government intends to introduce legislation that will give shareholders a binding vote on pay policy. The disclosure framework for the 'front half' is to be overhauled and the detailed disclosure requirements for executive remuneration will be amended to give greater transparency; the intention is to give shareholders more transparent, good quality information to enable them to hold companies to account so that executive pay is better linked to company performance.

Disclosure of directors' remuneration

5.223.1.1   Table 5.25 below illustrates how the links between remuneration and performance can be highlighted. Further examples may be found at corporatereporting.com.

Table 5.25 – Strategy and remuneration

SSE plc Annual Report 2012

At a glance

How has this Renumeration Report been put together?
In January 2012 the UK government recommended that remuneration reports should comprise two sections: one setting out how remuneration policy has been implemented in the previous year (for SSE, 2011/12); and one setting out future policy for Executive remuneration. With sections on Remuneration in 2011/12 (pages 75 to 79) and on Remuneration for 2012/13 and beyond (pages 80 to 83), this Report follows that structure.

What are the principles of the SSE Executive Remuneration Policy?
→ attract and retain Executive Directors who run the Company effectively for the benefit of shareholders, customers and employees;
→ adopt a competetive and straightforward approach to total remuneration, which meets shareholder expectation;
→ reinforce the culture and teamwork to deliver the long-term growth and sustainability of the business; and
→ set Total Remuneration Policy at levels which promote the long-term development of the business and reward individuals in line with performance.

What was new in 2011/12?
Colin Hood (Chief Operating Officer) retired from the company in October 2011. The Remuneration Comminttee confirmed the remuneration terms on exit which provided exactly what he was due under either his contract of employment or through the rules of the relevant incentive plans.

Colin Hood's existing responsibilities were shared between Gregor Alexander, Alistair Phillips-Davies, and selected Management Board members. With the new responsibilities in mind, Alistair Phllips-Davies and Gregor Alexander's remuneration arrangements were reviewed, resulting in both receiving an increase in basic pay of 10% with effect from 1 November 2011. There was no increase in salaries for the Executive Directors in 2010/11. No other terms were adjusted and their next formal pay review will be in April 2013. The cost of Colin Hood's retiral, including the pay enhancements to those taking on more responsibilities as a result, will be absorbed within a period of less than one year.

BIS launched a consultation exercise to improve both the reporting and governance arrangements in Executive remuneration. The Committee participated in the consultation exercise putting forward SSE's views. At the

March 2012 meeting the Committee agreed to adopt a number of the proposals at an early stage rather than wait until they become a formal requirement in 2013.

During the last year the Committee discussed the need to put in place a 'claw back' arrangement in both the main incentive plans from 2012 grants onwards. This would allow the Committee potentially to reduce payouts under these arrangements should there be any events such as material mis-statement of accounts, gross misconduct or something which causes significant reputational damage to the Company.

What issues did the Remuneration Committee take account of in making its decisions?
The Remuneration Committee Chairman's Introduction on page 75 and the table on page 79 summarise the issues that the Committee took account of in making its

decisions for 2011/12. They included positive aspects of performance, including effective teamworking, achievement of important personal objectives and another increase in adjusted profit before tax*. They also reflect the decision to adjust payments under the Annual Incentive Scheme to reflect the difficulties in which SSE found itself in relating to the use of sales aids in doorstep selling.

How has SSE presented one single figure for total remuneration for each Executive Director?
At SSE, what Executive Directors earn is made up of:

→ base salary;
→ benefits-in-kind;
→ cash awarded under the Annual Incentive Scheme;
→ shares awarded under the Annual Incentive Scheme and secured through continued employment; and

What is SSE's Total Executive Remuneration Policy?
Summary of remuneration policy

Minimum shareholding requirement equal to 100% base salary

How is the remuneration package structured?
Total Remuneration Policy (% each component element)

→ Base salary includes 1% to cover benefits-in-kind, namely a car allowance and private medical plan.
→ The pension element is the average of the present value of providing a single year of pension for the Executive Directors.
→ Target performance comprises annual incentive scheme awarded at target level (ie 50% of base salary) and, for the Performance Share Plan, an assumption that 50% of shares under award will vest.
→ Stretch performance is based on an annual incentive of 100% of base salary with exceptional targets being met and the Performance Share Plan is calculated based on the maximum grant at 150% salary which gives a range between 47%–64% in variable pay to recognise exceptional performance.

→ shares awarded under the Performance Share Plan, secured through continued employment and attaining performance criteria.

The calculation of what Executive Directors earned in 2011/12 is made up of salary, benefits-in-kind, cash awarded under the Annual Incentive Scheme for 2011/12 and shares awarded under the Annual Incentive Scheme and Performance Share Plan in 2008/09, but earned in 2011/12 as a result of continued employment (and, in the case of the Performance Share Plan, through performance over the three years against the criteria for awards).

The table opposite sets out what each Executive Director earned in 2011/12 on this basis.

What is the position with regard to members of the Management Board?
In addition to the three Executive Directors, SSE has seven Managing Directors who are also members of the Management Board, the role of which is summarised on page 58. On the same basis as that used for determining Executive Directors' earnings in 2011/12, the total earnings of the seven Managing Directors in 2011/12 was £2,313,00.

How does Executive Directors' remuneration compare with other financial dispersals?
The UK government has said that, to provide context, companies should outline how remuneration for Executive Directors compares with other dispersals such as dividends, capital and investment expenditure, taxation and general staffing costs.

SSE has set out the position for each of these areas in the table opposite. It shows that for every £1 spent on Executive Directors' earnings by SSE in 2011/12, £122 was paid in tax, £192 was spent on employee costs, £220 was made in dividend payments to shareholders and £524 was spend on capital and investment expenditure.

SSE's contribution to government revenues in the UK is also included in the table, and the overall position on taxation is set out on page 23. It is important to note that:

→ Executive Directors' earnings as described in this report are subject to taxation in the UK; and
→ in line with the countries in which it has substantial commercial operations, SSE is liable for taxation in the UK and Ireland only and does not use so-called 'tax havens' to avoid paying tax.

What did the Executive Directors earn during the year ending 31 March 2012?

	Base salary £000s	Benefits £000s	Cash incentive £000s	Subtotal £000s	DBP vesting value £000s	PSP vesting value £000s	Total (2012) £000s	Total (2011) £000s
Ian Marchant	840	19	158	1,017	170	–	1,187	1,382
Colin Hood	377	10	94	481	125	–	606	1,059
Gregor Alexander	516	16	123	655	98	–	753	816
Alistair Phillips-Davies	516	16	102	634	98	–	732	815
Total remuneration	2,249	61	477	2,787	491	–	3,278	4,072

Note: The shares earned under the DBP were awarded in respect of performance in the year to 31 March 2009 but were subject to continued employment with SSE until at least 31 March 2012, excluding Colin Hood who retired on 31 October 2011 and received these shares on his retiral. The value is based on the shares disclosed in table D and, in addition, dividend shares as follows: Ian Marchant – 2,076 shares, Gregor Alexander and Alistair Phillips-Davies – 1,192 shares, and Colin Hood – 1,385 shares. The shares earned under the PSP were granted in 2009 but were subject to continued employment with SSE until at least 31 March 2012 and to SSE's performance over the three years to that date in respect of Total Shareholder Return and Adjusted Earnings Per Share*. The valuation of the shares of both schemes is based on the closing price of 1,329p as at 31 March 2012. They will vest in June 2012. The cash payment under the Annual Incentive Scheme will be made in June 2012.

In addition, the Directors also participated in pension arrangements during the year to 31 March 2012 and accrued additional benefits under these arrangements. More information is given in table B on page 84.

Colin Hood's salary reflects earnings up to his leaving date of 31 October 2011 and his DBP vesting value reflects the vesting of the 2009 award. Alistair Phillips-Davies' and Gregor Alexander's salary reflects an increase in basic salary from £495,000 to £544,500 from 1 November 2011.

How do the earnings of the Executive Directors compare with other financial dispersals?

	2008 £m	2009 £m	2010 £m	2011 £m	2012 £m
Executive Directors' earnings[1]	5.1	7.0	4.5	4.1	3.3
Dividend payments to shareholders	502.8	551.9	618.5	659.8	716.9
Capital and investment expenditure	810.3	1,279.8	1,315.2	1,443.7	1,706.9
Contribution to government revenues in UK[2]	413.6	402.0	460.7	343.8	396.4
Staffing costs[3]	438.8	537.4	585.3	615.2	624.9

1. On same basis as 'What did the Executive Directors earn?' table.
2. Includes Corporation Tax, Employer's National Insurance Contributions and Business Rates.
3. Wages and salaries and share-based remuneration for all staff, as per note 6(i) of the accounts, excluding Executive Directors.

The Executive earnings show a reduction despite strong business performance for two main reasons:

→ a reduction in the number of Executive Directors during 2011/12 from four to three; and
→ the fact that despite strong underlying performance the long-term incentive plan did not pay out in 2010/11 or 2011/12 although it should pay out in future years if performance criteria are met.

Remuneration glossary of terms
STI – Short Term Incentive
LTI – Long Term Incentive
PSP – Performance Share Plan
BIK – Benefits-in-Kind
MSCI – Morgan Stanley Capital Index
TSR – Total Shareholder Return
EPS – Earnings Per Share
DBP – Deferred Annual Incentive Scheme

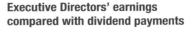

Executive Directors' earnings compared with dividend payments

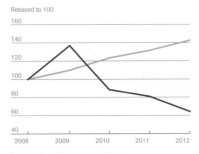

Rebased to 100

■ Executive Directors' earnings
■ Dividend payments to shareholders

NAPF remuneration guidelines

5.223.2 In November 2009, the National Association of Pension Funds (NAPF) wrote to the chairmen of FTSE 350 entities encouraging restraint over executive remuneration and stating that remuneration should be aligned with the long-term interests of shareholders. The NAPF stated that it is *"in the interests of pension funds as long-term investors that company management be well rewarded for delivering outstanding performance"* and made clear that:

■ Pay and performance should be clearly aligned, with a focus on risk. Bonuses should reflect profit levels. For example, if profits have decreased, bonuses should also be lower.

- Companies should explain in their annual reports how the longer-term interests of shareholders are balanced with those of management and how profits are allocated between capital, remuneration and dividends to shareholders.

- A significant part of any bonus payment should be deferred into shares.

- If performance conditions are adjusted because they are no longer realistic, companies should take account of the potential for economic recovery.

5.223.3 In addition to the recommendations described above, the NAPF has stated its support for the conclusions of the UK Corporate Governance Code.

5.223.4 The NAPF has also stated its support for the global remuneration principles, a set of guidelines on executive remuneration prepared by a group of UK institutional investors in 2007, applicable to both UK and overseas markets.

5.223.5 The global remuneration principles set out guidelines in three areas as follows:

- Formulation and implementation of policy. A clear statement of the objectives of remuneration policy should be provided. Companies should avoid paying more than is necessary and avoid rewarding departing directors for poor performance.

- Dialogue with investors. Such dialogue should ensure that remuneration policy for senior employees and executives is aligned to deliver company strategy that provides the best return to shareholders. Good behaviour should be encouraged and good performance recognised.

- Other factors. Where senior employees have significant equity holdings, the interests of directors and shareholders are better aligned. Remuneration should be appropriately balanced between long- and short-term elements and should incentivise and encourage retention. Care should be taken in benchmarking and any benchmarking process should be explained.

Further details of the global remuneration principles can be found within NAPF's 'Corporate Governance Policy and Voting Guidelines – 2010', available at www.napf.co.uk.

5.223.6 The NAPF refers to the ABI's guidelines for executive remuneration, anticipating that most institutional investors and issuers will use these as a benchmark for remuneration policy. The ABI's guidelines are described in the following section.

ABI guidelines for executive remuneration

5.223.7 The Association of British Insurers (ABI) published 'Executive remuneration — ABI guidelines on policies and practices' in December 2009. The principles, provisions and guidance represent best practice for listed entities and other entities are encouraged to observe the guidelines. The ABI summarised its views on executive remuneration in its position paper of the same date, as follows:

> *"Shareholders seek a constructive dialogue that results in remuneration policies that promote the creation of long-term sustainable value...*
>
> *Shareholders seek remuneration policies that encourage management to deliver long-term business performance in line with corporate strategy to deliver long-term value creation. Structures should be transparent and simple. Remuneration committees should be accountable to shareholders for their decisions and the use of discretion..."*

5.223.8 The core remuneration principles set out in the ABI's guidelines are:

- Remuneration policies and practices should promote longer-term value for shareholders. Remuneration policies should be clearly aligned with the company's objectives and strategy.

- Consistent with the UK Corporate Governance Code's recommendations, remuneration committees should comprise independent directors who scrutinise remuneration. High quality dialogue between boards and shareholders is important.

- Remuneration should be aligned with shareholder interests. Remuneration should be set at levels to retain and motivate executives and linked to individual as well as company performance. Benchmarks should be used with caution.

- The level of reward should be justified by performance and service contracts should be prepared appropriately to support this.

5.223.9 The ABI's more detailed provisions and guidance that support the principles described above cover remuneration committees and their responsibilities, guidance for base pay, bonuses, pensions and contracts and severance and guidance for share-based payment incentive schemes.

5.223.10 Full details of the ABI's guidance can be found at www.ivis.co.uk.

5.223.11 It is worth noting that in light of challenging economic conditions, in September 2008, the ABI drew specific attention to the following points:

- Remuneration policy should be fully explained and justified, particularly when changes are proposed. Shareholders will carefully scrutinise increases in remuneration, particularly in relation to salaries or annual bonuses.

- Where a company has underperformed and its share price dropped significantly, this should be taken into account when determining the level of awards under share incentive schemes. It is not appropriate for executives to receive awards of such a size that they are perceived as rewards for failure.

- Shareholders generally do not favour additional remuneration in relation to succession or retention, particularly where no performance conditions are attached.

- In the context of the consultation process for share incentive schemes, remuneration committees should ensure that shareholders have adequate time to consider the proposal and that their views are carefully considered. Relevant information related to the consultation should be clearly and fully disclosed.

RiskMetrics Group remuneration guidance

5.223.12 RiskMetrics Group's '2010 RiskMetrics U.K. Remuneration Guidance' is consistent with the NAPF's policy. It comprises general policies and practices as well as more detailed guidance on the components (basic salary, bonuses, long-term incentive plans and termination arrangements in service contracts) of remuneration packages. The general policies include the following:

- Remuneration and performance measures should be clearly linked with business strategy in order to motivate executives appropriately. Consideration should be given to the attitude to risk and behaviour that a remuneration package may drive.

- Shareholders should be fully consulted on remuneration policy proposals.

- Rewards for failure or poor performance should be avoided.

- Directors' remuneration should be consistent with pay and conditions across the company.

- Total remuneration is not, generally, expected to increase where profits have declined.

- One-off retention payments are not justified.

The full guidance can be found at www.riskmetrics.com.

Section V — Audit requirements

5.224 As indicated in the previous sections, SI 2008/410 requires part of the remuneration report ('the auditable part') to be audited. This requirement and the general provisions of the Act in relation to auditors' duties in respect of directors' remuneration information given in financial statements or accompanying them, are discussed below.

5.225 Section 412 of the Companies Act 2006 requires that the information in Schedule 5 to SI 2008/410 must be given in the notes to a company's annual accounts. [CA06 Sec 412]. Section 420 of the Companies Act 2006 requires that, in the case of quoted companies, a remuneration report must be prepared, which must contain the information required by Schedule 8 to SI 2008/410 and comply with any requirement of that Schedule as to how the information is to be set out in the report. [CA06 Secs 420(1); 412(1), (2)].

5.226 Section 498(1) and section 498(2) of the Companies Act 2006 require the auditors to determine whether the accounts (including the notes) and the auditable part of the company's directors' remuneration report (in the case of quoted companies) are in accordance with the accounting records and returns and are required to include a statement in their report if they are not in agreement. [CA06 Sec 498(1), (2)].

5.227 Section 498(4) of the 2006 Act requires that if the requirements of Schedule 5 to SI 2008/410 and, where a remuneration report is required to be prepared (that is, for quoted companies), the requirements of Schedule 8 to SI 2008/410 in respect of the auditable part of that report, are not complied with, the auditors must, so far as they are reasonably able to do so, include in their report the required information. [CA06 Sec 498(4)].

5.228 Section 497 of the 2006 Act requires that if a directors' remuneration report is prepared (that is, for quoted companies only – see para 5.6.3 for definition) the auditors shall report on the auditable part and state in their report whether in their opinion that part (the auditable part) of the directors' remuneration report has been properly prepared in accordance with the Companies Act 2006. [CA06 Sec 497(1)].

5.229 The auditable part of the directors' remuneration report is the part containing the information required by Part 3 of Schedule 8 to SI 2008/410. This has been discussed above under the heading 'Information subject to audit' from paragraph 5.163.

5.230 In October 2002, the APB issued Bulletin 2002/2, 'The United Kingdom Directors' Remuneration Report Regulations 2002'. The Bulletin discusses the auditors' responsibilities with respect to the unaudited part of the directors' remuneration report.

> **Example – Identification of auditable and non-auditable information**
>
> A quoted company is preparing its directors' remuneration report. The company is proposing to mix the auditable information and the non-auditable information within the remuneration report, rather than keeping them as separate parts. Is this acceptable under Schedule 8 to SI 2008/410?
>
> There is no requirement in SI 2008/410 to separate the auditable and the non-auditable information within the remuneration report, or even to state in that report which information has been audited and which has not. However, APB Bulletin 2002/2, 'The United Kingdom Directors' Remuneration Report Regulations 2002', considers the practical difficulties in describing, in the audit opinion, the scope of the audit when part but not all of a section in the annual report has been audited. It is insufficient for the directors and auditors of a company to assume that the user of the financial statements has existing knowledge to be able to determine which information has and which has not been audited.
>
> The bulletin suggests that the auditors should discuss the format of the directors' remuneration report with management before the year end and should agree, possibly by including terms in the letter of engagement, that the auditable and the non-auditable parts of the remuneration report will be clearly distinguished. Where this is the case, a cross-reference in the audit opinion to the identifiable audited part will satisfy the need to make clear the scope of the opinion.
>
> However, where the remuneration report does not clearly distinguish the auditable and non-auditable information, the audit report should identify specifically, by page and paragraph number or heading if necessary, each section of the directors' remuneration report that has been audited. This will need to be sufficient to enable the user to identify the information that has and has not been audited.

5.231 Also, under the Listing Rules, the scope of the auditors' report on the financial statements must cover the disclosures specified below. The auditors must state in their report if, in their opinion, the company has not complied with any of these requirements and, in such a case, must include in their report, so far as they are reasonably able to do so, a statement giving details of the non-compliance. [LR 9.8.12R]. The relevant disclosures are as follows:

- Detail of elements in the remuneration package (see para 5.165).
- Information on share options (see para 5.170).
- Details of other long-term incentive schemes (see para 5.189.2).
- Details of defined benefit schemes (see para 5.197).
- Details of contributions to money purchase schemes (see para 5.194).

[The next paragraph is 5.233].

Section VI — Group situations

5.233 Common problems arise with the disclosure of directors' emoluments in a group context. Consider the following examples where a director of a parent company has also been nominated to the board of one of its subsidiaries. In all the situations it is assumed that the director is remunerated by the parent company in connection with his services as director of the parent company, but also receives payment for services to the subsidiary (as set out in the examples below). It is also assumed that all the relevant information concerning emoluments is available to the reporting company and that both companies are private companies (that is, the relevant disclosures are governed by Schedule 5 to SI 2008/410).

Example 1 – Director paid by subsidiary

Where the subsidiary pays the director directly in respect of his services as a director of the subsidiary.

In this situation the parent company will need to disclose, as directors' emoluments, the aggregate of the amount paid to the director in respect of his services as a director of the parent company and the amount he receives in respect of his services as a director of the subsidiary. [SI 2008/410 5 Sch 7(2)]. This will be the case even if the parent is not preparing consolidated financial statements.

The subsidiary will also need to disclose the amount paid to the director by the subsidiary in respect of the director's services to that subsidiary, as directors' emoluments, in its own financial statements.

Example 2 – Payment passed back to parent

Where the subsidiary pays the director, but the director is liable to account to the parent company for the remuneration he receives in respect of his services as director of the subsidiary.

In this situation, the notes to the financial statements of the parent company need only disclose, as directors' emoluments, the amounts paid to the director in respect of his services as director of the parent company.

The amount paid by the subsidiary in respect of the director's services to that subsidiary, needs to be disclosed, as directors' emoluments, in the subsidiary's financial statements. Where, however, the director is subsequently released from the obligation to account for the remuneration, the remuneration must be disclosed in a note to the first financial statements of the parent company in which it is practicable to show it, and the remuneration must be distinguished from other remuneration. [SI 2008/410 5 Sch 8(2)].

Example 3 – Parent recharges subsidiary

Where the parent company pays the director directly and recharges the subsidiary for his services as a director of the subsidiary.

The aggregate amount that needs to be disclosed, as directors' emoluments, in the parent company's financial statements is the same as in example 1.

The notes to the subsidiary's financial statements must disclose, as directors' emoluments, the amount receivable by the director for services to the subsidiary, that is, in this situation, the amount recharged by the parent company in respect of the director's services.

Example 4 – Parent does not recharge subsidiary

Where the parent company pays the director directly, but no recharge is made to the subsidiary.

Again, the aggregate amount that needs to be disclosed, as directors' emoluments, in the parent company's financial statements is the same as in example 1.

The notes to the subsidiary's financial statements, however, must include details of the remuneration paid by the parent company in respect of the director's services to the subsidiary. An explanation to the effect that the charge for director's remuneration has been borne by the parent company may be useful, although there is no requirement in the Act to do so. If it is necessary for the parent company to apportion the director's remuneration, the directors may apportion it in any way they consider appropriate. [SI 2008/410 5 Sch 7(6)].

Practical difficulties in ascertaining remuneration

5.234 Practical difficulties may arise in connection with disclosure of remuneration in a subsidiary's financial statements where a director of the subsidiary is also:

- a director or employee of the parent and is paid by the parent; or

- a director of another subsidiary and is paid by that other subsidiary.

5.235 In such cases, it is often difficult to ascertain the emoluments of the director that are paid to or receivable by him in respect of his services to the subsidiary in question. This difficulty may be aggravated if there is no charge made to the subsidiary by the payer of the emoluments. It may also sometimes be aggravated by a desire on the part of either the parent or the subsidiary to limit the amount of disclosure in the subsidiary's financial statements, if, for instance, the parent-appointed director is more highly rewarded than other directors.

5.236 Paragraph 6 of Schedule 5 to SI 2008/410 states that the schedule requires information to be given regarding emoluments, pensions and compensation for loss of office only so far as it is contained in the company's books and papers or the company has the right to obtain it from the persons concerned.

5.237 As noted in paragraph 5.9 above, section 412(5) of the Companies Act 2006 states that *"...it is the duty of any director of a company, and any person who is or has at any time in the preceding five years been a director of the company, to give notice to the company of such matters relating to himself as may be necessary for the purposes of regulations under this section"*.

5.238 Where, despite the requirements of section 412 of the 2006 Act, there are difficulties in obtaining information one or more of the steps described below might be taken.

5.239 If the subsidiary is a party to the directors' service agreement, and that agreement stipulates what the director is paid in respect of his services to the subsidiary, then the information is contained in the subsidiary's books and papers and the subsidiary should disclose it.

5.240 If the subsidiary is not a party to the service agreement (possibly because the agreement is with the parent or a fellow subsidiary), the subsidiary or its directors should *'make reasonable efforts'* to obtain the information, for instance by asking the parent or fellow subsidiary for details of the terms of the service agreement, or by obtaining a detailed breakdown of any management charge.

5.241 If any fellow director of the subsidiary has obtained the necessary information in his capacity as a director of the subsidiary, he should disclose it to the board of the subsidiary. The information will then be under the subsidiary's control and it should disclose it.

5.242 If the information needed is not obtainable by any of the above means, companies often make an apportionment. This is relatively simple where a director is a director of both the subsidiary and the parent, but spends the vast majority of his time in an executive capacity on the subsidiary's affairs. It is less easy if the director is also a director of a large number of different subsidiaries. Schedule 5 to SI 2008/410 permits apportionment (see para 5.24.2 above). We suggest that where apportionment is relatively straightforward it may be the best way of determining the emoluments to be disclosed in the subsidiary.

5.243 The above steps may be summarised as follows:

- Inspect the subsidiary's relevant books and papers including service contracts to which it is party.

- Analyse any management charges for details of emoluments charged.

- Request information from other group companies that have service contracts with directors to which the company is not a party or from the director himself.

- Apportion where total emoluments are known and the apportionment can be made with a high degree of confidence and accuracy.

These steps should result in disclosure in the majority of cases.

5.244 If, in rare circumstances, the necessary information is not contained in the company's books and papers and the company does not have the right to obtain it from the director, the company is not required to disclose it (see para 5.236 above). In addition, the auditors would not be able to give the information required in their report (see para 5.10 above).

5.245 Where this situation occurs it might be that the financial statements would not give a true and fair view if no disclosure were made of the facts. Hence, in these circumstances, if the financial statements are to give a true and fair view, some narrative needs to be given.

5.246 We suggest that example 1 below and examples 2 and 3 in paragraph 5.247 would be appropriate notes for three situations that may arise where no information is available.

Example 1 – Recharge cannot be separately identified

A recharge is made to the subsidiary by a parent company or fellow subsidiary, but the management charge includes other costs and the emoluments cannot be separately identified.

'The above details of directors' emoluments do not include the emoluments of Mr X, which are paid by the parent company (fellow subsidiary) and recharged to the company as part of a management charge. This management charge, which in 20XX amounted to £95,000 also includes a recharge of administration costs borne by the parent company (fellow subsidiary) on behalf of the company and it is not possible to identify separately the amount of Mr X's emoluments.'

5.247 It is envisaged that this situation would be very rare as normally a full breakdown of management charges should be possible.

Example 2 – Non-executive role in subsidiaries

The director is an executive of the parent and also a director of a large number of other subsidiaries for which he carries on work. He is paid by the parent company which makes no recharge to the subsidiaries. His role is chiefly that of non-executive director of the subsidiaries overseeing the subsidiaries' affairs on behalf of the parent.

'The emoluments of Mr X are paid by the parent company. Mr X's services to this company and to a number of fellow subsidiaries are of a non-executive nature and his emoluments are deemed to be wholly attributable to his services to the parent company. Accordingly, the above details include no emoluments in respect of Mr X.'

Example 3 – Executive role in subsidiaries

The director is also a director of a number of other subsidiaries for which he carries on work. He is paid by the parent company that makes no recharge to the subsidiaries. His role is that of an executive director of each of the subsidiaries.

'The emoluments of Mr X are paid by the parent company which makes no recharge to the company. Mr X is a director of the parent company and a number of fellow subsidiaries and it is not possible to make an accurate apportionment of his emoluments in respect of each of the subsidiaries. Accordingly, the above details include no emoluments in respect of Mr X. His total emoluments are included in the aggregate of directors' emoluments disclosed in the financial statements of the parent company.'

5.248 It is suggested that where a similar situation applies, but the emoluments are paid by a fellow subsidiary, there should normally be a recharge. This is because the situation of a subsidiary paying emoluments of group directors normally only arises with a group services company and such a company would usually recharge for the services it performs. In such a case, the note would not be needed, because the appropriate amount to be disclosed should be ascertainable.

Annex 1 — UK Corporate Governance Code

The UK Corporate Governance Code is dealt with in detail in chapter 4. The main principles, supporting principles and related good practice provisions concerning directors' remuneration are set out below.

Section D of the UK Corporate Governance Code contains two main principles relating to directors' remuneration. The Listing Rules require all companies with a Premium Listing of equity shares to provide a statement on how they have applied the principles of the UK Corporate Governance Code and to give a statement confirming whether they have complied with its provisions (providing an explanation where they have not complied). The main principles, supporting principles and related best practice provisions are described below.

The level and make-up of remuneration

The first main principle concerning directors' remuneration states that levels of remuneration should be sufficient to attract, retain and motivate directors of the quality required to run the company successfully, but companies should avoid paying more than is necessary for this purpose. A significant proportion of executive directors' remuneration should be structured to link rewards to corporate and individual performance. [UK CGC D.1].

This is supplemented by a supporting principle, which states that performance-related elements of executive directors' remuneration should be stretching and designed to promote the long-term success of the company. The remuneration committee should judge where to position their company relative to other companies, but should use comparisons with caution in view of the risk of an upward ratchet of remuneration levels with no corresponding improvement in performance. They should also be sensitive to pay and employment conditions elsewhere in the group, especially when determining annual salary increases. [UK CGC D.1].

The following additional recommendations in relation to remuneration policy are made as part of the best practice provisions:

- The remuneration committee should follow the provisions in Schedule A of the UK Corporate Governance Code (2010), which offers additional guidance in designing performance-related remuneration schemes.

- Where a company releases an executive director to serve as a non-executive director elsewhere, the remuneration report should include a statement as to whether or not the director will retain such earnings and, if so, what the remuneration is.

- Levels of remuneration for non-executive directors should reflect the time commitment and responsibilities of the role. Remuneration for non-executive directors should not include share options but if, exceptionally, options are granted, shareholder approval should be sought in advance and any shares acquired by exercise of the options should be held until at least one year after the non-executive director leaves the board. Holding share options could be relevant to determining a non-executive director's independence.

[UK CGC D.1.1-D.1.3].

The best practice provisions also include the following relating to service contracts and compensation:

- Remuneration committees should carefully consider what compensation commitments (including pension contributions and all other elements) their directors' terms of appointment would entail in the event of early termination. The aim should be to avoid rewarding poor performance. They should take a robust line on reducing compensation to reflect departing directors' obligations to mitigate loss.

- Notice or contract periods should be set at one year or less. If it is necessary to offer longer notice or contract periods to new directors recruited from outside, such periods should reduce to one year or less after the initial period.

[UK CGC D.1.4-D.1.5].

Procedure

The main principle in this area is that there should be a formal and transparent procedure for developing policy on executive remuneration and for fixing the remuneration packages of individual directors. No director should be involved in deciding his or her own remuneration. [UK CGC D.2].

In support of this main principle are the following supporting principles:

■ The remuneration committee should consult the chairman and/or chief executive about their proposals relating to the remuneration of other executive directors. It should also be responsible for appointing any consultants in respect of executive director remuneration. Where executive directors or senior management are involved in advising or supporting the remuneration committee, care should be taken to recognise and avoid conflicts of interest.

■ The chairman of the board should ensure that the company maintains contact as required with its principal shareholders about remuneration.

[UK CGC D.2].

These principles are further supplemented by the following best practice provisions:

■ The board should establish a remuneration committee of at least three, or in the case of smaller companies (that is, those falling outside the FTSE 350 throughout the year immediately prior to the reporting year), two independent non-executive directors. In addition the company chairman may also be a member of, but not chair, the committee if he or she was considered independent on appointment as chairman. The remuneration committee should make available its terms of reference, on request and on the company's website, explaining its role and the authority delegated to it by the board. Where remuneration consultants are appointed, a statement should be made available (in the same way as described for the terms of reference) of whether they have any other connection with the company.

■ The remuneration committee should have delegated responsibility for setting remuneration for all executive directors and the chairman, including pension rights and any compensation payments. The committee should also recommend and monitor the level and structure of senior managements' remuneration. The definition of 'senior management' for this purpose should be determined by the board, but should normally include the first layer of management below board level. [Note that disclosure of the remuneration committee's activities throughout the year is considered to be good practice.]

■ The board itself or, where required by the articles of association, the shareholders should determine the non-executive directors' remuneration within the limits set in the articles of association. Where permitted by the articles, the board may, however, delegate this responsibility to a committee, which might include the chief executive.

■ Shareholders should be invited specifically to approve all new long-term incentive schemes (as defined in the Listing Rules) and significant changes to existing schemes, save in the circumstances permitted by the Listing Rules.

[UK CGC D.2.1-D.2.4].

Schedule A − The design of performance-related remuneration for executive directors

Schedule A of the UK Corporate Governance Code, which is referred to above, deals with the design of performance-related remuneration and includes the following:

■ The remuneration committee needs to consider whether the directors should be eligible for annual bonuses. If so, performance conditions should be relevant, stretching and designed to promote the long-term success of the company. Upper limits should be set and disclosed. There may be a case for part of the bonuses to be paid in shares to be held for a significant period.

■ The remuneration committee needs to consider whether the directors should be eligible for benefits under long-term incentive schemes. Traditional share option schemes should be compared to other kinds of long-term incentive scheme. Executive share option schemes should not be offered at a discount, except as permitted by the Listing Rules.

- Generally, shares granted or other forms of deferred remuneration should not vest, and options should not be exercisable, in less than three years. Directors should be encouraged to hold their shares for a further period after vesting or exercise, subject to the need to finance any costs of acquisition and associated tax liabilities.

- Any new long-term incentive schemes that are proposed should be approved by shareholders and should preferably replace any existing schemes or at least form part of a well considered overall plan, which should incorporate existing schemes. Furthermore, the total rewards potentially available should not be excessive.

- Payouts or grants under all incentive schemes, including new grants under existing share option schemes, need to be subject to challenging performance criteria reflecting the company's objectives, including non-financial performance metrics where appropriate. Remuneration incentives should be compatible with risk policies and systems.

- Normally, grants under executive share option and other long-term incentive schemes should be phased rather than awarded in one large block.

- Consideration should be given to the use of provisions that permit the company to reclaim variable components in exceptional circumstances of misstatement or misconduct.

- Generally, only basic salary should be pensionable. Remuneration committees need to consider the pension consequences and associated costs to the company of basic salary increases and any other changes in pensionable remuneration, especially for directors close to retirement.

[UK CGC Sch A].

Annex 2 — Directors' remuneration disclosure — decision tree

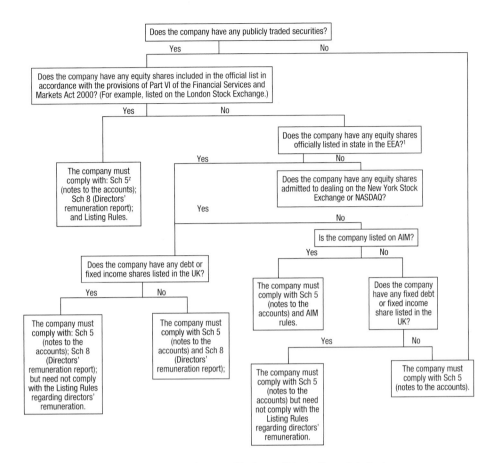

¹At the time of writing the EEA comprises the member states of the European Union plus Norway, Iceland and Liechtenstein.

²Note that paragraphs 2 to 5 of Schedule 5 to the 'Large and Medium-sized Companies and Groups (Accounts and Reports) Regulations 2008' (SI 2008/410) do not apply to quoted entities.

All of the above entities have also to comply with the Companies Act 2006 requirements concerning the content of the Directors' report.

Index

Locators are:
  paragraph numbers: 11.149, for Chapter 11, paragraph 149

Entries are in word-by-word alphabetical order, where a group of letters followed by a space is filed before the same group of letters followed by a letter, eg 'capital structure and treasury policy' will appear before 'capitalisation'. In determining alphabetical arrangement, initial articles, conjunctions and small prepositions are ignored.

Index

Index

Index

Index